D1558882

A Handbook of Divorce and Custody

A Handbook of Divorce and Custody

Forensic, Developmental, and Clinical Perspectives

edited by

Linda Gunsberg
Paul Hymowitz

THE ANALYTIC PRESS
2005   Hillsdale, NJ   London

Published by
    The Analytic Press, Inc., Publishers
    Editorial Offices:
    101 West Street
    Hillsdale, NJ 07642
    www.analyticpress.com

Designed and typeset by EVS Communication Networx, Point Pleasant, NJ

Library of Congress Cataloging-in-Publication Data
A handbook of divorce and custody : forensic, developmental, and clinical
    perspectives / edited by Linda Gunsberg, Paul Hymowitz
        p. cm.
    Includes bibliographical references and index.
    ISBN 0-88163-412-3
    1. Divorce–United States–Psychological aspects. 2. Custody of
    children–United States–Psychological aspects. I. Gunsberg, Linda.
    II. Hymowitz, Paul.

HQ834.D52 2005
306.89–dc22

                                                        2004057549

Printed in the United States of America
10 9 8 7 6 5 4 3 2 1

Dedicated to the Memory of
Joseph Goldstein
1924 – 2000
Sterling Professor Emeritus of Law, Yale University
and Psychoanalyst

Professor Goldstein coauthored *Beyond the Best Interests of the Child*, *Before the Best Interests of the Child*, *In the Best Interests of the Child*, and *The Best Interests of the Child: The Least Detrimental Alternative*. He was committed to the interface of law and psychoanalysis, particularly in the field of family law. Anna Freud, Albert Solnit, and Professor Goldstein viewed the child as a person in his own right. Photograph courtesy of Mrs. Sonja Goldstein.

Contents

Contributors List

Barry Bricklin, Ph.D. is Adjunct Associate Professor, Institute for Graduate Clinical Psychology, Widener University, and Executive Director, Professional Academy of Custody Evaluators, Wayne, PA.

B. J. Cling, Ph.D., J.D. is Associate Adjunct Professor of Forensic Psychology, John Jay College of Criminal Justice and St. John's University, New York City, and Editor, *Sexualized Violence against Women and Children: A Psychology and Law Perspective.*

Cynthia Dember, Ph.D. (retired) was Director of Psychology, Children's Psychiatric Center of the Jewish Hospital, Cincinnati, OH, and Adjunct Professor of Psychology, University of Cincinnati.

Robert Z. Dobrish, J.D. is a matrimonial lawyer in New York City, and a Fellow of the American Academy of Matrimonial Lawyers.

Gail Elliot, Ph.D. is Director, Child and Family Research, Bricklin Associates, and Executive Vice Director, Professional Academy of Custody Evaluators, Wayne, PA.

Vivian Fliman, Ph.D. is in private practice in Cincinnati, OH.

Michele Galietta, Ph.D. is Assistant Professor of Psychology, Psychology Department, John Jay College of Criminal Justice, New York City.

Patricia A. Grant, J.D. is a partner at Grant & Appelbaum, P.C. in New York City.

Martin Guggenheim, J.D. is Clinical Professor of Law at NYU School of Law, and Director, Clinical and Advocacy Programs.

Linda Gunsberg, Ph.D. (editor) is Chair, Family Forensics Training Program, Washington Square Institute for Psychotherapy and Mental Health, New York City, and Co-chair, Psychoanalysis and the Law Discussion Group, American Psychoanalytic Association.

Barbara B. Hauser, M.S.W., L.I.C.S.W., is Director, Family Service Clinic, Middlesex Probate and Family Court, Cambridge, MA, and Lecturer in Psychiatry, Harvard Medical School (at Cambridge Hospital).

Paul Hymowitz, Ph.D. (editor) is Clinical Assistant Professor of Psychiatry, New York Medical College, and Co-chair, Interdisciplinary Forum on Mental Health and Family Law.

Janet R. Johnston, Ph.D. is Professor, Administration of Justice Department, San Jose State University, CA, and coauthor, *In the Name of the Child*.

Steven Klee, Ph.D. is Chief Psychologist/Internship Training Director, Brookdale Medical Center, and in private practice in New York City.

Alan J. Klein, Ph.D., ABPP is in private practice in forensic psychology and specializes in family and criminal matters in New York State.

Barbara F. Nordhaus, M.S.W. is Assistant Clinical Professor of Social Work, Yale Child Study Center, New Haven, CT, and author of numerous articles on children and divorce.

Jack Novick, Ph.D. is Child and Adolescent Supervising Analyst, Michigan Psychoanalytic Institute, and Clinical Associate Professor at University of Michigan Medical School.

Kerry Kelly Novick is Child and Adolescent Supervising Analyst, Michigan Psychoanalytic Institute, and Child Development Director at Allen Creek Preschool.

Deborah Resnikoff, M.S.W. is in private practice in Corte Madera, CA.

Bernice H. Schaul, Ph.D., a clinical psychologist and psychoanalyst in private practice in New York City, is former Co-chair, Interdisciplinary Forum on Mental Health and the Law.

Elaine Schwager, Ph.D. is Faculty, Family Forensics Training Program, Washington Square Institute for Psychotherapy and Mental Health, New York City, and author of a book of poems, *I Want Your Chair.*

David L. Shapiro, Ph.D. is Associate Professor of Psychology, Nova Southeastern University, and coauthor (with L. E. Walker), *Introduction to Forensic Psychology, Clinical and Social Psychological Perspectives* (2003).

Moisy Shopper, M.D. is Clinical Professor, Child Psychiatry and Pediatrics, St. Louis University School of Medicine, and Training and Supervising Psychoanalyst (Child and Adult), St. Louis Psychoanalytic Institute (MO).

Ava L. Siegler, Ph.D. is Director, Institute for Child, Adolescent, and Family Studies in New York City, and author, *What Should I Tell the Kids? A Parent's Guide to Real Problems in the Real World.*

Susan W. Silverman, Ph.D. is Clinical Director, Growth and Recovery Program, Jacobi Medical Center, Bronx, NY, and in private practice in White Plains, NY.

Diana Siskind, M.S.W. is on the faculty of the New York School for Psychoanalytic Psychotherapy and Psychoanalysis, and is the author of three books on the treatment of children and their parents.

Albert J. Solnit, M.D. (deceased) was Sterling Professor Emeritus, Pediatrics and Psychiatry and Senior Research Scientist, Yale Child Study Center.

Judith Solomon, Ph.D. is Infant Mental Health Specialist, Department of Mental Health, Contra Costa County, CA, and coeditor, *Attachment Disorganization.*

Lora Heims Tessman, Ph.D. is a member, Boston Psychoanalytic Society and Institute, and author, *The Analyst's Analyst Within* (TAP, 2003) and *Children of Parting Parents* (1978).

Alan J. Tuckman, M.D., DLFAPA is Clinical Assistant Professor of Psychiatry, New York University College of Medicine, and Clinical Assistant Professor of Psychiatry, New York Medical College, St. Vincent's Hospital, New York City.

Alison Whitmer Tumas, J.D. is Adjunct Professor, University of Pennsylvania Law School, and Judge, Family Court of the State of Delaware, 1992-2004.

Judith Wallerstein, Ph.D. is author of numerous books on children and divorce and Founder of the Judith Wallerstein Center for the Family in Transition in Belvedere, CA.

James S. Wulach, Ph.D., J.D. is Professor of Psychology and Director, M.A. Program in Forensic Psychology, John Jay College of Criminal Justice, City University of New York, and in private practice in Millburn, NJ.

Acknowledgments

L awyers and judges are clamoring for developmental information about the children who are at the center of divorce and custody litigation. Their plea was emphasized at an interdisciplinary conference on Children and the Law sponsored by the New York Freudian Society in November 1997.

To this end, two projects emerged in 1997–1998. The first was this volume, *A Handbook of Divorce and Custody: Forensic, Developmental, and Clinical Perspectives*. The second was a training program in Family Forensics launched by Linda Gunsberg. Psychologists, social workers, and psychiatrists are trained in the developmental psychoanalytic framework and its application to family issues in Family Court and State Supreme Court. We extend our thanks to the following people at Washington Square Institute for Psychotherapy and Mental Health for their support in establishing and maintaining this program: Gerd Fenchel, Director of the Treatment Center and Dean of the Training Institute; Lawrence Birnbach, Chair of Training; Leslie Fenchel; and Joan Heitschel, Registrar. In addition, our thanks go to the candidates, graduates, and faculty for their spirited dialogue, which has stimulated our thinking about many of the issues tackled in this volume.

We would like to thank as well all of our contributors for the enthusiasm, hard work, and thoughtfulness they put into each and every chapter of this book. In addition, the coeditors wish to acknowledge the following people.

* * *

I wish to express my admiration for and thanks to Justice Elliot Wilk, New York State Supreme Court, who died in the spring of 2002. During his years presiding over matrimonial cases, he was unique both in his ability to integrate the legal and psychological aspects of a case and in his consistent respect for litigants and their children. Salvatore Guardino, Senior Court Officer, and Stephen Cumberbatch, Senior Court Clerk, Part VI, New York State Supreme Court, were responsible for maintaining the respectful climate in Justice Wilk's courtroom. They both maintained a quiet compassion for litigants in tragic situations.

A special appreciation goes to my longstanding legal mentors, Irving Shafran and Judith Coulston. Appreciation also to the members of the New York County Lawyers' Association Matrimonial Law Section, Custody and Visitation Subcommittee, for being a model for interdisciplinary collaboration between law and psychology.

Thank you to Rosa and Meaghan, who have allowed me to witness their courage in dealing with life's struggles and who have brought new meaning to Channukah.

My deepest love to my two children, Philip and Dana, who have begun their college studies. I am proud of both of you, and it is a privilege to be your mother.

To Joy Falkingham Day, who died of cancer on March 5, 2001. She fought hard to share every possible moment with her husband and two children.

And finally, my gratitude to Michael Cheatham, who kept a running count of the hours devoted to this book.

Linda Gunsberg

*   *   *

I offer sincere thanks to Stephen Herman for his initial encouragement of my work in forensics. In addition, he introduced me to the Interdisciplinary Forum on Mental Health and Family Law, where I have gone on to serve on its executive committee. The Forum is a model of the kind of collaboration between judges, lawyers, and mental health professionals to which this book is dedicated.

My thanks also to Sherrill Sigalow and Bernice Schaul, who have served as my mentors in doing custody evaluations.

Finally, love to my wife, Kay Sunstein Hymowitz, whose own writings on childhood and culture have been an inspiration, and to my three children, Dan, Nora, and Anna, who have consistently been there with their support, interest, and tolerance of all technical and personal glitches.

Paul Hymowitz

Preface

The marriage between mental health experts and the courts has not always gone smoothly. The health of this marriage has only grown more urgent as the offspring of the "custody wars" (Mason, 1999) keep proliferating. Close to half of our nation's children grow up in single-parent households, and many will experience the pain and trauma of their parents' divorce and custody battles, battles that highlight the uneasy nature of interdisciplinary collaborations. It is fortuitous that family law has captured headlines recently, bringing our children's plight into the public's consciousness. The year 2000 was particularly noteworthy, with the Elián González case and the Supreme Court's decision on grandparents' visitation (*Troxel v Granville*, 2000) making news and highlighting several major themes that appear in this volume (see chapter 10).

As practicing psychoanalysts and child psychologists, the editors aim to apply the contributions of psychoanalysis and developmental theory to the area of divorce and child custody. Our interest in doing so grew first out of our work as therapists of children and their families and then as forensic experts on custody matters. In 1997, our interest was piqued further at an interdisciplinary conference entitled "Children and the Law: Consistency, Compromise, and Conflict." At that conference, both Jacqueline Silbermann, the Administrative Judge for Matrimonial Matters in New York State, and Sondra Miller, Judge for the Appellate Division of New York Supreme Court, urged that forensic reports focus more explicitly on children's developmental needs. We have attempted to heed their call in generating this volume.

We are particularly mindful of the need for an ongoing dialogue between the legal and mental health communities, so often insulated, each within its own language and methodology. The work of

Goldstein, Freud, and Solnit (1973) was a seminal collaboration between the legal and mental health worlds, proposing public policies on behalf of children. Our volume follows their example by presenting the work of lawyers and judges as well as psychiatrists, social workers, and psychologists, who work closely with legal professionals on behalf of divorcing families. We anticipate that the book may serve as a guide or primer for both legal and mental health professionals who must at times feel themselves to be in the territory of the "other."

Mental health workers are often not only fearful of the adversarial system of the courtroom, but may be seriously uninformed about the law generally. They need to understand more about the legal/adversarial system and about the laws governing child custody disputes. In turn, lawyers and judges need to be better educated about child development, the psychodynamics of the parent–child relationship, and the psychology of parenting and its place in the human life cycle. If such education is achieved, each group could come to feel more at home in the other's territory.

The work of Goldstein et al. (1996) and the ongoing longitudinal studies of Judith Wallerstein and her colleagues (1980, 2000) have promoted the application of the psychoanalytic and developmental points of view to issues of family law and divorce. This volume follows in that spirit by applying a contemporary developmental psychoanalytic approach to the journey and travails of families in crisis.

REFERENCES

Goldstein, J., Freud, A. & Solnit, A. (1973), *The Best Interests of the Child*. New York: Free Press.
—— Solnit, A., Goldstein, S. & Freud, A. (1996), *Beyond the Best Interests of the Child*. New York: Free Press.
Mason, M. (1999), *The Custody Wars*. New York: Basic Books.
Troxel v Granville, 120 S. Ct. 2054 (2000).
Wallerstein, J. & Kelly, J. (1980), *Surviving the Breakup*. New York: Basic Books.
—— Lewis, J. & Blakeslee, S. (2000), *The Unexpected Legacy of Divorce*. New York: Hyperion.

Paul Hymowitz

Introduction

*M*r. and Mrs. Smith are an attractive dual-wage-earning couple in their late thirties. They are successful people, productive in their careers and involved with and loving to their two daughters. Yet they have become bitter enemies and are now accusing each other of abusive and negligent behaviors as spouse and parent. Mrs. Smith contends that her husband has cheated on her and is sexually inappropriate around the girls. Mr. Smith denies this contention and in turn states that his wife is an irresponsible woman who is too involved in her own activities to care for her children. Each parent has retained an ethical and experienced lawyer who finds his client to be a compelling and truthful individual. The judge in this case is a seasoned woman with a sharp legal mind, but new to matrimonial cases.

Faced with the myriad uncertainties of the cross-allegations and the distinct needs of children of different ages (one a twelve-year-old preadolescent and not the biological child of Mr. Smith, the other a five-year-old kindergartner), the court considers its options. One is to appoint a law guardian; that is, a lawyer who will represent the children. A second is to appoint a mental health professional to serve as a neutral expert, uniquely devoted to considerations of the specific needs of the children, as distinct from the rights of either parent or even from the children's stated wishes. To be qualified to function as a forensic expert in a custody dispute, a professional needs to have knowledge of family law, clinical skills, and a developmental perspective. In this case, the forensic mental health expert was also trained as a psychoanalyst, giving him skills that we argue would enable him to be especially sensitive to the underlying dynamics of the warring parents as well as the special needs of the two children.

The psychoanalyst focuses not only on the real relationships between child and parent, but also on their inner experiences, and on how a person's unconscious expectations of relationships rooted on early childhood (later manifested in part as transference reactions) in turn cast a silent influence over our daily lives. The psychoanalytic perspective reveals how such internal processes influence the sometimes irrational behavior of parents caught up in custody litigation. This perspective also helps professional experts identify their own unconscious forces.

The psychoanalytic approach dovetails well with the developmental one in that it adds a rich perspective on the inner mental life that enhances the developmental focus on the child in the framework of normative expectations. The study of development provides us with a timetable of unfolding social, emotional and cognitive capabilities in the context of an "average expectable environment." The developmental clinician then examines the individual child and her actual environment against that normative background. To this perspective, the psychoanalytically informed expert adds a focus on the child's evolving fantasy life (Pine, 1985), placing particular emphasis on how internal fantasies influence the developing child's actual behavior and relationships with others.

Consider the psychoanalytic-developmental approach in relation to the prominent forensic issue of child abuse allegations in the context of custody litigation. The analytic clinician is aware of the guiding role of fantasy, particularly sexual fantasies concerning the parents, in the growing child's imagination. He further knows of the special attention the oedipal child (ages three to six) may give to the parent of the opposite sex. Such sexually tinged fantasies might take the form, for example, of desires of the little girl to have a baby with her father, embellished, of course, from the child's limited perspective. Further, the child's oedipal longings can be heightened if she is spending more time alone with her father. Similarly, a boy whose father is absent from the scene may indulge in more active fantasies about his mother.

The child's mother, caught up in the throes of a custody battle and no longer trusting of her former partner and now adversary, might understandably become alarmed by her daughter's romantic desires and alert the authorities about her suspicions. To the clinician who states, "children don't lie," the psychoanalyst is inclined to add a reminder that young children do not always make adult distinctions between fantasy and external reality. Nevertheless, it must be emphasized that the mental health professional should always give recognition of the realities of child abuse and its destructive impact (see chapter 18).

Returning to the Smith family, the mother and her elder daughter (whom the father had officially adopted and to whom he had been especially close) had become allies; each had felt betrayed by Mr. Smith, who admitted to having an affair. Faced with serious accusations of child sexual abuse against Mr. Smith, the court restricted his access to his younger daughter to supervised visitation, during which time a forensic evaluation was ordered. In his evaluation, the forensic psychologist had to look for convergences from an array of data, including the case history, direct observations of each parent with the girls, and a psychological evaluation of the two adults. In this case, the evidence suggested that Ms. Smith's sense of betrayal, however understandable, had contributed to her making unfounded accusations about his sexualizing his relationship with his youngest daughter. The resurgence of oedipally infused romantic fantasies in the older girl likely increased her receptivity to her mother's accusations. Mr. Smith was assessed to be a relatively healthy man and loving father, who seemed to have an excellent relationship with the younger girl and spoke of his affair in contrite but open terms, citing a long period of mutual coldness and hostility in the marriage. The analytically oriented forensic expert was able to explain this family's dynamics in terms of the parents' (and stepdaughter's) unconscious motivations, while also empathizing with Ms. Smith's sense of betrayal (see chapter 8).

The courts are sometimes impatient with the psychoanalytic or developmental expert, who thinks in shades of gray rather than responding with specific answers. We analysts tend not to be comfortable making predictions. Human behavior will never be reducible to statistics. The analyst is most practiced at *explanations* of how a person's past contributes to and indeed may compel him to behave in his marriage, as a parent, or in the consulting room.

Faced with general questions about how well children of a given age can maintain an emotional tie to a parent from whom they will be geographically separated, the analytically trained clinician will want to know the history of a particular parent–child dyad, in addition to what is known to be developmentally appropriate, when considering specific visitation arrangements. For example, lawyers may reach a joint agreement to allow a father overnight visits with his one-year-old, who appears to be comfortable with her father, but the expert may raise concerns about what is known generally about the potentially disruptive effects of such a schedule on the infant's secure attachment to her mother, especially in high-conflict situations (see chapter 20 and Solomon and George, 1999).

This volume brings together a wide range of professionals dedicated to working in the legal arena with families in crisis. Psychoanalytic and developmental perspectives inform the contributors from the mental health field. We present the reader with the direct experiences of the various participants in such a crisis. The volume is divided into six sections, beginning with the individual perspectives of the various professionals, including a lawyer and a judge. The second section proceeds with the issue of parental psychopathology, often at the root of family conflict and turmoil. Section III concerns the range of the state's potential involvement with the family, from ensuring parents' rights to raise their children as they see fit through to the termination of parental rights. The remaining three sections are organized to roughly coincide with the progression that the divorcing family will face on entering the legal system. The fourth section deals with aspects of the actual forensic evaluation. Section V presents postdivorce legal arrangements in order to maintain the child's ties to both parents while protecting the security of the newly configured family unit. Finally, Section VI describes the emotional aftermath of divorce and a variety of therapeutic interventions.

Key themes can be traced through the chapters of this book. A primary theme, articulated by Guggenheim (see chapter 10), concerns the inherent conflict between the family's right to privacy and the state's commitment to promote the best interests of children. On the one hand, the legal system is mindful of the time-honored constitutional right of parents to raise their children free from government intrusion. On the other hand, the courts, in concert with mental health professionals, are attuned to determining the "least detrimental alternatives for the child" (Goldstein, Freud, and Solnit, 1973) when parents are neglectful, abusive, or in litigation against one another. The psychoanalyst is attentive to the best interests of the child, including the impact on her when her parent's authority is infringed on by the state.

A second theme, explicitly referred to by Solnit and Nordhaus (see chapter 11), is the increasing uncertainty about what (and who) constitutes a family in the new millennium. In the legal arena, this question is raised in terms of who is considered to have "standing" to claim his rights in relation to the child, such as rights to visitation. With the rise in new family configurations including single-parent households, test-tube babies, adoptive parents, blended stepfamilies, and gay parents, the right to legal standing has become ever more problematic. This uncertainty has only been exacerbated by the fact that marriage itself has become less clearly tied to the endeavor of child rearing; that is, married couples in larger numbers remain childless while single parenthood proliferates.

A third theme, related to the previous one, concerns the uncertain and problematic role of fathers in the lives of their children. Ironically, as the psychoanalytic focus on fatherhood has increased (Cath, Gurwitt, and Ross, 1982; Cath, Gurwitt, and Gunsberg, 1989), and the rise of the dual-wage-earner family and the stay-at-home dad have heightened fathers' actual involvement in day-to-day caretaking, the legal status of fathers' claims to equal parenting privileges remains shaky. There is some difference in emphasis even among our contributors, although they all agree that both parents should ideally be involved in their child's care. There are those who applaud the growing awareness of and sensitivity to the issues of domestic violence (see chapter 6) and the physical and sexual abuse of children (see chapter 18) and hold these concerns to be of paramount importance. Others argue that shifting family configurations and the absent father (see chapter 24) are harmful to greater numbers of children and may even contribute to the incidence of abuse. Similarly, in relocation cases, as noted by Hymowitz (see chapter 23), the security of the child's bond with the primary parent has had to be weighed against the desirability of keeping the child in close proximity to both her parents.

A fourth theme concerns the evaluation process itself: What is the proper role of the forensic expert and what is the "good enough" evaluation (see chapter 15)? The contributors present a range of approaches, from those who are more scientific and quantitative (for example, chapter 16) to those who would emphasize more subjective and individualized perspectives (for example, chapter 17). We would argue, in addition, that the psychoanalytically informed forensic expert has the tools to be particularly sensitive to the less conscious aspects of the process in both the family being evaluated and him- or herself.

The fifth concern is important to the forensic expert, that of maintaining a clear distinction between the role of therapist and that of evaluator. A good many of the contributors to this volume who do child custody evaluations were originally trained as clinicians and continue to devote much of their professional time to psychotherapy, an enterprise that typically relies upon the ability to empathize with one's patients. In contrast, the forensic evaluation requires a strict adherence to principles of neutrality and an objective detachment from all parties (see chapter 4). Complicating the evaluator's stance may be the attorney who tries to enlist him into a partisan role, which, if successful, will most quickly discredit the forensic expert in the eyes of the court. Yet, as Shopper vividly indicates in his chapter on parental alienation (see chapter 9), the divisive nature of many child custody cases tends to force one into taking sides.

Finally, a sixth theme concerns the question of the impact of divorce itself on the lives of today's children. Many parents agonize over the prospect of dissolving their marriages. They do not act impulsively, but proceed in the best way they know how. For the most part, the celebration of the onset of no-fault divorce laws, promoting the notion that divorce is a step in the direction of greater personal freedom and liberation, is long over. For example, Judith Wallerstein is regularly chided in the media for her supposedly Cassandra-like pronouncements about the perils of divorce, as in novelist Jane Smiley's (2000) attack on the gloom of the "Wallersteinians," in which she recounted what she calls "thank-God-for divorce" tales. It is ironic that Wallerstein and Resnikoff's contribution (see chapter 27), poignantly describes the resilience of a young man in navigating and surmounting the divorce of his parents early in his life. In contrast, a number of our contributors paint a more pessimistic picture of the lasting effects of divorce on children (see, for example, chapter 21). In a basic sense, such pessimism is less about the fact of divorce per se than about the poor health of some of today's marriages. And while this volume is child centered, the pain and loss suffered by parents on the journey from marital disharmony and divorce to new family formations is a focus of a number of our contributors as well.

Whether one thinks of it as a basic right of self-determination or a symptom of society's difficulties, divorce is going to remain a reality of modern life. Nevertheless, it is our hope that this book will help promote a dialogue that can allow professionals, working to help families in their journey from breakup to reconfiguration, to function in a more effective interdisciplinary collaboration. Ultimately, it is to the futures of our children and to their ability to thrive and feel hopeful about having families of their own that all our efforts are dedicated.

REFERENCES

Cath, S., Gurwitt, A. & Gunsberg, L. (1989), *Fathers and Their Families*. Hillsdale, NJ: The Analytic Press.
—— —— & Ross, J. (1982), *Father and Child*. Boston: Little, Brown.
Goldstein, J., Freud, A. & Solnit, A. (1973), *The Best Interests of the Child*. New York: Free Press.
Pine, F. (1985), *Developmental Theory and Clinical Process*. New Haven, CT: Yale University Press.
Smiley, J. (2000), There they go, bad-mouthing divorce again. *The New York Times*, September 12, p. 25.
Solomon, J. & George, C. (1999), The development of attachment in separated and divorced families: Effects of overnight visitation, parent and couple variables. *Attachment & Human Develop.*, 1:2–33.

Paul Hymowitz

Interlude I

The Courtroom
A Multidisciplinary Collaboration

Courtroom dramas reflect what appears to be an inherent conflict between parents' rights and children's rights. Attorneys represent the plaintiff and defendant, the mother and the father of the child or children whose custody is being contested. Then there is the guardian ad litem, or law guardian, who represents the child. This courtroom model suggests that the child's interests can clash with those of the parents. The mental health professional is called on to help the Court determine what custody and visitation plan is in the child's best interests. The Court (the judge) must not only weigh the child's interests and parents' interests but, in cases of abuse and neglect allegations in custody proceedings, the State's rights to intervene to protect the child must also be considered.

Judge Tumas (see chapter 1), matrimonial lawyer Dobrish (see chapter 2), matrimonial lawyer Grant and psychologist Klee (see chapter 3) offer different vantage points to the Court process based on their different responsibilities and functions toward any particular family. All provide the distinct flavor of their rich, personal courtroom experiences.

We remain unclear regarding an operational definition of "best interests of the child," yet we uphold "best interests" vigorously. Alternatively, "the least detrimental alternative" seems to be the standard upheld in divorce and custody cases. Somewhat unsettling is the question of how parents who are responsible for raising their children may have interests that conflict with those of their children. The discrepancy between the two positions, that of the parents and that of the children, poses a serious dilemma for all professionals involved in family litigation (see chapters 10–12, 15, 16, 19–23).

This problem is reflected in the United States' position as one of only two countries in the United Nations that has not ratified the 1989 United Nations Convention on the Rights of the Child. Our problem is that, if children's rights are highlighted, we assume parents' rights diminish. The issue of parents' rights has dominated American divorce courts for centuries (see chapter 12). An exquisite example of the conflicting interests of mother and father is the 1840 D'Hauteville legal battle, in the Philadelphia Court of General Sessions, for custody of their two-year-old son. This case has been analyzed by Grossberg (1996) in terms of shifting legal and social norms, and dominant gender beliefs.

Woodhouse (2000) formulates the congruence of parent and child rights in the novel terms of parents as *trustees* of the child; that is, parents act on behalf of the child's rights and in the child's best interests. The parents' responsibility in terms of a child's rights is very clearly defined in the State of Delaware, where, according to Tumas (see chapter 1), parties in a divorce action are required to sign an affidavit stating that their child has the "right to a continuing relationship with both parents" and the right to "know and appreciate what is good in each parent without one parent degrading the other."

This brings us to the question of the role of the law guardian. Grant and Klee (see chapter 3), and Tumas (see chapter 1) clearly distinguish between the child's best interests and the child's desires and wishes. It is the law guardian's role to represent the child's wishes, not the child's best interests as defined by the law guardian himself. In this capacity, it is crucial that a law guardian understand how to communicate with children of various ages. Grant and Klee make a plea for law guardians to seek training in the psychological, emotional, and social development of a child, issues of divorce, and family law.

In the process of representing the child, the law guardian must proceed cautiously in terms of contacts with the child's parents (Brandes, 2000), so that the child's interests remain independent. Too often, the law guardian is used by one or both parents as a way to achieve his or her own ends. The child and the law guardian thus become the parents' vehicle for expression of parents' rights. For example, in high-conflict divorcing families, where there is little agreement between parents on child-rearing issues, there is often controversy about access to the children. The parent who feels slighted may tell the children to call the law guardian to request more time. The children may do so, not telling the law guardian the origin of this request. The other parent, in an effort to protect his or her rights, might encourage the children to tell the law guardian to keep the visitation the way it is, also using the children as a vehicle for a parent's wishes.

In addition, the law guardian must be careful to not interfere with the parents' position as parents to the children. That is, a child who feels that the law guardian is making the decisions based upon the child's request feels empowered, but at the risk of appropriate parental authority being diminished and taken over by the law guardian. This is one form of the dilemma raised earlier between parents' rights and children's rights.

The Court process has been referred to as adversarial, but is it? Dobrish (see chapter 2) has a nice spin on this issue, in that he views the Court process as dynamic, a forum where "opposing positions are challenged and debated." He sees the presentation of findings by different disciplines as a corrective factor.

Again, this raises the issue as to how the disciplines can collaborate. First, collaboration does not necessarily mean agreement in findings. Collaboration may be not only seeing a case from different disciplinary perspectives, but also discovering different data. Herman and Sullivan (1997) discuss the dilemma of the trial court being concerned that it may be reversed on appeal if it does not follow the findings and recommendations of the forensic expert. In fact, it *is* collaboration when the Court disagrees with the findings of the forensic expert, as long as appropriate documentation for the disagreement is presented in Court and entered on the record.

Dobrish (see chapter 2) also points to the problems posed for attorneys representing parents when the forensic report does not favor their clients. He states that the forensic expert may start out neutral but is no longer neutral when he takes a position regarding which parent should have custody of the children. Although the attorney and client may feel that the forensic expert is no longer objective, the forensic expert's perspective is that he or she remains neutral *throughout* the evaluation, even after taking a position regarding custody. The expert's recommendations are not neutral, but his or her methodology for arriving at conclusions is neutral.

The issue of neutrality extends to the topic of "prepping" or "coaching" clients (see Dobrish, chapter 2). Furthermore, coaching occurs across the board. Parents prep their children for the forensic evaluation, for meetings with the law guardian, and even for meetings with the judge; law guardians prep the forensic expert by sharing their views on who should have custody, and law guardians influence judges in informal (off the record) conversations. The best way to ensure collaboration rather than collusion is to have all professionals work independently until they present their findings and recommendations.

Schaul (see chapter 4), and Wulach and Shapiro (see chapter 5) address the ethics of the mental health forensic expert in divorce and custody litigation. Because these contributors are psychologists, their comments are largely focused on the psychologist's professional conduct. Dr. Wulach served as chair of the Committee on Professional Practice and Standards (COPPS), which drafted the American Psychological Association 1994 Guidelines for Child Custody Evaluations in Divorce Proceedings. However, guidelines for ethical behavior and practice are available for all three major mental health disciplines involved as forensic experts: psychology, social work, and psychiatry (see references, this Interlude).

Schaul (see chapter 4) elaborates on the kind of training needed to perform competently as a mental health forensic expert. A top priority is in-depth knowledge of child development and how divorce impacts on the development of the child at different ages. This dovetails nicely with what the Court wants from the forensic expert (see Tumas, chapter 1). In order for the judge to render the most well-informed decision, she needs a detailed developmental assessment of the child or children in the family. The forensic expert sees all members of the family over time; most judges do not have the time or the expertise to gather this information. The forensic expert must be able to formulate this developmental assessment of the child and the family as a whole so that the judge can get a glimpse of the family dynamics and of how the child fits into the family, both when the family was intact and, now, in the process of divorce (see chapters 15–17).

Much can be said about the differences in the legal and psychological approaches to families in divorce and custody litigation. However, one important similarity is that judges and mental health professionals both appreciate the uniqueness of each family that comes before them. This shared appreciation for the family's uniqueness gives the psychoanalytic, developmentally trained expert entrée into the courtroom, with the possibility of making a significant contribution.

Finally, all professionals involved with a family in litigation need to address the issue of separation or termination of their contact with the family (see chapter 15). Fox (2000) reminds us that our goal is to preserve the relationship that the child has with both parents: "Children will have relationships with both parents after they leave the courtroom. Judges must preserve this."

REFERENCES

American Academy of Psychiatry and the Law (1995), *American Academy of Psychiatry and the Law Ethics Guidelines for the Practice of Forensic Psychiatry.*

American Medical Association (1994), *The Principles of Medical Ethics with Annotations Especially Applicable to Psychiatry.*

American Psychiatric Association (1988), *Child Custody Consultation.*

American Psychological Association (1992), *Ethical Principles of Psychologists and Code of Conduct.*

—— (1994), *Guidelines for Child Custody Evaluations in Divorce Proceedings.*

American Psychological Association (Division 41) and American Academy of Forensic Psychology (1991), *Specialty Guidelines for Forensic Psychologists.*

Brandes, J. (2000), The role of the law guardian. *New York Law J.,* June 27, 223(123):3.

Clinical Social Work Federation (1997), *Clinical Social Work Federation Code of Ethics.*

Fox, I. (2000), New voices: Listening to children. Presented, Family Law Symposium 2000: The American Family in the 21st Century, Philadelphia.

Grossberg, M. (1996), *A Judgment for Solomon: The D'Hauteville Case and Legal Experience in Antebellum America.* Cambridge, UK: Cambridge University Press.

Herman, W. & Sullivan, P. (1997), Court-appointed experts in child custody cases. *New York Law J.,* June 30, 217(124):7.

National Association of Social Workers (1996), *National Association of Social Workers Code of Ethics.*

National Organization of Forensic Social Work (1987), *National Organization of Forensic Social Work Code of Ethics.*

New York State Board for Psychology (1997), *Guidelines for Child Custody Evaluations.*

Woodhouse, B. (2000), Changing status of the child: From property to person. Presented, Family Law Symposium 2000: The American Family in the 21st Century, Philadelphia.

Linda Gunsberg

Chapter **1**

What Judges Want
(and Children Dream)

ALISON WHITMER TUMAS

*A*s a practicing judge who has heard testimony from mental health professionals in hundreds of custody cases over the past ten years, I thought it would be relatively easy to convey what judges want from such professionals. But, as I put pen to paper, I found that it was not. I frequently tell my colleagues that I will never have "heard it all." And, because each case is different and each family is unique, generalizations are difficult and risky. Then, I met Jonathan.

On the eve of his Bar Mitzvah, Jonathan found himself in my courtroom. He was at the center of a long, bitter custody dispute between his parents. As I tried to establish some rapport with him, he told me that he had recently finished writing an essay about a dream for English class. I asked him what he had dreamed about, expecting that he (like so many of his "global age" peers) would tell me that he hoped that peace would be achieved in the Middle East, racial strife would end in America, or violence would stop in our schools. But Jonathan's dream was much less worldly. He simply wanted the fighting—between his parents—to stop.

Jonathan's dream is the goal of judges who hear high-conflict custody disputes. And well-trained mental health professionals can make significant contributions to the attainment of that goal and the realization of the dream that so many children share with Jonathan.

DEVELOPING THE COMPLETE STORY

The mental health professional who is appointed by the court or selected by both parties (in contrast to the "hired gun" of one parent) is in a unique position. Unlike a party to a custody dispute who has a vested interest in the outcome of the litigation, and the attorney who represents the party who has an ethical obligation to advance her client's position, the mental health professional can offer an independent professional perspective (see chapters 4, 15, 16, and 17). And, unlike a judge whose opportunity to observe a family is limited to the courtroom and circumscribed by a burgeoning caseload, the mental health professional can assess and evaluate family members in a variety of settings over a period of time. In short, he can conduct the investigation that a judge cannot.

Developing the complete story requires evaluating all family members, as well as the partners of parents (whether stepparents or cohabiters) who may have a significant impact on the children who are the subject of the litigation. Developing the complete story also requires employing a variety of assessment tools, including interviews, psychological testing, home visits, and record reviews (see chapters 15, 16, and 17). And it necessitates corroborating the results with collateral sources. If time or resources do not permit a thorough evaluation, the mental health professional should decline to become involved, absent being retained for the limited purpose of assessing a psychological disorder. One-sided evaluations are virtually worthless to judges and impugn the integrity of the evaluator. And, they are rarely child centered. Most importantly, to the extent that such evaluations advance one party's position at the expense of the other's or overlook significant issues for a family, they not only fail to stop, but often escalate the fighting that Jonathan dreamed would end and that judges strive to eradicate.

RECOGNIZING PARENTAL STRENGTHS

Parties to high-conflict custody disputes (and the attorneys who represent them) frequently assume that their positions will be advanced by impugning the opposing party. Nothing could be further from the truth. Indeed, in Delaware (as in many jurisdictions), judges are required to consider a parent's compliance with his responsibilities as a child's joint "natural" custodian.[1] In addition, parties to a divorce action are required to sign an affidavit acknowledging that their children have the "right to a continuing relationship with both parents" and the "right to know and appreciate what is good in each parent without one parent degrading the other"[2] (see chapters 9, 19–23).

Among the best custody evaluations that I have ever received in a high-conflict case was one in which the psychologist who evaluated the parties and their children (as well as the parties' significant others) recognized that the focus of the evaluation was the best interests of the children (see chapter 11). The evaluator emphasized ways in which each parent's strengths could be combined to advance the girls' best interests. The evaluator's approach was decidedly (and refreshingly) child centered (see chapters 15–17). And, it had the beneficial effect of helping each parent realize that he or she had attributes to offer the children that the other did not. Three years later, the order that I entered with significant input from the psychologist remains in effect, neither previously litigious parent has since filed any actions against the other, and, reportedly, the girls are thriving. Although the fighting may not have ceased, it has waned.

EVALUATING ALLEGATIONS OF PATHOLOGY

While mental health professionals frequently perform custody evaluations in cases where the parties' mental health is not at issue, their expertise is essential in assessing allegations of pathology. Most judges do not have the time or the training to determine whether a parent is simply anxious about the litigation in which he finds himself or emotionally unstable. Most judges likewise do not have the ability to differentiate between occasional lapses in judgment and demonstrable propensities toward addictive behavior. Most importantly, judges do not generally have the aptitude to assess the likelihood that a parent who has committed an act of abuse against a child will repeat his or her behavior. Here, the expertise of an experienced mental health professional is invaluable (see chapters 6–9, 13–16, 18, 21–23).

Psychologists must, however, resist the use of psychobabble. If

---

[1] *See* 13 *Del. C.* §§701(a) and 722(a)(6).
[2] 13 *Del. C.* §1507(g)(1) and (4).

the dream of children who are at the center of high-conflict custody disputes and the goal of judges who decide them is to stop the fighting, the parents who are the parties to such disputes must have confidence in the integrity of the process. Just as lawyers who resort to legalese are viewed with skepticism, so too are psychologists who resort to psychobabble. Absent an explanation of what the tests are and what they are designed to measure, the MMPI-2 and Bricklin Scales (see chapter 16) mean little or nothing to parents (or judges) who are not trained to administer them or interpret the results. While parents may never accept psychological instruments that disclose their shortcomings, they must understand them.

ASSESSING THE CHILD'S WISHES

Most state custody statutes require that judges who decide children's living arrangements consider the children's wishes. Taking a child's wishes into consideration, however, can be as anxiety producing for a child as it is cathartic. Most children want their voices to be heard. On the other hand, one of the most poignant cases I have heard was one involving a seven-year-old girl who was in severe distress because she "[did] not know which parent to pick." Mental health professionals can play a significant role in assessing a child's wishes and allaying her concerns (see chapters 15–17).

Because mental health professionals have considerably more contact with the children who are at the center of high-conflict custody disputes than judges do, they have a better opportunity to assess a child's wishes than a judge does. Unlike a judge, who generally interviews a child on only a single occasion when the child's expressed wishes may be influenced by the parent who brought her to the interview, the mental health professional can (and should) schedule more than one session with a child, and should alternate which parent brings the child to the sessions. The mental health professional should base his assessment of the child's wishes not only on subjective interviews, but also on "objective" tests like the Bricklin Perceptual Scales (see chapters 15 and 16). Most important, the mental health professional (who has contact with a child before a judge does) should dispel the common misconceptions that the child will be asked to choose between her parents and that her choice will dictate the judge's decision.

Absent pathology, abuse, or "coaching," few children choose one parent over the other. Instead, many children express preferences in terms of their living arrangements, which may be as rooted in which parent retains the family residence and where the child's friends live, as a predilection for a particular parent. And, in most jurisdictions, a child's wishes are only one of a myriad of factors that a judge must consider in determining a child's legal custody and living arrangements. As early as possible in the litigation, children should be relieved of the burden of believing that their wishes will be case determinative.

Mental health professionals also can help educate judges who interview children to assess a child's wishes. While judges are becoming increasingly knowledgeable about the developmental stages of children and about the importance that a child's language development plays in a judge's interview of her, many have had no formal training about how to interview children (see chapters 4 and 18). Five-year-olds cannot be interviewed in the same manner as ten-year-olds, and there are ways to ascertain a child's wishes without putting her in the unenviable position of being asked whom she wants to live with. Mental health professionals can (and should) educate judges about the developmental level of the child whose custody is at issue and alert the judge to any special needs that the child has that may affect the judge's interview of her. Older children in particular are more inclined to accept the outcome of custody litigation if they believe that their voices have been heard. And, to the extent that the children who are the subject of the dispute accept the court's determination, the fighting between their parents is more likely to subside.

MAKING RECOMMENDATIONS THAT WILL MINIMIZE CONFLICTS

After the mental health professional has completed an assessment of the parties, their children, and any other persons who may have a significant impact on the children, she should make recommendations that will enable the family to move toward a peaceful, if not harmonious, existence. Such recommendations also must be developmentally appropriate (see chapters 15, 16, 19, and 20).

Among the worst recommendations I have ever received was that a six-year-old child reside with each parent every other school year. The psychologist who made the recommendation failed to consider that the boy (who already was lacking in self-esteem) would have to change schools every other year. Clearly, the evaluator was concerned only with eliminating the conflict between the boy's parents.

In order to make developmentally appropriate recommendations, the mental health professional not only must consider the child's needs now, but also in the future (see chapter 19). If the child has brothers or sisters who are the subject of the litigation, each child's individual needs must be examined and weighed against the general reluctance of judges to separate siblings. If further evaluation or treatment is warranted, the mental health professional should recommend what form it should take. And, he should consider the desirability of recommending that the judge enter a temporary order, and evaluate the efficacy of the temporary arrangement after the evaluation has been completed or treatment has commenced. All recommendations should be made with a view toward minimizing current and future conflicts, in an effort to avoid futher litigation.

JUDGES' WANTS AND CHILDREN'S DREAMS

What judges who decide high-conflict custody cases want and children who are the subject of the disputes dream is for the fighting to stop. Well-trained mental health professionals can play a significant role in achieving this goal by developing the complete story, recognizing parental strengths, evaluating allegations of pathology, assessing a child's wishes, and making recommendations that will minimize current and future conflicts (see chapters 4, 15–17, 19–23).

Chapter 2

A Lawyer's Considerations in Selecting a Mental Health Expert

ROBERT Z. DOBRISH

O ur system of justice is called the adversary system. Rather than determining the outcome of a controversy by ordeal or by battle, we do so by pitting lawyer against lawyer, trusting that, through the cauldron of negotiation or litigation, the truth will out. Attorneys will generally champion vigorously their clients' causes, giving them the benefit of any doubt. It is for the attorney to assert; the court to determine. Once retained, an attorney is charged with arguing his client's case as well as it can be done, provided that the positions taken are not false or frivolous. There is no exception carved out for custody cases. Nevertheless, where a child's safety, security, or well-being is at stake, most attorneys believe they are charged with a greater responsibility. Although it is not for an attorney to determine the outcome of a legitimate controversy, a responsible attorney may refuse to argue a position or cause with which he or she has a serious disagreement.

In litigation between individuals who were once in love there is often a great deal of bitterness and resentment. It is not unusual for litigants to desire some form of vindication to be achieved through court proceedings. Perceptions of past events are frequently skewed and attorneys are sometimes asked to pursue a course that is designed to do damage to the other litigant. Custody applications are commonly sought to gain leverage rather than achieve a benefit for the children. When such requests are made to responsible attorneys, they usually attempt to steer their clients away from this course and bring them back to a responsible reality. If a client refuses to alter this course, an attorney may refuse to represent that client. The discussion that follows is primarily based upon my personal experiences as a practicing matrimonial lawyer in divorce litigation for over twenty-five years.

We will assume that there is a legitimate controversy relating to custody or visitation and that the attorneys are responsibly representing their clients. In these situations, how do attorneys utilize mental health professionals and what do they look for in the professionals that they choose?

An attorney may become involved in the selection of a mental health professional in any number of ways. Of course, one may be called on to make a nonforensic referral in situations in which a parent may have an untreated mental or emotional disorder or suffer from alcohol or drug abuse, or it may be that a child has a severe behavioral or developmental disorder that requires treatment. Also, where there is a possibility that marital counseling could work, a referral might be made in that direction. In these situations, referrals will be very individualized and the selection process highly subjective. Generally, attorneys become involved in the selection of mental health professionals as experts (hereinafter "experts") in three ways: when they are to be utilized as neutral evaluators (see chapters 4, 15–18, 22, and 23), as advisors, or as witnesses. The selection process and considerations in each of these areas will be discussed separately.

EXPERTS AS NEUTRAL EVALUATORS

The word "neutral" is one that has a different connotation for mental health professionals and attorneys (see Interlude I). To a mental health professional it usually means that the determination is to be made in the interest of the child without regard for the wishes of either parent. To an attorney, a neutral is one who comes down on neither side (see chapters 10 and 12). Once an evaluator determines that one parent or the other should be awarded custody, the expert, from the lawyer's perspective, becomes partisan and loses all neutrality. Expert reports are usually written to justify a particular recommendation and are not in any way "neutral." The evaluation process is ideally perceived as a neutral one but, in reality, the evaluator is rarely neutral once the process begins. Nevertheless, we are presently committed to the use of the label "neutral evaluator."

There are times when judges select neutrals without consulting the attorneys. In some cases a guardian ad litem or law guardian for the child will be asked by the judge to make the selection. Often, however, the judge prefers that the attorneys agree on an expert; upon a failure to do so, a judge might ask that the attorneys each submit the names of several to the judge. In submitting names, it is preferred that the judge not know which attorney submitted which name(s).

Attorneys who are given the opportunity to submit names (whether to the judge or to the adversary) must decide whether they want to submit names that they think will (a) give their client an edge; (b) give their client an even break; (c) provide some other benefit (such as geographic desirability, cost appropriateness, age, gender, or style preference). The attorney must ask questions such as (1) whether an unknown is better than a known, but slightly flawed, candidate; (2) whether gender is a factor that is meaningful; (3) whether one can anticipate results or make predictions based on: (i) writings; (ii) past determinations; (iii) the reputation that a particular individual enjoys in the community. Reasonable people will disagree on these questions. However, just as in jury selection, where attorneys try to use their prognostic skills to guess which jurors will be sympathetic to their client's cause, so in expert selection the same skills are utilized.

What do attorneys do in order to conduct the *"voir dire,"* or questioning process, in this type of situation? They contact other lawyers who may have had experiences with these experts and, as a result, know more or different things about them; they try to obtain copies of curriculum vitae to determine what the expert has written or lectured about; and they speak to other experts, all to try to ascertain whether one expert or another might be more open to (for example) father or mother custody, joint custody, mid-week overnights, and the like. In addition, a Lexis/Nexis search may be made to find out whether that expert's name appears in any reported cases or articles. Other considerations might (and should) be cost and availability. Some experts take a long time to come to a result, some write long reports, some are stronger witnesses than others. Attorneys may also want to know whether an expert has a prior relationship with the other attorney or with the judge. The latter can sometimes be a problem.

In a recent visitation case a judge appointed a psychiatrist whom she knew socially, but who had not previously done forensic work. The psychiatrist wrote a report that came to the "right" result—the one the judge had anticipated. At a hearing, however, the psychiatrist got "caught" during cross-examination and retreated from the position taken in his report. On redirect, the expert was reluctant to back off and could not be rehabilitated. The judge, however, was able to intercede and lead the witness back to the desired result. A more experienced witness would not have stumbled in this manner in the first place. A witness who did not have a relationship with the judge might not have been so judicially malleable.

Some attorneys will tell you that jury/expert selection is a critical part of a case. Others feel that even when the selection is made solely by the judge, substantial justice is achieved because the process is generally designed to eliminate, at the very least, those who are disqualifiable or biased. Even where an attorney is not allowed any input into the selection, he or she may object once the selection is made. The fact is that a good expert will usually do good work. Therefore, most attorneys who are in the know will make the selection based on experience and reputation and forget about predilection, except in the broadest terms.[1]

EXPERTS AS ADVISORS

Attorneys also select experts to serve as advisors. This is apart from making telephone calls to pick someone's brain; this is where an attorney needs to sit down and work with the expert on the preparation of a case. This need might arise in situations where there is a claim that one party suffers from a mental disorder or disability which interferes with the ability to parent or, where there is a claim that certain behavior affects the determination (e.g., nudity, extended

---

[1]The amount of information an attorney obtains about a mental health professional during the selection process differs to some extent from the amount of information the attorney might seek to obtain for the purpose of cross-examination. For the latter purpose, an attorney would, in addition, attempt to obtain the transcripts of previous trials in which that expert testified as well as copies of reports written by that expert.

breast feeding, sexual preference, substance abuse, etc.). It comes up most frequently where there are important issues (and there are a myriad of them in these types of cases) that are beyond the ken of the attorney; such as: issues relating to cultural differences, attachment theory (see chapter 20), personality disorders, psychological testing, and indicators of abuse (see chapters 6 and 18). The advisor will, to some extent, help prepare the client for testimony, but will mostly prepare the attorney for trial. An attorney might want to know what the definitive or important texts, tests, or studies are and whether there are differing views or alternative hypotheses.

In this area, the attorney wants someone who is knowledgeable and flexible, someone who will not be averse to divining openings and walking through them, even if it means debunking one's own area of specialization by pointing out that there is inadequate research in a particular area, or the research is faulty, or the researchers themselves are biased. This will usually, then, be someone with whom the attorney has had dealings or someone whom the attorney knows is available for this type of assignment. Because the attorney works with this expert off the record, it is necessary that there be a rapport and an ease of communication between the two. When an attorney utilizes the services of an advisor, an attempt is generally made to have that advisor come under the umbrella of the attorney–client privilege so that all communications are shielded from discovery. This is done by having the attorney (rather than the client) employ the advisor and sometimes entering into a letter agreement setting forth the employment. This makes all communications part of the attorney's "work-product" and immune from subpoena or other discovery.

EXPERTS AS WITNESSES FOR ONE SIDE

The last and most common area in which an attorney has the opportunity to select an expert, whether or not there has been a neutral evaluation, is when the attorney wants a witness to testify. The pejorative term for such a witness is "the hired gun." In fact, such witnesses are often more than just helpful; they are critical. The areas in which an expert might serve as a witness are diverse. Often an attorney might want an expert to meet with or to administer testing to a client so that the expert can testify regarding the client's parenting ability. Although such a witness cannot testify regarding who might make the better parent or to relative merits, he or she can certainly testify regarding the particular qualities of the one person examined. Such a witness might also respond to hypothetical questions relating to the other parent (see chapter 1).

If there are particular weaknesses in a case or in the personality or behavior of the parent being represented, it is possible that a mental health expert will be able to provide testimony that will be helpful. The same is true if there is a claim that the personality or behavior of the other parent is harmful. Often an expert might be retained for a particular purpose, in which event the attorney has the ability to structure and shape the scope of the evidence that will be presented.

Another area for expert advocacy is peer review. While a mental health professional may not be able to make a custody recommendation without seeing all of the parties, he or she can certainly read a report and/or testimony and comment upon its thoroughness, methodology, consistency, the legitimacy of the conclusions reached, and whether alternative conclusions might have been reached by others or under other circumstances.

The reason it is important for the attorney to offer and for the judge to receive alternative theories through expert testimony is because judges want and must have a basis for each determination. We understand that it is for the judge, not the expert, to decide the case. In rendering a decision, however, every judge must state the reasons for making the determination as he or she is not given unfettered discretion: determinations must be reasonable and are subject to appellate review. If a neutral expert makes a recommendation contrary to the client's cause, the attorney must attempt to: (a) present evidence and argument that will cause the judge to disagree on a gut level with the neutral expert's recommendation; (b) attack the neutral expert to minimize the impact of the recommendation; and (c) present other expert evidence reaching the opposite conclusion that gives the judge a basis on which to decide against the recommendations of the neutral expert. In such cases, this "other" expert evidence becomes the critical evidence on which the case will be decided.[2]

---

[2]There are numerous cases in every jurisdiction in which judges disregard expert testimony and give reasons for doing so—reasons relating to cross-examination, inconsistencies, inadequate investigation, or the like. In each of these cases, the judge wanted to achieve a result different from the recommendation.

PREPARING A CLIENT FOR THE EVALUATION

One of the most controversial issues facing lawyers who handle custody cases is how to prepare a client for the interview with the mental health expert (whether appointed or privately retained). If an attorney's obligation is to assist in achieving the client's cause, surely that includes preparing a client for testimony, preparing a client for cross-examination, telling a client what clothes to wear to court, how to sit on the witness stand, how to express him or herself, and so forth. Why then would the same not hold true for preparing the client for the mental health examination which is no less critical?[3] Surely an attorney must prepare the client to some extent for the evaluation. On the other hand, explaining to a client what a mental status examination or a projective technique consists of, what kinds of tests might be administered, and what those tests are seeking to measure might be considered by many to be "cheating." Even more controversial might be having one's client pretested, handing a client a book on psychological testing, or having a mental health expert meet with the client prior to the evaluation to discuss the nature of evaluations (see Interlude I).

With a privately retained witness, the attorney and client can, to a great extent, control the flow of information about the client. Limiting that information is risky, however, since the other side could bring it out during cross examination.[4] Moreover, withholding important information from a retained witness might jeopardize the testimony in that case, as well as damaging any future relationship the attorney might wish to have with the witness. One must be very careful in this area.

CONCLUSION

The adversary system, like all other systems of justice that have been developed throughout history, is imperfect. Wise rules of law (such

---

[3]In one case, a client was told by an attorney to tell the neutral evaluator the truth and to hold back nothing. When asked about his dreams and fantasies, the client, a clergy person, disclosed having sexual fantasies about parishioners. Those disclosures appeared in the report and the case was lost.

[4]If the attorney and client failed to disclose to a retained expert extremely relevant information such as, for example, prior psychological testing, or the client's arrest or hospitalization record, and the withheld information were brought out during cross-examination, the retained expert might look foolish on the witness stand.

as determining custody in the best interests of a child) require judges and experts to use their discretion and, whenever discretionary power is given to imperfect administrators, there will be mistakes and even injustice. But this system has proven to be the best one yet devised. The process is a dynamic one. Opposing positions are stated, debated and challenged. No position is taken for granted. Determinations are reviewed. We do the best that we can and we arrive at a result, no matter how difficult it may be (and no matter how long it takes).

The reputation of any mental health expert is the key factor in expert selection. The same is true of attorneys. We must all maintain our integrity in these hotly contested, highly emotional proceedings so that we leave each case with our reputations not merely intact, but enhanced.

Chapter 3

Representation of the Child to the Court

The Law Guardian and Guardian ad Litem

PATRICIA ANN GRANT
STEVEN KLEE

C ustody and visitation disputes in divorce proceedings are probably the thorniest and most emotionally charged issues confronting our courts today. The court's objective in these situations is to determine what is in the best interest of the child or children involved. Increasingly, in recent years, our courts have relied upon lawyers who are appointed to serve as law guardians or guardians ad litem, to make recommendations concerning the best interests of the child. Despite the critical and delicate nature of the role of these court appointed attorneys, there are few meaningful guidelines with respect to their qualifications for appointment, the scope of their duties, and the amount of their fees.

Rapid growth in the use of such professionals in the absence of standards has led to serious abuses. Unfortunately, the role of the law guardian or guardian ad litem is most often not adequately explained to the litigants or the children and there is generally much confusion about what the role of a law guardian or guardian ad litem should actually be. In the simplest terms, a law guardian is an attorney who represents the child or children. In that capacity, he or she advocates the desires of the child in court proceedings. Law guardians must, by definition, be attorneys. A guardian ad litem, on the other hand, is appointed as an "arm of the court" to protect children who are unable, because of age or other incapacity, adequately to express their wishes. The guardian ad litem must consider the child's desires but, ultimately, is required to make an independent judgment and to express to the court an opinion as to what is in the best interests of the children. Because of this difference, guardians ad litem are generally appointed for younger children. In some states, the guardian ad litem is not required to be an attorney.

QUALIFICATIONS

There are virtually no qualifications or other criteria for appointment as a law guardian or guardian ad litem, other than a law degree in most cases. A background in psychology, psychiatry, or social work is not a prerequisite to appointment as a law guardian or guardian ad litem.

Recently, some states have begun to develop minimum standards for the training of law guardians (Curley and Herman, 1995). Before appointment, prospective guardians may have to complete some form of specialized training lasting from 8 to 12 hours. This training generally includes discussion of some or all of the following topics: child abuse and neglect; information about social service systems, including child welfare and protective services; child development; cultural and ethnic diversity; domestic violence; community resources; recent case law regarding divorce and custody.

While such training represents an improvement over the old system, there is unfortunately no system to measure compliance or competency. Training does not ensure an understanding of these concepts and there is no mechanism to evaluate guardian performance. Once training is completed, all that is required to maintain one's status as a qualified guardian is minimal continuing education hours.

THE DIFFICULTIES CONFRONTING GUARDIANS

Many conflicts confront the guardian ad litem. Trained as a lawyer who acts as an advocate for his or her clients, the guardian ad litem is asked to serve as the person who articulates the child's best interests or needs, even if they conflict with the apparent wishes of the child, the nominal client (Moore, 1996). Absent general psychiatric or developmental psychological training, it is difficult to imagine how a guardian ad litem can effectively pursue her mandate to represent those interests. We believe that the guardian ad litem's lack of psychological sophistication may have dire consequences in this situation.

A law guardian, on the other hand, must represent the wishes and position of the child, even when they are in conflict with the guardian's own judgment. Many law guardians confront this ethical dilemma. These lawyers must have the ability to analyze and focus on the power dynamic inherent in the parent/child relationship and they must achieve a balance between advice and information and undue persuasion and coercion. A law guardian who finds little tolerance for a child's ambivalence and decision swings may begin to involve the child less and less in the decision-making process. Alternatively, a law guardian who becomes overattached to a child may lose perspective as to the overall court proceeding and its objectives. The law guardian must remember that there is a fine line between trying to understand a child and attempting to work therapeutically (Freedman et al., 1993). Lawyers, as professionals, are not meant to be, nor are they qualified to be, therapists or surrogate parents.

In general, law guardians are asked to insinuate themselves into a family system that is undergoing a tremendous degree of turmoil. Their exact role within this system may be unclear to the parents, the child, and to the guardians themselves. Such ambiguity can lead guardians to become overly intrusive when feeling protective of the children. Similarly, the lack of a clearly defined role can lead others to withdraw, thus providing a noticeable lack of involvement. A guardian who is sensitive to a child's plight might react in what she believes to be a caring and attentive manner. However, this concern may be viewed skeptically by the parents who see the guardian as conspiring with their children to find negative information about their parenting. These same children, while comforted by a guardian's attention, may begin to feel guilty about providing any information regarding their parents' behavior. Despite such feelings, the parents may be too frightened to share their concerns about their children's discomfort with the guardian for fear of alienating her, while the child may not be sophisticated or informed enough to do so.

In these high-conflict, traumatic situations, it may be more appropriate to have properly trained mental health professionals engaged in this task rather than attorneys. At the very least, we suggest that law guardians or guardians ad litem be required to undergo a certification process which involves a meaningful training program designed and operated by mental health professionals in conjunction with lawyers.

THE EMOTIONAL ISSUES

It may be useful to examine issues that commonly arise in custody and visitation disputes. Typically, the children are residing with one parent and the noncustodial or nonresidential parent has a visitation or parenting schedule. The children have often lived through severe hostility and conflict while their parents were together, which may now take the form of interference with visitation, angry comments by one parent against the other, attempts to "bribe" the children through gifts and privileges, and, in extreme cases, extensive, concerted efforts seriously to malign the other parent (parental alienation syndrome). The guardian must be aware of these dynamics and monitor the child's reactions to the parent's behavior. While it is natural for a lawyer to form his own opinion of the parents, he must remember that most children desire to maintain a loving relationship with both parents.

Children may feel responsible for their parents' break-up and, if they are old enough to be asked, they are likely to feel extremely guilty about choosing one parent over the other. Guardians need to be aware that children forced into choosing sides may feel anxious, guilty and/or ambivalent. Or they may develop an inappropriate sense of empowerment. Custody disputes may also involve cases of abuse and neglect. Guardians need not only to be educated concerning the signs and symptoms of abuse, but about how to communicate effectively with children about abuse.

Custody disputes almost invariably involve issues of change. Children may be required to change homes, schedules, and schools and give up much of what is familiar to them. There may be issues that require separating siblings. The impact of these changes may be different for children of varying ages, thus requiring guardians to have some knowledge of developmental issues. Guardians must be aware that their decisions and recommendations may radically change a child's life. Therefore, the reasons for these decisions must be separated from personal emotional reactions. At the very least, a guardian who is uncertain about what is best for the child or children she represents must be knowledgeable enough to consult other experts for their advice and guidance (Galatzer-Levy, 1999).

PAYMENT OF FEES OF LAW GUARDIANS AND GUARDIANS AD LITEM

Just as there are no qualifications for law guardians or guardians ad litem, or standards governing their appointment, there are no standards with respect to their fees. In fact, payment may come from the government, or, more likely, from one or both parents. Most frequently, it is the moneyed spouse who pays the guardian's fees. Sometimes the fees are divided by the parents in proportion to their income. It is troubling to consider the potential reaction of a guardian to the refusal, or inability, of a parent to pay his share of the fees. It may be more appropriate and less prejudicial to the parties and the children to have the state or county pay the fees, which should be fixed at a uniform, reasonable amount. This would obviate negative reactions to a parent who cannot or will not make the required payments.

CASE EXAMPLES

Consider the case of three small children (the oldest was eight years of age), who lived with their mother while their father fought for sole custody. In this case, there were issues of race (the parents were an interracial couple), extended family (one parent had extensive extended family who were involved with the children), and constancy for the children (school, friends). The guardian ad litem proposed that the children be moved to the father's home because the mother's house was "untidy," a proposal that overlooked the children's emotional needs. This example highlights one of the potential pitfalls in employing a guardian who lacks psychological sophistication.

In another case, a law guardian with little knowledge or sophistication in the field of mental health, and with little common sense—decided to use the child he represented as a pawn. He joined with one parent's counsel and supported her unfounded allegations without any independent investigation. It was troubling to hear a law guardian in court objecting, on technical grounds, to questions whose answers he would have been eager to hear if he had been truly acting as the child's advocate. In this case, in which the law guardian could have caused irreparable harm to a child, perhaps without even realizing it, the law guardian joined in an application to suspend contact between the child and one parent premised on an unsubstantiated and demonstrably false allegation. Fortunately, the judge refused to "rubber-stamp" the application. In most cases, the requests or recommendations of a law guardian or guardian ad litem are routinely granted and accepted by the court.

Often, however, guardians serve a crucial role in helping children through the stressful process of divorce. When properly trained, they can protect a child's rights, disseminate information in a meaningful and constructive manner, and instruct the parents and the court in how best to deal with the children involved in the case. Although there is much to criticize about the present system, with its conflicts and potential emotional dangers to children and parents, it must be emphasized that there are law guardians who intervene appropriately and perform valuable services. Two examples spring to mind.

In one case, although the law guardian for the children sharply criticized one parent and appeared to be biased against him, it took little hindsight to recognize that she had observed grossly inappropriate conduct by that parent, and had truly averted a catastrophe as a result of that parent's ignorance with respect to his own children. In that case, neither parent had the capacity to be objective about the situation. Both parents were destroying their children by using them as pawns in the divorce. And the destruction would have gone unchecked had the law guardian not intervened, no matter how unfair and harsh her intervention appeared at the time. In retrospect, she likely saved the children's emotional lives or at least controlled the damage that was being done to them.

In a second case, a law guardian with tremendous psychiatric knowledge and insight was appointed after a long period of time during which one of the parents had used the children as bargaining chips—which is not unusual in highly charged matrimonial disputes. The mother withheld visitation from the father in an attempt to extract financial benefit. The law guardian here was strong and psychologically sophisticated. It was clear that her involvement diffused the situation; the case was settled, and the children finally gained meaningful access to both parents.

We believe that some law guardians are so imbued with their own sense of power and importance that they lose all perspective. In one case, a law guardian who had been more or less indifferent to the plight of his clients (in nearly eight months, he had briefly seen the children on two occasions and consistently refused to return telephone calls about serious issues that arose during the proceedings) took umbrage at something counsel for one of the parties did, made it known that he had consulted with the highest ranking judge in the court in which the proceeding was pending, and then continued to grandstand in an attempt to prove his point by accepting a speaking engagement about the case while the matter was pending and over the strenuous objection of one of the parties. This particular case points to a number of ethical issues and raises serious questions and concerns about the role of a law guardian. It is also illustrative of a case in which a law guardian is so unresponsive and disinterested as to be an ineffective representative of the children. If a law guardian is simply another lawyer in the case who happens to represent the children instead of one of the parents, should he or she have ready access to judicial officials and be in a position to receive ex parte advice from them?[1] We think not. If a lawyer for one of the parents acted in this manner, severe disciplinary action could result against that lawyer. The rules need to be more clearly enunciated in order to prevent such conduct by law guardians.

RECOMMENDATIONS

Given the importance of the role of law guardians and guardians ad litem, it is recommended that more states consider appointing mental health professionals in custody and visitation disputes, or disputes involving abuse allegations. Perhaps mental health professionals should replace lawyers altogether as guardians ad litem. However, when law guardians (who are lawyers by definition) are appointed, it is urged that they undergo mandatory educational training that

---

[1]In New York, this is prohibited conduct, but it appears that the rules in some boroughs are relaxed for some law guardians nonetheless.

addresses issues such as child development, the dynamics of abuse and neglect, the psychological implications of divorce, and factors affecting the best interests of the child. If mental health professionals are appointed as guardians ad litem, they should be well informed in the field of family law.

In New York, the legislature has recently attempted to grapple with some of the problems involving law guardians, although much remains to be done. Certain "favorites" were being appointed time and again, and other qualified individuals were being ignored. Patronage was and is rampant, at least in some boroughs of New York. Beginning in mid-2003, the amount of annual compensation that may be earned by law guardians or guardians ad litem was severely circumscribed. In addition, the legislature limited the number of high-paying cases each law guardian could take each year. This is a step in the right direction, but clearly not all that is required. Patronage needs to be curbed, truly qualified people need to be appointed, and there needs to be an annual review of the work of law guardians—perhaps by truly confidential evaluations from lawyers on both sides. Issues such as the firing of a law guardian by her client need to be addressed.[2] Although these issues may appear simple to resolve, we believe they are not quite as simple as they may sound. Truly meaningful mechanisms must be established to report suspected or perceived guardian abuses. We do not believe such mechanisms exist.

Fees for those who serve as law guardians and guardians ad litem should be standardized. At the present time, at least in New York, guardians are paid as little as $25 an hour, and as much as $400 an hour and more. Fee disputes between payor-parents and guardians are common and questions arise as to whether the court who made the appointment should sit in judgment of these fee disputes.

In summary, we have argued that law guardians and guardians ad litem ought to be well trained in family law and have some meaningful education in child development, rather than a course consisting of a lecture of a few hours with no measure of comprehension or capacity. We urge that guardians ad litem be appointed for children

---

[2]Since law guardians or guardians ad litem are appointed by the court, they are not susceptible to the usual rules governing the attorney–client relationship. If children dislike their guardians, they are not free to fire them without making an application to the court that involves complicated issues beyond the scope of this chapter.

up to at least the age of thirteen. Guardians must work in tandem with trained senior mental health professionals (and, as we have suggested above, perhaps mental health professionals should replace lawyers altogether as guardians ad litem) to help monitor transference and countertransference issues. Continued appointments as law guardian and/or guardian ad litem should be based upon past performance and openness to meaningful continued training. We believe that trained senior mental health professionals should review the performance of law guardians or guardians ad litem on at least an annual basis to evaluate their performance and make recommendations as to whether they should continue to receive appointments.

REFERENCES

Curley, P. S. & Herman, G. (1995), Representing the best interests of children: The Wisconsin experience. *J. Amer. Acad. Matrimonial Lawyers,* 136:123–136.

Freedman, M. R., Rosenberg, S. J., Gettman-Feizien, D. & Van Scoyk, S. (1993), Evaluator countertransference in child custody evaluations. *Amer. J. Forensic Psychol.,* 11:61–73.

Galatzer-Levy, R. M. & Kraus, L., eds. (1999), *The Scientific Basis of Child Custody Decisions.* New York: Wiley.

Moore, N. J. (1996), Conflicts of interest in the representation of children. *Fordham Law Rev.,* 64:1819–1856.

Chapter 4

Considering Custody Evaluations
The Thrills and the Chills

BERNICE H. SCHAUL

While the majority of clinicians might never want to have anything to do with the legal system, I believe that working in the area of divorce and custody litigation can in fact be one of the most exciting and gratifying professional experiences that one can have. After more than twenty-five years of conducting custody evaluations, I still find this work to be extraordinarily fascinating, complex, and stimulating. It is an arena that taps into and expands many of the clinician's natural interests and skills and can be filled with intellectual and emotional challenges. Each time an evaluation begins, the clinician is confronted with an unfolding drama in which multitudes of variables are operating. Not only do the parents and the children have major roles in what is taking place but the personalities, proclivities, and belief systems of the attorneys and caseworkers are also often just as critical to the final outcome of a case. And, each time, it is the clinician's task to understand the wide range of forces at play in the family, both internal and external, and to make sense of all the available information. No matter how many similarities and themes we can recognize from one case to the next, each divorcing family is unique. As such, each one also deepens our understanding of what parents and children are experiencing in this most stressful of life situations.

The families that are referred for custody evaluations are a small and unique subset of all of those that are in the process of divorcing.

They are not the clients who might be seen in one's practice who are struggling earnestly to work through the anxiety and loss that divorce often entails. Instead the referred family is one in which an impasse has occurred, tensions are rising, and animosity may be building to a rapid boil. The divorce has triggered for one or both parents an angry and adversarial response and, no matter what reasonable arguments are offered, little can be done to move beyond the stalemate that has taken shape. The lawyers may have fanned the flames of contentiousness or been the voices of reason but, despite everyone's best efforts, it has been impossible to craft an agreement which is satisfactory enough to both parties.

Janet Johnston (Johnston and Campbell, 1988; Johnston and Roseby, 1997) has written eloquently about the many powerful emotional forces that can impel parents to sustain conflicts with their estranged spouses. When a psychological evaluation is ordered by the Court, it strongly suggests that these emotional forces are being expressed in the courtroom. It is recognized that at least some of the issues blocking a resolution of the case are *psychological*, not *legal*, and therefore the door has been opened for the kind of input that lawyers and judges are not equipped to provide. It is at this juncture that the clinician first has contact with the family. The evaluation becomes the vehicle with which to examine and elucidate what emotional forces and factors are operating in the family interaction as a whole as well as in the parents and children individually. Hopefully, through the process of careful assessment, the clinician can provide the court with enough insight, clarification, and practical recommendations to contribute to the resolution of what has become an acrimonious and intractable situation.

For those professionals who are intrigued by these unique circumstances, the possibility of playing a role in a high conflict divorce situation can be quite compelling. Yet caution and humility are qualities necessary to those who embark on the task of conducting custody evaluations. Just as we know from the analytic situation that there are layers and layers in the internal world, so it also is in this unusual world in which legal and psychological problems intersect. After years of doing this work and observing the changing legal and psychological climate, there are several caveats that I would offer to those who gingerly approach this exciting field.

SPECIALIZED KNOWLEDGE IS ABSOLUTELY NECESSARY

Although it may seem self-evident that one needs training in the area of custody evaluations, it is surprising how frequently some clinicians assume that they can simply expand their practices to include this particular undertaking. In an era when managed care has narrowed the range of options available to mental health practitioners, the possibility of doing custody evaluations might seem appealing. However, without a healthy respect for the uniqueness and the complexity of this work, the clinician may be embarking on a path in which he or she will be doing more harm than good. The results of an evaluation from an ill-equipped clinician are often disastrous for families who subsequently may be forced to live with poorly conceived and inappropriate custody arrangements that have been recommended and then court-ordered.

There are several excellent detailed resources available for informing oneself about the "how to" of conducting a custody evaluation (Schutz et al., 1989; Stahl, 1994, 1999). Categories of information to be elicited, specific interview questions, observational techniques, special complex issues, and report writing are all discussed. There are also professional guidelines for conducting custody evaluations promulgated by the American Psychological Association (1994), the Association of Family and Conciliation Courts (1994), and the American Academy of Child and Adolescent Psychiatry (1997), among others, that provide perspectives on this complex task (see chapter 5). Before even considering whether or not to do this kind of work, the clinician should be familiar with all of this literature and become "forensically informed."

In addition, the clinician should be conversant with the extensive body of clinical and research literature that discusses the multiplicity of psychological factors that affect families of divorce. For example, a great deal has been studied and written about the impact of a child's age at the time of divorce, parental psychological functioning, level of parental conflict, family composition, and different custodial arrangements. Again, the clinician should be informed and aware of past and present developments in the field. The outstanding work of Wallerstein (Wallerstein and Kelly, 1980; Wallerstein and Blakeslee, 1989, 2003; Wallerstein, Lewis, and Blakeslee, 2000),

Hetherington (Hetherington and Kelly, 2002), Kalter (1990), Garrity and Baris (1994), and Hodges (1991), to name just a few, all offer considerable insight into the issues at play in the divorce situation.

Although there are few actual training programs available for learning the necessary skills, there are other means to do so. Conferences, lectures, workshops, and symposia on child custody evaluations are periodically offered by the Association of Family and Conciliation Courts, for example. In addition, finding a mentor or supervisor is advisable, much as it is in other aspects of clinical training. This affords the novice some guidance in learning what psychological variables are most relevant to the legal system and how best to communicate information to the courts. As one gains some experience, participation in a forensic peer group in which custody cases are discussed offers an opportunity to exchange perspectives with other clinicians doing this work. Finally, the clinician seeking to do forensic work should also have grounding in the prevailing case law and customary approaches to custody issues in the particular court system in which he or she will be working.

The clinician must have highly developed skills in the assessment of adults and children, both in terms of personality functioning and in terms of the parameters of what constitutes normal and disturbed reactions to divorce in the family. A developmental understanding of the child's reactions and needs when divorce takes place is obviously absolutely critical. For example, recognizing how the infant and toddler's normal attachment and security needs will be affected by parental separation or how the older child's increasing cognitive and emotional capacities impact on their behavior are common issues that arise. In a high-conflict divorce, a good-natured and easygoing two-year-old may become tense and cranky when traveling between two parents whom he genuinely loves. A six-year-old who claims she does not like "the schedule" might be hearing the custodial parent's words reverberating in her head. An adolescent whose spirit has been crushed by years of being overwhelmed by a parent who pressures him relentlessly may not be able to express, or even know, his true feelings in an interview with a forensic evaluator. In short, clinicians must have the insight and knowledge that will allow them to understand how situational variables interact with developmental processes, temperament, and personality factors for each child they evaluate.

Perhaps the most critical aspect of the evaluation and of the ultimate health of the family is the assessment of the personality and parental competencies of each of the parents. It is our role to appreciate the many variables impinging on the parents during the divorce process and to assess what may be enduring patterns of behavior and what may be acute reactions to a crisis. Compassion for the disorganizing effect of divorce as well as an attunement to the basic mental health, the interpersonal issues, and the individual strengths and weaknesses of the parents is absolutely necessary. Can the parent provide "good enough" care to the child to support healthy development? Are the parent's own narcissistic needs so profound as to interfere with appreciating the child's separate needs and experiences? Can the parent act with a modicum of civility so that sufficient communication can take place with the other parent? Is the parent conscious of his or her own tendencies to blame and/or sabotage the other parent and can he or she control impulses toward destructive behavior? It is clear that in this work a multilayered assessment is necessary, in which the forensic evaluator must be able to consider and balance many different factors before coming to any conclusions.

There are developmental issues for the adults as well as for the children in the family, and the thoughtful clinician should be considering both. For the parent, the divorce is a critical *developmental moment*, in which his or her sense of identity and place in the world is being threatened. Suddenly the attachments and the life that have defined the parent's identity for five or ten or fifteen years are torn asunder. Reactions to this rupture can be powerful. For some parents it may be devastating, blinding them temporarily to the needs of their children. A father may feel that his sense of potency and place is being undermined when rigid limits are set on the times when he can see his children. A mother may feel attacked and threatened when the child she has cared for every day goes off with a father who abandoned her for another woman. These moments in a parent's life can be difficult and exceedingly painful. It is critical that the clinician understands as much as possible the components of what is actually driving and motivating the adults involved in a custody dispute, appreciating what may be a short-term reaction and what may be a more enduring pattern. To do otherwise would be a disservice to the parents and the children.

THE QUANDARY OF SELF-REPORT
(OR THE ROLE OF REALITY)

In few other clinical situations is there as much motivation, or perhaps need, to distort reality as in custody evaluations, at times unwittingly and at times intentionally. Given that self-report (that is, each family member's subjective version of events) is the primary source of information we have, there are inherent difficulties in learning about what has actually gone on in the past. Parents often tell diametrically opposed stories, and discerning "reality" is no simple task. Uncertainties about the objectivity of family members' reports pervade the clinical interaction and require a healthy degree of skepticism on the part of the evaluator. At times, parents are so driven by their own wishful thinking or distorted perceptions that their capacity for balanced thinking or, even more significantly, their sense of reality has been seriously compromised. Whereas in the treatment situation patients have some incentive to explore openly their experiences and to expose their true thoughts and feelings in the hopes of alleviating distress, this is often not the case in custody matters. In fact, parents are understandably wary and anxious about being evaluated and they worry about being misunderstood or judged poorly. They feel threatened and want to present themselves in the best possible light.

Nonetheless it is the evaluator's task to know as much as possible about what has actually taken place in a family. While the factors are complex when it comes to distortions, the savvy clinician who does this work must be particularly attuned to the opportunities for misrepresentation and manipulation, conscious and unconscious, in both parents and children. Sorting through what is reality, as well as recognizing the limitations as to what is truly knowable and what is not, is not simple, yet it is an extremely important piece of conducting a thorough and competent evaluation.

While we understand what is said in the traditional therapeutic setting as an expression of the client's *subjective emotional experience* in the forensic evaluation, we need to probe more deeply into the concrete details of life to try to also discover what *objective* reality has been. In some sense the forensic evaluator becomes a "detective of divorce," as one particularly astute eight-year-old commented during an interview, and a careful and thorough inquiry is one of the best tools we have to accomplish our goals. We want to learn not only what parents and children think and feel, but how they behave and what they have done and continue to do in their lives. The clinician is often bombarded with thinly veiled self-congratulatory commentary and disowned denigrating remarks about the other parent. As such, it becomes particularly important to carefully distinguish between a parent's opinions about events and the details of what in fact occurred.

One needs to be able to frame non-threatening questions that elicit specific information about a range of areas of life, as well as to be alert to differentiating between intellectualized commentary and genuine understanding of a child's needs. Conversations may be rife with declarations about being the "primary parent" or "Mr. Mom," but it is always necessary to explore what these labels mean to any particular adult. For example, when a father who worked at home as a writer reported that he had been the "primary parent" while the mother attended graduate school full-time, inquiry was made about the details of the childcare arrangements. Discovering the facts that a baby-sitter was present during most of the time that the father was at home and that the mother took over childcare the moment she returned home made the father's version of reality questionable.

Sometimes clients are tacitly encouraged by their attorneys to emphasize certain points, to frame their conversations with the clinician in particular ways. Less than ethical attorneys may even suggest that parents lie, either by omission or by commission. When parents are ashamed about things they have done, they may welcome such advice. Their own needs to disown or cover up their behavior, rather than address it openly, become operative. Illustrative of this point is the father who, in the sway of his passions, encouraged his secret lover to try to nurse his infant daughter, unbeknownst to the child's mother. He understandably wanted to deny this episode. More generally, a parent who was explosive or one who was absent or inaccessible for long periods might well feel that revelations about these aspects of the family history would not be in his or her self-interest. Clearly, the way parents handle these issues tells us something about who they are and how they function, yet knowing as much as possible about the reality of what has taken place is perhaps more important.

For some particularly disturbed or narcissistic parents, the need to revise the family history can be quite powerful. When faced with abandonment and the vulnerability and rage that it can precipitate, reality often takes a back seat to a revised version of the family history. Initially a parent might be quite cogent, but often as the case unfolds one learns how skewed and distorted his or her reports may be. In a particularly poignant case, for example, a physically disabled, infantile, and emotionally dependent mother said she still loved her husband and refused to give him a divorce. Nonetheless, she continually accused him of trying to kill her by allowing her wheelchair to roll down the street, and frequently repeated this accusation to their two sons. A disturbed parent may truly come to believe the reality of his or her perceptions and, at times, indeed, there may be a shred of emotional truth in these statements. It is critical, however, that the clinician always keep in mind the powerful individual and family dynamics at play and the degree of emotional disturbance involved and suspend judgment until an in-depth inquiry has been concluded.

Of course, the fact that we are able to hear not only both parents' versions of reality but also the children's versions is quite helpful when trying to understand family history, particularly if rigid alignments have not yet formed. As we listen to all the family members, the opportunities to develop working hypotheses about what has taken place expand enormously. The various perspectives that the forensic clinician has access to, in contrast to the professionals who hear only one side of the story, allow us to have a fairly balanced view of the family. For example, when a mother said that without question she encouraged visitation and wanted her two children to have a relationship with their father, it sounded convincing. However, when her bubbly six-year-old and more guarded eight-year-old both explained that "mommy says if we sleep over at daddy's she'll cry and cry and cry," it raised serious questions about the mother's reports, as well as about what really takes place in the family. These children were young enough that their spontaneity allowed a fairly free discussion of what occurred in the home, thereby providing some potential insight into the reality of the communications in the family.

That said, it must be remembered that children, like adults, are in the sway of emotional currents during a divorce and that some of their reports must also be listened to with caution. Frequently, legal professionals look to the children as a source of information and assume the veracity of their statements. Not only can this be an enormous burden for a child, but it also ignores the realities of the panoply of factors that influence children's communications. Any child whose family is in the midst of a high-conflict divorce is feeling a great deal of pressure, usually both internally and externally. Depending on his or her developmental stage and individual personality, not to mention the dynamics in the family, a child may have great difficulty expressing himself freely or even knowing what he thinks and feels. Young children may not be accurate reporters because momentary needs and emotions affect them. Older children may form alliances that preclude openness and honesty and block their ability to discuss events in an evenhanded way.

Finally, access to collateral sources of information also enhances our ability to understand and appreciate the reality of what has taken place in the family, above and beyond the subjective perceptions of the parents and the children. Although it must be remembered that all "reporters" bring their own subjectivity and biases to the situation, at times the information provided by a therapist, a teacher, and a nanny can shed valuable light on a troubled situation. Not surprisingly, many therapists are advocates for their patients, but some provide balanced information that is useful. In one case, when a father insisted his desperate wife's departure from the home with their two-year-old daughter was a complete shock, the reports of three marriage counselors the couple had seen revealed otherwise. Apparently, in all three treatments the father exploded with rage and refused even to speak about the possibility of separation whenever the mother began discussing the topic. Sensitive teachers, another possible source of information, often can share perceptions and describe events that are revealing. Similarly, although nannies may become heavily identified with one parent or the other, at times they can provide information that is quite useful.

Ultimately it is incumbent on the forensic evaluator to put all of the data together in ways that shed light on the personality functioning, the family dynamics, and the reality of the family history. It is imperative in this process to recognize the importance of validating information and to possess a healthy level of skepticism about the reports being provided. That said, it is also important to be sensitive to and have compassion for what may be driving and motivating the distortions that take place. Our role is not to condemn or indict but to understand and to clarify, with effective family functioning as the eventual goal.

THE LEGAL PERSPECTIVE VERSUS
THE MENTAL HEALTH PERSPECTIVE

Although all of the professionals involved in custody cases may be perceptive, reasonable, and sensitive human beings, when it comes to dealing with these highly conflicted matters, the language that mental health and legal professionals use is often not even remotely similar. The prism through which an attorney, as an advocate, sees his client's case is different from the prism through which a judge weighs the issues, though both share a belief in arriving at "fairness" in the context of case law and certain procedural rules. The perspective that a clinician takes in trying to make sense of the fray that is being played out in his or her office is, however, vastly different from either of these perspectives. As a consequence it may be difficult to create a meaningful and useful dialogue about the issues that are of emotional concern. While we are all ostensibly familiar with and concerned about "the best interests of the child," how these best interests are translated into reality can be vague. Appreciation for some of the implications of the differing professional perspectives is critical.

Clinicians doing a custody evaluation speak to children and try to understand where they are developmentally, whether they are functioning within a normal range, and how they are currently affected by the divorce that is taking place. We make certain assumptions about what may be positive for a child and how best to plan for them, given their ages, their histories, and their temperaments. We try to understand all the relationships in the family and what each parent's strengths and weaknesses are and, given all of these factors, how best to ensure that the child will thrive and will not spend years warding off the burden of parental pathology or high levels of conflict. We are eager to ensure that a child will have meaningful relationships with both parents that take place in something other than a war zone. We must also recognize when and how to protect children from destructive situations and destructive relationships. Although much of the work may involve assessing the parents' functioning, there is little question that our focus is on how to best protect and support a healthy environment for the child.

The legal system, in contrast, emanates from an entirely different set of assumptions. It is an adversarial system that tends to focus on fairness and entitlements. It is also a system in which attorneys attempt to shape reality around what their own clients are seeking. They use all their skills to promote their client's position in the best ways they possibly can. Clients who are disturbed or malevolently motivated present a problem for thoughtful lawyers. The lawyers are not responsible, however, for the well-being or needs of the children (with the exception of the law guardian, the child's attorney) as long as what they are seeking appears reasonable.

Judges must hear the facts from all sides, weigh the issues, and eventually resolve the case. As part of that responsibility, they may try to encourage or even pressure the parties to come up with an equitable arrangement. Recognizing that it is far better for parents to resolve the issues themselves, the Court does what it can to avoid a trial that will be costly and painful for everyone. The judge is concerned with fairness and, while the "best interests" standard takes precedence, the judiciary is called upon to balance the needs of all parties. Since the most vocal participants in this process are often the parents (as represented by their attorneys), their needs and wishes, not surprisingly, may overshadow those of the children.

What these differences in perspective translate into in a case can vary enormously. Dilemmas inevitably arise in which the *rights* of the adults are pitted against the *needs* of the children, when the pressure to settle the case obscures the need to protect the child's welfare. When the child becomes akin to property that is to be divided *fairly* and when one party presses relentlessly to *win,* the chances that the child's emotional safety and stability will be threatened and distorted multiply exponentially. In the heat of the adversarial process, then, the ability to support the healthy unfolding of development may well be seriously compromised.

Given these often opposing attitudes, it is also not surprising that, in the courtroom, psychological assumptions about a child's needs at a particular developmental stage can be derided as "biases" or cast in a questionable light, if it serves an attorney's purpose. Developmental assumptions and observations that may be viewed as self-evident among clinicians are not necessarily shared by the legal system. The clinician's conclusions, therefore, may require a level of explanation or justification that is not ordinarily necessary when speaking to colleagues within their own profession: this can be intimidating and difficult if one has not prepared for this eventuality. That said, even when explanations are clearly provided and well-substantiated, a judge may have his or her own opinion about what is right for children and may be unmoved by "expert" clinical input.

Discussions about access arrangements for infants and toddlers in particular can generate intense disagreements about what is best for a child, probably because these are the children who cannot speak for themselves at all. The clinician who makes recommendations about access can easily be caught in the crossfire between attorneys whose clients have different beliefs and wishes. Since any recommendation is to some extent based on developmental theory and research, as well as on the forensic evaluation of the parties, an aggressive attorney or even a judge may dismissively suggest that the evaluator's conclusions are only an opinion, not a fact.

In one case, an ill-conceived access arrangement was implemented for a vulnerable and high strung two-year-old, alternating residences every four days, despite the fact that the father had previously been virtually uninvolved in childcare. When the little girl became agitated, clinging, and could no longer sleep through the night or remain in her nursery school classroom, the mother sought help from the Court. The father's attorney derided the psychologist's observations about the child's "regression" and "distress" and the Court was unwilling to make any changes in the schedule. This case reveals that what may be compelling and self-evident to a clinician trained in child development is often seen quite differently by other professionals in the legal setting. A judge may assume that the problem will pass with time, and an attorney might argue that the reports are grossly exaggerated or that the child's upset is in reality the custodial parent's fault. Such are the dilemmas that arise over and over when these two very different disciplines try to resolve the contentious issues of a young child's "best interests" in a high-conflict divorce.

Above and beyond these theoretical questions, the courtroom situation often raises complex issues of *credibility*. On the one hand, courts generally do not want mental health professionals to draw conclusions about whether or not a particular person is credible in his reports, since technically it is only the judge who can make this decision. On the other hand, the clinical process inevitably involves assessing the reliability and validity of an individual's reports and presentation. Particularly when parents, and even children, present markedly different descriptions of events, it is incumbent on the clinician to make some determination as to how much distortion exists and what may be motivating the reports of different family members. Certainly the clinician must draw some conclusions about what has taken place in the family in order to make recommendations, yet the boundary between what is the Court's terrain and what is the clinician's is murky at best. While the clinician should not be drawn into making definitive statements about the "truth," there are many situations in which the legal and mental health perspective as to the "facts" may be at odds with one another.

As if these problems were not daunting enough, the structure and procedures of a trial and providing testimony are hardly conducive to examining and exploring clinical issues. The rules that govern how direct and cross-examination can take place can be bewildering and it is often disorienting for an evaluator to grasp the nuances of the legal dialogue. Of course, attorneys do not ask questions in order to elicit an understanding of the family's problems. Rather they are seeking to undermine or bolster the clinician's findings, depending on who their client is, and they structure their questions to do just that. They look to assign blame and to discredit the other parent and, if necessary, the clinician.

In the legal setting, learning the basics of the courtroom process is a necessity in order to allow oneself to achieve a comfort level on the witness stand. The evaluator must also be well prepared to explain the often complex dimensions of the functioning of parents and children to lawyers and judges who do not speak a psychological language. Since many laymen find clinical concepts fuzzy and insubstantial, it is critical to be able to describe issues in clear and cogent ways, making connections between what we have learned about personality functioning and family dynamics and what we can expect and anticipate about future parenting. Despite our best efforts, we must also recognize that our ability to be heard and to influence will be tempered by a legal system that often is at odds with a psychological perspective.

CONCLUSION

Without question, conducting custody evaluations requires a particular kind of intellectual slant, a tolerance for hostility, and a willingness to allow for ambiguity and uncertainty in the process of pursuing understanding. Clinicians have a unique contribution to make in the forensic arena and the challenge to do so in a thorough, insightful, and cogent way can ultimately provide us with tremendous professional rewards. It must also be recognized that there will be injustices as well as serious disappointments in how the system operates. Notwithstanding this reality, when the custody evaluation fosters psychological awareness and sensitivity in the courtroom, there exists a remarkable opportunity to have a substantial positive impact on parents and children who are coping with the turmoil of divorce.

REFERENCES

American Academy of Child and Adolescent Psychiatry (1997), Practice parameters for child custody evaluation. *J. Amer. Acad. Child & Adoles. Psychiat.*, 36:10 Supplement, 57–67S.
American Psychological Association (1994), Guidelines for child custody evaluations in divorce proceedings. *Amer. Psychol.*, 49:677–680.
Association of Family and Conciliation Courts (1994), Model standards of practice for child custody evaluations. *Family & Conciliation Courts Rev.*, 32:504–513.
Garrity, C. & Baris, M. (1994), *Caught in the Middle.* San Francisco: Jossey-Bass.
Hetherington, E. M. & Kelly, J. (2002), *For Better or for Worse.* New York: Norton.
Hodges, W. F. (1991), *Interventions for Children of Divorce.* New York: Wiley.
Johnston, J. & Campbell, L. (1988), *Impasses of Divorce.* New York: Free Press.
—— & Roseby, V. (1997), *In the Name of the Child.* New York: Free Press.
Kalter, N. (1990), *Growing up with Divorce.* New York: Fawcett Columbine.
Schutz, B., Dixon, E., Lindenberger, J. & Ruther, N. (1989), *Solomon's Sword.* San Francisco: Jossey-Bass.
Stahl, P. (1994), *Conducting Child Custody Evaluations.* Thousand Oaks, CA: Sage.
—— (1999), *Complex Issues in Child Custody Evaluations.* Thousand Oaks, CA: Sage.
Wallerstein, J. (1991), The long-term effects of divorce on children: A review. *J. Amer. Acad. Child & Adoles. Psychiat.*, 30:349–360.
—— & Blakeslee, S. (1989), *Second Chances.* New York: Ticknor & Fields.
—— & —— (2003), *What about the Kids?* New York: Hyperion.
—— & Kelly, J. (1980), *Surviving the Breakup.* New York: Basic Books.
—— Lewis, J. & Blakeslee, S. (2000), *The Unexpected Legacy of Divorce.* New York: Hyperion.

Chapter 5

Ethical and Legal Considerations in Child Custody Evaluations

JAMES S. WULACH

DAVID L. SHAPIRO

*T*here are significant legal and ethical constraints on mental health professionals performing child custody evaluations, which must be carefully considered at the clinician's peril. At the national level, the most relevant ethical standards for psychologists are the Guidelines for Child Custody Evaluations in Divorce Proceedings (American Psychological Association, 1994), drafted by the Committee on Professional Practice and Standards (COPPS), while the first author was chair.

GUIDELINES

The Guidelines are intended to be only aspirational, meaning that they are not intended to be either mandatory or exhaustive. Nevertheless, failing to follow them has crucial consequences. The Guidelines are an attempt to apply the principles of the American Psychological Association's Ethical Principles of Psychologists and Code of Conduct (APA, 1992) to child custody evaluations. If there is an ethical complaint against a psychologist, a finding could not be sustained on the basis of the Guidelines alone, since an actual violation of the Ethical Principles must have occurred. However, as the Guidelines apply the Ethical Principles to the custody arena, violations of the Guidelines would often be ethical violations as well. For

45

example, one precept in the Guidelines states that psychologists must gain specialized competence to perform custody evaluations. This precept mirrors Ethical Standard 2.01 (APA, 2002), which requires that psychologists provide services only within the boundaries of their competence.

It should be noted that psychologists who deviate from the Guidelines risk ethical inquiry not only from the American Psychological Association. Many state psychological associations adopt the APA Ethical Standards as their own, and the Guidelines would be relevant in such hearings as well. Psychologists testifying in custody cases are frequently cross-examined about their fidelity to the Guidelines. Deviations from the Guidelines may be used in malpractice cases to document that psychologists did not maintain professional standards of care in their assessments. Finally, state licensing boards incorporate into their regulations many of the ethical principles relevant to child custody evaluations.

According to the annual reports published by the Ethics Committee of the American Psychological Association, the number of complaints generated as a result of custody evaluations are consistently high, in some years second only to those complaints that have resulted in loss of licensure at the state level (e.g., sexual misconduct). As complaints to ethics boards and state licensing boards by custody litigants occur quite frequently, psychologists are advised to adhere quite carefully to the Guidelines, not only to support the best possible professional practice, but also in the interests of risk management.

The Guidelines are focused on child custody and visitation determinations, but not on proceedings in which parents are being charged with abuse or neglect by the state, when their rights may be terminated. The Guidelines stress that the central purpose of the custody evaluation is to assess the best psychological interests of the child. While the court may determine custody or visitation on various legal considerations, the psychologist's expertise and focus must be the child's psychological needs, and these must remain paramount over the interests of the parent. Some psychologists may erroneously believe that their role is to present the best case for the party who retained them, or they become seduced into presenting that case by the retaining attorney. However, it is clear that this position may be inimical to the child's psychological needs, and hence a violation of the Guidelines.

In addition, Standard 2.04 of the Ethics Code (APA, 2002),

requires psychologists to base their judgments on "established scientific and professional knowledge." An opinion must be consistent with and derived from the data, not from the viewpoint of a particular advocate. Guideline V-1-C of the Specialty Guidelines for Forensic Psychologists is even more specific (Committee, 1991). While aspirational in nature, psychologists who represent themselves as experts should consider the Specialty Forensic Guidelines in directing their activities. Guideline V-1-C speaks of the need to maintain objectivity and scientific integrity in approaching a task in the forensic area, seeking out data that will test plausible rival competing hypotheses before rendering a conclusion or opinion. Only after this process has been followed may a particular position be advocated.

The Custody Guidelines (as contrasted with the Forensic Specialty Guidelines) stress that the focus of an evaluation should be on parenting capacity, the psychological and developmental needs of the child, and the resulting fit between parents and child. The psychopathology of the parents is relevant, but only in its impact on the child's functioning, and is not determinative in and of itself. Thus, even parents who are mentally ill, in some cases, may have a significant role to play in their child's upbringing. For example, a schizophrenic mother, whose delusions are controlled with medication and do not involve her children, may be a preferable custodial parent to a physically abusive father with a personality disorder. She may even be a preferable custodian to a father with no diagnosis who is totally absorbed with his professional life, with little available time for his children.

The importance of evaluating the "fit" between the parents and child recognizes that differing parenting styles may have varying impacts on different children. A democratic parenting style may be ideal for a well-behaved and quiet child, yet a hyperactive child may require a more authoritative approach. Consequently, it would seem essential that the psychologist must evaluate each child separately, as well as together with each parent in order to determine the best fit.

The Guidelines emphasize that the psychologist must function as a neutral and objective expert, providing information in a balanced and impartial manner. The psychologist must be competent in the assessment of children, adults and families, and must be familiar with relevant legal standards. If expertise is required in areas outside of the psychologist's competence, the psychologist must seek additional consultation or supervision. This may mean that the psychologist must obtain a limited opinion from an expert in areas such as alcoholism or child abuse, if the psychologist is not proficient in those specialties. The expert would issue a separate report on the issue of alcoholism, for example, which the psychologist would then use in arriving at his or her recommendations and conclusions. This requirement of the Guidelines is anchored in Ethics Code Standard 2.01(a) (APA, 2002), which requires psychologists to practice only within the bounds of their competence, which in turn is based on "education, training, and supervised experiences." Of some interest is how closely this statement tracks the Federal Rules of Evidence which defines an expert as someone qualified by virtue of knowledge, skill, education, experience, and training.

The psychologist must become aware of and strive to overcome personal and societal biases, which might impinge upon an objective evaluation and recommendations. For example, in cases involving homosexual spouses or lovers, psychologists' feelings either for or against such sexual orientations must be held in abeyance, while pertinent professional literature is reviewed and the individual impact of such behavior upon the children is carefully considered. Other biases may include a preference for maternal or paternal custody at various ages in a child's life, which also must be verified by a literature review and investigation of the impact on the particular family to be evaluated. Likewise, the Ethics Code, in Standard 2.01(b) requires that, when these cultural, racial, or other factors significantly affect psychologists' work, psychologists must "obtain the training, experience, consultation, or supervision necessary to ensure the competence of their services, or they make appropriate referrals." Specialty Guidelines for Forensic Psychologists (Committee, 1991) require an even greater obligation of the psychologist: If any of these attitudes might reasonably impact on the evaluation, they must make this known in advance to the person or persons seeking their services [Forensic Guideline IV A (2)].

DUAL RELATIONSHIPS IN CHILD CUSTODY EVALUATIONS

Greenberg and Shuman (1997) list many compelling reasons why therapeutic and forensic roles are "irreconcilable": (1) The client is different; (2) the privilege is different; (3) the cognitive set is different; (4) the areas of competency are different; (5) the amount of scrutiny applied to the information differs; (6) the amount of structure differs; (7) the amount of "adversarialness" differs; (8) the goals are different. The individual who has established a therapeutic relationship cannot simply "shift gears" and become impartial and objective.

The Custody Guidelines urge psychologists to avoid multiple relationships in their evaluations and treatment. In particular, they should avoid performing assessments in cases where they have previously been or are a psychotherapist for the child or family. Treating psychologists, when they are asked to testify in a custody proceeding, are urged to limit their testimony to factual information, and avoid giving recommendations or opinions regarding custody or visitation issues. It is regrettable that naïve psychotherapists often respond positively to their divorcing patient's pleas for a letter testifying to their excellent mental health and parenting skills, and then recommend that the parent receive custody or increased visitation. Such letters are a violation of the Guidelines for two reasons. First, there is a dual relationship, in which the therapist's role in understanding the psychology of the patient is subverted by a legal advocacy role. Second, the therapist has not evaluated all parties and the children in a neutral and objective manner in making conclusions. Such recommendations are an invitation for the spouse to sue or make a complaint to the professional ethics board and state licensing board.

The entire area of dual or multiple roles in forensic work is misunderstood by many psychologists. Feeling that they "know" the client very well from the therapeutic context, they seek to answer forensic questions, which not only require objectivity and neutrality, but a much broader data base than in psychotherapy. Standard 3.05 of the Ethics Code urges the avoidance of multiple roles if they are likely to impair objectivity, or cause harm or exploitation. This guideline is unfortunately not specific enough for much forensic work. The Forensic Specialty Guidelines (IV D) provide more detailed guidance, requiring that psychologists recognize the inherent role conflicts and seek to avoid them; when it is absolutely impossible to do so, they need to proceed with sensitivity and caution.

INFORMED CONSENT

In performing evaluations, psychologists must obtain informed consent and a waiver of confidentiality from all adults, and must inform children about the evaluation, to the extent that they are able to understand. Participants in an evaluation must be informed about the limits of confidentiality, which hardly exists, except perhaps in extreme cases where the release of information may put the health or life of a child or spouse in danger. It is best that the evaluating psychologist prepare a contract or statement of custody evaluation policies and procedures, that both parties can sign, which specifically obtains informed consent and a waiver of confidentiality.

Likewise, the Ethics Code, in Standard 3.11, requires the provision of "appropriate information beforehand" about the nature of the services to be provided. This, coupled with Standard 4.02, which speaks about discussing the limits of confidentiality and the foreseeable uses of the information generated, provides an excellent baseline for an informed consent document. Many psychologists mistakenly fail to communicate these confidentiality limitations to clients resulting in misunderstanding and bitterness of the people being evaluated.

PSYCHOLOGICAL TESTING

Psychologists are urged to use multiple methods of data gathering, including clinical interviews, observation, psychological tests, and data from outside sources. They are urged to interpret data in a cautious manner, neither overinterpreting nor inappropriately interpreting interview or assessment data. Of all the custody guidelines, this is perhaps the most frequently violated. For example, an elevated L or K score on the MMPI, suggesting that the party is defensive and trying to present as overly virtuous, can be over interpreted into a conclusion that the person is a liar with something to hide, who should not have custody. However, such profile patterns are common in custody evaluations, where relatively normal parents anxiously minimize their faults so as not to lose custody of their children. Tests with norms that have not been standardized on forensic custody populations should be used with caution, with their limitations noted in the report.

What is needed is careful empirical research performed in custody situations, to determine what the "normative" degree of defensiveness is, and then to compare the degree of defensiveness of a particular individual. Despite a variety of interpretative systems claiming to have forensic norms, there are no well-established norms for use in custody evaluations, although Bathurst and Gottfried (1997) have performed an excellent initial study of normative data for the MMPI-2 in child custody litigation. The psychologist must, therefore, use his or her clinical judgment in assessing the degree of defensiveness in a given profile, as required by the Ethics Code.

Ethical Standard 9.06 directs psychologists to be sensitive to situations where particular norms or interpretations may not be applicable. This Standard also requires taking into account any factors that might affect the accuracy of interpretations and indicating any significant limitations of their interpretations. If a test were normed on a clinical sample, and a psychologist were conducting a custody evaluation, the normative group is different and might require a statement in the report about the limitations and validity and reliability of test results in this population.

OPINIONS ABOUT INDIVIDUALS NOT EVALUATED

The Guidelines state that psychologists must not give opinions regarding the psychological functioning of individuals whom they have not personally evaluated, such as spouses accused of misconduct by the other spouse. This is such a widespread abuse that a section of the Ethics Code addresses it specifically. Standard 9.01b states that, "Psychologists provide opinions about the psychological characteristics of individuals" only after they have conducted an examination of the individual adequate to support their statements or conclusions. Only after "reasonable efforts" made to conduct such examinations are unsuccessful, can the psychologist make any conclusory statement, and then only by limiting the nature and extent of conclusions and recommendations.

DOCUMENTATION

Psychologists must maintain careful records of all data obtained during the evaluation, with the expectation that other psychologists and the courts may review it. Such data include unexpected telephone calls from the parties and their attorneys, where it is recommended that the psychologist keep dated notes to ensure protection against later scrutiny.

In the Specialty Guidelines for Forensic Psychologists, from which the Ethics Code language is in fact derived, the statement is again even more specific. "This standard, i.e. for documentation, is higher than the normative standard for general clinical practice" (Guideline 6B). Forensic psychologists "incur a special responsibility to provide the best possible documentation under the circumstances."

LEGAL CONSIDERATIONS

The legal standard for custody/visitation determinations in most jurisdictions is "the best interests of the child" (Uniform Marriage and Divorce Act S402, 9A ULA 561, 1987). This standard is extremely broad, and allows the court to make decisions regarding legal and physical custody, as well as timesharing arrangements based upon the fact-specific details of each case. However, the statutes of many jurisdictions have somewhat differing lists of considerations for the court to take into account in determining the child's best interests. For example, several jurisdictions have a statutory bias in favor of joint custody, unless one parent is unfit, or unless there is substantial evidence that joint custody would not be in the best interests of the child. In addition, case law in each state may interpret such statutes differently.

It is important for the custody evaluator to be aware of the statutory criteria for making custody/visitation determinations, as well as relevant case law in the state where the assessment is performed. While adherence to legal criteria in a report may help the court in translating psychological concepts into statutory criteria, the law may create ethical dilemmas when such criteria conflict with the psychologist's standard of "best psychological interests of the child." For example, in states where joint custody is mandated unless there are substantial indications of parental unfitness, the psychologist may determine that the psychological best interests of the child favor the custody of one parent, but that the less preferred parent is not unfit. Ethical Standard 1.02 requires that if ethical responsibilities conflict with the law, "Psychologists make known that their commitment is to the Ethics Code and take steps to resolve the conflict in a responsible manner." Sometimes this will require documentation of a letter to an attorney explaining the nature of this ethical conflict and suggesting ways of resolving it.

The issue of a legal maternal preference rule is another in which there is a potential conflict between the "best psychological interest" standard and the law. Several jurisdictions follow the rule that children should be raised in the custody of their mothers, except in cases of maternal unfitness. Other states follow a modified version of this rule, called the "tender years doctrine", in which maternal preference is given added weight during the early years of the child's life (Trenkner, 1977). In such jurisdictions, the psychologist's determination of "best psychological interest" may sometimes conflict with maternal preference. As with other legal standards, the psychologist should follow the Guidelines and make recommendations based upon the "best psychological interest," while stating the alternative possible outcome if the maternal preference rule is applied, as the psychologist understands it.

RECOMMENDATIONS TO THE COURT

In a conflict between legal standards and the standard of the Guidelines, that is, best psychological interests of the child, it is recommended that the evaluating psychologist, if he or she chooses to make recommendations, do so using the criteria of the Guidelines. The psychologist should then note that the legal criteria might necessitate an alternative outcome, which should be described. If the psychologist were to make recommendations based on the legal criteria alone, while ignoring the Guidelines, he or she might be violating ethical principles. However, the Guidelines also emphasize that the psychologist should be familiar with relevant legal criteria, so that the findings are relevant to actual law. The recommended approach encompasses both aspects of the conflict. It should be noted that those psychologists who limit their reports to the presentation of psychological data alone, without making custody recommendations, on the theory that such ultimate issues should be left to the court, avoid this issue.

There is a great deal of controversy in the field regarding whether or not psychologists should address such ultimate issues, or where the conclusions from the data end and where the ultimate issue begins. There are respected opinions on both extremes. In actual practice, however, many judges will expect an opinion on the ultimate issue and some may even refuse to admit testimony or a report unless the psychologist has done so.

RISK MANAGEMENT STRATEGIES

Having considered the ethical and legal factors in custody evaluations, it is now useful to consider risk management strategies. Before beginning to perform child custody evaluations, it is important for the psychologist to consider whether he or she is willing to evaluate people in stressful, at times hostile and always litigious circumstances. The psychologist should be ready, not only for vigorous cross-examination if the case proceeds to trial, but also for a complaint to the state licensing board or a malpractice suit by the loser in a case. In some jurisdictions it has been estimated that 25 percent of all contested custody evaluations result in a complaint.

Financial arrangements must be clarified before the evaluation begins. Psychologists should not misrepresent their services for insurance reimbursement purposes, by billing the time as a psychotherapy or health service, rather than as a forensic assessment. Ethical Standard 6.06 requires that psychologists, in their report to payors for services, accurately state the nature of the research or service provided.

The "loser" in a custody battle may be the one to make complaints about custody matters to ethics and state licensing boards. While such complaints are often not justified, it is essential that the evaluator perform the evaluation in as fair and objective a manner as possible, so that there will be no appearance of bias or favoritism. The evaluator should strive to spend roughly equal amounts of time with each party. The use of psychological tests on the parents and children is customary for psychologists, so that a failure to use a standard test battery should be justified. On the other hand, if psychological tests are utilized, the psychologist should be familiar with the use of such tests in forensic contexts, and be prepared to discuss the standardization sample, reliability, and validity of the test on the witness stand.

The psychologist should be prepared emotionally for complaints, even if he or she performs evaluations with the highest standard of professionalism. It is recommended that the psychologist review his or her malpractice insurance, and select one of the several nationally recognized companies that specifically provides legal reimbursement for complaints before state licensing boards and professional ethics boards.

Before proceeding with custody evaluations, the psychologist should review the Custody Guidelines, the Ethical Principles of Psychologists, the Forensic Specialty Guidelines and any relevant state ethics codes, rules and regulations of the state licensing board, or state guidelines. For example, in New Jersey, the Board of Psychological Examiners issued custody guidelines that are much more specific and detailed than the APA Guidelines and largely supplant the Guidelines in that state.

The psychologist should not perform custody evaluations without the specialized training recommended by the Guidelines. Supervision or consultation is highly recommended for the beginning custody evaluator. The best defense against any complaint or suit is a carefully documented file, with all interviews, tests and telephone contacts described in detailed notes, written with this eventuality in mind. If a psychologist is challenged by a complaint or the threat of a suit, it may be necessary, at times, to withdraw from a case if one's objectivity is affected, just as a therapist may recommend transfer of a patient if one's countertransference interferes with successful treatment.

If a psychologist is informed of a lawsuit or complaint, or even threatened by one from a party in the custody dispute, it is recommended that legal advice be sought immediately, before speaking or writing to anyone involved in the custody case. Even speaking to a colleague could result in that colleague being compelled to testify if later revealed. Following the legal consultation, the psychologist then may be required to inform one's malpractice insurer. A decision must be reached on whether to continue or withdraw from the case. Finally, a strategy for informing the attorneys or the judge must be developed, as well as a strategy for responding to the legal action or the threat of it.

SUMMARY AND CONCLUSIONS

While the caveats expressed in this article may seem forbidding, psychologists who practice with high standards and careful risk management can experience considerable professional satisfaction from performing child custody evaluations. There is opportunity to provide significant psychological input into crucial judicial determinations that will affect the child and family throughout life. Such information can lead to healthier outcomes that are sensitive to the needs of the child(ren), and that provide for appropriate psychological and social services to minimize conflict and facilitate growth during one of the most turbulent phases of family life.

REFERENCES

American Psychological Association (1992), Ethical principles of psychologists and code of conduct. *Amer. Psychologist*, 47:1597–1611.
—— (1994), Guidelines for child custody evaluations in divorce proceedings. *Amer. Psychologist*, 49:677–680.
—— (2002), Ethical principles of psychologists and code of conduct. *Amer. Psychologist*, 57:1060–1073.
Bathurst, K. & Gottfried, A. W. (1997), Normative data for the MMPI-2 in child custody litigation. *Psycholog. Assess.*, 9:205–211.
Committee on Ethical Guidelines for Forensic Psychologists (1991), Specialty guidelines for forensic psychologists. *Law & Human Behavior*, 6:655–665.
Greenberg, S. A. & Shuman, D. W. (1997), Irreconcilable conflict between therapeutic and forensic roles. *J. Profess. Psychology: Res. & Pract.*, 28:50–57.
Survey of American Law (1985), *11 Fam. L. Rep.*, 3015, 3019.
Trenkner, T. R. (1977), Modern status of maternal preference rule or presumption in child custody cases, *70 ALR 3d 262* (1977).
Uniform Marriage and Divorce Act S402, 9A ULA 561 (1987).

Interlude II

Parental Psychopathology and Its Impact on the Child

*T*he chapters in this section address a variety of situations in which the parent behaves in destructive and pathological ways. Such behavior is invariably characterized by the adult's egocentricity and inability to empathize with his child. Despite and even because of that parent's faulty development, his or her influence over and impact on the child can be profound. In fact, each of this section's contributors sensitively depicts how the intergenerational transmission of the parental psychopathology occurs insidiously and mostly has an impact on the unconscious of the child. If the chapters herein tend to have a pessimistic tone, it is perhaps inevitable when addressing the warping of the child's developmental potentialities via the impact of parental disturbance and related marital conflict. We believe this interference with optimal development, with its long-term implications, must be faced squarely before addressing, in subsequent sections, the remedial impact of legal interventions and ultimately, therapeutic approaches.

Jack Novick's (1997) presentation of his work on the concept of soul blindness, with its videotaped segments of the ABC News coverage of the Jessica DeBoer case, was profoundly moving. The Novick and Novick chapter (see chapter 7) conveys the spirit of that presentation, with its focus on the unseen need of the child for validation of her experience. Hinted at, as well, in the development of a child deprived of such reflective attunement, is the atrophy of her own empathic capacity. One can only speculate about the limitations of such a child's ability, as a future parent, to provide "soul" nurturance to her own children.

Gunsberg's chapter (see chapter 8) on incest and the parental affair might be taken to illustrate one form of profound soul blindness. Although she devotes most of her attention to the impact of such an affair on the spouse who is "driven crazy" by it and on the child, questions must still be raised about what "blindness" could allow the "infidel" (or unfaithful parent) to act with such blatant disregard for family boundaries and for his child's developing sense of self–other differentiation (to note just one developmental task that would be distorted). Gunsberg's discussion of Freud's insights about how the taboos of primitive societies come to be replaced by internalized prohibitions (in the form of the superego) in people of "advanced" societies is relevant here. Is it possible, as the boundaries of the family have both expanded and become less well defined, that the internalized prohibitions against incest are no longer so effective? If so, the pathology of the adulterous parent can well become the legacy of the child.

The syndrome of parental alienation is described by Shopper (see chapter 9). It may well be that a person who feels betrayed or injured could become an alienating parent who, consciously or not, seeks to preserve the child's "purity" by turning him or her against the other parent. Shopper achieves considerable explanatory power over the baffling and all too common phenomenon of alienation by subsuming it under a broader category which he terms "disorders of created reality." It is enlightening to view again the process by which a developmental disorder of one individual—in the instance of alienation, a parent's own failure to have successfully negotiated the separation-individuation phase (Mahler, Pine, and Bergman, 1975)—is transmitted to another, in this case the child.

Parental alienation represents a situation in which false allegations of parental abuse of a child are often part of the alienating parent's vilification of the reviled ex-partner. In contrast, Siegler's chapter (see chapter 6) on domestic violence reminds us that aggressive conflict is a real and terrifying presence in all too many families. Siegler brings passion to bear in describing the destructive impact that violence and its threat can have, and calls upon the courts to take a clearer stand against domestic abuse and to weigh it more heavily in the course of custody litigation. She also brings her knowledge of psychoanalysis to the fore in delineating precisely how the concept of "identification with the aggressor" describes the mechanisms by which domestic violence lives on in the child. She again reminds us, it is the perpetuation of the parental psychopathology in the child that is the insidious counterpart to the direct impact of that pathology on the family.

REFERENCES

Mahler, M., Pine, F. & Bergman, A. (1975), *The Psychological Birth of the Human Infant*. New York: Basic Books.
Novick, J. (1997), Soul blindness: A form of externalization. Presented at conference Children and the Law. New York City, November 1.

Paul Hymowitz

Chapter 6

Home Is Where the Hurt Is

*Developmental Consequences
of Domestic Conflict and Violence
for Children and Adolescents*

AVA L. SIEGLER

A STATEMENT OF THE PROBLEM

*A*s we move into the twenty-first century, divorce has shifted from an extraordinary to an ordinary event. However, the developmental reverberations for children of divorce, particularly those whose parents are locked in perpetual conflict, remain of serious consequence.

When the battle between parents escalates, there can be no victors, only casualties and survivors. Warring parents, preoccupied by the intensity of their conflict, are able neither to perceive the destruction they wreak upon their children, nor to meet adequately their parental responsibilities for nurturing. Of particular poignancy is the fact that, regardless of the outcome for the adults involved, children and adolescents caught in the crossfire of intimate aggression are always left to deal with bitter lessons. Most learn that a parent they love can frighten; many learn that a parent they love can hurt; and most tragic of all, some learn that a parent they love can kill. It has been estimated that over ten million American children live each day in a domestic atmosphere of fear, cruelty, and coercion (Holden, Geffner, and Jouriles, 1998).

This chapter maintains that, in addition to clearly grievous assaults like battering, marital rape, or the murder of one parent by another, there is a destructive spectrum of adversarial, antagonistic, and abusive behavior between cohabiting adults that is frequently revealed in divorce and custody proceedings. This spectrum includes pervasive verbal abuse (including shouting, criticism, relentless sarcasm, and humiliation), threats and coercion (including manipulation, emotional blackmail, and domination), and unpredictable physical outbursts (including hitting, punching, shoving, breaking objects, and kicking). All of these behaviors constitute a direct developmental danger to children and adolescents. Indeed, a youngster raised in a family that can be located at any point in this spectrum is likely to suffer a wide variety of grave psychological consequences. These include a generalized increase in anxiety and fearfulness, stress-induced bodily complaints, attentional and learning difficulties and serious behavioral disorders (depression, suicide, drug and alcohol abuse, and delinquency). Cruelty and conflict leave profound scars on the mind (Furstenberg and Cherlin, 1991; Davies and Cummings, 1994; Ellis, 2002). In addition, whenever one parent becomes the victim of the other parent's verbal or physical abuse, the children in that family are always deprived of the proper parental nurturance and care of both the abuser and his victim.[1]

Although parents often seek a divorce because of a history of heightened conflict between them, any antagonistic or abusive pathology that has previously existed is likely to escalate during and immediately after divorce proceedings, increasing the developmental threat to the children. This makes thoughtful custody and visitation determinations, based on a general knowledge of child and family development, as well as upon a specific knowledge of each individual member of the family, crucial to any attempt to secure the children's well-being.

A PSYCHOANALYTIC DEVELOPMENTAL PERSPECTIVE ON AGGRESSION

While full reflection on the phenomenon of aggressive behavior (male or female) lies outside the scope of this chapter, some comments on

---

[1]When reporting information about domestic violence, I shall be using a male pronoun to denote the abuser and a female pronoun to denote the victim. Of course, while males are overwhelmingly the aggressors in physical violence, acts of cruelty and hostility can be inflicted by either sex on the other.

the ways in which anger and aggression ordinarily come to be modulated and controlled in development are relevant to our concerns, because it is when modulation and self-control fail that abusive and violent behavior emerges.

The potential for aggression lies within all of us and is not confined to any one class, gender, economic level, racial background, ethnicity, or specific family structure. However, the taming of individual aggression is essential to the survival of a society. As Freud stated in 1930, "The fateful question for the human species seems to me to be whether and to what extent their cultural development will succeed in mastering the disturbance of their communal life by the human instinct of aggression and self-destruction" (p. 145).

Without the ability to restrain one's own impulses for the sake of another, there can be no meaningful human relations. Achieving restraint over these impulses is no easy task in development. Family life is the way a society teaches children the crucial tasks our social order needs them to learn. Parents socialize children in two basic ways: first, by virtue of the values and standards that are directly and deliberately taught to them and second by virtue of the model of control that a parent offers the child for identification and internalization.

In particular, it is in the earliest years (two to six) that parents must teach their children how to modulate the normal aggressive impulses that all of us possess. The young child learns self-restraint by being restrained through parental limits and discipline; he learns consideration by being treated with consideration; he learns empathy by being treated empathically, and he learns to understand and respect the rights of others by being treated with understanding and respect within his family. By the end of the oedipal phase (plus or minus seven years), we expect these character virtues to have become internalized. How well one is able to accomplish this developmental task depends upon how well one has been initially nurtured and disciplined.

From this perspective, then, *the capacity for violence emerges as a failure in human development.* Any person who has been temperamentally endowed with strong aggressive impulses; possesses little self-awareness, self-regulation, or self-control; struggles with poor frustration tolerance; and, most critical of all, appears to have an inability to feel pity, is at high risk for violence (Freud, 1930). The absence of control over aggressive impulses becomes particularly relevant in intense interpersonal relationships like partnering and parenthood, both of which require an enormous capacity to defer one's own needs in order to tend to the needs of another.

PSYCHOLOGICAL CONSEQUENCES
OF DOMESTIC CONFLICT AND VIOLENCE
FOR CHILDREN AND ADOLESCENTS

While being afraid is a normal part of being human and crucial to our survival, fearfulness is unnaturally intensified in children raised in conflict-filled homes. In particular, as I have indicated elsewhere (Siegler, 1993), throughout the course of development all children must be able to master five basic fears—fears of the unknown, fears of being alone, fears about the body, fears of the voice of conscience, and fears about the self. Youngsters raised in a climate of domestic conflict and violence are often unable to muster either the confidence or competence they need to cope with their fears and are left weakened and vulnerable. In addition, children and adolescents who have been raised in conflict-laden families suffer significant psychological consequences:

1. Domestic cruelty and conflict present children with an adversarial paradigm of interpersonal relationships that teaches them that hostility and aggression are an ordinary and acceptable outcome of emotional encounters.
2. Parental conflict causes children to fear the very adults with whom they are intimate and on whom they are dependent, which causes them to become anxious, distrustful, and persistently apprehensive (if they identify with the victim) or aggressive, confrontational, and oppositional (if they identify with the aggressor).
3. A parent who is psychologically or physically abused is likely to become psychologically or physically incapacitated, which cripples her caregiving capacities, while a parent who is abusive and loses self-control becomes dreaded and feared. Therefore, domestic conflict essentially deprives children of the nurturing and protective services of *both* parents, leaving them emotionally orphaned.
4. In potentially violent domestic situations, children must remain constantly vigilant, mobilizing all their energies for

appeasement in anticipation of the first sign of the abuser's anger. The resultant environment of impending doom compromises the children's ability to function, particularly in situations requiring concentration, such as in school.

5. Children or adolescents who are raised in an atmosphere of domestic violence live in terror that they or their parents will be hurt, and in guilt that they are helpless to do anything about it. This terror makes children, and particularly teenagers, feel ashamed about their inability to stop the hostilities between their parents. Experiences of this sort emphasize youngsters' weakness in the face of adult power and erode their self-regard.

6. And finally, children who actively attempt to interfere between their fighting parents are put at direct risk for injury, or even death.

In order to evaluate the impact of domestic aggression on the children and teenagers in an individual family, we must know as much as we can about the nature of the conflictual circumstances. *First, did the children overhear the aggressive encounter or did they witness it?* Second, *what were the specific details of the abusive event?* Was it a screaming match with broken plates? Did one parent punch or kick the other? Was a weapon used to intimidate or assault a parent? Knowing the intensity and parameters of the domestic conflict enables the examiner to evaluate its subsequent effects on the children. Third, *the frequency of the conflict is important,* because it enables us to understand more fully the child's experience of daily life in his family. Repeated exposure to relentless aggression can be much more damaging to a child than the experience of an isolated explosive episode. Since trauma can be cumulative, symptomatic consequences for children mount over time, and, in addition, these symptoms are not easily alleviated. It can take years for a child's symptoms to diminish, even after the stress has ceased. Fourth, *the sex, temperament, and personality of the child or adolescent must be taken into account.* We cannot simply predict the nature of a traumatized reaction from the parameters of the traumatic event. A fearful, sensitive, wary child may be easily overwhelmed by events that a bold, sturdy, confident child can absorb emotionally.

However, even when we know the nature, intensity, and frequency of the marital conflict, and the sex, temperament, and

personality of the youngster, we are still not in a position to understand its impact until we know the age of the child and her phase of
development. Because the young child's comprehension of events is
limited by her cognitive immaturity, a traumatic experience leaves
the child particularly vulnerable to developmental damage. Since
reactions to trauma are informed by the child's phase of development, *children of different ages observing the same event are likely to
comprehend it in entirely different ways and assign it entirely different
meanings.*

CASE EXAMPLES

I would like to discuss briefly three cases from my practice that demonstrate the ways in which a child's emotional life (at three different
developmental stages) can be compromised by parental cruelty, conflict, and violence.

The Young Child at Risk

Mr. and Mrs. M had been married for more than eight years and
were now in the process of separating. Each wanted sole custody of
their four-year-old son, Edward, the mother insisting that her husband was hostile and verbally abusive, and the father maintaining
that his wife was neurotic and anorectic. Mr. M, the owner of a car
dealership, did indeed have a history of mistreating employees, while
Mrs. M, a bank teller, had a history of anorexia, including a prior
hospitalization when she was an adolescent. Both parents were
strong-willed and verbally confrontational, but there was no physical
violence in the home. They described themselves as "fighting like
cats and dogs." Often their arguments were shaped by the father's
cruel taunts about his wife's thin body (for example, "You're not a
woman, you're a dried-up piece of shit").

Edward was another source of antagonism between them. The
father maintained that Mrs. M "babied" Edward, kept him all to herself, isolated him from the real world, and was "turning him into a
faggot." The mother insisted that the father continuously frightened
and humiliated Edward in the same ways he frightened and humiliated her. She maintained that her husband's brutal hectoring of
Edward required that she protect him and keep him away from his

father whenever she could. She stated that Mr. M often taunted and threatened her in front of Edward. For instance, he would state, "When I go into court, I'll tell them that you're crazy. You were in a loony bin. You're no fit mother for Edward." She also reported that Mr. M would try to manipulate Edward during their arguments, telling him, "Wouldn't you rather stay with Daddy, Edward?" or promising Edward a puppy if Edward would tell the judge he wanted to live with his father. Edward had been subjected to his parents' endless arguments since he was born. By the time he was two years old, he was displaying symptoms of chronic intestinal distress, including alternating constipation and diarrhea. In addition, he was a poor eater and a poor sleeper who suffered from frequent nightmares.

On examination, Edward presented as a slight, pale-skinned, and anxious little boy. He was exceptionally sensitive to sounds, and started when the door to an adjacent apartment closed or a truck revved its engine in the street. He reported nightmares about "sharks coming to bite him" and he was flooded with worries about his family, including the idea that his house could burn down while everyone was in it. In Edward's drawings of his family, he portrayed himself standing close to his mother. Both figures were small and tucked into a corner of the page, while his father was drawn looming over them at some distance.

Because of his intestinal sensitivities, Edward had recently undergone medical testing and had been diagnosed with incipient ulcerative colitis. Since his parents had entered into divorce proceedings, Edward's attacks had been occurring more frequently and his physical condition was worsening. In addition, it was clear that Edward was already at considerable emotional risk. He was obviously intimidated by his father and physically cringed when his father approached him during their joint interview. In his joint interview with his mother, Edward was more relaxed, but also more "clingy" and dependent. His fearfulness had already interfered with his ability to normally identify with his dad and begin to separate from his mom—ordinary, preoedipal developmental tasks (Freud, 1905; Erikson, 1963). In addition, Edward's early and prolonged overexposure to his parents' ongoing confrontations had produced a high level of generalized anxiety that was triggering and/or contributing to his serious somatic symptoms.

Children under five years old like Edward, who live in an atmosphere of cruelty and coercion, appear to experience pervasive

behavioral disruptions. At this age they are the most easily frightened and overwhelmed, the most dependent on a parent's care, and
the least autonomous or resourceful. During preoedipal phases, children normally learn how to separate from their parents and function in the larger world, develop a sense of an intact and competent
body, and establish self-regulation and self control. Any or all of these
accomplishments are likely to be compromised in an atmosphere of
relentless parental conflict.

On examination, children this age are often unable to express
anger directly at their parents or even to acknowledge their fears
about their family to others. Instead, they display a great deal of
anxiety, worry, and insecurity. They often cling and cry if they are
separated from their mothers, and appear oversensitive and
overreactive to stimulation. They may become paralyzed whenever
they hear screaming, start at loud noises in the street, or burst into
tears if scolded at school.

In addition, if a child this young has directly witnessed physical
fighting between his parents, this traumatic experience interferes
with the normal developmental shift that ordinarily takes place at
this age, from resolving conflict through physical action (using your
body) to resolving conflict through language (using your words). Since
these children have been exposed to a terrifying lack of parental
control as well as a parental inability to differentiate between right
and wrong at the very time when they are attempting to internalize
socially acceptable behavior, they are unable to regulate their own
strong feelings, easily succumbing to emotional storms or temper
tantrums.

Because the relationship between mind and body is so intertwined at this early stage in development, youngsters persistently
subjected to an atmosphere of parental conflict are likely to react as
Edward did, with an array of physical symptoms, including colds,
headaches, sore throats, colitis, asthma, ulcers, enuresis and enco-
presis, allergies, tics, insomnia, and nightmares. Further, longitudinal studies have demonstrated that these physical symptoms are apt
to persist as lifelong patterns of illness (Rosenbaum and O'Leary,
1981; Zill, Morrison, and Coiro, 1993; Osofsky, 1995; Holden,
Geffner, and Jouriles, 1998).

Finally, because the thinking of a young child is still quite magical and egocentric, it is not unusual for a two- to six-year-old in a
conflict-filled family to come to believe that *he* is the cause of his

parents' conflict and to absorb blame and take responsibility for the events around him. This is the young child's way of trying to control damaging parental outbursts ("If I'm good, Mommy won't yell").

Edward, torn between his warring parents, was at both emotional and physical risk. The forensic evaluation, which took about three months to complete, was able to provide him with some psychological sanctuary, as well as an opportunity to express many of the anxious and angry feelings that were literally "eating him up inside."

Toward the end of the forensic process, both parents were informed that Edward's life was endangered by their antagonism, and that I would be recommending immediate psychotherapy for him. Sole custody was recommended for the mother who had always been Edward's primary caregiver. Since she and the father were not only antagonistic toward each other but disagreed on how to raise Edward, joint custodial arrangements would only have perpetuated their relentlessly hostile engagement with one another, increasing the psychological and physical risk to Edward.

Parent guidance was recommended for both parents to help them understand the impact of their behavior on Edward's symptoms. Supervised visitation was recommended for Mr. M for the first six months because of Edward's apprehension. Mr. M was encouraged to bring his sister or mother to supervise these meetings. It was strongly recommended that Mr. M complete a series of parent education lectures before he was permitted to see Edward alone. Unsupervised visitation was not advised until Edward's physical condition had stabilized and his psychotherapy was in place. After six months, it was recommended that Mr. M see Edward unsupervised for a half day each weekend. Mr. and Mrs. M were advised to meet regularly with Edward's therapist in order to learn how to provide a more secure environment for Edward's growth. Because of the grave nature of the child's symptoms, a reevaluation of this family was recommended for the following year.

The School-Aged Child's Struggles

Mr. and Ms. L, the parents of two girls, Nicole and Nina (eight and ten years old), were in the midst of a prolonged custody battle, with the father insisting on joint custody while the mother was insisting on sole custody. While they both deeply cared about their daughters, they were resentful of each other, and their screaming arguments often escalated into explosive behavior that included throwing objects, shoving, and pushing. The rage of both parents was easily triggered, and neither possessed much self-control. Nicole and Nina spent a lot of time in their room during these arguments, trying to shut out the sounds of their parents' fights by listening to television. They loved both their parents and were often terrified that one parent or the other would be hurt.

Mr. L, a wine salesman, had refused to leave the marital home despite difficulties in the marriage over the past ten years. He maintained that, if his wife wanted a divorce, she could leave, but he was "staying put." Conflict between the couple had worsened since the wife had begun a relationship with another man, and made known her wishes to dissolve the marriage. Since they both occupied the marital residence during their extended custody proceedings, both parents remained in close and bitter contact on a daily basis.

As the battle dragged on, Nicole and Nina began to experience many problems at school. They appeared distracted and unable to concentrate in class, repeatedly forgot to hand in homework, and frequently failed tests. Teachers described the sisters as "out of it" and "in their own world." As Nicole and Nina withdrew from academic engagement, they also became socially disengaged. Isolating themselves from their friends, they became increasingly dependent on each other, shutting everyone else out. For the few months prior to my meeting with them, both Nicole and Nina had been refusing to leave their house to attend school at all.

On examination, both girls seemed withdrawn and inattentive. Their mood was both anxious and depressed, and they roamed apathetically around the office, unable to become engaged by any specific toys or games. If either child began to play, she soon stopped, appearing restless and distracted, and turned to the other for comfort.

In response to projective testing, the stories the sisters told were filled with catastrophic themes. Nicole saw parents and children dying in floods and volcanoes erupting, while Nina described tornadoes destroying towns and being trapped in a "cave-in." Both of them expressed affection and concern for their parents. When asked to draw their family, both girls included pictures of neighbors and aunts and uncles, as if they needed (or wished to have) lots of people around them to keep things safe, since they could not count on their parents for security.

Erikson (1963) described latency as the phase of development when the seven- to ten-year-old child must begin to separate from her family and move out into the world at large, embracing the goals of learning and productivity. Riddled with fears about their parents' welfare and expending all their energies to obliterate their parents' daily battles, Nina and Nicole were preoccupied with defending themselves by shutting off and shutting down, withdrawing from the academic world. ("What you don't know can't hurt you.") The relentless parental conflict in their daily lives also prevented them from addressing, modulating, and sublimating their own anger and anxiety into sports activities, game playing, drawing, or reading. Instead, they were in emotional retreat, seeking sanctuary from rather than mastery over the developmental challenges they faced. Their social, emotional, and intellectual growth were already profoundly compromised.

Older children who live with domestic conflict can call on more intellectual ability to analyze and understand the situation than children under seven years old. The positive aspect of this intellectual maturity is that a ten-year-old's thinking is more rational and less idiosyncratic. However, the negative aspect is that their more sophisticated cognitive abilities also enable them to "imagine the worst." This realization of impending danger or damage (to a parent or to themselves) can fill a child's mind, leaving no room for learning, growth, or pleasure. Since seven- to ten-year-olds spend most of their lives in school, they need to be able to concentrate, work, and endure frustration. They are also required to get along with others, develop their physical abilities, tolerate differences among their peers, and consolidate social skills. Living in a home shaped by conflict compromises the child's ability to absorb the lessons society urges upon them. How can a child like Nina concentrate and produce when her home does not provide an emotional haven for her development? How can a child like Nicole learn acceptance, tolerance, and compromise in a climate of parental cruelty, bitterness, and antagonism?

It is typical to find the kinds of symptomatic learning problems (attentional difficulties, an inability to focus on work, and poor memory skills) that we see in Nicole and Nina when children become preoccupied with their parents' problems. In addition, since children from conflict-filled homes are fearful and ashamed about what goes on in their families, and may have been directly warned by their parents not to talk about family affairs, they may try to keep others at a distance, and shrink from making or maintaining friendships.

Forensic recommendations called for the husband to leave the marital home immediately, without prejudice as to its later disposition. Mr. L, while initially resistant, eventually chose to establish a residence near Nicole and Nina's school. He was given liberal parenting time during the week and saw the girls alternate weekends. It was recommended that Mrs. L have sole residential custody of the children because of the level of antagonism between the parents. However, the father was given joint decision-making power with regard to education, camps, medical/psychological treatment, and religious schooling, since the couple's conflicts were based on their hostilities towards each other as marital partners rather than on any child-rearing disagreements. In fact, Mr. and Mrs. L had always been able (when not preoccupied with their own resentment toward each other) to effectively co-parent their children. Finally, full neuro-psychological evaluations were recommended for Nicole and Nina to determine the best way to support their development. Both tutoring and psychotherapy were recommended to enable them to attend school and regain a feeling of positive self-regard.

The Adolescent Breakdown

Thirteen-year-old Tomas was the only child of his father and his mother. Mr. A, a trucker, was a volatile and often violent man with a history of alcohol abuse. Mrs. A, a hospital worker, was an obese woman who suffered with adult-onset diabetes. Mr. A was often on the road for weeks at a time but, when he returned home, he went drinking with his friends and often returned home in an irritable and abusive mood. His anger was usually directed against his wife and her inadequacies, particularly as a sexual partner. Their fights often escalated into physical violence. On one occasion when Tomas tried to defend his mother, his father slammed him against a wall, breaking his wrist. This incident was not reported to the authorities, as neither his mother nor Tomas was willing to press charges. After this incident, Mrs. A would often go to sleep in Tomas's bed, attempting to avoid her husband's sexual demands.

Tomas alternated between trying to take care of his mother (making sure she ate well, took her insulin shots, and stayed out of his father's way) and trying to leave her (by running away from home). While her husband was driving cross-country, Mrs. A, with the support of her coworkers at the hospital, filed for divorce. When Mr. A returned and learned of her efforts to separate from him, he became enraged and beat her up. Mrs. A, through an attorney, sought and was granted an order of protection against her husband, who was compelled to leave the apartment. Mrs. A hoped that she and Tomas would be protected from her husband now, and that things would "settle down." Shortly after Mr. A moved out, however, Tomas's school notified her that he had not attended classes for several months. When Mrs. A confronted Tomas, pleading and crying for him to "be a good boy," he promised, but the next day when Mrs. A returned home from work, he was gone. Tomas was found three weeks later by his maternal uncle, living in an abandoned building with home-less teenagers and sharing their stash of crack. Tomas's behavior terrified his mother. She also felt bewildered because she had al-ways believed that Tomas was more like her, and now he seemed to be behaving more like his father.

Adolescence is the developmental bridge between childhood and adult life. But there are five major tasks that must be accomp-lished before the child can cross over into the adult world: First, the teenager must be able to psychologically separate from old fam-ily ties; second, he or she must be capable of creating new peer at-tachments; third, he or she must be able to establish a mature sexual identity and begin to explore a sexual life; fourth, he or she must be able to form new ideas and find new ideals to admire; and fifth, by the end of adolescence, he or she must form a sense of identity and begin to consolidate his or her character (Siegler, 1997).

A climate of domestic violence compromises the possibility of healthy development in all of these areas. Most importantly, both psychic identity and sexual identity are likely to be distorted, since the adolescent in a violent home is compelled on a daily basis to choose between identifying with the *victim* or the *victimizer*. This narrows and dichotomizes developmental opportunities, skews the normal process of identification, and interferes with the establish-ment of healthy masculinity or femininity. Adolescent boys like Tomas are taught through their exposure to violence that being a man means being aggressive.

Once they take their violent fathers as a model, a developmental process called "identification with the aggressor" is set in motion. These teenage boys, then, may themselves become abusive toward their girlfriends. Also studies have shown that later on, when they become parents, their aggressiveness persists and becomes a stable personality characteristic. In adult life they are more likely to become abusive toward their own children, carrying the terrible lessons they have learned into the next generation (Straus and Gelles, 1990). On the other hand, adolescent girls who live in an atmosphere of domestic conflict and violence are more at risk for identifying with their victimized mothers. As they move into male–female relationships, they may mistake cruelty and control as strength and love, and passively remain in abusive liaisons of their own making.[2]

On examination, Tomas appeared sullen, withdrawn, and depressed. Once he began to talk, it was obvious that he felt equally threatened by his father's violent abuse and his mother's increasing dependency on him. Leaving home seemed to be the only way to escape his emotional dilemma. Tomas felt that living on the streets was preferable to living with a brutal father or a mother who slept in his bed. Further exploration revealed that Tomas's abuse of drugs was serving several different functions for him. First, it offered him a way to separate from his vulnerable mother. Second, it helped him feel more like his powerful father, and enabled him to leave home, as his father had. Third, drugs offered Tomas a way of obliterating his feelings of guilt about abandoning his mother. Tomas's adolescent development was already dangerously derailed.

In order to help Tomas regain self-control, protect him from his self-destructive impulses, and address his substance abuse problems, immediate placement in a residential drug rehabilitation unit was recommended. Despite his history of domestic violence, Mr. A had asked for visitation with Tomas whenever he was not on the road. He protested that he had never "intentionally" hurt Tomas and was angry that anyone would stand in the way of his "parental rights." Tomas, however, refused to see his father, and coercive visitation would only serve to replicate Tomas's traumatic experiences of his father's tyranny. It was recommended that the mother be given sole custody of Tomas, and it was strongly suggested that Mr. A address his alcoholism, which was directly linked to his episodes of violence.

---

[2]Note, however, that these processes are not always bound by same-sex identifications. Since boys and girls identify with both their mothers and their fathers, the reverse, while much less common, could be the outcome as well. That is, an adolescent boy could identify with his helpless mother, while an adolescent girl could model her behavior after her aggressive father.

No visitation was recommended until Mr. A was able to maintain sobriety for a minimum of six months.

FORENSIC CONSIDERATIONS

The predominant legal position regarding high-conflict and violent families often makes it difficult to protect children. Courts are loath to separate a parent from his child, even under dire circumstances. As little as a decade ago, judges in custody and visitation proceedings, as well as court-appointed forensics, would not always conclude that verbal or physical abuse of a wife necessarily made a father unfit. In fact, all too often an abusing husband could continue to be seen by the courts as a "good" father. The Pikul case (*O'Guinn v Pikul,* 1987), in which the presiding judge gave custody of two young children to the father, Joseph Pikul, who was accused (and later convicted) of bludgeoning his wife to death, is a case in point. In that case, the court put great reliance on the "fact" that this father had never directly abused his children, as well as on the "fact" that the children, in forensic examination, professed affection for their father.

From a psychological point of view, both of these "facts" bear close scrutiny. In relation to the first "fact" (that a violent father may be a fit father if he has never directly abused his children), it is important to recognize that violence need not be a specified act limited to one person and one person alone. Indeed, violence is often uncontrollable and unpredictable. An abuser is usually someone who lacks appropriate self-regulation and self-control over anger. Even more significant is the finding in many studies of a close correlation between spousal abuse and eventual child abuse, particularly as the child gets older (Rosenbaum and Leary, 1981; Straus and Gelles, 1990; Davidson, 1995). That is, continued violence by one parent toward another increases the likelihood that violence towards the developing child will be subsequently enacted as well.

In regard to the second "fact" (that a child's "love" for a parent demonstrates that parent's fitness), it is unfortunately all too common to find that children love and are loyal to those who abuse and hurt them. Not only will these children not reveal the emotional, physical, or, for that matter, sexual abuse to which they have been subjected, they will often go to great lengths to shield their abusive parent from outside detection. This loyalty often seems incomprehensible to observers. But, in fact, children will sometimes sacrifice themselves in the hope of transforming an abusive parent into a benign parent. They will maintain, for example, that they deserve the abuse, no matter how arbitrary or severe. From a psychoanalytic perspective, making oneself responsible for provoking violent events is always psychologically preferable to the idea that violence emerges from an unpredictable and uncontrollable parent. When a child maintains that parental violence is the child's fault, it is also possible to believe that he or she some has control over catastrophic events. (The child reasons, "I am bad. Daddy is good. I made him angry. If only I were better, he wouldn't hurt me. Therefore, I can control his violence by being good.")

In 1990, Congress passed a joint resolution encouraging the courts to deny custody to any parent who had taken violent action against the other parent. Following suit, in the last decade, thirty-eight states have passed statutes requiring the court to take domestic violence into account when considering a child's best interest in custody determinations. Additionally, many states recognize that, if a parent flees, relocates, or is compelled to leave a child because of domestic violence, that factor should not weigh against the victimized parent in determining custody or visitation.

It is necessary to understand the impact of less severe but more widespread forms of domestic cruelty. It is important for the courts to recognize that the parent who, during the marriage, lies, manipulates, and deceives, who uses coercion, threats, and intimidation to get his way, who is verbally abusive, domineering, and demeaning, is going to continue to use these modes of control during and after the divorce proceedings. Just as victims of domestic violence are often more at risk once they have separated from their abusers so, too, after a divorce resolution, these verbally abusive, controlling spouses are likely to continue and even escalate the hostilities towards their partners through hostile phone calls, faxes and letters, spying and stalking, stealing or vandalizing papers and property, returning the children late or not at all with some inadequate excuse, and most damaging of all, consistently demeaning and undermining the other parent to the children, alienating their affections. If a climate of coercion and control existed in the marriage, it is likely to continue after the marriage ends. This likelihood has profound implications for the determination of custody and visitation arrangements, because the very process of reaching these arrangements can provide an abusive spouse with endless opportunities for manipulation and control over his partner. Sometimes the abuse previously reserved for the spouse may, after the marriage ends, be turned towards the children, since the victimized partner no longer functions as a buffer between the child and the abusive parent.

Joint custody arrangements, though currently very much in favor as an expedient solution to the exhausting legal battles between warring parents, should always be carefully examined in cases where there is a high potential for relentless conflict. If a husband and wife have not been able to cooperate with each other while sharing a home, it is not psychologically credible to believe that they will do so when they are no longer bound by mutual goals and ties. The relentless strife that is perpetuated through ineffective joint custodial arrangements ceaselessly erodes the development and mental health of the children compelled to live in such arrangements.

It may be instructive to take note of a study (Reidy et al., 1989) of joint custody in California, a state which has a presumptive joint custody statute. Over sixty-eight percent of the judges polled reported that joint custody determinations produced (at best) neutral and (at worst) poor results. It should not surprise us to learn that vengeful, acrimonious parents make poor partners. If the best interests of the child are to be served, the courts should remain extremely cautious in making joint custody awards, which can perpetuate the malevolent dynamics of the marriage throughout the children's lives. In high-conflict marriages, joint custody has been found to be a poor option and an ill-advised solution.

RECOMMENDATIONS

How, then, can justice be served and the development and emotional health of children be secured during divorce proceedings?

1. In order for judicial relief to be offered in a timely manner, conflictual and violent cases need to be identified and docketed expeditiously.
2. Relevant temporary orders that protect both the parental victim and the children need to be made. Judges should err on the side of protecting the reportedly abused parent when examining any allegations of aggressive behavior.

3. In all high-conflict cases where the welfare of a child or children is involved, a forensic examiner who has experience in child development should be appointed as quickly as possible to examine all parties. This forensic child specialist will not only be capable of making recommendations to the court regarding the child's emotional well-being, but her presence during the height of these adversarial proceedings provides an opportunity to scrutinize volatile parents. In addition, the mere presence of a forensic consultant can provide ongoing support for frightened children as well as safeguard their welfare during and after the custody proceedings.

4. In those divorce cases in which cruel and relentless conflict is apparent, the forensic examiner should be instructed by the court to make immediate interim recommendations regarding the feasibility of joint residence in the marital home. If shared occupancy is not feasible, the more aggressive parent should be required to leave the marital home immediately (without prejudice as to the subsequent disposition). Family relations deteriorate rapidly during separation and divorce proceedings, which can go on for years. Keeping adversarial parents confined in the same living space can only enflame an already heated situation, putting the children at greater developmental risk.

5. A history of domestic abuse should always be a primary concern and visitation determinations and a thorough investigation of the abusive parent should be immediately conducted. Legal or residential joint custody in this situation will only perpetuate further abuse and endanger the children's welfare.

6. The court should not be reluctant to institute supervised visitation in any case where the child might have reason to fear a parent, and no visitation in those cases where a child would be directly at risk. A dangerous parent can be much worse than no parent. The child's best interests should always supersede parental rights.

7. In those tragic cases where a parent has been murdered (unless the murder was in self-defense), the law would be best served if the presumption against the accused or convicted surviving parent could be rebutted only through demonstrating that the child would suffer more if placed in any other custodial arrangement.

CONCLUSIONS

As a society, it is time for us to acknowledge that a pervasive climate of coercion and conflict within the home does, indeed, constitute an emotional assault upon the child, and to realize that fear of the abusive parent and fear for the abused parent undermines the child's ability to develop normally. Children trapped in these painful circumstances are compelled to develop defenses which may become lifelong characterological patterns of behavior. As we have indicated, these children may model the violent behavior of the aggressor or the vulnerable behavior of the victim. Or they may become what we call "parentified" or "pseudo-mature" kids who look good on the surface, exhibiting autonomy and self-sufficiency, while underneath this façade they are actually severely anxious, depressed, or suicidal. We have also seen that living in an unpredictable, hostile environment may prove so stressful that the children of these families develop profound physical symptoms that reflect their heightened sense of bodily danger or display significant attentional disabilities which interfere with intellectual motivation and academic achievement.

Finally, children and adolescents who have directly witnessed acts of domestic violence often suffer from a wide array of symptoms that can be described as posttraumatic stress disorder (PTSD). Veterans of domestic wars, these youngster are wary, vigilant, and distrustful of others and experience the nightmares, dissociation (including memory loss and fugue states), and flashbacks (recurrent, painful thoughts and images) that mimic the well-documented suffering of shell-shocked, battle-weary soldiers. All of the above responses (identification with the aggressor or the victim, somatic complaints, pseudo-maturity, self-destructive behaviors, and posttraumatic stress disorder) are pathological. They all constrain and distort the child's ability to make use of her emotional and intellectual resources and to become a productive citizen of our society.

This chapter emphasizes that, in all violent and conflict-filled homes, there is a climate of apprehension and antagonism that both systematically undermines the capacity of the victim and aggressor to function as parents and significantly compromises the psychological and physical welfare of children, both in the present and for the future. For that reason, it is of the utmost importance that mental health professionals, law enforcement officers, legal observers, and the courts of our land pay close attention to the fate of these children. Youngsters who have been raised in a crucible of family conflict, cruelty, and violence are likely to become either our next generation of abusers or our next generation of victims.

REFERENCES

Davidson, A. (1995), Child abuse and domestic violence: Legal connections and controversies. *Family Law Quart.,* 29:357–387.
Davies, P. & Cummings, E. M. (1994), Marital conflict and child adjustment: An emotional security hypothesis. *Psycholog. Bull.,* 116:387–411.
Ellis, E. M. (2002), *Divorce Wars.* Washington, DC: APA.
Erikson, E. (1963), *Childhood and Society.* New York: Norton.
Freud, S. (1905), Three essays on the theory of sexuality. *Standard Edition,* 7:135–243. London: Hogarth Press, 1953.
—— (1930), Civilization and its discontents. *Standard Edition,* 21:64–145. London: Hogarth Press, 1961.
Furstenberg, F. & Cherlin, A. (1991), *Divided Families.* Cambridge, MA: Harvard University Press.
Holden, G., Geffner, R. & Jouriles, E., eds. (1998), *Children Exposed to Marital Violence.* Washington, DC: APA.
Huesmann, L. R., Eron, L. D., Lefkowitz, M. M. & Walder, L. D. (1984), Stability of aggression over time and generations. *Develop. Psychol.,* 20:1120–1123.
O'Guinn v Pikul, April 29, 1988, unpublished decision by Justice Kristen Booth Glenn.
Osofsky, J. (1995), The effects of exposure to violence on young children. *Amer. Psychologist,* 50:1–7.
Reidy, T. J., Silver, R. M. & Carlson, A. (1989), Child custody decisions: A survey of judges. *Family Law Quart.,* 23:75–80.
Rosenbaum, A. & O'Leary, K. D. (1981), Children: The unintended victims of marital violence. *Amer. J. Orthopsychiatr.,* 51:692–698.
Siegler, A. L. (1993), *What Should I Tell the Kids?* New York: Dutton.
—— (1997), *The Essential Guide to the New Adolescence.* New York: Dutton.
Straus, M. A. & Gelles, R. J., eds. (1990), *Physical Violence in American Families.* New Brunswick, NJ: Transaction Publishers.
Zill, N., Morrison, D. & Coiro, M. (1993), Long-term effects of parental divorce on parent-child relationships, adjustments, and achievement in young adulthood. *J. Family Psychol.,* 7:91–103.

Chapter 7

Soul Blindness

A Child Must Be Seen to Be Heard

JACK NOVICK

KERRY KELLY NOVICK

*E*ver since its beginnings over a hundred years ago, psychoanalysis has been a revolutionary doctrine, calling for a new view of ourselves and our world. Recently, psychoanalysts have tended to focus on clinical and technical applications of psychoanalytic concepts but, from the time of Freud's "Interpretation of Dreams" (1900), psychoanalytic concepts were also applied to and were in turn influenced by factors outside the consulting room. As Esman (1998) demonstrates, psychoanalysis has always been an applied science; the need to reaffirm the mutual influences of psychoanalytic concepts and other aspects of society and culture is even more relevant today than ever before.

EXTERNALIZATION AND SOUL BLINDNESS

One of Freud's first discoveries was the concept of "defense," which we have seen as a person's need to blind himself, not to see things in himself or others which threaten the stability of his or her self-image

An early version of this paper was first presented at the conference "Children and the Law: Consistency, Compromise and Conflict," presented jointly by the New York Freudian Society Committee for External Affairs and the Interdisciplinary Forum for Mental Health and Family Law, New York State, November 1, 1997.

(Novick and Novick, 1970). A major aim of psychoanalysis is to help a person become aware of his or her defenses, to have the choice of more adaptive ways of self-protection, and to allow for the integration of different parts of the personality. This leads to a more effective self, able to respond creatively to the exigencies of reality. The capacity to look clearly and accurately at what comes from within and from without is one of the products of healthy development.

Adaptive functioning is always susceptible to stress from many quarters. Divorce has a particularly strong impact, at all levels of the adult's personality. Adults in such a situation often have to deal with powerful feelings of anger, frustration, failure, anxiety, and hurt; they may also feel helpless in relation to their spouse and to external demands. This can not only produce personal disarray and preoccupation, but adults may then also invoke defenses against these feelings, rendering them at such times blind to many aspects of life including the needs, indeed, the very separateness and individuality of their children.

We have described families in which the parents are blind to the real personalities of their children, where parents use the defense of externalization to deal with their own anxiety or pain (Novick and Novick, 1970). Externalization is the attribution to another person of parts of one's own personality, irrespective of the other's characteristics. When this is a parent's way of relating to a child, the child's reality is denied—a particular form of the defense graphically described by Wurmser (1994, 1996) as "soul blindness."

There are many instances in life and clinical work that illustrate parallels between clinically derived psychoanalytic knowledge and understanding from other sources. "Soul murder" and "soul blindness" are evocative phrases that capture the destructive effect of pathological psychological mechanisms. These terms come from literature: Goethe referred to soul murder (Wurmser, 1994) and many of Ibsen's female characters are victims of soul blindness and themselves become soul blind (for example, the character Nora in *A Doll House* [Ibsen, 1879]).

Our early studies indicated that children who are the objects of parental externalizations show severe disturbance in their self-esteem and difficulty integrating positive aspects of their functioning as well as in developing a realistic self-image. Not only are these children unseen by those around them, they also lose the capacity to see themselves clearly. If parents are blind to a child's reality, the child in turn may grow blind to herself; then, as she grows up and becomes a parent, she too may be blind to the reality of her child's basic needs, tempo, and desires. In this way soul blindness can become a family trait passed on through generations.

Since externalization violates the child's existing and developing personality, it constitutes an abuse in itself. In our work we have suggested that concrete instances of sexual or physical abuse take place in the context of a pre-existing abusive relationship that often includes externalizations visited upon the child (Novick and Novick, 1994, 1996). Externalizations are fueled by feelings of helplessness, guilt, or shame and then, bolstered by social attitudes, become part of situations of discrimination and divisiveness. Dehumanization of the other, a blindness to shared humanity and individuality, effected often by externalization of repudiated, uncomfortable, "bad" parts of the self, is often a precursor to abuse. Shengold (1989) has movingly described the impact of actual events of abuse as "soul murder." Here we explore some of the precursors, the psychic mechanisms that go into "soul blindness," which is in turn a precondition for assaulting another.

FROM SOUL BLINDNESS TO EMPATHY

The Case of Max

Max's (a pseudonym) parents separated soon after his birth and were divorced six months later. Custody was disputed and his father's lawyers persisted in petitioning for repeated custody evaluations after each disposition. Each party accused the other of emotional and physical abuse and sued for sole custody. The fourth court-ordered evaluation was done when Max was three years old. By this time Max had been asked to leave three daycare settings because he was disruptive and unmanageable. He spoke very little, erupted into aggressive behavior at the slightest provocation, and had little mastery of self-care. The various psychologists came up with dire diagnostic formulations, such as autism, pervasive developmental disorder, and sensory integration dysfunction. All the mental health professionals noted the potential traumatic effect on Max of the cumulative strain from the continuing uncertainty and repeated evaluations.

The last evaluation recommended that the parents seek guid-ance for parenting and explore whether Max would benefit from psychotherapy. The mother was generally a very intelligent, caring person, but it became clear that neither she nor Max's father could see beyond their own rage at each other and their panic that Max would be taken away. Neither parent could imagine Max's lifelong experience of uncertainty or the impact of the parents' anxiety and fury at each other. They had not seen Max's developmental delays or behavioral difficulties as signs of his own inner stress. Rather, each took Max's dysfunction as a direct result of bad treatment by the other parent. Max's parents' own feelings of victimization, failure, and damage had been externalized onto Max and they seemed blind to his own psychic reality.

Each of the psychological evaluations had noted the deleterious impact on Max of the uncertain and unsettled custody situation and the disruptive visitation schedule that had the child transferring residences every other day. But neither judges nor attorneys seemed to see the seriousness of these issues and the legal battle continued. At this writing, Max was six years old and about to start elementary school. He still remained partly under the shadow of inconstant and negative early experience.

Guidance work with Max and his mother was gradually enabling her to move from soul blindness to an ability to empathize with Max as a separate person suffering his own pain. She was helped to address his uncertainty and his belief that he would be asked to choose between his parents. Max regained some developmental momentum: he began to put his feelings into words rather than actions, gained some mastery of his impulses, developed self-care skills and the beginnings of concern for others. These gains allowed for more definitive determination that he was not suffering from any primary organic disorder, but rather had been traumatized by the acrimonious custody battle. He was able to attend regular kindergarten, but remained vulnerable to sudden rages at times of separation and transition.

How can we ensure that parents, judges, therapists, teachers, attorneys, and court officials are not blind to the needs of those who cannot defend themselves, for instance, children in custody disputes? Empathy is not something mystical, but an active use of one's cognitive and emotional responses to imagine oneself in the place of the other. The infantile developmental step of acknowledging the separateness of self and other is followed by a stage of generalizing from oneself so that the separate other, whether human or not, is seen as having characteristics similar to oneself (Mahler, Pine, and Bergman,

1975). If development does not proceed past this point, generalization will continue as a basis for a kind of pseudo-empathy that understands others only in terms of the self. Understanding oneself as unique, and therefore understanding the uniqueness of others, is a stance achieved only gradually throughout childhood and adolescence. This conceptual capacity is under constant pressure from feelings of aloneness and anxiety and the consequent operation of defenses. Empathic capacity cannot be taught, and it is often diminished in the heat of divorce, but it can sometimes be restored through the intervention of a therapist able to convey understanding of the embattled adult while aligning with his or her attributes as a concerned parent (see chapter 26).

The Case of Jessica

Let us turn to some notorious judicial proceedings of several years ago to illustrate further the complexity and subtlety of understanding issues of empathy and soul blindness. We assume that there are few readers who would dispute the assertion that children need the security of continuity of positive parental care for optimal development—and to be able to find creative solutions to the conflicts that life brings. The ingredients of security are many and varied; an important early sign is the loving mutual gaze between parent and child. The experience of pleasure and its reflection in the eyes of a parent are important validators of the baby's sense of self. The abrupt loss of such continuity can be traumatic, with immediate and long-term deleterious effects on the child. However, there are developmental specialists, who argue that continuity of care is often less important than other factors, such as the legal rights of adults and the primacy of biological ties (Kagan, 1996; Lewis, 1997). As one eminent psychologist said in relation to the case of Jessica DeBoer (the two-and-a-half-year-old child who was returned from Michigan in 1993 to her birth parents), "Blood calls to blood" (Horner, 1993). He and many others have argued that a child's separation from longstanding caretakers can be done in such a way as to minimize any short-term effects and avoid any long-term harmful impact. What does this mean in terms of how we think about children as individuals, how we see the specific child as a person with unique experience and needs?

Proponents of different points of view have used the case of

Jessica DeBoer to bolster their respective arguments over the relative importance of the individual child's experience. We will not go into the details of the DeBoer case but, to summarize, quote from the flyleaf of the book *Losing Jessica* (DeBoer, 1994): "On August 2, 1993, Robby and Jan DeBoer were forced to give up the little girl that they had raised, since infancy, for two and a half years. In a decision that shocked the entire country, the courts ruled that Jessi DeBoer was to be taken from the only parents and the only home she had ever known and given back to the biological parents who were virtual strangers to her." The case had a galvanizing effect on those of us who live in Ann Arbor, Michigan. Psychoanalysts, psychologists, and law professors left their offices to volunteer their professional services to try to avert a tragedy in the making, a pain that should have been avoidable.

About six months after a screaming, distraught Jessi was transferred to her biological parents, there was a nationally televised follow-up. In this television report we see the three-year-old, renamed Anna by her biological parents, playing happily with her toys and showing the interviewer her room. We see her cuddling up to her biological parents, calling them Mommy and Daddy, and playing with her new baby sister. In this follow-up there are clips of the testimonies of the developmental experts, a child psychoanalyst, two professors of developmental psychology, and an infant psychologist,[1] predicting possibly serious immediate and later consequences—loss of toilet mastery, regression in speech, nightmares, and inconsolable crying. One expert witness likened the course of personality development to the building of a house, whose foundation and internal construction have to be solid in order to withstand later stresses. Invisible cracks or faults in the foundation may only become significant much later, when life brings extra pressure to bear on the personality. Whether or not Jessica developed immediate regressive symptomatology, the foundation of her personality would be compromised by the experience of rupture of her earliest secure relationships.

In the television interview (Sawyer, 1994), Jessica/Anna is shown to be cheerful in her new large extended family, and said to be show-

---

[1]Among the expert witnesses were David Brodzinsky, Rutgers University; Jeree Pawl, University of California; Elinor Rosenberg, University of Michigan; Vicki Bennett, University of Michigan; Beth Clark, and Jack Novick, New York Freudian Society, University of Michigan.

ing none of the symptoms predicted by the experts. An unnamed psychologist who was asked to comment on the films of the child is quoted in the television program as saying that Jessica/Anna, "is adjusting very well."

There is a very brief segment of that hour-long interview when the interviewer asks Jessi/Anna if she remembers Pear Street, the home of her first family in Ann Arbor. Jessi's face changes and the psychologist describes this as "understandable reserve." It is presented as a positive reaction and the interview proceeds unchecked, with the repeated implication that the whole experience has had little impact on the child. This program has been used and will be used again to demonstrate that all the predictions of the experts on the harmful effects of separation can be dismissed as nothing more than scare tactics. According to these critics, the law prevailed as it should.

We have suggested that a psychoanalytic perspective emphasizes empathic sensitivity as a starting point (Novick and Novick, 1994). A thoughtful child psychoanalyst would want to take time to "feel with" the child (Novick and Novick, 1998), and be open to the possibility that her observable pleasure may be an expression of an adaptive transformation or a defensive submission to the needs of others to deny any trauma. In our view of this television segment, we see a performance quality in Jessi's laughter, as she repeatedly turns to check the adults' reactions. The tone of her laugh is brittle and high-pitched, as if driven by anxiety rather than joy. When asked about her first home on Pear Street with her adoptive parents, her movements slow, her hand goes to her mouth and two fingers to her nose, her face goes still, and her eyes go dull and blank. As if a shutter has closed, she seems to be looking nowhere. For that moment, she has the unseeing look of traumatized children. It is a look of withdrawal and closing down, of rendering oneself blind to protect against unbearable perceptions.

When we have presented this paper, accompanied by video taken from the television followup, there has been a consistent response from child clinicians who have noted the similarities between Jessi/Anna's look in the film and that of children worldwide who have been subjected to overwhelming stresses. The way we see the film leads us to ask whether the child's sadness is an insignificant reaction to having been reminded of her previous family or the indication of a defensive withdrawal, a traumatic shutdown, the beginning of soul

The two-and-a-half-year-old girl known as Jessica cries as she is strapped into a car seat and taken away from the home of Jan and Roberta DeBoer Monday August 2, 1993, in Ann Arbor, Mich. Jessica, who is at the center of a two-state custody battle, was taken and given to her biological parents, Dan and Cara Schmidt of Blairstown, Iowa. Photograph © AP/Wide World Photos.

blindness. The picture does not provide any definitive answers,[2] but, if it raises questions, then it has helped all of us take a step from soul blindness to empathic understanding.

Indeed the case of Jessica DeBoer, with its heart-rending photographs of a little girl dissolved in tears and panic as she was taken from the only parents she had ever known, did begin to remove the scales from the eyes of the nation. Articles in national newspapers and magazines, and special programs and newscasts on national and worldwide television, brought attention to the many children in situations similar to Jessi's. Hundreds of thousands of letters and calls poured into the local committee organized to defend Jessica. Within a short time the "Justice for Jessi" group had gathered concerned individuals and eminent legal and mental health experts into a national grassroots organization, "Hear My Voice," advocating for the

---

[2]Followup material on Jessica/Anna's subsequent development is difficult to obtain. It is known that her biological father eventually left the family, as he had done on two previous occasions with two former families, that letters and gifts from the adoptive parents have been returned unopened, and that the biological family has refused available professional support offered by local psychologists.

rights of all children to have a stable, secure family. This organization has subsequently succeeded in influencing changes in custody legislation and practices in many states.

In the legal arena, Jessica's case gave rise to a "best interest" ruling by Judge William Ager that leaned heavily on the testimony of a child psychoanalyst. As the case continued through the legal system, dissenting judges and justices at every level[3] gave weight to the child's own needs, citing the evidence of Jessi's experience of the events that were overtaking her life. By July 1993, the American Bar Association Presidential Working Group on the Unmet Legal Needs of Children and their Families issued a report called "Children at Risk" that called for lawyers to be specially trained in representing the interests of children. The legal establishment began to see children with new eyes.

Perhaps as a society we are beginning to see each child as a separate person and hear each story as unique. But the process of seeing clearly, of moving from soul blindness to empathy, starts as an effort of the imagination within each individual. Only when we have the courage to look clearly at ourselves, without the fog of defenses, will we be truly capable of empathy with small children caught up in the affairs of adults.

REFERENCES

American Bar Association (1993), America's children at risk: A national agenda for legal action. *Report of the Presidential Working Group on the Unmet Legal Needs of Children and Their Families.*

B.G.C. Nos. A-64, A-65 (1993), Supreme Court of the United States. Dissent: Justice Blackmun with whom Justice O'Connor joins, dissenting, July 30.

DeBoer, R. (1994), *Losing Jessica.* New York: Doubleday.

Esman, A. (1998), What is "applied" in "applied" psychoanalysis? *Internat. J. Psycho-Anal.,* 79:741–756.

Freud, S. (1900), The interpretation of dreams. *Standard Edition,* 4 & 5. London: Hogarth Press, 1953.

Horner, T. (1993), Best interest of the child hearing: Trial transcript. Washtenaw County Circuit Court, Ann Arbor, MI. Judge William Ager. Expert testimony, February 3.

---

[3]Dissent by Justice Levin, Michigan Supreme Court, July 16, 1993. Dissent by Justice Blackman joined by Justice O'Connor, United States Supreme Court, July 30, 1993.

Ibsen, H. (1879), *A Doll's House*. In: *Henrik Ibsen: The Complete Major Prose Plays*, trans. R. Fjelde. New York: Farrar, Straus & Giroux, 1978.

In re Baby Girl Clausen (1993), Nos. 96366, 96441, 96531, 96532. Michigan Supreme Court Dissent. Dissent by Justice Levin, July 16.

Kagan, J. (1996), Three pleasing ideas. *Amer. Psychol.*, 51:901–908.

Lewis, M. (1997), *Altering Fate*. New York: Guilford Press.

Mahler, M. S., Pine, F. & Bergman, A. (1975), *The Psychological Birth of the Human Infant*. London: Hutchison.

Novick, J. & Novick, K. K. (1970), Projection and externalization. *The Psychoanalytic Study of the Child*, 25:65–95. New York: International Universities Press.

—— & —— (1994), Externalization as a pathological form of relating: The dynamic underpinnings of abuse. In: *Victims of Abuse*, ed. A. Sugarman. Madison, CT: International Universities Press, pp. 45–68.

—— & —— (1996a), *Fearful Symmetry*. Northvale, NJ: Aronson.

—— & —— (1998), An application of the concept of the therapeutic alliance to sadomasochistic pathology. *J. Amer. Psychoanal. Assn.*, 46:813–846.

Sawyer, D. (1994), *American Journal*. ABC Television, February.

Shengold, L. (1989), *Soul Murder*. New Haven, CT: Yale University Press.

Wurmser, L. (1994), A time of questioning: The severely disturbed patient within classical analysis. In: *The Annual of Psychoanalysis*, 22:173–207, ed. J. A. Winer. Hillsdale, NJ: The Analytic Press.

—— (1996), Trauma, inner conflict, and the vicious cycles of repetition. *Scand. Psychoanal. Rev.*, 19:17-45.

Chapter 8

Betrayal of the Family

The Parental Affair as Family Incest

LINDA GUNSBERG

*E*ven in this era of moral permissiveness, shock and perhaps even horror register when traditional family boundaries are violated. The blurring of boundaries, particularly in the area of sexual relations that can be characterized as incestuous, has been an issue addressed by all societies, notwithstanding that what constitutes boundaries and boundary violations varies from one society to another.[1] For the purpose of this chapter, I define family incest as sexual relations between a spouse and a member of the family of the other spouse, whether or not this person is related to the other spouse by blood (for example, the wife's sister-in-law); sexual relations of a spouse with a biological child, adopted child, or stepchild; sexual relations between siblings; sexual relation between a spouse and someone who is treated like "one of the family," such as a babysitter, nanny, housekeeper, or employee (outside of the home); and sexual relations between a spouse and a "family friend."

Although these are general guidelines, any family may include someone as "family," such as a friend, based on its own criteria. Of course, there is a societal taboo against sexual relations between family members related by blood (see chapter 18). There is also an unspoken taboo against sexual relations between any two people considered "family" by the child or a spouse.

---

[1] One of the most significant laws of Mesopotamian civilization was the Code of Hammerabi. Of the 282 laws within the Code, 73 pertained to sexual and marital relations. Incest, adultery, and rape were punishable by death (Lerner, 1986).

91

The purpose of this chapter is to address both the short-term and long-term impact on the family members, especially children, when there is a sexual boundary violation within the family, particularly between the mother or father and someone who is considered a family member. The dishonesty and lies that often accompany such violations will also be addressed.

Sexual boundary violations may result in divorce between spouses. How much weight will be given by a court in a divorce and/or custody proceeding to such family boundary violations when assessing the issue of parental fitness (see chapter 18)? The psychological impact of the parental affair as family incest will be illustrated in two publicized cases—Freud's case of Dora, an eighteen-year-old adolescent whose father involved her in his affair with Frau K.; and the Woody Allen and Mia Farrow custody case regarding three of their children—as well as in the psychotherapy of two children and one adult exposed to incestuous parental affairs.

ANTHROPOLOGICAL DATA REGARDING SEXUAL BOUNDARY VIOLATIONS

In his attempts to understand the role of oedipal and castration complexes in young children and in child and adult neuroses, Freud (1912–1913) turned to anthropological data to examine the social boundaries established by tribal peoples in Australia, Polynesia, Melanesia, and parts of Africa. All of these peoples were organized in clans. Each clan had a common ancestor, known as a totem. The totem, usually an animal, was the protector of the clan and, in return, the clansmen had a sacred obligation to the totem. People sharing the totem were forbidden from having sexual relations and from marrying. Often, violation of these social codes was punishable by death, whether or not the sexual relations resulted in pregnancy.

Sexual relations were forbidden not only within the immediate family unit (for example, between a man and his mother or between a man and his sisters), but also between persons of the opposite sex within a clan. Thus, the concept of family was extended to the entire clan, beyond blood ties. Sexual relations within the clan were taboo, and the prohibitions established in this regard were referred to as "avoidances."

Freud (1912–1913) emphasizes that, because tribal peoples have such an intense fear of incest and do not trust the ability of clan members to contain such intense longings through internal measures, strict external prohibitions must be established by the group and adhered to by all clan members. This is the function of the taboo.

Freud (1912–1913) believed that the child's incestuous longings toward his or her opposite-sex parent are the focus of oedipal phase development, with the further elaboration of an internalized super-ego (moral conscience) available to regulate those intense longings. Incestuous wishes become unconscious (repressed) and if and when they erupt, are dealt with by the internal structural agencies of the ego and superego. Thus, according to Freud, in more civilized societies, the need for such strong external prohibitions diminishes.

Unresolved oedipal longings, nevertheless, become the core of child and adult neurosis. In this chapter, several cases will be examined in which internal controls were not sufficient to prevent the breakthrough of incestuous longings into incestuous behavior. Perhaps since Western social codes rely heavily on individual sense of responsibility and do not offer strict punishment for incestuous behavior between persons considered "family," as tribal clans did, such temptations and violations are acted out more readily.

INFIDELITY: PSYCHOLOGICAL CONSIDERATIONS

Contemporary psychodynamic contributions regarding infidelity do not explicitly focus on incestuous sexual boundary violations within the marriage. The most comprehensive and coherent understanding of the psychological aspects of infidelity is offered by Lusterman (1989, 1995, 1998). Lusterman defines infidelity, offers a stage model for the various phases of infidelity, and addresses the impact of infidelity on children.

According to Lusterman (1989), infidelity is a secret. The unfaithful spouse (the person who breaks the marital contract) maintains the position towards the betrayed spouse (the partner in the marriage who discovers the spouse has been unfaithful) that the monogamous marital relationship has never been broken.[2]

---

[2]For the purposes of this chapter, the unfaithful spouse refers to the husband and the betrayed spouse refers to the wife, since, statistically, a greater number of marital affairs are initiated by the husband. The dynamics described hold true, however, whether the unfaithful spouse is the husband or the wife.

Stage 1 occurs prior to the onset of the affair (Lusterman, 1989). Although the partners to a marriage in which infidelity occurs report minimal marital problems during the early years, careful examination indicates there have been significant difficulties in self-disclosure and communication between spouses.

Stage 2 marks the onset of the affair, when one partner begins to look outside the marriage for greater intimacy, excitement, and pleasure, while the other partner seems content in the marriage and unaware of the changes in her spouse's feelings.

Stage 3 is cold rage, when evidence that a spouse is having an affair becomes available, yet is denied by the betrayed spouse. The betrayed spouse distances him- or herself from the spouse and often becomes irritable. These behaviors on the part of the betrayed spouse allow the unfaithful spouse to justify having and continuing the affair.

Stage 4, characterized by hot rage, occurs when the betrayed spouse can no longer deny the existence of the affair. At this stage, the betrayed spouse's anger, confusion, and shame reach heightened proportions, leading to a marital crisis. It is in this stage that the betrayed spouse can experience suicidal and/or homicidal feelings.

Lusterman (1989) addresses the phenomenon of the unfaithful spouse driving the betrayed spouse crazy. This phenomenon begins in stage 3, cold rage, and continues through stage 4, hot rage. For example, a wife who has repeatedly seen evidence that her husband is having an affair may confront him. He denies these accusations and requests for the truth, telling his spouse that she is crazy, leading her to revert to the denial stage and believe that her spouse has been, is, and will continue to be faithful to her and the marriage. The continued lying that accompanies this "protracted marital infidelity" (Lusterman, 1995) serves to weaken the betrayed spouse's grasp on reality and heighten her feelings that her sanity is at stake and that she, in fact, may be crazy. When the reality of the infidelity can no longer be ignored by the betrayed spouse, she feels her whole life is in shambles.

Because of the erosion of the betrayed spouse's sense of self esteem, she becomes less effective in her parenting. She becomes overwhelmed by and obsessed with the affair. The betrayed spouse may feel the need for the children to side with him or her against the unfaithful parent (Lusterman, 1990, 1991). The loss of a spouse, the loss of a sense of family as one thought it existed, and perhaps the perceived loss of one's children that the betrayed spouse may experience if the children do not feel betrayed in the same way he or she does, can lead to insensitive and even destructive treatment toward the children.

Involvement of Children in a Parent's Infidelity

The unfaithful parent may involve a child in his or her affair without consideration of the consequences to the child. (Once the child realizes that the parent has involved him or her in the affair, the child loses trust in the parent and feels used [Lusterman, 1998].) Most important, the child can no longer rely securely on family boundaries and lines of communication as they formerly existed. For example, the unfaithful parent may tell his child about his affair and require that the child keep it a secret. The very act of involving the child in the affair violates the parent–child boundary and creates both an unhealthy closeness with the unfaithful parent and an unnatural distance from the parent from whom the secret must be kept. This inappropriate closeness with the unfaithful parent and concomitant disloyalty and distance from the betrayed parent may intensify the child's guilt over knowing and keeping the secret.

The unfaithful parent may divide the siblings from each other by telling one or some of the siblings but not all of them, swearing those "in the know" to secrecy and creating distance from the siblings who have not been told. Alternatively, the betrayed parent may confide in one or more but not all of the siblings about the affair. He or she may hope that the children who are told will keep the affair a secret from the other children, side with him or her when the marriage dissolves, and distance themselves from the errant spouse.

Children are always adversely affected by a parent's infidelity (Papp, 1993; Lusterman, 1998). Younger children feel a heightened sense of insecurity and often exhibit regressed behavior, while older children may act out by vandalizing, shoplifting, becoming aggressive with other children, and even threatening to commit suicide. Adolescents, who are struggling so hard with their own sexuality, rely on their parents for models of appropriate boundaries of sexual behavior. A parent's unfaithfulness may actually frighten the child whose sexual fantasies are already heightened in adolescence and are intensified by the parent's boundary violations. The adolescent may fear that the unfaithful parent may not be able to contain his sexual impulses towards him or her.

The Affair and Its Impact on the Betrayed Spouse

Abrahms Spring and Spring (1997) claim that the betrayed spouse suffers serious loss to the sense of self. There are nine specific losses identified. First, there is loss of identity, as a result of which the spouse perceives him- or herself in negative rather than positive terms. Second, the spouse loses the sense of being special to someone, since the affair indicates that he or she is disposable. Third, the betrayed spouse loses self-respect in the process of trying to win the unfaithful spouse back. Fourth, the spouse loses self-respect in the recognition that he or she has denied, sometimes over a long period of time, the unfaithful spouse's hurtful actions. Fifth, the betrayed spouse feels he or she has lost control over thoughts and actions; he or she cannot stop thinking about the affair. Sixth, there is a loss of a sense of order and justice within the marriage and in society: rules of conduct, to which the betrayed spouse has adhered, have been violated by someone whom he or she trusted. Seventh, there is a loss of faith: how has God allowed this to happen to me? Eighth, there is a loss of connection with others. Friends sometimes turn away and the betrayed spouse wonders whom he or she can talk to about the infidelity. Finally, there is a loss of sense of purpose and, in some cases, even the will to live. Thoughts of suicide and even suicide attempts may be triggered.

Often, the unfaithful parent's affair stimulates "transgenerational injuries" (Abrahms Spring and Spring, 1997). Both spouses may have histories of growing up in families in which one or both parents had affairs and of having been drawn into secret alliances with either or both of their parents. The need to repeat one's own parent's affair may override the anticipatory guilt which might otherwise occur at the thought of causing pain to one's spouse and children, as well as one's own principle-based moral self-image (Hoffman, 2000).

The Affair and Its Impact on the Unfaithful Spouse

Less attention has been given to the psychological effects of the infidelity for the spouse who has the affair than for the spouse who has been betrayed. The lying and deception often does not stop once the affair has been discovered. The unfaithful spouse frequently continues to lie about various aspects of the affair, including its date of onset. He or she lies to create a false family history, which now conflicts with the family history of the other parent, their children, and others. This lying confuses the children. The unfaithful spouse/parent seems to be unconcerned about the impact of his actions on his spouse and children and often blames the spouse for his or her own transgressions and their effects on the marriage. The lying either has been or becomes part of the character structure of the unfaithful spouse. The lying may be a defense against confronting the loss of the family unit as it once existed and his or her responsibility for that loss and for the damage that has been inflicted on the family.

The unfaithful spouse, as a parent with whom the children identify, becomes a flawed role model for moral values, conscience, and trust, and honesty in human relationships. Sadly, once he or she is seen for what he is, he is no longer trusted by his children, as they become suspicious in their relationships to him as well as in their relationships to others in their lives.

Although the character flaws of the unfaithful parent are recognized at some point by the children, it is not uncommon for children to behave as if they quickly forgive the unfaithful parent. First, this is due to their desperate need to have continued relationships with both parents. Second, depending on the developmental level of the children, they may be both cognitively and emotionally unable to understand fully the meaning of family betrayal and family incest.

The Parental Affair as Family Incest: Betrayal of the Child

The psychoanalytic/developmental literature has not focused specifically on the parental affair as family incest (Strean, 1980). Thus, we are only in the beginning phase of observing children from this perspective. The following are my preliminary observations based upon the individual psychotherapy of eight children; six children whose fathers have had incestuous affairs as defined in the beginning of this chapter, and two children whose mothers have similarly been unfaithful spouses and committed incestuous affairs in their marriages. These preliminary observations may parallel findings pertaining generally to the larger category of extramarital affairs, of which incestuous family affairs are a subgroup.[3,4]

The child is the biggest loser in this kind of family scenario. First and foremost, the child lacks integration in her life narrative and life experience and becomes confused. She has two separate existences, one with mother and one with father and father's girlfriend/wife. The child is told by both parents that certain pieces of information cannot be shared with the other parent. Thus the child is forced to lie. For example, the child is often required to lie to the mother when asked whether the father's girlfriend is present when the child spends time with the father. In addition, the mother may not want the father to know who visits her house or whom she is dating. The child gets from each parent different stories about family chronology, the nature of the relationship between the father/unfaithful spouse and his new girlfriend, and about the onset of this relationship. The tragic result is that the child feels she cannot trust either parent, which in turn leads to distrust of others with whom the child is involved, such as friends, teachers, and other adults in the present and in the future.

There are verbalized and unverbalized questions as to the character and authenticity of people. The child's basic premise is that she will be lied to, so she must take a hypervigilant stance with others who may lie to her. There is a hypersensitivity to accuracy and historical truth. Furthermore, the family betrayal may be reenacted in future love relationships, either with friends or in romantic relationships. The child may later become the betrayed spouse and/or the unfaithful spouse.

Another form the infidelity takes is that the child feels betrayed by the father/unfaithful spouse who has a new family (children) with

---

[3]The same holds true for the overlapping symptomatology of some children who have suffered any kind of trauma and children who have suffered the specific trauma of divorce.

[4]I have chosen to group my preliminary observations regarding children of parents involved in incestuous family affairs, since no single case illustrates all the symptoms, behaviors, feelings and fantasies described in this section.

another wife. The child feels cast away by the father and, in this sense, identifies with the mother/betrayed spouse.

The child caught up in this type of family betrayal often manifests psychological symptoms. Suicidal feelings and attempts are reported, as well as despair. The child is responding not only to the family disruption as a result of the parental affair, but particularly to the disintegration of the devastated mother, who in turn deteriorates in her parenting skills, albeit temporarily. Depending upon the child's developmental level, she may or may not understand that the parental affair is wrong, especially if she has had a previous relationship with the woman (father's girlfriend) and likes or loves her.

The child may manifest a host of psychosomatic symptoms and patterning and transition disturbances (headaches, nausea, stomachaches, sleep disturbances, and school phobias). The psychosomatic symptoms are often related to the guilt the child feels for lying to either parent. Although chronic physical symptoms may be hazardous to a child's physical health, these symptoms do play an important role in alerting the psychotherapist to the internal conflict being waged. When the symptoms disappear, the psychotherapist wonders whether some of the family issues have been resolved (for the child, not necessarily for the family) or whether the battle has gone underground. That is, has the lying become part of the child's character structure and does the lack of reported guilt indicate dissociation or superego lacunae?

Finally, school problems often emerge for children with such family circumstances. The child is distracted; she is thinking about family problems. The child is unmotivated as a learner. The school becomes a safe haven for the child and a place to rest, not a place to work. The child is inhibited about knowing, and about telling, which affects her desire to learn. Does she want to know what is unknown? Is learning lying, or is learning obtaining helpful knowledge? These issues are residues from learning about the parental affair. Now, learning about something new may be experienced as disruptive and confusing, sending the child again into a state of questioning the accuracy of what she sees, thinks, and feels. Similarly, the child may not wish to learn about herself in psychotherapy.

CASE ILLUSTRATIONS

Freud's "Dora" Case: The Incestuous Ties
Between Dora's Family and the K's

Dora was brought to Freud (1905) for psychoanalysis shortly after her eighteenth birthday. She had insisted that her father break off relations with family friends, Frau and Herr K, and then had written a suicide note which her parents found. Dora had also developed neurotic symptoms, which included a nervous cough and hoarseness of the throat (Freeman and Strean, 1981).

Dora's father had contracted tuberculosis when Dora was six years old. He had been nursed back to health by Frau K. The two families became very close. Dora looked toward Frau K as a mother-substitute, shared secrets with her, and loved her very much. Whenever Dora stayed at the K's home, she shared Frau K's bedroom. On numerous occasions, Dora took care of the K's two small children. She witnessed with her own eyes the development of a romantic relationship between Frau K and her father.

Also, Dora had a fondness for Herr K, who took her for long walks and gave her presents. When Dora was 14 years old, Herr K kissed Dora on the lips. When Dora was eighteen, shortly before she consulted Freud, Herr K had professed his love for Dora, indicated that he and his wife were not having sexual relations, and proposed marriage to her.

Dora told her parents about these two incidents, but neither of them believed her. Her parents asked Herr K about his advances toward Dora, which he denied. Dora went into a rage when Frau K also refused to believe her allegations, and commented that all Dora knew about sex was what she read in books. The girl felt betrayed.

To Dora, involvement with the K's felt incestuous on two accounts. First, she witnessed with her own eyes the development of a romantic relationship between Frau K and her father. Second, she was being pursued romantically by her father's friend, the husband of the woman with whom her father was having an affair.

Dora felt everyone she loved had failed her by not believing her. She felt used by her father whom she felt had handed her over to Herr K as a gift so that Herr K would not interfere with his (her father's) involvement with Frau K. She felt her father hurt her "as he made her part of his promiscuous sexual life" (Freeman and Strean, p. 179).

Dora's father, in bringing her to Freud for treatment, seemed less concerned about whether Dora would be helped by Freud than with whether Freud would continue the lie that he (Dora's father) had begun—which was that all he had with Frau K was a friendship. As Glenn (1980) points out, Dora's analysis with Freud was actually sabotaged by her father because he was afraid that psychoanalysis could expose the truth about his involvement with Frau K.

In fact, Freud and Dora were working at cross purposes: Freud was interested in discovering "psychic reality" and Dora was interested in "historical truth" (Erikson, 1964, p. 169). Erikson (1962) states that the actuality of events is particularly important for adolescents, as this is related to their concerns about fidelity. That is, one must be loyal to the objective truth, as well as truth in relations with other people. By not confronting the fact of her father's affair, Dora exhibited a "fatefully perverted fidelity" (Erikson, 1964, p. 172). By denying the truth of her allegations, Dora's parents, Herr K, and his wife, Frau K, contributed to Dora's feeling crazy.

In describing her father and her understanding of his character flaws, Dora told Freud: "He was insincere, he had a strain of falseness in his character, he only thought of his own enjoyment, and he had a gift for seeing things in the light which suited him best" (Freud, 1905, p. 34). The long-term effects of her father's conduct are described by Deutsch (1957), who states that, as a middle-aged woman, Dora continued to accuse those around her of infidelity. Scharfman (1980) attests to the poor outcome in relations with men when women fail in their earlier relationships with their fathers. Dora's father used her and lied to her, and this model of interactions with men plagued her for the rest of her life.

Woody Allen v Mia Farrow: Incest Within the Family

This matrimonial case involving the custody of three children of Woody Allen and Mia Farrow was tried by Justice Wilk in the New York State Supreme Court (Allen v. Farrow, 1993). Woody Allen's request for custody followed the discovery of his sexual relationship with Mia Farrow's adolescent daughter, Soon-Yi, who was adopted during Farrow's former marriage to Andre Previn, and allegations of child sexual abuse of his seven-year old daughter, Dylan.

At the trial, Woody testified, "I didn't envision that I would maintain necessarily a long relationship with her. I felt nobody in the world would have any idea about it except Soon-Yi and myself."

> Justice Wilk: "Wasn't that enough? . . . That *you* would know that you were sleeping with your children's sister?"

> Woody: "No, I didn't see it that way. She was an adopted child and Dylan was an adopted child. I did not conceive of this as a sister relationship between the kids. A lot of kids were adopted and Soon-Yi was older" [*Allen v Farrow*, 1993: cited in Justice Wilk's opinion, June 7].

The following is an excerpt from Woody's interview with *Time* magazine reporter Walter Isaacson (1992), in which Isaacson tries to get Woody to address his concept of family, moral responsibility to the members of his family unit, and identity as a father figure.

> Isaacson: But wasn't it breaking many bonds of trust to become involved with your lover's daughter?

> Woody: There's no downside to it. The only thing unusual is that she's Mia's daughter. But she's an *adopted* daughter and a grown woman. I could have met her at a party or something.

> Isaacson: Were you still involved with Mia when you became interested in Soon-Yi?

> Woody: My relationship with Mia was simply a cordial one in the past four years, a dinner maybe once a week together. Our romantic relationship tapered off after the birth of Satchel, tapered off quickly.

> Isaacson: What was your relationship with Soon-Yi when you first started going over there to visit your children?

> Woody: I never had an extended conversation with her. As a matter of fact, I don't think she liked me too much. The last thing I was interested in was the whole parcel of Mia's children. . . . I spent absolutely zero time with any of them. This was not some type of family unit in any remote way. I didn't find any moral dilemma whatsoever. I didn't feel that just because she was Mia's daughter, there was any great moral dilemma. It was a fact, but

not one with any great import. . . . These people are a collection of kids, they are not blood sisters or anything. . . . It wasn't like she was my daughter.

Isaacson: Do you consider your relationship with Soon-Yi a healthy, equal one?

Woody: Who knows? . . . The heart wants what it wants" [pp. 59–61].

In a dramatic letter to Woody, Moses, age 14, expressed his feelings about his father's affair with his sister.

You can't force me to live with you. . . . All you want is the trust and relationships you had in the beginning of the time. You can't have those worthy things because you have done a horrible, unforgivable, needy, ugly, stupid thing, which I hope you will not forgive yourself for doing. . . . I hope you get so humiliated that you commit suicide. . . . You brought these things to yourself, we didn't do anything wrong. Everyone knows you're not supposed to have an affair with your son's sister including that sister, but you have a special way to get that sister to think it's OK. Unfortunately, Soon-Yi hadn't had a serious relationship before and probably thought, "OK, this is a great chance to see what a serious relationship is like." That's probably why she did it. . . . I just want you to know that I don't consider you my father anymore. It was a great feeling having a father, but you smashed that feeling and dream with a single act.

I HOPE YOU ARE PROUD TO CRUSH YOUR SON'S DREAM [*Allen v Farrow*, 1993 cited in Justice Wilk's opinion, June 7].

Justice Wilk tackled the thorny issues of family boundaries, relations, and morality very directly and gave them great weight in his decision regarding custody. In the Court's opinion, he writes:

When asked how he felt about sleeping with his children's sister, he responded that "she (Soon-Yi) was an adopted child and Dylan was an adopted child." He showed no understanding that the bonds developed between adoptive brothers and sisters are no less worthy of respect and protection than those between biological siblings [*Allen v Farrow*, 1993 cited in Justice Wilk's opinion, June 7].

The Court went on to state that

> the fact that Mr. Allen ignored Soon-Yi for ten years cannot change the nature of the family constellation and does not create a distance sufficient to convert their affair into a benign relationship between two consenting adults. . . . He had no consideration for the consequences to her, to Ms. Farrow, to the Previn children for whom he cared little, or to his own children for whom he professes love [*Allen v Farrow*, 1993, cited in Justice Wilk's opinion, June 7].

Rayson: Is It My Fault or Daddy's Fault?

Rayson was two and a half years old when his mother and father separated. To him, the separation was concretized by his recognition that his father and mother no longer slept in the same bed, although they still lived together. When he was out in the park playing with his dad, a young woman came up to them on several occasions and they played together. It was not long before he connected this woman with his parents' separation.

Rayson told his mother that he had played in the park with this woman, and he wanted to know if he had done something wrong. "I won't play with her again, mommy, I promise." He felt that he, by playing with this woman, caused the marital breakup. One and a half years later, he continues to play out themes of broken houses that are vulnerable to outside assault. He feels his mother offers him security and he now holds his father responsible for the parental breakup.

Sandra: Bereft, Discarded, and Replaced Like Mother

Sandra, now an eight-year-old, was six when her parents separated. Her father left her mother after his affair with the children's babysitter was exposed. He had given Sandra a beautiful gold necklace when she was three, for her birthday. The necklace had the inscription, "daddy's girl."

Daddy remarried and had another daughter. Although Sandra was excited about having a little sister, other feelings emerged when the necklace broke. She was bereft, sobbing in her mother's arms. Her mother understood the significance of the necklace for her daughter; that Sandra was daddy's number one girl before his affair had begun, and before his new daughter was born. The mother offered to ask the father to have the necklace repaired or replaced, and said that Sandra, in the mother's words, "would always be daddy's number one girl." For Sandra, the theme of family incest developed along two lines: the babysitter was father's wife and mother of the new half-sister, and the new baby girl was the creation of the family incest.

Sandra's stepmother (formerly the babysitter) wants Sandra's recognition as a mother figure, which Sandra refuses to give. It is possible that the stepmother requires Sandra's acknowledgment in this way so that she can put aside the reality, which is that she and Sandra's father were involved in an affair within the marital home, right in front of Sandra and Sandra's mother. Sandra aligned herself with her bereft mother and chose to take care of her mother by staying home from school and sleeping in the same bed with her.

Hanna: Her Father's Betrayed Lover

Hanna thought she was the only one of three sisters who knew about her father's affair with his secretary. The secretary was treated like a member of the family. Hanna's mother was never told of this affair. She would send Hanna on long weekend trips with the father, and Hanna and her father would sleep in the same hotel room. Hanna fantasized she was adored by the father, and the most preferred of the three daughters. She also fantasized that her mother chose her to "entertain" the father since she was dramatic and funny.

Hanna had few boyfriends in her teen and adult years. At one point, she gave serious thought to adopting a child and becoming a single parent. She felt she could not have a relationship with a man or become a mother until her father died. Hanna dated primarily married men, identifying with her father's secretary's role in her father's life.

Hanna experienced a great blow when she found out that one of her two sisters also knew about the father's affair because he told her as well. Symbolically, Hanna was no longer the prized daughter with whom father was having an affair. He was secretly having an affair with each daughter without telling the other. When discovered, this secret led to a sense of betrayal for Hanna, as if she had been two-timed by her father. Her intense psychic connection with her father continues to this day, along with a fiery sibling rivalry with the other sister whom father had told about his affair with his secretary. Hanna is in her late fifties, unmarried, and childless.

THE COURT'S RESPONSE
TO THE INCESTUOUS PARENTAL AFFAIR

When the husband or wife moves for a divorce and custody trial, the unfaithful spouse (father) often looks good, "well-heeled." He has psychologically been detached from his wife (and even children) for some time and has had time to find another partner. The betrayed spouse (mother) of the parental affair may look rageful, disturbed, and even crazy. By this time in the family's chronology, the affair has been exposed, and the wife may have made a suicidal attempt and perhaps been psychiatrically hospitalized. The unfaithful spouse refers to his wife as crazy, emotionally unstable, and a suicide risk. Based on the above, he alleges she is an unfit mother and seeks sole custody of his children.

The unfaithful spouse/father needs to annihilate the original family unit which involves the children's relationship to their mother. Thus, he denies the affair's negative impact on everyone by making a new family and attempting to integrate the children of his first marriage into it. By seeking and winning custody of the children and continually working toward diminishing their relationship with their mother, he tries to erase the parental affair from family history.

For example, a vengeful unfaithful spouse/father who had an affair with his children's babysitter tried to scare his wife into agreeing to a divorce and giving him very generous time with his children. He told the children that their mother was crazy. He added that they now have two mommies, their mother and his new girlfriend. In addition, he told his wife, "Don't worry, I'll keep going back to court to get more time with the kids and in two years, you won't have them at all."

The betrayed parent/spouse comes to Court with the following agenda. She needs the Court to serve as a public forum to expose the husband and the husband's affair. She needs him to acknowledge the affair, that is, the existence of the affair, which he may have refused to do. According to Lusterman (1998), she needs the above transitional steps to be taken in order for her to move on with her life. Finally, she may be looking to the Court to respond morally to her husband's infidelity and betrayal of her and the children. In some cases, the wife may delight in the Court's punitive response to the husband. She needs these steps to be taken so she can feel whole again. These are the betrayed spouse's conscious motivations.

The Court may not respond and, therefore, will disappoint the betrayed spouse who is looking for verification that the parental affair actually did take place and for punishment of the errant spouse. By viewing the family from the child's best interests standard, the Court is looking at the family through a different lens. The forensic expert, when recommending custody and specific visitation guidelines, plays a critical role in helping the Court assess the impact of the parental affair and lying by the unfaithful spouse on the children. Personal emotional reactions to the above by the judge, the attorneys, the law guardian, and psychotherapists treating family members will be somewhat contained by the forensic expert's focus on the impact, in as objective terms as possible, on the children.

CONCLUDING REMARKS

In the past, a parent who betrayed his or her family by having an affair could expect to be punished financially by the Courts. For example, if a wife had an affair, the court might deny her alimony. If a husband had an affair, the wife might receive greater child support and alimony awards. The Court functioned similarly to the ancient Hammurabi Code, as an external presence ensuring that violations of codes were addressed as serious offenses. Now, with men and women entering the divorce court on a level playing field, parental affairs are often not considered relevant.

The Court, by not addressing parental affairs in its custody determinations, ends up indirectly condoning such actions, which are extremely damaging to children in both the short term and the long term. Justice Wilk, in the *Allen v Farrow* (1993) case, did not turn his back on the Court's responsibility to raise the moral, ethical, and familial violations committed by an unfaithful father. This kind of confrontation by the Court regarding the moral fabric of marriage and family requires legal expertise, psychological sensitivity, and the capacity to enter the gray zone—the land of subtleties.

REFERENCES

Abrahms Spring, J. & Spring, M. (1997), *After the Affair*. New York: Harper Perennial.

Deutsch, F. (1957), A footnote to Freud's "Fragment of the analysis of a case of hysteria." *Psychoanal. Quart.*, 16:159–167.

Erikson, E. (1962), Reality and actuality. *J. Amer. Psychoanal. Assoc.*, 10:451–474.

—— (1964), *Insight and Responsibility*. New York: Norton.

Freeman, L. & Strean, H. (1981), *Freud and Women*. New York: Frederick Ungar.

Freud, S. (1905), Fragment of an analysis of a case of hysteria. *Standard Edition*, 7:3–122. London: Hogarth Press, 1953.

—— (1912–1913), Totem and taboo. *Standard Edition*, 13:1–74. London: Hogarth Press, 1955.

Glenn, J. (1980), Freud's adolescent patients: Katharina, Dora and the "homosexual woman." In: *Freud and His Patients*, ed. M. Kanzer & J. Glenn. New York: Aronson, pp. 23–47.

Hoffman, M. (2000), *Empathy and Moral Development*. New York: Cambridge University Press.

Isaacson, W. (1992), "The heart wants what it wants." *Time*, August 31, pp. 59–61.

Lerner, G. (1986), *Creation of Patriarchy*. New York: Oxford University Press.

Lusterman, D. D. (1989), Marriage at the turning point. *Family Networker*, 13(May/June):44–51.

—— (1998), *Infidelity*. Oakland, CA: New Harbinger.

—— (1995), Treating marital infidelity. In: *Integrating Family Therapy*, ed. R. Mikesell, D. D. Lusterman & S. McDaniel. Washington, DC: American Psychological Association, pp. 259–269.

Papp, P. (1993), The worm in the bud: Secrets between parents and children. In: *Secrets in Families and Family Therapy*, ed. E. Imber-Black. New York: Norton, pp. 66–85.

Scharfman, M. (1980), Further reflections on Dora. In: *Freud and His Patients*, ed. M. Kanzer & J. Glenn. New York: Aronson, pp. 48–57.

Strean, H. (1980), *The Extramarital Affair*. New York: Free Press.

Woody Allen v Maria Villiers Farrow, also known as Mia Farrow (1993), New York State Supreme Court, New York County, No. 68738/92.

Chapter 9

Parental Alienation

The Creation of a False Reality

MOISY SHOPPER

*P*arental alienation is a confusing, perplexing legal and psychological problem that often defies simple or even complex remedies. Alienation may occur in a variety of settings: in an intact stable marriage, during adolescent turmoil, in a divorce/custody dispute, or in a reconstituted family between a stepparent and stepchildren.

Alienation by definition involves the estrangement or transfer of feelings away from one person and often onto another. Within a family, attempts at alienation may take the form of criticism and bad-mouthing of a parent or an emphasis on the mistakes or inadequacies of the parent. However, not all such parental behavior is in the interest of alienation. A parent may criticize another as a way of "evening the score" or *anticipating a criticism* such as might occur in a stable but sadomasochistic marriage. In other instances, a parent may love the spouse but point out faults so that the child disidentify rather than identify with the specific character or behavioral faults of the spouse. If the criticizing parent is not motivated to estrange the child from the other parent but to have a more realistic appreciation of that parent's strengths and inadequacies, effects on the children may vary according to age. For a younger child, the distinction between disidentifying with a character trait versus disidentifying with the parent as a whole may be beyond the child's developmental abilities. In most cases the older child perceives that there is no denunciation of the parent as a whole but only of a circumscribed aspect of that parent's behavior.

In contrast, in its most severe form, "Parental Alienation Syndrome" (Gardner, 1985), "Medea Syndrome" (Wallerstein and Blakeslee, 1989), or the "Malicious Mother Syndrome" (Turkat, 1995), alienation refers to a concerted attempt, conscious or not, to disrupt a child's affectionate relationship with the other parent and coopt all of the child's affection and loyalty onto oneself. In the course of the alienation, the other parent is portrayed in such a demonized and dehumanized fashion as to render that person unfit for either affection from or a positive relationship with the child (Stoltz and Ney, 2002).

DISORDERS OF CREATED REALITY

Alienation in any setting or cause can best be viewed theoretically and clinically as a subtype of what I have termed "disorders of created reality" (Shopper, 1992). While not a recognized diagnostic category[1] I find it unifies conceptually what are otherwise considered separate and distinct entities. "Disorders of Created Reality" refer to situations in which a person's own autonomous sense of reality testing and reality appreciation are devalued and/or overwhelmed and replaced by a different reality through the actions of another. This occurs in *folie à deux* (Anthony, 1970), cults (Galanter, 1982; Langone, 1993), Munschausen by proxy[2] (Meadow, 1993), mass hysteria (Medalia and Larsen, 1958; Jacobs, 1965; Lee and Acherman, 1980), false allegations of sexual abuse (Meadow, 1993; Silber, 1994), and "parental alienation syndrome." In the typical *folie à deux*, a psychologically

---

[1]It is unlikely that this designation will achieve acceptance in the next revision of the American Psychiatric Association's *Diagnostic and Statistical Manual of Mental Disorders 4th Edition* since there is a preference for categories determined more by behavioral manifestations than by psychodynamic or structural criteria. I think this concept is useful because the phenomena described are not illusions, fantasies, or delusions. Rather, they are a deviation in reality appreciation that has been created, suggested, or inculcated by an outside source. This phenomenon has been depicted in the play *Angel Street* and its film version, *Gaslight,* and what Dorpat (1985) and Calef and Weinshel (1981) have called "gaslighting."

[2]Munchausen by proxy is a form of child abuse where the parent, often the mother, creates and/or reports a serious medical illness in her child, often an infant. When the child is older, the child, too, provides the false information of illness.

stronger person (the inducer) creates a belief system in a subservient, suggestible person to the point where the latter has a belief system, delusional though it may be, identical to that of the inducer. Upon separation from the inducer, the other person may, after a period of time, spontaneously regain his or her former state of reality testing. Anthony (1970) describes several cases of *folie à deux* in children in which the child's "reality testing often clashed with the needs of object relations, the mother frequently making the acceptance of her delusion a test of loyalty (to the mother)" (p. 576). He links *folie à deux* to failures in separation-individuation, in which, on an intrapsychic level, there is a "poor differentiation of self and object representations" (p. 592).

PARENTAL ALIENATION IN INTACT MARRIAGES

It is not unusual in an argumentative, sadomasochistic marriage for one party to constantly devalue the other. When a mother tells her son, "I hope you don't grow up to be like your father," it is not intended to encourage closeness between father and son. When a father uses the children as confidantes to discuss the unhappiness of his marriage to the mother and to cast blame on the mother this, too, serves to alienate. When the child becomes a confidante to a parent, superficially it seems as though the child and parent are drawing closer together, and achieving greater intimacy. In actuality, for the child to be drawn into the parental bedroom and to be privy to parental intimacies is not only overwhelming and/or overstimulating to the child but, even more important, the child is alienated from the demeaned parent and has lost the demeaning parent (see chapter 8). The child is no longer a child whose parents' first and only emotional concern is the child's welfare. Instead, via the shared secret, the shared confidence, the child suddenly enters the world of adult relationships, adult emotions, and adult conflicts, far beyond the child's capacity to manage, much less to understand. The parent who cares for and nurtures the child is replaced by a parent who requires the child's support and loyalty.

Deprecation, devaluation, and denunciation of the spouse can occur within an intact, stable marriage. In these marriages the depreciation is not a consequence of divorce but exists as part of a stable but disturbed home atmosphere. The parent may have a variety of motives, conscious and unconscious. Some of these may be narcissistic issues that lead to interfering with the child's same-sex gender identification, sex role identification, separation/individuation, desexualization of the parental relationship, and effective resolution of oedipal conflicts. The child is used by the parent for narcissistic regulation and, finally, as a vehicle for repetition and mastery of the parent's parents' behavior when the parent was a child.

In a most extreme form of devaluation, Stoller (1966) reported on mothers of children with serious gender identity problems. The mothers he described embarked on a course of devaluation and degradation of the father, regarding him as worthless and expendable. Their sons, in a variety of overt and covert ways, were encouraged to identify with the mother—not just with her character attributes, but also her femininity. As the father is devalued, so too is his maleness and his masculinity. The father is sufficiently emotionally passive and/or withdrawn from the home to allow this to occur. Even when physically present, such a father fails to provide any counter-balancing force favoring his son's maleness. I would like to emphasize that it is not the father's absence, per se, but rather the mother's attitude toward that absence. A father may be absent because of a service commitment or a business or educational endeavor. However, generally a mother values her husband and enjoys his masculinity and thus fosters and encourages a child's relationship with the father even *in absentia*. In fact, the mother may elevate the importance of the work or mission that necessitates the father's absence from the home. Recognizing the importance of gender identity, such a mother encourages stereotypical "male" activities and interests as well as calling upon males from the community (male coaches, male tutors) and the extended family (uncles, grandfathers) to be role models during the father's absence.

Pathological alienations should not be confused with the normal albeit painful parental alienation that occurs in the course of adolescence. This alienation is adolescent induced, may involve both parents in unstable and varying degrees, and should be considered part of the adolescent's attempt to cope with maturational issues such as sexual maturity, masturbation, desexualization of parental relationships, and separation/individuation. As intense as it may be for all concerned, it is readily reversible when there is a real family crisis or where the adolescent needs the power and approval of the parent (for example, an illness, obtaining a driver's license, or college visits).

Cordiality with one parent can abruptly end only to surface later with the other parent, with motives for the transformations murky at best.

THE ROLE OF GEOGRAPHIC MOVES IN ALIENATION

After a divorce a parent may seek to relocate, as what held him or her to a geographic locale during the marriage may no longer prevail post-divorce (see chapter 23). Whatever the cogency and realistic aspects of a geographic move, an adversary can interpret the move as that parent's wish to escape the jurisdiction of the divorce court and disrupt visitation of the non-custodial parent. E-mail, letters, and telephone calls are insufficient replacements for the face-to-face prolonged parent/child contact that is characteristic of evening visitations and weekend sleepovers. The younger the child, the greater the disruption. Parents, attorneys, and the courts need to have a high index of suspicion when petitioned by a custodial parent to remove the children from the immediate geographic area. However, differentiating between "good faith" motives and the wish to alienate the other parent from the children may call for the expertise of a psychodynamically trained forensic evaluator for whom the "best interests of the child" will be a determining consideration.

REMARRIAGE AND STEPPARENTS

When the motivation for a geographic move stems from the custodial parent's remarriage, the non-custodial parent's relationship is even more threatened.[3] Whether associated with a geographic relocation or not, the remarriage of the former spouse shatters ubiquitous fantasies of eventual reunion. For the noncustodial parent, remarriage by the custodial parent may be perceived as a narcissistic injury involving not only the loss of power over the former spouse, but the feeling that the former spouse now has a new protector/defender/supporter. The noncustodial parent also has the fear that he will become obsolete and redundant as the child develops a close

---

[3]For the purposes of this chapter, I will discuss the common scenario, in which the mother is the custodial parent and the father has visitation.

relationship with the stepparent (see chapter 8). The younger the child at the time of remarriage, the weaker the internalized mental representation of the relationship with the non-custodial parent. A mental representation relatively weak in duration, stability, intensity, and/or positiveness is more readily eclipsed by a knowledgeable stepparent eager to establish such a relationship (Shopper, 2001). The stronger the mental representation of the noncustodial parent, the less likely it is that such an eclipse will occur, even if the actual relationship with that parent is terminated by absence of visitation or by death.

Many noncustodial parents faced with a former spouse's remarriage believe themselves to be in a disadvantageous and vulnerable position to sustain their parent/child relationships. For many, this results in repeated "motions to modify," citing changed circumstances favorable to increasing the times and opportunities for maintaining oneself as an enduring presence in the child's life. Some non-custodial parents who earlier had placed children rather than their careers on the back burner realize that they and the child have missed out. As a result, they may not be as important to the child as they would have liked. With the remarriage of the ex-spouse, the fantasy is that the stepparent will want to replace the biological parent in the child's affection (see chapter 12). Regretting their career aspirations, absences from the home, and hurried child caring, this parent feels extremely vulnerable to replacement by the "in house" stepparent. A parent so threatened, whether the threat is based in reality or resides more in fantasy, will often attempt to interfere with the former spouse's remarriage, with geographic relocation, and especially with the child's attachment to the stepparent. A postdivorce parent, threatened by anticipated and fantasied alienation and replacement by a stepparent, may retaliate in advance, with his or her own efforts at alienating the child from the stepparent.

An excellent illustration is *Gotwald v Gotwald* (1986),[4] a notorious case receiving front page newspaper attention in Nashville. Neither an attentive, caring father or husband in his first marriage, Mr. Gotwald remarried. His new wife was childless. When his ex-wife planned to marry an outstanding and well-respected physician, the ex-husband offered to have an extended visitation with their three-

---

[4]I was asked by the mother's attorney to be their expert witness, which gave me access to all the written data.

year-old son, allegedly so the ex-wife could have more time to prepare for her wedding. At the end of the visitation, the father brought
the child to the pediatrician, alleging the son had told the father of
sexual and physical abuse perpetrated by the mother's fiancé. The
pediatrician reported the allegations to the child protective agency,
which removed the child from the mother's home and gave custody
temporarily to the father. This action was deemed necessary because
the mother not only did not believe the allegations but emphasized
her fiancé could not have had the opportunity much less the intent.

When the child was brought to the therapist by his mother, he
made no allegations; when he was brought by his father, he repeated
and elaborated the allegations. I testified as an expert witness. Although the case was decided in the mother's favor, the mother's
engagement did not endure the publicity and problems, and she
was burdened with huge legal expenses. The father, more a biological father than a psychological father to his son, would probably have
been readily eclipsed by this "almost" stepfather. However, the child
sustained the greatest loss, loss of an involved caring stepfather and
the experience of a biological father who, for his own narcissistic
motives, induced a "disorder of created reality" and who created a
harried, perplexed, and overwhelmed mother.

PARENTAL ALIENATION SYNDROME

As previously noted, an extreme form of disorders of created reality
is the form of alienation occurring in divorce/custody conflicts labeled "Parental Alienation Syndrome" by Gardner (1985). He refers
to a family interaction in which a child adamantly refuses to visit the
noncustodial parent, claiming that this parent is mean, abusive, un-
caring, and otherwise unloving toward the child, often buttressed
with (false) allegations of physical and/or sexual abuse against the
noncustodial parent. Gardner views the child as having been "programmed" by the custodial parent, even though the child often takes
full responsibility for his/her refusal. Gardner (1992) emphasizes that
Parental Alienation Syndrome is not simply the "programming" of a
child by a parent. The child has his or her own reasons and unconscious dynamics for being adamant and unyielding about non-visi-
tation. Wallerstein and Blakeslee (1989) described the same clinical
constellation but referred to it as the "Medea Syndrome," alluding

to the vengeful betrayed Medea of Greek myth "in killing her children, Medea destroys the symbols of the marriage," (p. 195). They argue that "Modern Medeas do not want to kill their children but they do want revenge on their former wives or husbands—and they exact it by destroying the relationship between the other parent and the child. In doing so they severely damage and sometimes destroy the child's psyche as well" (p. 196). Turkat (1995) prefers a different term, "Divorce Related Malicious Mother Syndrome," a concept derived from his clinical practice. He emphasizes that these mothers "unjustifiably punish" (p. 254) their divorced husbands by alienating the child and interfering with the father's access to the children even to the point of violating the law. Kelly and Johnston (2001) prefer to speak of the "Alienated Child," which they define as one whose behavior and negative feelings "are significantly disproportionate to the child's actual experience with that parent" (p. 251). They believe this emphasis on the child is "more objective and neutral" (p. 251) and shifts the focus from the "programming" parent.

For our purposes, the mother is assumed to be the alienating parent and the father the one alienated. Gardner (1985, 1992, 2002), Wallerstein and Kelly (1980), and Turkat (1995) remark that this may reflect the greater number of mothers given physical custody, their often unfavorable financial settlements, their greater problems in the job market and remarriage, and their perceived powerlessness in areas other than their children. With changing gender attitudes in the courtroom and more favorable outcomes for the mother, a growing number of fathers have taken to alienating their children from their mothers. It may be too early to have accurate incidence statistics.

Clinically, the child's denunciation of the parent seems to be a rehearsed litany. The accusations against the alienated parent are presented with vehemence; some accusations are totally contrived. With others, a real event is grossly misinterpreted, while at other times no specific event can be cited. There is simply a blanket denunciation and degradation of the parent. Perceiving him- or herself the victim of the parent's badness, the child shows no guilt. Even more striking is the absence of ambivalence. The alienated parent has no redeeming qualities, past or present.

The custodial parent may verbally support the visitation but take the position that she cannot change the child's mind and believes that the alienated parent is perfectly capable of doing all of the horrible things that the child alleges. However, the bottom line is that she will not forcibly compel a visitation that the child views as frightening, traumatic, and unwelcome. While the mother may seem cooperative with the visitation, on a deeper level she is only too pleased with the child's negative stance. This stance is a product of a prolonged period of her devaluation by and hostility toward the alienated parent prior to the divorce and certainly exacerbated by the divorce proceedings and outcome. For such a custodial parent it is as though, because she has divorced the children's father, she expects and insists the child(ren) do likewise. To love the other parent or even to want visitation with or accept presents from him is tantamount to betrayal. The child clearly perceives that the custodial parent cannot tolerate this degree of perceived "disloyalty." The preservation of the child's relationship with the custodial parent hinges on renunciation of the relationship to the non-custodial father. Once visitation ceases, the reality input of visitation with the father, which might correct the mother's denigration of him, also ceases. Without exposure to a countervailing reality, the child readily succumbs to the demonized picture inculcated by the mother. The similarity to Anthony's (1970) *folie à deux* is striking.

Some children, in the presence of the alienated parent, will fight vigorously to avoid the visitation. Other children, when visitation is enforced, will settle into a comfortable and somewhat friendly relationship with the parent whom they so vehemently denounced a short time before. When there is interaction with the father, the mother's denunciation of him is no longer realistically tenable. While this makes the child's position vis-à-vis the alienating parent more tenuous and uncomfortable, perhaps this child is healthier than the child who has relinquished all relationship to the alienated parent. In more severe instances the child, who may still love the alienated father, cannot show it out of fear that the mother's hostility and devaluation, currently aimed at the noncustodial father, would then be directed against the child. The legendary Medea killed her child. Such may be the cost of nonalienation.

CASE EXAMPLE

After a third petition for postdivorce visitation was brought by the estranged father, I was asked by the court's *guardian ad litem* to evaluate Fred, a ten-year-old boy who adamantly refused visitation with his noncustodial father. There had been two prior evaluations and three prior psychotherapists. The boy was insistent that the father was abusive, assaultive, and in all other ways a bad person. He repeatedly refused visitation. His mother stated her position, that she would tolerate visitation despite her devaluated view of the father, but she would not force visitation on her son as it was against his will. (For example, she would not carry him bodily into a car.)

When I saw Fred for the first time, I asked him about his school, hobbies, almost everything but the parental conflict. Impatiently, he interrupted his replies, all too eager to begin his recitation of the father's bad attributes which justified his refusing visitation. When it finally did become the topic, he expressed himself with eloquence, earnestness, and great emotion. However, his words and comments about the father were repetitive; they seemed memorized and delivered by rote. There was not the slightest indication of ambivalence toward the father. The father was totally bad, without a single redeeming quality. In a later interview I noted that, at one time, his mother was very pleased with his father—for example, when they first married. He startled, looked confused, became perturbed, and recovered his composure as he repeated his tirade of allegations against the father.

He echoed his mother's comments that he did not need a father, his family provided all that for him, especially since he had an older brother (Andrew). However, he remembered very little about his brother. When I noted that he was three years old when his brother left for an East Coast college, he was surprised, puzzled, had a momentary look of sadness, and then started a spontaneous tirade of abusive and demeaning remarks about his father. In my office, he was curious about many of the play and decorative items on the bookshelves and tabletops, but was exceedingly cautious about touching and handling them, needing my reassurance that it was permissible to look at, touch, and handle these objects. He made pronouncements with certainty, namely that the hourglass timer was five minutes, but after timing it for twenty seconds, lost patience. Simple puzzles were tackled with force rather than trial and error. Though he was bright, articulate, and well informed, he was doing very poorly in school. In addition, he intruded on and provoked other children and misbehaved. At home he slept poorly, wet the bed, and had repetitive nightmares of killing and/or being killed.

It was difficult to interview Ms. A as she told me when *she* would find it possible (convenient) to meet with *me*. Her replies to my questions were terse, nonresponsive, and in general, there was a stonewalling noncommunicativeness. With pointed, persistent questioning, the following story emerged.

Ms. A was a musician who left Russia with her mother and her seven-year-old son, Andrew (from her first marriage). She stated there had been no formal divorce from her first husband but that he was in agreement with her leaving. At the airport, Andrew asked why all the people were crying. He had been under the impression that everyone was taking a plane to go on a Black Sea holiday. It was at that point that he was told that they (he, mother, and maternal grandmother) were leaving the country. Although a full-sized harp was taken, no photos of Andrew's father were taken, nor were any letters or telephone calls exchanged in the ensuing twenty-two years. Once she arrived in the United States, Ms. A taught in her field and met and married an American man who was captivated by her intelligence and her air of culture and refinement.

After four years of marriage they had a child, Fred. Mr. A adopted Andrew, paid for Andrew's private school education and fees for a variety of lessons and activities, and set up a sizable trust fund for his higher education. However, the language of the home continued to be Ukrainian and the father felt totally excluded from conversations. The maternal grandmother continued to live with them, doing the childcare and babysitting for both children. Although both sons were bilingual, only Ukrainian was spoken in the home, ostensibly because the grandmother was "too old to learn English."

I would hypothesize that the parental alienation of the current father was a continuation of the mother's *and* grandmother's devaluation of men in the lives of her children. While the mother was barely superficially cooperative, there were many areas of inquiry to which she was noncommunicative, evasive, and even mute. When I asked to meet with the grandmother, even offering to supply an interpreter, they conspired to get the grandmother's physician to say it would be detrimental to the grandmother's high blood pressure. Later, when I spoke to the physician, I found that, rather than telling the physician that it would be a psychiatric interview to gather information about Fred, the mother and grandmother had told the physician that the grandmother was to testify in court and be cross-examined. For legal reasons, the *guardian ad litem* could not get the court to order her appearance for an interview.[5] The court did not agree with my recommendation of a period of foster care combined with enforced, supervised visitation. Supervision was recommended not for Fred's protection but for observation purposes.[6] Several years later, despite further litigation and continued court involvement, brief and unsatisfying visitations occurred only when the mother's child support was threatened by court order. The boy's treatment with another therapist exerted no beneficial effect.[7]

CRITIQUE OF THE PARENTAL ALIENATION SYNDROME

While Gardner speaks of the mother "programming" the child (which he uses synonymously with brainwashing), I believe it to be a poor choice of terminology. Both terms imply a conscious deliberate effort on the part of an active inculcator and a passive recipient. Although many divorcing parents know or are told that they should not "involve" their children in their divorce, it is very difficult for parents to abide by that advice even if it is their conscious wish to do so. Others profess verbal agreement but neither understand the concept nor appreciate the harm that may ensue when it's not followed. For the unusually angry vulnerable parent, the narcissistic need for revenge and emotional possession of the child prevails. What Gardner calls programming, I would regard as nothing more than the child's awareness of one parent's conscious and unconscious attitudes toward the other, as witnessed in the vicissitudes of the minute to

---

[5]Of interest, but not surprising, is that Fred accused the father of being able to manipulate all the prior doctors, evaluators, and therapists to say things favorable to the father's viewpoint.

[6]Optimally, the enforced visitation should be supervised and witnessed, not for the child's protection but for the father's protection. A witness of the visitation may be needed to rebut the child's allegations of the father's bad behavior, and to bear witness to the child's apparent enjoyment of the visitation. Often, once in the mother's orbit, the child may feel obliged to once again accuse the father and shout his (the child's) nonenjoyment of the visit.

[7]By the time these cases come to court, they have attained a certain measure of chronicity. Even if all the expert recommendations are appropriately considered by the court and equally appropriate court rules are promulgated, it is unrealistic to believe that chronicity and intense emotional positions will readily change. Although one's access to the family members et al. ends with the evaluator's report and testimony, long-term follow-up should be attempted, if only for one's own edification.

minute, day to day marital relationship. Each custodial parent will have his or her particular and specific ways of encouraging alienation and devaluation of the noncustodial parent. However, when one parent threatens the child with a disruption of their relationship, the child then settles the loyalty conflict with unambivalant loyalty to the threatening parent and unambivalant alienation from the other (Anthony, 1970).

Certainly in the course of a divorce/custody dispute, allegations, real and fantasied, are prominent and plentiful. Divorcing parents learn that allegations of sexual abuse against the other parent create a marked and often insurmountable disadvantage for the latter in custody disputes (see chapter 18). However, allegations of sexual abuse should not automatically be considered a strategy in the divorce proceedings since, as Schultze (1997) points out, sexual abuse may actually have occurred and may trigger a spouse to seek a divorce. Or, once the parents separate and file for divorce, the child may feel more comfortable to disclose the sexual abuse, or the narcissistic hurts, disequilibrium and loss accompanying divorce may so unsettle a parent's existing defenses that sexual abuse may then occur.

To tie issues of true or false allegations of sexual abuse to parental alienation as Gardner has done may be accurate in a percentage of cases, but clarity is best served if the two issues are considered separate and independent of each other. Faller (1998) makes this point even more forcefully.

Many in the legal profession regard Gardner's "Parental Alienation Syndrome" as not meeting the standard of acceptable scientific and technical evidence as defined by U.S. Supreme Court decisions in Daubert (1993) and Kumho (1999). As Justice Williams (2001) notes, the trial judge has a "gate keeping" function with respect to the admissibility of the evidence presented. Williams enumerates the problems with Parental Alienation Syndrome. and cautions us that "the admissibility of Parental Alienation Syndrome and/or Parental Alienation should *not* be benignly taken for granted" (p. 278). Gardner (2002) responds and continues to advocate for Parental Alienation Syndrome.

TREATMENT IN PARENTAL ALIENATION

A court ordered psychiatric or psychological examination can be very useful in clarifying the issues and assessing the degree and nature of parental alienation. Courts need to recognize that the longer an alien-ating situation continues, the more difficult it is to treat and to reverse. Identifying and taking clear and unequivocal corrective measures in high-risk conflict and alienation situations is essential. In cases of early or mild alienation, giving both parents an opportunity to ex-press and vent their angers, frustrations, and misperceptions can be a valuable therapeutic measure. In moderate and severe cases, simply venting with their attorneys or the *guardian ad litem* is insufficient, and parents may need to seek their own therapists. For a five-tier classification of gradations of severity see Lee and Olesen (2001).

It is necessary for judges, attorneys, and mental health profes-sionals to work together and utilize each other's expertise in working toward the best interest of the child. This partnership of judge, at-torney, and mental health professional is necessary since mere judi-cial orders often can be and are evaded. Similarly, the advice and suggestions of mental health professionals are often ignored. Efforts by the judge and the mental health professional must be facilitated by the attorneys if any treatment plan is to be potentially successful.

The appointment of a special master or a staff member of the court's child protective team often represents the court's presence and pressure in securing cooperation with the court's orders (see chapter 26). I would like to emphasize the need for continued involve-ment and supervision by the court. If family members are mandated into a psychotherapy process, the confidentiality of each treatment should be respected except for reporting as to the patient's atten-dance and "cooperation."

Alienation cases are among the most difficult cases to treat ei-ther legally or psychotherapeutically, as there is no motivation ema-nating from the parent who has perpetrated the alienation. In fact, that parent is more likely to be covertly obstructionist and uncoop-erative. During the post-divorce period of alienation, the child's re-ality testing has been undermined by the alienating parent and cannot be corrected until satisfactory contact between the child and the alien-ated parent is ongoing. Until such time, the reality proposed by the alienating parent becomes and remains the "created reality" of the child. The alienating parent is not likely spontaneously to seek treat-ment or to seek treatment for the child even if there are ample symp-toms of disturbance in both as treatment would be seen as tending to undo and interfere with the alienation. Thus, therapy must be mandated by the court.

The therapist has to be skilled and sufficiently aware that an alienating process is occurring and that the therapeutic alliance with the alienating parent is, at best, tenuous. This alliance becomes non-existent should the alienating parent perceive the therapist (or the process) as un-doing the alienation. In addition, the therapist stands the risk of a countertransference reaction, whereby the therapist supports the reality presented by the alienating parent, thus becoming that parent's ally in the fight for the allegiance of the child. Courts frequently do not see the need to separate the child from the alienating parent. To suggest foster care when the court sees the alienating parent, as both fit, competent, and well-meaning, may strike the court as unreasonable. To place the child with the alienated parent as recommended by Gardner (1992) would certainly be difficult for the courts to contemplate, especially so when many courts are obligated to ascertain a child's custody preference prior to making a definitive custody ruling. On the face of it, such a change in custody *seemingly* goes so greatly against the "best interest of the child" as to make it appear untenable. However, Levy (1992) notes, "If parents who engage in PAS [Parental Alienation Syndrome] know that aware judges may give custody to the innocent parent, and perhaps even apply sanctions against parents who use a child to prevent the other parent's access to the child, the PAS, which is itself a form of child abuse, may suffer a fatal and well deserved setback" (p. 277).[8]

Cartwright (1993) concurs and advises the courts to have little patience for negotiations when the alienating parent is insincere and unmotivated to correct the situation. Foster care or placement with an unaffiliated blood relative might find greater acceptance. Many courts are unaware that, apart from the loss suffered by the alienated parent, the very fact and intensity of the alienation may cause irreparable harm to the child. In my jurisdiction, the courts have seen a sufficient number of Parental Alienation cases and have come to regard parental alienation as a form of child abuse. As a result, they are more ready to institute more drastic solutions, such as placement outside the alienating home. Even with such placement, there is no guarantee that the child's reality testing, and loyalties can be sufficiently corrected as to allow for beneficial visitation with the

---

[8]Yet if the court were to recognize parental alienation as a form of child abuse, judges would have less reservation about enforcing separation of the child from the alienating parent.

alienated parent, especially if the alienation has been going on for several years. In some jurisdictions, there are newspaper reports of mothers who would rather spend time in jail (in contempt of court) than allow the child to have visitation with the other parent or the relatives of the other parent. Certainly, the combined resources of judicial intervention (discretionary power), court-offered services, and the private sector of competent therapists offer the best hope for treatment in these extremely difficult situations.

REFERENCES

Anthony, E. J. (1970), The influence of maternal psychosis on children—*Folie à deux*. In: *Parenthood*, ed. E. J. Anthony & T. Benedek. Boston: Little Brown.
Calef, V. & Weinshel, E. M. (1981), Some clinical consequences of introjections: Gaslighting. *Psychoanal. Quart.*, 50:44–66.
Cartwright, D. F. (1993). Expanding the parameters of parental alienation syndrome. *Amer. J. Family Ther.*, 21:205–215.
Clawar, S. S. & Rivlin, B. V. (1991), Children held hostage: Dealing with programmed and brainwashed children. *Section of Family Law, American Bar Association*.
Daubert v Merrill Dow Parmaceuticals Inc. 500 U.S. 579 (1993).
Dorpat, T. L. (1985), *Denial and Defense in the Therapeutic Situation*. New York: Aronson.
Faller, K. C. (1998), The parental alienation syndrome: What is it and what data supports it. *Child Maltreatment*, 3:100–115.
Galanter, M. (1982), Charismatic religious sects and psychiatry: An overview. *Amer. J. Psychiat.*, 139:1539–1548.
Gardner, R. A. (1985), Recent trends in divorce and custody litigation. *Acad. Forum*, 29:3–7.
—— (1992), *The Parental Alienation Syndrome*. Cresskill, NJ: Creative Therapeutics.
—— (2002), Parental alienation syndrome vs. parental alienation: Which diagnosis should evaluators use in child-custody litigation? *American J. Family Ther.*, 30:101–123.
Gottwald v Gottwald, #86-463-111. Chancery Court, Davidson County, Tennessee (1986).
Jacobs, N. (1965), The phantom slasher of Taipei. *Soc. Problems*, 12:318–328.
Kelly, J. B. & Johnston, J. R. (2001), The alienated child—A reformulation of the parental alienation syndrome. *Family Court Rev.*, 39:249–266.
Kumho Tire Co. v Carmichael 119 S. Ct. 1167 (1999).
Langone, M. D., ed. (1993), *Recovery from Cults*. New York: Norton.
Lee, R. L. & Ackerman, S. (1980), The sociocultural dynamics of mass hysteria. *Psychiatry*, 43:78–88.

Lee, S. M. & Olesen, N. W. (2001), Assessing for alienation in child custody and access evaluations. *Family Court Rev.*, 39:282–298.

Levy, D. (1992), Parental alienation syndrome: A guide for mental health and legal professionals. *Amer. J. Family Ther.*, 20:276–77.

Meadow, R. (1993), False allegations of abuse and Munchausen syndrome by proxy. *Arch. Dis. Child.*, 68:444–447.

Medalia, N. Z. & Larsen, O. N. (1958), Diffusion and belief in a collective delusion: The Seattle windshield pitting epidemic. *Amer. Sociolog. Rev.*, 23:180–186.

Metnick, M. F. (1998), Parental alienation: A continuum of responses in high-conflict divorce. In: *Serving the Needs of the Child Client* (The Children: Law Manual Series), ed. M. Ventrell. Denver: National Association of Counsel for Children.

Schultze, R. (1997), Evaluating medical and mental health testimony in child sexual abuse cases. *Wiley Family Law Update*. New York: Wiley.

Shopper, M. (1992), Disorders of created reality. Presented to the Michigan Psychoanalytic Society, Ann Arbor, MI.

—— (2001), Stepfathers: Varieties and job description. In: *Stepparenting*, ed. S. Cath & M. Shopper. Hillsdale, NJ: The Analytic Press.

Silber, T. J. (1994), False allegation of sexual touching by physicians in the practice of pediatrics. *Pediatrics*, 94:7425–7425.

Stoller, R. J. (1966), The mother's contribution to infantile transvestic behavior. *Internat. J. Psychoanal.*, 47:384–395.

Stoltz, J. M. & Ney, T. (2002), Resistance to visitation: Rethinking parental and child alienation. *Family Court Rev.*, 40:220–231

Turkat, I. D. (1995), Divorce related malicious mother syndrome. *J. Family Violence*, 10:253–264.

Wallerstein, J. S. & Blakeslee, S. (1989), *Second Chances*. New York: Ticknor & Fields.

—— & Kelly, J. (1980), *Surviving the Break-up*. New York: Basic Books.

Williams, R. J. (2001), Should judges close the gates on PAS and PA? *Family Court Rev.*, 39:267–281.

Interlude III

Parents' Rights and Responsibilities

We guard our freedoms zealously in this country. Foremost among them is the freedom to rear our children however we see fit. Yet the state has taken on itself the guardianship of the child's best interests in situations where parents are deemed to be abusive or neglectful or when two fit parents become legal adversaries. The contributors in this section address issues that involve actions of the state that might be placed along a continuum from least to most restrictive of a parent's freedoms. Although the focus of the section is on parental rights and responsibilities, a number of the authors note how other interested parties, from stepparents to grandparents, have also claimed the courts' attention.

As Solnit and Nordhaus (see chapter 11) delineate the novel family configurations and complex legal dilemmas that the courts face, one can infer how difficult it often is now to establish a sole "psychological parent." Their reminder of Anna Freud's dictum to put oneself inside the "skin of the child" is a timely call to maintain our focus on the child's experience of the parent even as society's changes seem to be ever accelerating. They note that one crucial component of the child's experience concerns his or her sense of time and the importance of achieving solutions that are within the child's tolerance for delay.

Galietta's discussion (chapter 14) of the wrenching issues involved in termination of parental rights cases reflects just such a "skin of the child" perspective. While remaining sensitive to the rights of the biological parents, she applauds efforts by the legislature to improve the efficiency of the abuse and neglect courts in the service of the child's emotional needs for timely solutions. She further warns

127

of the need to be wary of the forensic expert's inclination to sympathize with the individual who faces a permanent loss of parental rights where the child's safety and welfare have proven to be at stake.

Guggenheim (chapter 10) identifies the common underlying principle of the two headline family law cases of the year 2000 and goes on to underscore the essential Constitutional guarantee of the family's right to privacy. His legal argument on behalf of protecting the family's privacy, of course, is restricted to situations in which a fit parent supercedes the state's investment in the child. In contrast, Klein, viewing the issue of parental rights from a mental health perspective, notes that it is often only with family discord that such rights become an issue at all. He suggests that a focus on parental "obligations" might help to bridge what, in today's society, at times appears to be a conflict between parents' and children's rights.

Silverman (chapter 13) and Galietta (chapter 14) each address situations in which the state's *parens patriae* role is most overt. Here we have come full circle from Guggenheim's examples, in which the state's powers have been correctly circumscribed. While sensitive to the complex and often conflicting issues facing mental health professionals and the legal system alike within the penal system, Silverman remains particularly attuned to the "fragile bond" between mother and child. Of additional interest is her exploration of the cultural clashes that ensue once the state becomes involved in child rearing. The racial and cultural issues in divorce and custody merit far more attention than we were able to give them in this book and have been insufficiently studied.

Paul Hymowitz

Chapter 10

When Should Courts Be Empowered to Make Child-Rearing Decisions?

MARTIN GUGGENHEIM

*A*merican popular culture is deeply connected with the law. Rarely does a year go by without several legal cases capturing the attention of the American public. The year 2000 was no exception. What was perhaps somewhat unusual was that two cases which achieved center stage were in the field of family law. This chapter presents a happy opportunity to discuss important principles of family law with an audience already somewhat familiar with the background details.

THE ELIÁN GONZÁLEZ CASE AND THE GRANDPARENT VISITATION CASE

The first case involved Elián González, the six-year-old Cuban boy who came to the United States in a life-raft with his mother, who drowned at sea (*González v Reno*, 2000). The case concerned the right of a Cuban child to be permitted to remain in the United States over the objection of his only living parent (or, depending on how one sees the matter, the right of his American relatives to petition an American court to allow him to remain over the father's objection). The second case, dubbed the "grandparent visitation case," was widely discussed when the Supreme Court of the United States decided it in June 2000 (*Troxel v Granville*, 2000). This case involved the right of grandparents to visit grandchildren over the objection of the children's parents.

On one level, these two cases appear to have little in common. What connects them is that both involved efforts by nonparents to obtain a court order concerning a child's upbringing over the parents' objection. The central issue raised by both cases concerns the power of the state—whether through the legislature or the courts—to interfere with, and overrule, a parent's child-rearing choices. The question of when and why state officials (commonly judges) may be empowered to force parents to make child-rearing decisions over the parents' objections raises profound constitutional questions of the relationship of the citizen and the state.

Simply stated, American law generally assigns to parents the authority to make all child-rearing decisions for their children. And, in order to discourage people from taking the law into their own hands, when someone other than a parent wants something to happen to a child which the parent opposes, the law generally requires the nonparent to sue the parent in court. This is what happened both in *González* and in *Troxel*.

A second overlapping characteristic of both cases is that both sought (unsuccessfully) to have the case decided on the basis of what was in the children's best interests. In *González*, Elián's best interests were never reached because the case was decided on grounds that precluded courts from even asking what was in his best interests. Instead, Immigration officials ruled that only Elián's father could file an application for asylum to remain in the United States. Federal courts agreed with that conclusion. As a consequence, because Elián's father did not want his son to remain in the United States, there was no petition for asylum to consider. In the absence of such a petition, there was no jurisdiction to keep Elián in the United States, and he returned to Cuba. Elián's relatives complained that Elián never had his day in court and, particularly, that the way the case was decided deprived any court of deciding what was in Elián's best interests.

In *Troxel*, the best interests standard was the basis for the original trial court's awarding visitation to the grandparents. But the Supreme Court explicitly rejected that standard as appropriate for deciding the case. Indeed, the Court went so far as to hold that the use of the "best interests" standard to order the parents to allow the grandparents visitation could violate the federal Constitution. In *Troxel*, the paternal grandparents of two grandchildren sued the children's mother pursuant to a Washington statute that permitted nonparents to petition a court for visitation rights and authorized courts to grant such visitation rights only if "visitation may serve the best interest of the child."

The Supreme Court declared the statute unconstitutional as applied. Although no majority decision was achieved, the plurality opinion declared the Washington statute unconstitutional because it "effectively permits a court to disregard and overturn any decision by a fit custodial parent concerning visitation whenever a third party affected by the decision files a visitation petition, based solely on the judge's determination of the child's best interest" (p. 67). In particular, the plurality opinion criticized the trial court because it failed to accord the determination of [the mother] any weight. The trial court made only two findings: (a) the grandparents are part of an extended family; and (b) the children would benefit from visiting with them.

"These 'slender findings,'" the plurality held, combined with the trial court's "announced presumption in favor of grandparent visitation and its failure to accord significant weight to [the mother] already having offered meaningful visitation to [the grandparents], show that this case involves nothing more than a simple disagreement between the [trial] court and [the mother] concerning her children's best interests" (p. 72). The plurality added that "the Due Process Clause does not permit a State to infringe on the fundamental right of parents to make child-rearing decisions simply because a state judge believes a 'better' decision could be made" (pp. 73–74).

WHO SHOULD MAKE CHILD-REARING DECISIONS: PARENTS, CHILDREN, OR JUDGES?

The question remains, why should parents be able to make decisions for their children when others (even judges) could conclude that such decisions are not in the child's best interests? A different, but also important, question is, when should children have rights of self-determination under American law? Both the *González* and *Troxel* cases raise the first question. It is not clear whether either raises the second because in neither case is it evident what the children themselves actually wanted. But it is important to acknowledge that empowering parents to make decisions for their children *dis*empowers all others. First, it disempowers judges from supervening parental decisions. Second, it disempowers children from taking actions opposed by their parents.

What justifications are there for allocating to parents child-rearing decisions that must be respected in court unless the parents are unfit? Although the Constitution does not expressly confer upon parents the right to rear their children without undue interference by the state, rights of this nature have been found implicit in a number of constitutional guarantees. The Supreme Court has recognized that the freedom of parents and families against unnecessary state intrusion is within the Constitution's protections of privacy (*Griswold v Connecticut*, 1965), liberty (*Cleveland Board of Education v LaFleur*, 1974, pp. 639–640; *Wisconsin v Yoder*, 1972, pp. 230–234; *Stanley v Illinois*, 1972, p. 651; *Pierce v Society of Sisters*, 1925, pp. 534–535), and personal integrity (*Stanley v Illinois*, p. 651; *Griswold v Connecticut*, p. 500; *Poe v Ullman*, 1961, pp. 551–552).

AMERICAN CONSTITUTIONAL PRINCIPLES

In the first significant parents' rights case, the Supreme Court held that the liberty protected by the Due Process Clauses of the Fifth and Fourteenth Amendments encompassed the right to marry, establish a home, and bring up children (*Meyer v Nebraska*, 1923). A statute forbidding the teaching of the German language was invalidated as an impermissible infringement on the freedom of parents to have their children learn a foreign tongue if they wished. The Court considered the practice, endorsed by Plato and others, of removing children from their homes for training by "official guardians" and concluded:

> Although such measures have been deliberately approved by men of great genius, their ideas touching the relation between individual and State were wholly different from those upon which our institutions rest; and it hardly will be affirmed that any legislature could impose such restrictions upon the people of a State without doing violence to both letter and spirit of the Constitution [p. 402].

Relying on *Meyer*, the Court two years later struck down an Oregon statute requiring children to attend public schools. In *Pierce v Society of Sisters* (1925), the Justices found that this statute unduly interfered with the right of parents to select private or parochial schools for their children and that it lacked a reasonable relation to any purpose within the competency of the state. The Court wrote:

> The fundamental theory of liberty upon which all governments in this Union repose excludes any general power of the State to standardize its children. . . . The child is not the mere creature of the State; those who nurture him and direct his destiny have the right, coupled with the high duty, to recognize and prepare him for additional obligations [p. 535].

In *Prince v Massachusetts* (1944), the Court wrote that "[i]t is cardinal with us that the custody, care and nurture of the child reside first in the parents, whose primary function and freedom include preparation for obligations the state can neither supply nor hinder" (p. 166). *Prince* nevertheless held that this freedom could be limited by the state to the extent necessary to protect children from serious hazards to their physical well-being. The Court sustained the conviction of a minor's guardian for violating a child labor law by permitting the child to vend evangelical newspapers pursuant to the missionary tenets of the child's and guardian's religion. "Parents may be free to become martyrs themselves. But it does not follow they are free . . . to make martyrs of their children" (p. 170).

In *Roe v Wade* (1973), the Court restricted state power to forbid abortions, holding that a woman's decision whether to bear a child is within the sphere of privacy "founded in the Fourteenth Amendment's concept of personal liberty" (p. 153). The Court noted that, even though privacy is not explicitly mentioned in the Constitution, a "guarantee of certain areas or zones of privacy" has been constitutionally recognized in connection with "activities relating to marriage, procreation, contraception, family relationships, and child rearing and education" (pp. 152–153). Similarly, the Court invalidated a scheme of mandatory leaves for pregnant public school teachers because that scheme unnecessarily interfered with the decision to raise a family: "freedom of personal choice in matters of marriage and family life is one of the liberties protected by the Due Process

Clause of the Fourteenth Amendment" (*Cleveland Board of Education v LaFleur*, 1974, pp. 639–640). Summarizing its cases, the Supreme Court has said:

> The absence of dispute [concerning the fundamental nature of the parent-child bond] reflect[s] this Court's historical recognition that freedom of personal choice in matters of family life is a fundamental liberty interest protected by the Fourteenth Amendment [*Santosky v Kramer*, 1982, p. 753].

The upshot of this body of case law is that parents have a constitutional right to the care, custody, and control of their children. This right includes the right to be free from interference by the state in the rearing of the child and in the child's instruction, so long as the parent discharges certain obligations to support the child, provide for his or her health and safety, and ensure his or her education and welfare. Because of the fundamental nature of these rights, state intrusion into the upbringing of children or the integrity of the familial relationship is permitted only after a showing has been made that a weighty state interest justifies disturbance of the parent–child bond and cannot be achieved in a less disruptive manner.

WHAT ABOUT THE BEST INTERESTS OF CHILDREN?

Can these principles be reconciled with a child-friendly legal system? Is it proper that courts are not permitted to consider for themselves what is in a child's best interests? Finally, what about a child's right of self-determination? These questions need to be briefly addressed before concluding the discussion of *González* and *Troxel*.

Although empowering courts to decide what is in a child's best interests may appear on its surface to advance children's rights, it is not perfectly clear why this is so. If courts were free to disagree with a parent about what is in a child's best interests, the state (through the judiciary) would be empowered to make child-rearing decisions. But such empowerment would not necessarily translate to children being better off. The conflict of power would be between two sets of adults: parents and judges. But in both cases, children's fates would be determined by someone other than the child.

Nonetheless, it might be argued, we should still prefer a scheme by which state officials are permitted (and obliged) to make decisions based on what furthers a child's best interests. This argument implicitly assumes such a determination is (a) more or less objective and (b) relatively easy to reach. Nothing could be further from the truth.

Although the "best interests" test is alluring, it is important to appreciate its deficiencies. In the words of one author, the best interests test "is not properly a standard. Instead, it is a rationalization by decision-makers justifying their judgments about a child's future, like an empty vessel into which adult perceptions and prejudices are poured" (Rodham, 1973, p. 513). In addition, the test is inherently indeterminative, in part because we simply lack the tools to make intelligent predictions about the future (even though this is an implicit feature of intervening) and in part because of the absence of any single set of social values one is to use (Mnookin, 1975, p. 257).

A virtue of existing law is that parents are protected even from having to justify and defend their parental choices when the most that can be said about the exercise of their choice is that it is not in their child's best interests. Even tolerating legal action to review parental child-rearing choices has a dramatic impact on the well-being of children. As Joseph Goldstein and his colleagues remind us:

> Children . . . react even to temporary infringement of parental autonomy with anxiety, diminishing trust, loosening of emotional ties, or an increasing tendency to be out of control. . . . At no stage should intrusion in the family [which the authors define as conducting a hearing] be authorized unless probable cause for the coercive action has been established in accord with limits prospectively and precisely defined by the legislature [Goldstein, 1979, p. 25].

Fit parents have the constitutional right to raise their children as they deem appropriate, even when others could reasonably disagree and claim the child's best interests would be served by a different approach. Goldstein (1977) has reasoned, for example:

> State policy toward child rearing revolves around attempts to answer this question: will children become what this society most wants if parents are left to follow their own stars in child rearing and if plural subcultural groups are free to shape norms of child rearing for parents, or if the more inclusive state community is permitted to intrude and set limits on both parental and small-group impositions on children? The answer to this question surely

must be that there can be no conclusive answer favoring one contestant over the other.

Though it may seem paradoxical, that answer is a central guide for court review of state child rearing policy. If there can be no such conclusive answer, courts should properly insist that the question remain adequately open [p. 650].

THE CHILD'S RIGHT TO SELF-DETERMINATION

Finally, there is the question of the rights of children to make decisions for themselves. Many of the rights adults enjoy under American law are designed to enhance autonomy. Our laws not only restrict government intrusion into the private affairs of Americans, they also provide substantive freedoms to Americans to make individual choices about the kind of life to lead. Law treats children differently than adults in a great many ways. This differential treatment derives from one fundamental notion: Adults presumptively have the reasoning capacity to make important decisions for themselves; young children do not. As the Supreme Court has said, "unlike adults, [children] are always in some form of custody. . . . Children, by definition, are not assumed to have the capacity to take care of themselves" (*Schall v Martin*, 1984, p. 265).

At the same time, the law recognizes that the category of "childhood" is very broad and that disabling seventeen-year-olds from having any autonomy rights is very different from disabling seventeen-month-olds. For this reason, the Supreme Court has recognized that children are "persons" within the meaning of the Fourteenth Amendment, with their own liberty and privacy interests. American law sensibly grants to older minors (commonly called "mature minors") certain autonomy rights, at least when they can demonstrate the general presumption that they lack the maturity to make wise decisions about their future is inappropriate as applied to them. So, for example, older minors can leave school and join the work force without parental permission before reaching adulthood. They can even obtain an abortion without parental permission (*Bellotti v Baird*, 1979).

Virtually none of the rights young children enjoy under American law have anything to do with advancing their autonomy. Many of these "rights" would be disabilities if applied to adults. Our most enlightened laws exclusively applicable to children would be regarded as repugnant if applied to adults. Requiring adults to attend a program for six hours per day five days a week for more than forty weeks each year, for example, would obviously constitute a significant restriction on liberty. Yet compulsory education laws are a prominent example of what we characterize as children's rights.

Current law has not established a bright line distinguishing between minors who have limited rights of self-determination and those who do not, principally because determining who is a "mature minor" probably is best resolved on a case-by-case basis. But there are no substantive rights to self-determination that six-year-olds enjoy under American law. For children this young, American law requires that all significant decisions about their future be decided by a responsible adult acting on the child's behalf. In most cases, this means the parents.

CONCLUSION

The court clearly was correct in *González* in concluding that, under American law, parents are entitled to speak for their six-year-old children. Because Elián's father did not want his son to seek asylum in the United States, the only choice was to deny jurisdiction to consider an asylum application and permit the father to choose where to live with his family. Had the court sought to prevent Elián's father from deciding whether Elián should return to Cuba, it would have gravely threatened the liberty of all Americans. Similarly, the Court's decision in *Troxel* adheres to long-established principles that restrict judges from second-guessing child-rearing decisions that do not endanger the well-being of children.

It is not a sleight of hand to suggest that children reciprocally enjoy constitutional rights to be raised by their parents free from governmental interference (or from interference by relatives who seek to rely on the courts). By allocating child-rearing choices to parents (and thereby limiting the power of state officials to make child-rearing choices), American society maximizes pluralism and the diversity of ideas through a decentralized child-rearing scheme. This, in turn, optimizes the benefits of participatory democracy, which is at the core of American political theory. The legal system's insistence on private ordering of familial life ultimately guards against state control of its citizens.

REFERENCES

Bellotti v Baird, 443 U.S. 622 (1979).

Cleveland Board of Education v LaFleur, 414 U.S. 632 (1974).

Goldstein, J. (1977), Medical care for the child at risk: On state supervention of parental autonomy. *Yale Law J.*, 86:645–680.

—— Freud, A. & Solnit, A. (1979), *Before the Best Interests of the Child*. New York: Free Press.

González v Reno, 212 F.3d 1338 (11th Cir. 2000) (*affirming* 86 F. Supp. 1167) (S.D. Fla. 2000).

Griswold v Connecticut, 381 U.S. 479 (1965).

Meyer v Nebraska, 262 U.S. 390 (1923).

Mnookin, R. (1975), Child-custody adjudication: Judicial function in the face of indeterminacy. *Law & Contemp. Problems* 39:226–293.

Pierce v Society of Sisters, 268 U.S. 510 (1925).

Poe v Ullman, 367 U.S. 497 (1961).

Prince v Massachusetts, 321 U.S. 158 (1944).

Rodham, H. (1973), Children under the law, *Harvard Educ. Rev.*, 43:487–510.

Roe v Wade, 410 U.S. 113 (1973).

Santosky v Kramer, 455 U.S. 745 (1982).

Schall v Martin, 467 U.S. 253 (1984).

Stanley v Illinois, 405 U.S. 645 (1972).

Troxel v Granville, 530 U.S. 57 (2000).

Wisconsin v Yoder, 406 U.S. 205 (1972).

Chapter 11

Divorce and Custody in a Changing Society

ALBERT J. SOLNIT
BARBARA F. NORDHAUS

*I*n a recent report in *The New York Times,* "Is Social Stability Subverted If You Answer 'I don't'" (Lewin, 2000), the subtitle is, "Fears for Children's Well-Being Complicates a Debate over Marriage" (p. 11). The report states that "about a third of the births in this country are to unmarried mothers." The article further states "over the last few years family scholars have learned that many—perhaps half—of single mothers who give birth are living with the baby's father." It goes on to state, "Whatever their views on marriage, family scholars agree that, for children, two caring adults are better than one: between them they are likely to have more money, more time, more resources in case of emergency. At the same time, there is clear evidence that co-habiting couples break up more often and sooner than married couples, disrupting children's lives."

Given changing conditions and patterns of family structure and functions (Shapiro, Shapiro, and Paret, 2001). what can psychoanalytic theory and psychoanalysts contribute to our understanding of divorce and especially to better knowledge in the service of the child's best interests?

We start and end with efforts to put ourselves in the "skin of the child"—as advised by Anna Freud (personal communication to Albert J. Solnit, 1973). From the child's point of view, divorce would not be permitted to law or by custom. When there is a de juris or de facto divorce, however stormy or difficult the relationship between two parents, the child enters into a lifetime effort to put Humpty Dumpty together again.

There is ample psychoanalytic and clinical evidence that children who have primary significant relationships, starting in early infancy, experience the separation of the caring adults as a breaking-up of their world, an experience that at best is a significant loss and at worst a painful, damaging trauma. "So long as the child is part of a functioning family, the preservation of that family serves her developmental needs" (Goldstein et al., 1996, p. 88). This view acknowledges that, once the family fails in its function (as in abuse, abandonment, failure to provide available and accepted treatment for life-threatening illnesses or injuries, or when separating parents cannot agree about custody and visitation), it is our value preference that the child's interests should be paramount. After all, it is the adults who have the need and capacity to be responsible for nurturing, guiding and protecting children, and it is the adults who have the authority and autonomy to make decisions for the child.

Psychoanalytic child development together with other disciplines (developmental psychology and sociology) has documented that each child needs and should have a continuity of affectionate care and guidance from at least one adult who wants the child. These adults interpret the realities of life and law for the child and provide appropriate protection throughout childhood.

It is of great importance that such care and attachments not be postponed beyond the child's tolerance of waiting for such a relationship. Indeed, the passage of time in achieving a stable arrangement that is in the best interests of the child is a risk factor to the child's development. From the point of view of the child's best interests, the law, as well as our customs and practices, should work together to avoid the corrosive passage of time. Complying with adult-friendly legal processes to achieve fairness for contending adults, or to search for an ideal solution that is in the best interests of adults, does not protect the child's best interests. From the child's point of view, the best is the enemy of the good[1] (Roosevelt, 1900). All in all, once a family breaks up, once there is a divorce, there is no

---

[1] Theodore Roosevelt (1900) quoted the Church of England's Archbishop Benson who said in a letter he wrote to his chancellor, "I do not want the best to be any more the deadly enemy of the good. We climb through degrees of comparison" (p. 225).

solution without some risk to the child. Thus, the child is best served, less harmed, by having a least detrimental alternative in a time space that is responsive to the child's tolerances and capacities.

The above guidelines need translation and interpretation in a wide variety of traditional and nontraditional situations that will confront the child in this new millennium. The following list is not exhaustive, it is intended to leave room for newer, less expected conditions that will become the subculture in which children will face the losses associated with divorce.

As family structure and functions have changed over the past decades (Shapiro et al., 2001), the ripple effects on children of separation and divorce have reflected the following: (1) significant increases in single working parents, as a result of separation or divorce; (2) increased numbers of divorcing parents in conflict about custody and visitation associated with one or both parents relocating to geographically widely separated living and working sites; (3) remarriages resulting in families that include stepparents and half-siblings; (4) an increase in the break up of families in which children are being raised by homosexual couples, by infertile parents who have had children after a divorce through the use of newer reproductive technologies such as artificial insemination, frozen stored fertilized ova, and surrogate mothers; (5) conflicts regarding international abduction of children by one parent wanting to separate from the other parent, thus forcefully taking custody in an international setting; (6) increasing claims by grandparents and other members of the extended family with regard to custody and visitation after separation and divorce; (7) increased numbers of long-term foster parents involved in custody and visitation conflicts.

Throughout these vicissitudes of life for children of separating and divorcing parents there are the challenges of how to follow the principles of putting ourselves into the skin of the children and of using least detrimental alternatives within a dynamic framework of psychoanalytic child development knowledge.

In summary, for the new millennium, we believe that child experts can contribute to the complex issue of children experiencing divorce by emphasizing the following:

When parents separate, the child's loss sets the scene for finding the least detrimental alternative for that child in a timely manner. "Timely" refers to the child's developmental capacity to tolerate waiting to have her needs served. These needs include being wanted, having a continuity of affectionate care, guidance, and protection, and having a reasonable expectation of permanency.

Our view is based on the psychoanalytic theory of object relations. This orientation emphasizes the biopsychological need of children to internalize and identify with caring adults. This process enables children to use relationships as an internal resource that fosters healthy self-esteem and the capacity to empathize with others. Such a process gradually supports a progressive development that will enable them, when they are adults, to take charge of themselves and their lives in a socially constructive manner, including their interest in and commitment to parenthood.

REFERENCES

Goldstein, J., Solnit, A. J., Goldstein, S. & Freud, A. (1996), *The Best Interests of the Child.* New York: Free Press.

Lewin, T. (2000), *The New York Times,* November 4, Section B, p. 11.

Roosevelt, T. (1900), *The Strenuous Life.* New York: Century. Derived from chapter 8, "The Best and the Good" published in *The Churchman,* March 17, 1900.

Shapiro, V. B., Shapiro, J. R. & Paret, I. H. (2001), *Complex Adoption and Assisted Reproductive Technology.* New York: Guilford Press.

Chapter 12

The Rights of Parents and Stepparents

Toward a Redefinition of Parental Rights and Obligations

ALAN J. KLEIN

*N*umerous attempts have been made to clarify those factors that can be used to determine the best interests of the child (Uniform Marriage and Divorce Act, 1974, Michigan Child Custody Act, 1970). These standards focus on the ability of the parent to provide for the emotional, physical, educational, and social needs of the child. Although custody determinations are made daily by the courts, from a psychological point of view, it can easily be argued that the best interests of the child are met by being raised by parents who love each other and love the child. Anything less is not in the child's best interests. Since divorce is likely to have a negative impact on the emotional well-being of the child, the problem becomes one of finding the least damaging solution. As a result, the courts have turned increasingly to mental health experts to assist in unraveling the complicated emotional needs and issues which arise in the course of custody litigation.

PARENTAL RIGHTS AND PARENTAL OBLIGATIONS

In legal terms, the issue of custody gradually shifted, during the first half of the twentieth century, from the rights of ownership of the child to the needs of the child (Mason, 1994). Parents of intact families are generally willing to make sacrifices for the benefit of their children, such as waiting on long lines at Disneyland rather than relaxing on a Caribbean beach, because they see it as part of their responsibility to their children. In an intact and functional marriage, parents assume that they have certain obligations in the raising of their children. It is the parents' responsibility to their children to provide a secure physical and emotional environment, to encourage their growth, and to help them develop effective socialization skills. It is rare to hear parents in this situation talking about their rights as parents. The position taken here is that, when parents divorce or separate, they do not suddenly acquire a new set of parental rights, but rather, continue to have the same parental obligations to their children that they have always had. The act of divorce does not and should not relieve a parent of the responsibilities and obligations of being a parent.

The term "right" is often associated with the parent's right to have continued contact with his or her child. It is generally held that, unless contact with a particular parent is found to be toxic to the child, that parent has a "right" of access to the child. Beyond this narrow definition, describing a parent's responsibility to the child as a "right" may be a serious misnomer. There is an implicit assumption that it is in the best interests of the child to maintain a relationship with his or her parents. If this is true, and it is to the benefit of the child to have contact with both parents, then the parent has the duty to provide that contact and nothing should be done that would interfere with a parent's ability to meet that commitment. It is evident that we recognize the financial obligations of parents, and the law provides harsh punishments for those who fail to meet them. This is not to suggest that one can legally punish an uninvolved or selfish parent, but that the concept of continuing obligation should extend beyond financial support.

MISUSE OF PARENTAL RIGHTS

When couples separate, one parent's desire for revenge or feelings of vindictiveness toward the estranged spouse can be cloaked under the guise of parental rights. Perceiving one's parental relationship with a child as a right may imply a sense of ownership, which then places the focus on the parent and away from the child. This can lead to situations that are far from the child's best interests. The parent who becomes concerned with exercising his or her rights may begin acting in ways that will likely cause the child to suffer.

Conscientious parents do enjoy spending time with their children, but seldom would insist that the child be with them to the exclusion of any other activity. An example of this is the case of G v N. Mr. G and Ms. N were never married and, in the course of their relationship, they had a child, C. When the relationship ended, C was three years old. The Court issued an interim custody arrangement in which each parent had an equal amount of time with the child and the child moved between the two homes every third day. Ms. N, like many parents in similar situations, viewed the days that the child was in her custodial care as "her time" and jealously guarded her prerogatives during these periods. Any attempt to provide some continuity between the child's life with the father and her life with her mother were resisted as interference in the mother's time with the child. The father had enrolled the child in nursery school, but the child was not allowed to attend her nursery school "graduation" because it fell on one of the mother's days and the mother was not about to relinquish her "right" to do whatever she pleased on her days. This child soon found herself in a bizarre situation in which she led two separate and distinct lives with no continuity between the time she spent with each of her parents. She attempted to provide her own solution to the problem. She became increasingly withdrawn and isolated, and by doing nothing in both situations, she managed to maintain her loyalty to them both.

The parent who becomes more concerned with his or her "rights" than the needs of the child poses a threat to the present and future well-being of the child. In effect, the child becomes an object in the struggle, the prize that symbolizes winning or losing. However, once the hill has been won, it becomes of little concern. A case in point is that of R v R. The father sued for a reversal of custody shortly after the mother asked for an increase in child support. He claimed that, since he had remarried, it would be in the child's best interests to be with his loving, caring father in a two-parent home and that the mother was neglectful, as indicated by the boy's poor school attendance record. The fact that he perceived his son as an object and not an obligation was clearly indicated in his contact with the school. The father only asked for information regarding attendance records.

The guidance counselor felt constrained to volunteer the fact that his son was doing well in school.

The parent who is more concerned with rights than obligations, is likely to have great difficulty in shifting perceptions and behaviors once the issues of the divorce are resolved. The primary importance of the child has been minimized. Subsequent obligations are likely to be perceived as onerous and responsibilities may be shifted to more disinterested third parties.

THE ROLE OF THE STEPPARENT
IN PARENTAL OBLIGATIONS

The courts often have a difficult time deciding which of the two parents is the more fit in the process of assigning custody. This decision becomes even more complex when there are one or two other adults who are to become involved in the rearing of the child. Although it is felt that the primary responsibility for the child rests with the parent, a third party who enters into a romantic relationship with one of the parents after the divorce becomes involved, to varying degrees, in the day-to-day life of the child (Gregory et al., 1993).[1]

There is a psychomythology that has developed around the term "stepparent." The wicked stepmother is an ominous, inimical, lurking figure in childhood stories. This cultural perception is often reinforced when an estranged parent sees the stepparent as being poised to supplant his or her role. These perceptions remain regardless of the actual good behavior of the stepparent and often in the face of absent or neglectful behaviors of the actual parent (Bray and Kelly, 1998).

There are times when the stepparent can be a positive and effective force in supporting a parent in meeting his or her obligations. In the case of E v W, Mr. E had gradually grown apart from his children. Although he continued to pay for their support, he became less and less involved with his children. Approximately five years after his divorce, he remarried. His new wife had also been divorced and had children of her own. However, she had a good working rela-

---

[1]Some parents become involved in a live-in relationship with another individual to whom they are not married. Since these people are, for all intents and purposes, stepparents, the term "primary caregiver" is used to describe both married and unmarried stepparents.

tionship with her children's father and felt that Mr. E's estrangement was not good for him or his children. With her encouragement, he attempted to renew his contacts with his children. His ex-wife resisted, maintaining that he had alienated himself from the children and for him to come back into their lives would not be in their best interests. The children, who felt that their father had abandoned them, did not want to re-establish a relationship; they expressed concerns that if they were to become involved with him, he would again disappear from their lives. The stepmother's willingness to assume the obligation of repairing the father's relationship with the children was a deciding factor in renewing his visitation with the children, and the final outcome was positive.

The point at which a stepparent becomes involved is a critical factor. When this involvement occurs a considerable period of time following the divorce, the pattern of the relationship between the parent and child has been established. There may be any number of adjustment difficulties, but the complexities are considerably less than when the prospective stepparent is immersed in, and a party to, the divorce proceedings. The future spouse has a vested interest in the outcome of the divorce. Unlike the estranged parent, who has experienced the history of the relationship, some of it good and some bad, the prospective partner is likely to have heard and experienced only the negative factors.

Just as a parent is likely to feel threatened by someone usurping his or her role, the stepparent may also feel threatened by the ex-spouse and is likely to become an active force in the custody battle, often to the detriment of the children. The case of *J v J* provides an extreme example of this. Mr. J initiated the divorce and "wanted it all." He threatened to take the children away from his ex-wife and to "destroy" her unless she acceded to his demands. His fiancée became an active and willing participant in his plans. She made frequent and disparaging comments to the children regarding their mother, pointed out all of her deficiencies, promoted and abetted the conflicts that often exist between teenage daughters and their mothers, and constantly presented herself as their ally. Mr. J supported these attempts, pointing out how wonderful his fiancée was and how bad their mother was. Despite the fact that the court agreed with the expert that these behaviors were not in the children's best interests and awarded custody to the mother, the combined efforts of the father and stepmother were ultimately successful in alienating the children from their mother.

Not all stepparents who become co-conspirators act as blatantly as the father's fiancée in the case described above, but some may exhibit behaviors that are no less detrimental. The mother of a six-year-old boy who was the product of an interfaith marriage became involved with an individual who had deep and openly expressed prejudices. When the boy tearfully told his father that he should not be Jewish any more because Jews were bad and were going to Hell, the father sued to reverse custody. Although the mother possessed adequate parenting skills and did not share her boyfriend's views, her judgment in the choice of mates interfered with her ability to maintain her parental obligations. Only under the threat of losing custody did she sever the relationship. The potential stepparent who actively becomes involved in the battle between parents may feel that he or she is supporting a loved one, not recognizing that this form of support is not only damaging to the child, but is likely to inflame the intense feelings of anger and resentment already present in family members. The relationship between the child and the parent who is being supported may suffer irreparable harm. Equally detrimental to the child is the parent who expresses negative attitudes and feelings toward a potential or actual stepparent. It is not uncommon in divorce to find fathers who are willing to have mothers remain the primary custodial parent, but who become enraged if their ex-spouses become involved with another man.

In many cases, it is a stepparent who is forced to assume the primary role of parent who may then find that he or she has gotten more than he or she bargained for. The child, who has emerged from being the focus of one battle between his parents, is now the focus of a renewed struggle between a parent and stepparent. William C, a six-year-old boy, became depressed when his father continually made disparaging remarks about his new stepfather. This man was making reasonable attempts to provide an intact home life with his new family. He took an interest in the boy's activities, played games with him, and helped him with his homework. He did not attempt to supplant Mr. C's role as father and in fact encouraged it. William liked his stepfather, but felt that his positive feelings represented a betrayal of his father and could find no way to resolve the conflict.

THE STEPPARENT AND FORENSIC EVALUATIONS

When mental health experts are asked to assist the courts in making custody determinations, a nearly impossible task is set. The expert is asked to make predictions regarding future behaviors based on the presentations of individuals who are undergoing what is likely to be the most stressful time of their lives. As complicated as this may be, the situation becomes even more uncertain as multiple "parents" become involved. In addition to all the considerations of a forensic evaluation of parents with respect to custody of the child, an equally intensive evaluation of future stepparents must be conducted. It has often been argued that children may be better off in a two-parent family and that one parent's intention of marrying after the divorce will provide a healthier and more effective environment for the child. This argument may have merit if that environment does not contain the toxic elements described above. Whether this is or will be the case becomes the task of the forensic evaluator.

As in any custody evaluation, the willingness of a parent to foster a positive relationship between the child and the other parent is a factor which is given considerable weight by the courts in determining the best interests of the child. The parent who focuses on his or her obligations as a parent is more likely to perceive an ongoing relationship with the other parent as a positive factor in the life of the child. In evaluating a stepparent married to a custodial parent, that individual's willingness to promote and maintain a relationship between the child and the noncustodial parent becomes a vital concern. As noted in the case histories previously discussed, the third party can either facilitate or hinder this relationship. Particular attention should be given to the language the future stepparent employs. The individual who narrates a rote repetition of the allegations of the parent, wholly supports the future partner, and denigrates the other parent is highly suspect. Such individuals will often speak in glowing terms of the positive relationship they have with the children and gloss over any potential difficulties. Insight into the feelings and needs of the children may be lacking. A cautionary note needs to be raised here. Some individuals may manifest these behaviors out of naïveté and their ability to co-parent may be improved through education and training. Caregivers can be helped to understand the impact that their behaviors have on the children and to develop strategies for more effective co-parenting.

In any evaluation for custodial fitness, attempts are made to assess individual strengths and weaknesses in light of the needs of the child as well as knowledge and skills in parenting. This assessment is equally important when assessing a stepparent. Does this individual have an awareness of potential difficulties and problems that may arise in the future? All too often, the phrase "If I only knew then . . ." is heard. The extent to which the parent and stepparent have been able to discuss and review their strategies for coping with the new family unit should be reviewed. By examining the role that the primary parent has played in the lives of the children in the past, indications of future behavior may be surmised.

In summary, determinations regarding the best interests of the child are difficult enough when trying to decide between mother and father. When a parent enters into a new romantic relationship, including re-marriage, decisions regarding the best interests of the child must take into account three or possibly four caregivers. In some instances, the issue becomes one of father versus stepfather and mother versus stepmother regarding who will be the primary caregivers. It is here that the distinction between parental rights and obligations becomes most crucial for the forensic evaluator. The manner in which stepparents have dealt with their obligations to their own children can provide important indicators about the way that they will interact and influence the environment of the children in a blended family. The willingness, as well as the ability of the stepparent to assist in meeting parental obligations is one that should be given great weight in making custodial recommendations.

REFERENCES

Bray, J. & Kelly, J. (1998), *Stepfamilies*. New York: Broadway Books.
Gregory, J. D., Swisher, P., Scheible, S. & Wolf, S. (1993), *Understanding Family Law*. New York: Matthew Bender.
Mason, M. A. (1994), *From Father's Property to Children's Rights*. New York: Columbia University Press.
Michigan Child Custody Act (1970), No. 91 (M.C.L.A. Sec. 722.21 et seq.).
Uniform Marriage and Divorce Act (1974), Uniform Laws Annotated, 9A.

Chapter 13

When the State Has Custody

*The Fragile Bond of Mothers and
Their Infants on the Prison Nursery*

SUSAN W. SILVERMAN

T he sanctity of the mother–infant bond has long been the cornerstone of psychoanalytic and developmental perspectives about healthy human functioning. Yet it is difficult to imagine a more precarious relationship than that of an incarcerated mother and her baby. And as ever-increasing numbers of women make their way into the correctional system while pregnant, notions about the best interest of the child and the role of mental health professionals working in these settings require closer examination.

According to a national survey of female offenders, almost 6 percent of women in American prisons and jails enter the system while pregnant (Bureau of Justice Statistics, 1999). In response, prison nurseries have sprung up in a number of states (for example, Florida, New York, Massachusetts, Virginia, and Wyoming). These nurseries, which allow mothers and infants to remain together for 12 to 18 months (and ideally to leave prison together), are intended to be an insurance policy of sorts for the early psychological well-being of the infants and are hoped to provide an incentive for incarcerated mothers to turn their lives around. The nursery is the concrete expression of hope, on the part of all concerned, that the experience of day-to-day closeness and bonding of mother and baby will be transformative and provide a detour past the prison's revolving door. Whether this is actually true has yet to be determined: there is little systematic follow-up on the women and children of these prison nurseries.

A profile of 90 women and their infants incarcerated at a state correctional facility from June 1990 through April 1993 conducted by the State of New York Department of Corrections Services (1993) reveals that close to 60 percent of the women did not go home with their babies; the infants had to be placed with others. Of those infants who left the nursery without the mother, 51 percent went to a grandparent; 31 percent to a relative or friend, 11 percent to foster care, and 7 percent to the father.

Mental health professionals working in prison settings are often called on to play important roles in the lives of incarcerated mothers and their children by facilitating family visits and helping maintain contact with the children through foster parents. Yet nowhere is their potential impact greater than in the prison nursery. Here, psychologists and social workers are expected to screen mothers for inclusion in the nursery program, assess mothers' pre- and postpartum functioning in the prison milieu, provide psychoeducation and individual and group therapy, *and* participate in decisions about whether to separate infants from their mothers. The mental health professional functions as both evaluator and therapist. In no other setting is there such a merging of roles that are inherently contradictory and potentially unethical.

Consider the typical scenario: Once a woman has been accepted for the nursery and her baby is born, the child is then in the physical custody of the Department of Corrections. After several months, circumstances—usually of a disciplinary nature—arise that necessitate a decision about whether or not to separate mother and baby. Until this point, the mental health professional has functioned as therapist to the mother and therefore has some idea how this particular mother might experience the stress of such a separation (for example, depression, anxiety, posttraumatic stress, even psychotic decompensation). But now the therapist is asked to make a custodial recommendation.

In civil custody cases, the guideline is quite clear: decisions are made in "the best interests of the child." In forensic settings such as the prison nursery, however, this guideline is compromised for two primary reasons: (1) the mental health professional who provides important input for such decisions has heretofore been acting as a therapist/advocate for the mother, making it extremely difficult to offer an unbiased assessment of what action should be taken; (2)

perhaps even more critical is the fact that the "best interests of the child" often run counter to the best interests of the institution whose mandate it is to maintain security by managing inmates in the easiest and most expedient way. A closer look at the structure and functioning of the prison nursery, along with several vignettes, will highlight the kinds of experiences and issues mental health professionals can expect to face in a correctional setting.

STRUCTURE AND FUNCTION OF THE PRISON NURSERY

At the Correctional Facility nursery where I worked as a psychologist, women are prescreened with a number of factors taken into consideration: presentencing report, psychological/psychiatric history, and disciplinary background. Collateral interviews with family members and caretakers of the mother's other children are also conducted. Residence on the nursery is open to all pregnant inmates with short sentences because they may be eligible to leave the facility by the time the baby is a maximum of 18 months old. Exclusion criteria are basic and obvious: a history of violence, child abuse, or neglect. Space is limited to approximately 25 to 30 beds. The final decision to allow a woman to reside on the nursery is made by the deputy superintendent with input from representatives of a number of disciplines: a psychologist and/or social worker, corrections counselor, and the nursery manager (a civilian employee who functions as "mother" to the mothers).

At first glance, few things seem as incongruous as infants in prison. Prisons are simply not equipped to provide the kind of secure, stimulating experiences we know infants need to grow, thrive, and master developmental tasks. Correctional facilities are certainly not set up to allow for the flexibility in schedule that new mothers need to adequately respond to their babies. On the nursery, however, every effort is made to put the infants first, at least as much as is possible in an environment structured around security issues. Required activities such as count (i.e., the checking of inmates, number and location), meals, and attendance at drug programs are scheduled around infant needs.

Because the correctional facility where I worked is populated exclusively by women serving sentences for drug-related crimes, substance abuse treatment is a high priority for all inmates, including mothers in the nursery unit. Attendance at recovery programs such as Alcoholics or Narcotics Anonymous, self-help groups, and optional academic classes (many women at the prison complete their General Equivalency Diplomas) must be squeezed into a tight schedule that is already exhausting because of the demands of caring for an infant.

When the women are away from the nursery in the afternoons participating in these programs, infants are cared for by inmate babysitters who are screened by the nursery manager, administrative personnel and, if available, a psychologist or social worker. Additionally, nursery mothers are encouraged to fill in for each other whenever possible. Mornings generally consist of baby-care activities and classes on infant nutrition and development, parenting skills, and other health-related issues, such as postpartum recovery, sexually transmitted diseases, and contraception. Mental health professionals are also called on to give psychoeducational classes on such topics as postpartum depression and self-esteem issues. Especially popular among the mothers are arts-and-crafts classes in which the women learn how to make items for their babies. Babies' birthdays are celebrated with parties complete with cake and photos. Such occasions are both highly anticipated and appreciated and serve to normalize the experience of having infants in the prison milieu.

The medical needs of the mothers and their infants are attended to by staff nurses, who are on the unit in the morning, and a registered nurse, who is on call 24 hours a day. An outside pediatrician and a public health nurse maintain hours on the nursery several times a week. Interestingly, breastfeeding is not permitted, primarily because it interferes with the structured demands of prison life and also because of the risk of an HIV-infected mother passing on the virus to her baby.

MULTIPLE SOURCES OF STRESS

Although the nursery is regarded as a place of privilege within the prison, the mothers who reside on it say it carries its own unique sources of stress. Unlike their counterparts in the general population, nursery mothers serve two masters: their babies and corrections authorities. Mothers and babies share rooms (usually two mothers with their infants room together) and because individual infant waking and feeding schedules are rarely in sync, sleep deprivation is a serious concern.

For many women, meeting the demands of the nursery along with the demands of the institution is an impossible task. One mother commented, "There's a lot of stress for us. With my first son, if I got too stressed, I could walk away for a few minutes and let him cry and then, when I was calmer, I could go back and deal with him. Not in here, you can't do that. Someone will say that you are letting your baby cry. There's always someone looking over your shoulder. In here, you can't say something like, `My baby is driving me crazy and I want to wring his neck.' Someone might take you literally. So that's not an acceptable feeling. But what mother doesn't feel like that sometimes?" (Clark, 1996).

CULTURAL DIFFERENCES

A woman's cultural heritage can clash with nursery rules about what makes a "good" mother, and hence, about what constitutes appropriate mother–infant interaction. The African-American mother's tradition of braiding her baby's hair often appears harsh to those outside the culture and is frowned upon on the prison nursery. Also against prison regulations is the ear piercing of infant girls by Latina mothers (which is often done when mothers are on furlough) because of concern that the earrings might become unfastened and be swallowed by the baby. Ideas about discipline and feeding are culturally based and become yet one more battleground upon which the mother and the prison system face off. The authoritarian structure of the prison system not only impacts on the mother's ability to parent in a way that is consistent with her culture but may also affect her ability to parent her infant *at all* if it is decided that her customs are not consistent with the system's sanctioned norms. "Bottle propping"—having the bottle "propped" but not held by the mother, is a common practice for many of the mothers, and results in disciplinary action that can lead to the mother being removed from the nursery and her infant being sent home.

The power of such issues should not be underestimated as they extend to the very definition of the mother's role as primary caretaker of her baby. Such a notion has long been at odds with practices in

African-American and Latino cultures, both of which adopt a broader view of the mothering role. In Latino families, *hijos de crianza* (which literally means "adopted children") refers to the practice of transferring children from the nuclear family to another within the extended system in times of crisis (Garcia-Preto, 1996). African-American families are accustomed to similar practices. In addition, children are commonly adopted and reared by extended family members who are better equipped, either financially or in terms of their current circumstances, than the children's parents (Boyd-Franklin, 1989; Billingsley, 1992). Extending help and exchanging resources are the norm. Frequently, in families with a large number of children, older children also take on mothering roles.

Such differences in values, beliefs, and roles are often viewed pejoratively when they run counter to the prevailing culture. Inasmuch as these representations of "appropriate," "right," or "true" mothering are internalized, intrapsychic clash is inevitable. Many women come to believe that they have been poor mothers because they have not been the sole caretakers of their children. More insidious is the underlying message that these women cannot be trusted to make sound choices for their babies.

The unfortunate truth is that many nursery mothers have lost other children to foster care or adoption. Hearing the details of such events is bound to stir strong feelings, particularly among mental health professionals who have children of their own. Vigilance about the possibility of one's own conscious and unconscious prejudices against incarcerated mothers who have been unable, for myriad reasons (substance abuse, domestic violence, neglect, their own prior abuse), to keep custody of their other children, must be paramount and ongoing. Intensely negative feelings and judgmental attitudes are often communicated in subtle ways such as body language, tone of voice, and facial expression. Therefore, diligent self-monitoring becomes a crucial part of the clinician's job.

UNRESOLVED DEVELOPMENTAL ISSUES

Although the mothers can and do vent, both in group sessions and privately, on many of the issues that impact their life on the nursery, other issues are not as easily voiced. Ambivalent feelings about pregnancy and motherhood are ubiquitous among women, but for incarcerated women in particular, questions about their willingness and ability to parent their children are cast in high relief against the confluence of circumstances that led them to prison: poverty, drugs, abusive relationships. Many of these women have had poor early relationships with their own mothers; giving birth to a new baby reactivates a minefield of unresolved developmental issues.

For many women, pregnancy and parenthood, even without the additional stressor of incarceration, are periods of immense turmoil. Successful negotiation of both these critical developmental transitions requires an ability to tolerate and process intense affective states. This is not an easy task for women who have relied on drugs and alcohol to manage painful aspects of their inner lives. Powerful emotions cannot be tolerated, nor can they be medicated away now that the mother is incarcerated. Instead, they are split off and acted out in ways that are idiosyncratic and related to each woman's particular developmental history. "The baby often [becomes] a silent actor in a family tragedy" (Fraiberg, Adelson, and Shapiro, 1980, p. 163).

E is an example of a mother who inherited a legacy of emotional overload and learned helplessness. A 38-year-old African American, E struggled with addiction to a variety of substances before her crack use and lifestyle finally landed her in prison. She admitted to being high during the early months of her pregnancy and indeed her infant son showed some signs of developmental delay. The baby's father was a "friend" who made no effort to see or support E or their son. E left behind two other children, a 12-year-old-son who was being cared for by her maternal grandmother, and a 6-year-old daughter who was being cared for by E's own mother. E expressed tremendous guilt about her previous treatment of her older children, particularly in light of her intense involvement with her new baby boy on the nursery. E also struggled with a number of "extraordinary" stressors while in prison: symptoms of a yet-undiagnosed, life-threatening medical condition and the painful death of an aunt whom she idealized and regarded as her mother. The aunt was someone E could rely on never to reject her no matter what kind of trouble she had gotten herself into. "I could always go to my aunt. My mother would just fall apart. She could never handle anything." E had ruminated endlessly about her fear that her aunt would die while she was in prison. E's ability to parent her son began to deteriorate almost immediately after she learned that her aunt had indeed died from rapidly advancing cancer. Chronically an anxious woman, E became even more so. She resented having to respond to her baby when he cried. She was put on warning after being observed by correction officers treating the infant roughly. E was clearly overwhelmed and unaware that she had begun to respond in ways that her own mother had responded to her, becoming flustered, impatient, dismissive. E's aunt had been a soothing presence; she had been able to listen to E's problems without becoming overwhelmed.

The death of E's aunt left her feeling guilty and furious at her aunt for leaving her helpless to fend for herself. She was also angry at her baby for ceaselessly demanding care when E was mourning the loss of her own caretaker. Guilt feelings about letting her aunt down by being incarcerated were also particularly strong.

E was eventually able to pull herself together after a rather precarious period when staff seriously considered having to remove her and her baby from the nursery. E began to recover when she realized that her aunt could not be brought back to life no matter how helpless she became. She was on her own now with no one to turn to—neither her mother nor the drugs she had previously used to escape. The help and support from the structure of the nursery experience was instrumental. E let the nursery become her "aunt." E herself believed that she would not have survived had she been out on the street.

THE IMPACT OF PREVIOUS LOSS

"Maternal bereavement," a term most often used to describe a mother's reaction to the loss of a child through death (Theut et al., 1989), is also a useful way to understand the multi-dimensional loss sustained by incarcerated mothers who are separated from their children for reasons other than death (e.g., loss to a social service agency prior to incarceration or as a direct consequence of incarceration). In addition to the actual loss of the child is the loss of the woman's representation of herself as a good, caring, competent mother. Nursery mothers experience a reactivation of feelings of guilt and shame over the loss of their other children. In some cases, the press of these feelings helps the mother take her life in a whole new direction.

B, a 35-year-old Latina, left behind six children in foster care before coming to prison and giving birth to a baby girl. She also had another daughter who was being cared for by her mother. B was outspoken, labile, and needy, and no one on staff would have bet that B would remain on the nursery and eventually go home with her baby. Her strength proved to be her desire to change and her willingness to talk about painful issues concerning the death of her father from alcoholism and her open hostility toward her mother, whom B saw as the reason for her father's downward slide.

B was devoted to her new baby and she often cried about her other children. Many times she called home wanting to talk to the daughter in her mother's custody but her little girl refused to come to the phone. Despite B's pleas, her mother rarely brought B's daughter up to see her. B was increasingly able to reflect on the kind of mother she had been to her other children. "I thought getting drunk and acting silly in front of them was fun," she remarked one day, looking appropriately horrified. Her time in prison, which enabled her to get clean and to learn how to parent her new baby, fostered her resolve to reunite her family. B went home with her baby girl and eventually was able to get all of her other children back. She also returned to school and trained as a nursing assistant. She is one of the nursery's biggest success stories.

SUMMARY

These vignettes represent the most positive outcomes of the prison nursery experiment. When the experiment works, women get the opportunity to be the kind of mothers they were unable to be on the outside. Babies have the chance to experience that which most of us believe is their birthright: care and nurturing in a safe, secure environment. But the truth is that not every mother and child fares well, and when the experiment breaks down, the damage done is profound, long lasting, and extremely difficult—if not impossible—to repair.

Although few can argue with the good intentions on which the prison nursery was conceived, many questions about its functioning and efficacy remain to be answered: Do babies belong in prison? Does the structure itself preclude nurturing, effective parenting of an infant? What about the possibility of trauma to both mother and infant if and when separation becomes necessary? What happens to these mothers and their babies after release? There are no clear-cut answers to any of these questions because more work needs to be done. Only systematic follow-up can tell us whether this road paved with good intentions is headed in the right direction.

One thing we do know is that mental health professionals are faced with the Herculean task of bolstering and strengthening the mother/infant bond within the confines of a rigid and uncompromising structure. We are asked to play the dual role of therapist and evaluator, which runs counter to our training, our clinical judgment, and our ethical code. One cannot be an advocate for mother, infant, and correctional system simultaneously. Nor can one be expected to switch roles with shifting circumstances: therapist for the mother on one day, messenger for the system on another, and protector of the "best interests of the child" on still another. This dilemma in some ways echoes that facing incarcerated mothers, who are confronted with the multiple and conflicting demands of their own rehabilitation as they simultaneously work to shape a better destiny for their children.

REFERENCES

Billingsley, A. (1992), *Climbing Jacob's Ladder.* New York: Simon & Schuster.
Bloom, B. & Steinhart, D. (1993), *Why Punish the Children?* National Council on Crime and Delinquency.
Boyd-Franklin, N. (1989), *Black Families in Therapy.* New York: Guilford Press.
Bureau of Justice Statistics. (1999), Special report on women offenders (NCJ 175688). Washington, DC: U.S. Department of Justice, December.
Clark, J. (1996), Lessons from a prison nursery: The mothers' experiences. Paper presented by Sister Elaine Roulet, Director of the Children's Center at Bedford Hills Correctional Facility at the Zero to Three National Training Institute, Washington, DC, December.
Fraiberg, S., Adelson, E. & Shapiro, V. (1980), Ghosts in the nursery: A psychoanalytic approach to the problems of impaired infant-mother relationships. In: *Clinical Studies in Infant Mental Health,* ed. S. Fraiberg. New York: Basic Books, pp. 163–172.
Garcia-Preto, N. (1996), Latino families: An overview. In: *Ethnicity & Family Therapy,* ed. M. McGoldrick, F. Giordano & J.K. Pearce. New York: Guilford Press, pp. 141–154.
State of New York Department of Corrections Services (1993), *Profile of Participants, The Bedford Hills and Taconic Nursery Program in 1992.*
Theut, S. K., Pederson, F. A., Zaslow, M. S., Cain, R. I., Rabinovich, B. A. & Morihsisa, J. M. (1989), Perinatal loss and parental bereavement. *Amer. J. Psychiat.,* 146:635–639.

Chapter 14

When Families Cannot Be Healed
The Limits of Parental Rights

MICHELE GALIETTA

E xperts have noted that the tension between the state's interest in maintaining parental liberty and family privacy juxtaposed with the state's interest in protecting children from harm (see chapters 10 and 13) has produced one of the most complex and confusing areas of law (Melton et al., 1997). Child welfare legislation has evolved through a combination of state and federal initiatives. The relationship between federal and state legislation pertaining to child welfare has shifted over time. At times, states have influenced national changes with progressive or innovative state legislation. At other times, Congress has encouraged changes in state regulations through use of financial incentives to promote specific social policy goals (Shotton, 1990) or by mandating legislative changes.

Early efforts to protect children originated at the state level. New York's Society for the Prevention of Cruelty to Children, established in 1875, was a private agency that received public funding and was granted authority by New York State to intervene in the lives of abused and neglected children (Levine and Wallach, 2002). Within thirty-five years, most states followed suit and enacted similar legislation. Another important event in the development of child welfare legislation was the publication of an article by Kempe and colleagues (1962) alerting physicians to particular patterns of injuries indicative of what the authors referred to as "battered child syndrome." Subsequently, state legislatures enacted laws mandating physicians to report suspected abuse to child protection authorities.

Federal child protection legislation originated with the Social Security Act of 1935, which incorporated child welfare under the auspices of public welfare departments, but did little to encourage specific actions that should be taken on behalf of children. In 1974, Congress passed the Child Abuse Prevention and Treatment Act (CAPTA), which reinforced state efforts to establish classes of professionals responsible for reporting abuse and neglect. This act was revised several times and established a national plan for a comprehensive child protection effort based on policies emphasizing prevention of removal, reunification of families, and treatment in communities. The Adoption Assistance and Child Welfare Act (1980) added to existing legislation by establishing "reasonable efforts" requirements and tying them to state funding (Shotton, 1990). While child welfare policies have shifted at times in accordance with prevailing social norms and political tides, the courts have generally given the rights of biological parents substantial weight. However recent legislation has, to some degree, limited the rights of biological parents.

The 1997 Adoption and Safe Families Act (ASFA) explicitly stated that the health and safety of children must be the principal consideration in all child welfare proceedings. Subsequently, the Strengthening Abuse and Neglect Courts Act of 2000 (SANCA) was passed with the purpose of improving the administrative efficiency and effectiveness of the nation's abuse and neglect courts, as well as to facilitate application of additional measures intended by ASFA. While these companion acts provide financial and other support to states for the purpose of improving the availability and quality of services available to children and their families, they also include mandatory timelines for determining whether children removed from their homes can safely return to their homes or whether other permanent alternative situations should be pursued. Permanency hearings must now be held within one year of a child's entry into foster care. This legislation allows that reasonable efforts to preserve the family can take place concurrently with reasonable efforts to find a safe, stable, permanent placement for a child.

Moreover, the acts require that the state *must* move to terminate the rights of any parent whose child has been in foster care for 15 of the last 22 months (see chapter 13). They also stipulate circumstances in which reasonable efforts to reunite the family are not required. For example, when the parent has subjected a child to "aggravated circumstances" defined as abandonment, torture, severe sexual abuse (see chapter 18) or chronic physical abuse, when the parent has committed or aided in the murder of a sibling of the child in question; or when the rights of the parent to a sibling of the child have been terminated. In such cases, the state is required to hold a permanency hearing within 30 days and to make reasonable efforts to facilitate adoption or another suitable permanent arrangement. These changes in the courts make it even more likely that mental health professionals will be asked to assist in making difficult decisions involving potential revocation of parental rights.

This new emphasis on permanency planning for abused and neglected children offers an opportunity for mental health professionals to educate the court and to positively affect the lives of many abused and neglected children. Where in the past many children would linger in foster care for indeterminate periods, the courts will now be looking for recommendations about the likelihood of reunification and whether such action would be in the best interests of particular children. Further, if a parent's rights are revoked, the court will be seeking information about various permanency options. Mental health professionals will be able to provide a valuable service by evaluating the social and psychological needs of a child and ensuring that appropriate services to meet those needs are included in any permanency plan. While such issues have always played a role in the involvement of mental health professionals in Family Court proceedings, the new legislation makes it more likely that such considerations will be prominent.

TERMINATION OF PARENTAL RIGHTS PROCEEDINGS

Who Initiates TPR Proceedings?

Parents may voluntarily permanently revoke their rights to a particular child resulting in Termination of Parental Rights (TPR). However, involuntary TPR proceedings may only be initiated in a few ways. First, the state may initiate TPR proceedings at any time following removal of the child, provided that reasonable efforts to reunite the family have been made. The state may initiate TPR proceedings immediately, without attempting to reunite the family, in cases where AFSA or state statute does not require efforts to reunify the family. As described above, such cases include serious sexual abuse of a child, murder of a sibling of the child, or if a parent's rights to a sibling have previously been terminated. Second, TPR may be triggered automatically (the state is compelled by law to initiate proceedings) if a child has been removed from the home for a particular period of time (Melton et al., 1997). Lastly, in some states third parties may petition for TPR on behalf of a child. The role of third parties, for example, foster parents, with regard to TPR proceedings varies widely in accordance with various states' legislation.[1] In New York, foster parents may initiate TPR proceedings if a child has resided in their home for 12 months (NY Soc. Serv. Law § 392[2][c]).

Procedures for TPR Proceedings

The process of TPR usually occurs in a single proceeding. However, in some states TPR takes place in a bifurcated process. In states with bifurcated proceedings, two distinct hearings are held. First, a "factfinding" hearing is held. The purpose of this hearing is to determine whether certain statutory conditions are met before proceeding with TPR. Usually this portion of the process deals with the question of whether the child meets the definition of an "abused and neglected child," or whether the parent is "unfit."

The second stage of the process is the dispositional hearing, the purpose of which is to determine who should have custody of the child. If the facts in the first portion of the process do not support a finding of unfitness, the judge must dismiss the case. Even if the judge dismisses a case, he has the discretion to determine whether the child should be returned to the parent immediately or should remain in foster care until the parent can provide a safe environment for the child. If the conditions of the statute are met and the parent is found to be unfit in the factfinding phase by "clear and convincing evidence,"[1] then during the dispositional hearing, the judge is charged

---

[1]In the past, foster parents could only advocate for their interests in the dispositional phase. If a child was found to be permanently neglected (or a parent found unfit), then the foster parents (particularly if they proposed to adopt the child) could present evidence to clarify why they believe it would be in the best interests of the child for the foster parents to be awarded custody. Recent legislation allows foster parents in certain states to initiate a TPR proceeding.

with choosing the course of action that is in the best interest of the child. For example, a child could be returned to the parent, remain in foster care temporarily, or be legally separated from the biological parent in which case the child can be adopted or made a permanent ward of the state. In states with single-process TPR the proceedings are essentially the same, although they take place at one hearing.

At the dispositional phase, testimony by mental health professionals may be especially helpful. It is appropriate to testify about the potential benefits and risks inherent in various dispositional options. Information about attachments which exist for the child and the child's attachment capacity is frequently presented. Providing an accurate description of the specific developmental, social, educational, and emotional needs of the child is extremely valuable to the court. It is particularly helpful to clearly present any special needs a child has and the services necessary to meet those needs.

Some authors have argued that the process of TPR is weighted in favor of the state, citing the fact that the state generally has more access to mental health professionals than parents typically do (Melton et al., 1997). However, parents are afforded certain due process rights, such as the right to notice and the right to counsel, throughout the duration of the proceedings. One factor that distinguishes TPR from other types of custody decisions is the fact that, when a decision is made to terminate the rights of a parent, the decision is permanent and irrevocable once affirmed on appeal.

Prior to TPR, parents are given a time frame determined by the social service agencies and the court in order to change whatever circumstances led to the placement of their child. In most states, agencies are required to make "diligent" or "reasonable" efforts to rehabilitate the parent through counseling, drug treatment, parent education, and anger management classes. Agencies attempt to make informed clinical decisions about a parent's efforts at change, and more importantly their success or failure at improving actual caretaking skills. Should the agency find a complete lack of effort by the parent, or find that despite considerable efforts by the parent and agency the parent is still not capable of providing a minimally adequate environment for the child, proceedings to terminate rights will be initiated.

The Role of the Judge in TPR Proceedings

Most judges have a sober respect for family privacy and are reluctant to make a decision so final as TPR. However, it is becoming increasingly clear that maintaining children in "legal limbo," depriving them of a permanent home, is in itself "abusive" to children (Melton et al., 1997). Judges must balance the rights of the parent with the needs of a child. They are required to think rationally and to work within proper legal guidelines while listening to material which is often profoundly disturbing and emotionally charged.

Preliminary Research on Judges' Decisions on TPR

Galietta (1998) looked at a sample of New York judges and asked them to list all the factors they consider in determining the best interests of children in TPR decisions. Judges listed the following factors (in order from most to least important) they considered when applying the best interest standard at the dispositional stage: the social service agency's attempts to reunite the family, efforts of the parents to contact the child and parent's compliance with treatment recommendations, child's prospects for adoption, prior extent of abuse and risk of future harm to the child, duration of out of home placement, demographics (age or sex of child) and any special needs of child, recommendations of other parties such as the law guardian, psychologist, social worker, social supports available to the family such as extended family or homemaker services, qualities of the biological parent including parenting skill, and the presence and current status of the child's siblings.

Of significant import in the design of this study is the fact that judges were asked to use the best interest standard at the dispositional phase of the proceeding, subsequent to a finding of parental unfitness by a clear and convincing standard of evidence, where at which point New York statute dictates that the best interest of the child shall be the sole criteria for the determination. Despite this fact, judges included efforts the agency had made at reunification, and efforts of the parents (not demonstrated parenting ability) as primary factors they consider in deciding what is best for a child. This indicates that, even in states with bifurcated TPR proceedings, decision making in the two phases often blurs together. This is important because the best interest may be obfuscated by factors other than those directly pertaining to the best interests of a child.

Judges indicated that, in New York, most TPR hearings were "defaults," that is, the parent was not present at the hearing, despite notice. Finally, many judges indicated that they would like New York statutes necessitating "diligent efforts" at reunification be modified or eliminated as they often conflict with the best interest of the child.

Psychological Issues Pertaining to TPR Proceedings

In his seminal paper considering child and family policy in this country, Melton (1987) argued that much of family law and policy has been based on mythological views of children and family life, views which are often contradicted by empirical reality. Repucci and Crosby (1993) similarly noted society's underlying belief that "the private autonomous family is the institution best suited to provide for the best interests of society's children" (p. 2). They contended that this belief is the basis for the assumption that "in general, state intervention into families is a negative occurrence" (p. 2). In many cases these assumptions are correct. It is probably true that, given the realistic alternatives for children, many are best raised in their own homes, even if parenting is not optimal (see chapter 10). Providing intensive in-home services and offering the child enrichment opportunities may be the best alternative (Besharov, 1986; Advisory Board on Child Abuse and Neglect, 1992). In some cases however, parenting capacity is so severely impaired that even with intensive services and training, significant change is not possible (Willet, Ayoub, and Robinson, 1991; Adnopoz, 1996).

Commonly held assumptions about children and families may obfuscate what is in the best interest of any individual child, particularly if that child's circumstances contradict the schemas we hold about what "families" are like. Experts caution that both judges and mental health professionals may bias determinations of parental fitness in termination of parental rights proceedings (Newman, 1989; Leonard, 1991; Azar and Benjet, 1994; Azar et al., 1995). Operating under the assumption that all mothers have an innate capacity and desire to love their children,[2] may put a child's safety at risk. Additionally, overidentification with the child victim gives rise to rescue fantasies that may prevent the professional from recommending return to an adequate, albeit flawed environment.

Case Illustration

The following scenario was developed from a composite of cases provided by the author's experience and that of colleagues. It illustrates how both schemas about families and countertransferential feelings may negatively impact on a TPR evaluation.

> Dr. S is a clinician who has been appointed by the Court to evaluate Samantha Jones and to assist the Court in determining the best interests of this child. The state recently initiated proceedings to terminate Ms. Jones's rights to Samantha. At a recent fact-finding hearing, Samantha was found by clear and convincing evidence to be a "permanently abused or neglected child." The Court has asked Dr. S to provide information to aid in the disposition of this case. The Court may terminate Ms. Jones's rights and free Samantha to be adopted by her foster care parents or may suspend judgment for one year if it is determined to be in the best interests of the child to do so.
>
> Samantha Jones is a three-year-old child who has been in the custody of the state for the last two years. She was placed subsequent to a finding that her mother had neglected her needs. The state investigation revealed that Samantha was physically abused. Samantha was not taken to general medical appointments and frequently remained in dirty diapers for long periods of time. Samantha was originally removed from her mother's care because Ms. Jones brought her to the emergency room stating that the child had fallen off her bed and hurt her arm. Doctors in the emergency room took x-rays and found that

---

[2]This assumption has been called into question by research studies pertaining to primate parenting behaviors (e.g., Harlow and Harlow,1965). This research has demonstrated, for example, that female monkeys raised without mothers were subsequently found to be incapable of successfully nurturing their own offspring. While not directly testable in humans for ethical reasons, both clinical experience and the overrepresentation of abusive/neglectful behaviors in mothers with histories of maltreatment speak to the fact that many attachment behaviors seem to be learned.

Samantha's fractured arm was the result of someone twisting the arm. Additionally, they found evidence of at least five older fractures at various stages of healing.

On meeting Ms. Jones for the first time, Dr. S was struck by her fragility and child-like demeanor. During the course of the evaluation Ms. Jones stated that she wants to attend parenting classes and that she never attended before because she "didn't have her head together." Ms. Jones stated tearfully that she was very lonely and missed her daughter terribly. When asked why she had not attempted to contact her daughter during the entire placement, Ms. Jones could not provide an answer. She told Dr. S that she had never before had anyone who listened to her. Ms. Jones spoke of her own abusive past and expressed a wish to be treated by Dr. S. Dr. S told Ms. Jones that she was an evaluator for the court and could not treat her, but that she was glad she trusted her and would be glad to provide her with a referral.

On meeting Samantha, Dr. S was impressed with her friendliness and open demeanor. Dr. S noted that Samantha did not appear to have any recollection of her biological mother. The child appeared to be healthy and well taken care of and was meeting developmental milestones appropriately. She was brought to the meeting by Ms. Jackson, her foster mother. Although Dr. S did not formally meet with Ms. Jackson, she noted that the child appeared to have a warm and trusting relationship with her foster mother.

In her recommendations to the court, Dr. S emphasized the importance of the mother–child bond that occurred at birth, and the importance for Samantha of knowing her mother and her history. She noted in her opinion that Ms. Jones appeared to love her daughter very much and suggested that it would be in the best interests of Samantha that Ms. Jones be given another chance to take advantage of treatment services.

The case of Samantha and Dr. S is problematic for several reasons. While professionals disagree about the ethics involved in giving ultimate-issue opinions, it may be problematic that Dr. S met only with the mother and yet testified about the *best* dispositional option. The role of Dr. S in this case was to provide information about the relative risk of various dispositional options. Ideally, Dr. S would have objectively assessed Samatha's attachment to both her biological mother and her foster mother. At this stage of a TPR proceeding, the central issue is whether severing the legal relationship between

Samantha and Ms. Jones would be consistent with or detrimental to Samantha's best interests. Dr. S made an error by blurring the criteria for decision making in the two stages of the TPR process. Dr. S's observations about Ms. Jones's intentions to participate in treatment and have her daughter back hold little relevance to her actual parenting capacity or to what is in the best interests of Samantha at this stage of the TPR process.

While Ms. Jones's apparent interest in "straightening out for her daughter" is relevant, as is the question of whether the state made reasonable efforts to assist Ms. Jones, these questions are perhaps more pertinent to one of several dispositional reviews of the case that took place prior to the TPR proceedings. In the jurisdiction in which this hypothetical child welfare case takes place, these issues would have been discussed in the factfinding phase. In the dispositional phase, the role of the psychologist is to provide information that directly pertains to the best interests of the child. In other words, what are the child's particular needs and where can they best be met?

Samantha appeared to have bonded satisfactorily with her foster parent. Samantha appeared to be developmentally on schedule. Information about any special needs Samantha might have should have been presented to the court. Ideally, a forensic evaluation such as this would include thorough assessment of all of the dispositional options for Samantha. A home visit with the foster mother would also be appropriate, if possible.

Had the evaluator in this case taken the time to closely examine her feelings and considered their possible influence on her thinking, it is likely that she would have attended more to the child's best interests *at the time of the evaluation.* For example, she might have focused more on the child's positive attachment to her foster mother. She might have considered the potential deleterious consequences of prolonging a relationship with a biological mother who has demonstrated no behavior indicating motivation or likeliness to improve her parenting. Failure to consider these factors illustrates the subtle manifestation of countertransference and its potential consequences in TPR proceedings.

One possible scenario that can be particularly dangerous involves positive misattributions about a parent's motivations and actual parenting capacity. Even regular attendance at parenting classes does not necessarily indicate improvement in parenting skills.

Parenting skills must be directly assessed, to the extent possible. Taking an overly optimistic view of a parent's intentions and suggesting extensions when permissible may reduce the guilt clinicians feel when they recommend TPR. In the scenario described above, the result of these feelings is prolonging the limbo of foster care for children. As argued above, in other cases the consequences may be far more devastating, as a child can ultimately be returned to an unsafe environment.

TREATMENT FOR ABUSED AND NEGLECTED CHILDREN WHO HAVE BEEN INVOLVED IN TPR PROCEEDINGS

Children whose parents' rights have been terminated are by definition "abused or neglected." Therefore, it is essential that therapists treating such children have a current understanding of the consequences of child abuse, as well as treatments effective for particular types of child abuse. Cicchetti and Olsen (1990) summarized the pervasive negative effects associated with maltreatment as follows:

> Taken in tandem, the findings of the theoretically guided studies on the sequelae of child maltreatment underscore the devastating impacts that maltreatment phenomena have upon the functioning of these children. Specifically, maltreated children manifest impairments on all the early stage-salient developmental issues (e.g., the development of a secure attachment, the development of an autonomous self, communicative development, and peer relations). They also show deficits in each domain of development (affective, cognitive, social, social-cognitive, and linguistic), and are at heightened risk for the development of behavior problems and later psychopathology [p. 275].

In addition, many children who are affected by TPR have been exposed to drugs prenatally, making it more likely that they will have physical anomalies and neurological difficulties and that they will require specialized services. Sadly, despite the fact that these children are at high risk for a host of problems, including psychological, educational, social, and health-related difficulties, it is a reality that their treatment needs are frequently unmet, even if a child is in the care of the state (Melton et al., 1997).

Part of the difficulty involved in treating children who are affected by TPR is that, in addition to being abused/neglected, they have the additional burden of coming to terms with the parental termination process and its meaning. Being legally disconnected from a biological parent may have multiple meanings for both the child and the therapist. Both child and the therapist may be confronted with conflicting feelings. It is crucial that the therapist never assume the meaning of the experience for the child. The therapist should avoid "pulling" for labeling of the event as either traumatic or positive. This is where a position of neutrality can be most beneficial. Children may have extremely varied responses to TPR. For a severely abused child, TPR signifies safety and the end of an emotional limbo. It also signifies the end of the fantasy that mother will "get better" or "love me." The end of this fantasy often marks the beginning of a difficult process in which the child must confront the fear that mother is gone because the child was unlovable and bad.[3] Further complicating treatment is the fact that the meaning ascribed to the event may change over time and with a child's development in various domains.

CONCLUDING REMARKS

Both current research and recent legislative initiatives support the provision of services for families in cases where reunification is possible, and also support timely efforts to terminate rights in cases where reunification is not the appropriate course of action. It is crucial that children receive adequate physical, social, educational, and psychological treatment as soon as abuse or neglect is discovered, and for as long as is needed. Recent legislative changes make this an optimistic time for child advocates, but whether such legislation will successfully accomplish the goal of improving child welfare outcomes for children who are abused and neglected remains to be seen.

Termination of parental rights cases are perhaps the most serious decisions undertaken by the Family Courts. David Pelzer (1997), a former foster child whose mother's rights were terminated, illustrates

---

[3]This task is often complicated by the fact that, in many cases, the child was told that he or she was bad, evil, or unlovable during episodes of abuse. Subsequent behavioral problems (e.g., lying or disruptive behaviors) are common in foster children and often evoke negative responses from people, which serve to further reinforce the belief that they are damaged, bad, or not worthy of love.

this fact, "There is no doubt in my mind that had I stayed with my biological mother much longer, I would have definitely been killed" (p. 305).

REFERENCES

Adnopoz, J. (1996), Complicating the theory: The application of psychoanalytic concepts and understanding to family preservation. *The Psychoanalytic Study of the Child*, 51:411–421. New Haven, CT: Yale University Press.

Adoption Assistance and Child Welfare Act (1980).

Adoption and Safe Families Act of 1997, Pub. L. No. 105-89, 105th Cong. Available online. http//thomas.loc.gov. (the law is listed under H.R. 867).

Advisory Board on Child Abuse and Neglect (1992), Creating caring communities: Blueprint for an effective federal policy on child abuse and neglect. Washington, DC: Author.

Areen, J. (1985), *Cases and Materials on Family Law*. New York: Foundation Press.

Azar, S. T. & Benjet, C. L. (1994), A cognitive perspective on ethnicity, race, and termination of parental rights. *Law & Human Behavior*, 18:249–268.

—— —— Fuhrmann, G. S. & Cavallero, L. (1995), Child maltreatment and termination of parental rights: Can behavioral research help Solomon? *Behavior Ther.*, 26:599–623.

Besharov, D. J. (1986), The misuse of foster care: When the desire to help children outruns the ability to improve parental functioning. *Family Law Quart.*, 20:213–231.

Child Abuse Prevention and Treatment Act of 1974, Pub. L. No. 93-247.

Galietta, M. (1998), A therapeutic jurisprudence study: New York State judges and their interpretation of the law regarding termination of parental rights decisions. Presented at the meeting of the American Psychology and Law Society, Redondo Beach, CA, April.

Harlow, H. & Harlow, M. (1965), The affectional systems. In: *Behavior of Nonhuman Primates, Vol. 2*, ed. A. Schrier, H. Harlow & F. Stollnitz. New York: Academic Press, pp. 287–334.

Leonard, A. S. (1991), From law: Homophobia, heterosexism, and judicial decision making. *J. Gay & Lesbian Psychother.*, 1:65–91.

Mann, E. & McDermott, J. F., Jr. (1983), Play therapy for victims of child abuse and neglect. In: *Handbook of Play Therapy*, ed. C. E. Schaefer & K. J. O'Connor. New York: Wiley, pp. 283–307.

Melton, G. B. (1987), The clashing of symbols: Prelude to child and family policy. *Amer. Psychol.*, 42:345–354.

—— Petrila, J., Poythress, N. G. & Slobogin, C. (1997), *Psychological Evaluations for the Courts*. New York: Guilford Press.

Newman, S. A. (1989), A tale of two cases: Reflections on psychological and institutional influences on child custody decisions. *NY Law School Rev.*, 34:661–678.

Pelzer, D. (1997), *The Lost Boy*. Deerfield Beach, FL: Health Communications.

Repucci, N. D. & Crosby, C. A. (1993), Law, psychology, and children: Overarching issues. *Law & Human Behavior,* 17:1–10.

Shotton, A. C. (1990), Making reasonable efforts in child abuse and neglect cases: Ten years later. *California Western Law Rev.,* 26:223–256.

Strengthening Abuse and Neglect Courts Act of 2000, S. 2272, 106th Cong, 2nd sess. (2000).

Willet, J. B., Ayoub, C. C. & Robinson, D. (1991), Using growth modeling to examine systematic differences in growth: An example of change in functioning of families at risk of maladaptive parenting, child abuse, or neglect. *J. Consult & Clin. Psychol.,* 59:38–47.

Interlude IV

The Forensic Expert's Challenge

*Making Recommendations
in the Best Interests of Children*

T wo chapters in this section offer comprehensive frameworks for the family forensic evaluation (Gunsberg; Bricklin, and Elliot). Gunsberg's approach (see chapter 15) is guided by the developmental psychoanalytic framework, and Bricklin and Elliot (see chapter 16) offer a systems-specific perspective. Different in many respects, they share the same respect for unconscious processes at work in the family members who are being assessed. In addition, they are both committed to home visits as an important source of data about the parent–child relationship. Finally, they both try to elicit information about the child's preference for custody and visitation *indirectly* via responses to the PORT (Perception of Relationships Test), projective tests, or play.

Schwager (see chapter 17) and Cling (see chapter 18) offer chapters about specific dimensions of the family forensic evaluation. Schwager makes a plea for assessing the parent's capacity to respond to the spiritual and creative aspects of the child when the court is making child custody decisions. Schwager argues that these aspects of the child are critical to his inner life and self-esteem; neglect or annihilation of these aspects of the child by the parent has been referred to as soul murder (Shengold, 1989).

Cling addresses the complicated issue of child abuse allegations within child custody disputes. She highlights the contribution of fantasy and unconscious processes both in the parent making the allegations and in the child who is the focus of the alleged sexual abuse. She comments on the impact of sexual abuse allegations on the family, whether true or false, particularly on the relationship between the identified child and the accused parent.

When doing forensic evaluations of families going through divorce, we must be respectful of the ways in which parents have structured their family's life. That is, if parents have mutually decided that the children will be cared for by the mother, and their decision works, it is not our task to recommend change. Our recommendations, if they involve changes in family functioning, must not only be convincing in terms of how the family can function better, but also must require small (not dramatic) shifts that can be realistically accepted and accomplished by the family members. When recommendations for custody and visitation are too far from what can be accepted by the family, the family responds by not implementing the court's decisions, with frequent returns to the court for modifications in these arrangements.

Bricklin and Elliot are absolutely correct in their assertion that parental capacity can only be evaluated within the parent–child dyad. In describing the Bricklin Perceptual Scales (BPS) as an attempt to operationally define the best interests of the child criterion and also to maximize the child's input in the custody decision by developing a test that taps the child's perceptions of the parents, Bricklin (1984) states:

> (1) Even parents *not* engaged in adversary battles often misrepresent themselves when observed, while parents actively engaged in custody battles *almost always* do; (2) Even if one could secretly observe competing parents, there is no clear way to recognize behavior in a child's best interests, since what is most important is not what parents do but how a particular child at a particular time *utilizes* what the parents do; and (3) Children often reveal their reactions to parental behavior unconsciously in *nonverbal* behaviors, rather than in what they say [p. 11].

In Bricklin and Elliot's chapter, reference is made to parental attunement to the child's symbol systems and information processing strategies. That is, it is important to assess how the child ascribes meaning to his or her world and what the capacity of the parent is to understand this and exchange information with the child. How the child ascribes meaning and how well the parent understands this meaning are also the concern of Schwager in her chapter.

Furthermore, attention must be given to the defenses and dynamics of the child and how these impact on a parent's parenting. That is, the parent–child relationship is dynamic, with two active participants affecting each other. A good family forensic evaluation, especially one that takes place over time and involves a home visit, becomes a microcosm of how parental decisions are made and how a child responds to the parenting styles and behavior of his parents (see chapters 4, 15, and 16).

Every forensic expert in the field of child custody and visitation has preferred dimensions along which parental capacity is assessed. Although there is some overlap, there are many dimensions that are unique to the particular forensic evaluator, often colored by his or her own theoretical position and views of parenting. Some overlapping dimensions include capacity for nurturance and empathy, degree of parental conflict, ability to co-parent or collaborate around the children, and psychopathology as it affects parenting (Jenuwine and Cohler, 1999). It is important to address the psychopathology of both parents in relationship to parenting, since the noncustodial parent's psychopathology can be as damaging to the child's well-being as that of the custodial parent. Assessing this dimension carefully may be an important determinant in tailoring an access schedule. Parental psychopathology affects not only present, but future parenting; continued exposure to a parent's psychopathology leads to internalization and unconscious transmission of this psychopathology to the next generation (see chapters 4, 15, and 16).

Black and Cantor (1989) offer several dimensions that are not usually mentioned in the literature. They include the parent's capacity for separation and individuation, identity organization or sense of self, reality testing and impulse control, and motivation and ability to improve parenting skills. Gardner (1999) and Gunsberg (see chapter 8) suggest the parent's moral character is also a critical consideration.

Three issues have come to the foreground recently in family forensic evaluations. First, when psychological testing results are reported, we need to know who has administered the psychological tests and who has scored and interpreted the data and written the psychological testing report. Although psychological testing has been integrated into forensic evaluation in general for over fifty years, within the family forensic arena, psychological testing has come to the forefront within the last two decades.

A second problematic issue is the forensic expert's interview of psychotherapists working either with the parents or the child. The treatment process can be affected when a psychotherapist is interviewed by the forensic expert who includes the findings from this interview in the report to the Court. This can have an effect similar to that when a psychotherapist testifies directly in the custody trial. The forensic expert often interviews the psychotherapist with particular *forensic questions* in mind. He translates what he finds out from the psychotherapist into data that he can use to answer issues of parental psychopathology, child custody, and visitation. However, psychotherapists should not be offering, nor should they be asked, to give their opinions regarding custody and visitation. Psychotherapy data come from different levels of awareness. Often the psychotherapist may not make clear what inferences are being made by the psychotherapist and what was actually said by the parent or child in treatment.

Furthermore, if one parent is in treatment and the other is not, these data are available about only one parent. This situation can be misinterpreted as meaning that the parent who undergoes psychotherapy is more troubled than the parent who is not in psychotherapy when it may actually be that the parent in psychotherapy is more motivated to work on his or her problems so that they do not interfere with parenting of the children.

A third problem that has emerged fairly recently is what has been referred to as "demarcated joint custody" or "zones of responsibility." This kind of joint custody arrangement has been tried with high-conflict divorce litigants. However, it often raises more problems than it solves. First, there is the battle over which parent gets which areas. Second, these zones, although they can be separated intellectually, in reality interface with each other or, more often than not, collide with each other. Parents then argue which zone has priority, "mine or yours." Locked in the same kind of conflict between the two parties that has historically taken place, the parents are unable to resolve their differences, and the conflict must then be resolved by a third party. The court, paralleling the parental decision-making impasse, brings the child (somtimes inappropriately) into the picture as a tie-breaker, via the law guardian. The child may resent being taken away from the tasks and joys of childhood and pulled into these conflicts and, at the same time, feel guilty about taking a position, which his parents translate into a test of loyalty. Also, the child can feel too empowered. The most serious problem, however, is the outcome—insufficient *integration* of decision-making about the child. How then does a child feel "whole"?

REFERENCES

Black, J. & Cantor, D. (1989), *Child Custody*. New York: Columbia University Press.

Bricklin, B. (1984), *Bricklin Perceptual Scales*. Furlong, PA: Village Publishing.

Gardner, R. (1999), Guidelines for assessing parental preference in child-custody disputes. *J. Divorce & Remarriage*, 30:1–9.

Jenuwine, M. & Cohler, B. (1999), Major parental psychopathology and child custody. In: *The Scientific Basis of Child Custody Decisions*, ed. R. Galatzer-Levy & L. Kraus. New York: Wiley, pp. 285–318.

Shengold, L. (1989), *Soul Murder*. New Haven, CT: Yale University Press.

Linda Gunsberg

Chapter 15

The Developmental Evolution of the Family Forensic Evaluation

LINDA GUNSBERG

The purpose of this chapter is twofold. First, it offers the reader a psychoanalytic/developmental conceptualization or frame work that can be used in evaluating children, parents, and their families for the court. Second, a case is presented that follows the psychoanalytic methodology offered. This is not a "how-to" chapter; rather, it attempts to expose the reader to the multiple variables that need consideration when doing family forensic evaluations.

THE PSYCHOANALYTIC DEVELOPMENTAL POSITION

Psychoanalysis has been committed to a developmental model for almost one hundred years, since Freud (1905) proposed sequential stages for the understanding of psychosexual development (Tyson and Tyson, 1990). His interest in developmental stages was continued by his daughter, Anna Freud. She studied normal child development before turning her attention to psychopathology. Others (Erikson, 1950; Colarusso and Nemiroff, 1981) have suggested that development continues throughout the lifespan. Although in childhood and adolescence development leads to structural changes and new developmental stages, development in adulthood leads more often to adaptive reorganizations of previously existing structures or levels attained (Tyson and Tyson, 1990).

Anna Freud used an observational methodology. However, she went beyond traditional academic developmental psychology, which derived its meaning "solely from conscious behaviors with little or no understanding that one behavior might have multiple unconscious determinants" (Mayes and Cohen, 1996). Thus, the psychoanalytic observer both *records and interprets* the events of the moment.

Anna Freud then organized her observations and developed the metapsychological profile (A. Freud, 1965), which charted a child's development along multiple lines simultaneously. Areas included drive development, ego and superego development, regression and fixation points, conflicts, and assessment of general characteristics such as frustration tolerance, sublimation potential, and overall attitude towards anxiety. She looked at the child's path within a particular developmental line as well as across lines. She observed the harmony or disharmony across the lines of development. She saw development as both discontinuous, and continuous and cumulative. Discontinuity is evidenced within each developmental line in terms of achievable steps. However, even though consolidation occurs and takes the form of steps, phases, or stages, there is an overall progression through the developmental process, which emphasizes continuity in child development.

Anna Freud also emphasized progressive and regressive forces in development. That is, when there is conflict and/or a catalyst to move forward, the child is vulnerable when taking new steps; as a result, in the process of progression, there may be regression. The child may temporarily revert back to a previous comfortable stage, at a lower level on the developmental ladder, in his transition to a higher developmental level. Although there are general guidelines for the achievement of stages within particular developmental lines (certain chronological ages), the emphasis is less on whether it has been achieved by a certain age than on the child's progression through the developmental steps at his own pace.

In addition, Anna Freud posited that, once a child passes through a lower developmental stage, this stage does not disappear. It remains in the child's repertoire forever, co-existing with higher-level stages. Thus, a child, within the same developmental line may have achieved a higher level of functioning but may function on several developmental stages within that developmental line either simultaneously or successively.

Although Anna Freud shared with Piaget in cognitive development (Piaget, 1958; Flavell, 1977) and Mahler in the separation-individuation process (Mahler, Pine, and, Bergman, 1975) a common commitment to the concept of phases or stages in development, her metapsychological profile would essentially subsume their interest in particular lines of development. She was interested not only in the observable changes in the child's behavior in relationship to an external event, but in the child's internal experience of the event as well (Mayes and Cohen, 1996). Thus, a further psychoanalytic contribution is that behavior observed is multiply determined by both conscious and unconscious factors.

Tyson and Tyson (1990) beautifully summarize the developmental process as the following:

> The word process should be emphasized, for no one point or pattern ever recurs, and no one system is ever a fixed and final attainment; new additions or modifications may be made throughout life. Furthermore, if we consider the infinite complexity of all the elements cascading together in the developmental process, a large measure of unpredictability is characteristic, and yet there is a predictability and stability to the overall pattern. Also, no one system is superordinate nor can any one system be considered in isolation from the others; no one system is causally related to, derived from, or explanatory of another. Rather, all are interdependent, but the relationships among them are not strictly proportional. It is the integration among the systems, however, that promotes adaptation at increasingly higher levels of psychological functioning [pp. 33, 36].

THE FAMILY FORENSIC EVALUATION:
A GLIMPSE INTO THE INTERNAL WORLDS
OF PARENT AND CHILD

In a forensic evaluation, the forensic expert is evaluating the family and each member of the family at a time of disruption, separation, and divorce (see chapter 4). At times of crisis and potential trauma, parenting is subject to unconscious pulls and irrational thoughts and behavior even more than usual. The forensic expert must try to distinguish between behavior that is temporary and connected to the family upheaval and behavior that is more constant and therefore potentially indicative of serious parental dysfunction.

Wallerstein and her colleagues (Wallerstein and Blakeslee, 1989; Wallerstein, 1997; Wallerstein and Corbin, 1999) have reported a transitory diminished capacity in parenting associated with the upheaval of divorce in which the parent seems less able than usual to differentiate the child's needs from the parent's needs. Two associated themes emerge in such parents. First, there is a conscious and, in many cases, unconscious wish to abandon the child at the same time as the marital breakup. Although the underlying motivations for this wish may not be available (and they vary from parent to parent), the child feels the abrupt shift in the parent's behavior. The child fears being abandoned and may evidence "hypervigilant tracking" of the parent as well as a heightened anxiety that can interfere with developmental progress and dominate the child's inner world. For example, Betty Broderick, shortly after her husband left her, drove her children to her husband's house and left them there in a confused state.[1] Although this behavior was shocking to her children and to others, it was on some level an attempt to get her husband to return to her (Stumbo, 1993). Another theme associated with the temporary rejection of a child at the time of marital breakup is an intensified need of the parent for the child to take care of the parent (Tessman, 1975).

Although these two behaviors on the part of the parent can be transitory, their effects and impact on the child may not be transitory. In fact the child, even after the parent's parenting capacity is restored to normal, may continue to be hypervigilant, expecting another abandonment by the parent, or may continue to feel responsible for keeping the parent alive, subordinating his own interests and welfare to that of the parent. Furthermore, even when this abrupt change in the parent is explained to the child either by the recovered parent or by a mental health professional, the child may continue to feel responsible for the onset and continuation of the behavior and feel he or she was "unlovable" (Wallerstein, 1997).

Psychoanalytic theory has shown there is no one-to-one correspondence between real world experiences and the inner world's

---

[1]Betty Broderick, the wife in a highly publicized California divorce case, later killed her ex-husband and his new wife as they slept in their marital bed. She was convicted and sentenced to a jail term, leaving her four children essentially orphaned.

registry of these experiences. The inner world images are subject to distortion, fantasy, and other elaborations, such as cumulative previous experiences with a particular person. The inner world is also subject to the activity of defensive operations and, to a great extent, is not available to us consciously, yet it rules our behavior and thoughts, often in irrational ways.

Fraiberg, Adelson, and Shapiro (1987) speak poignantly to this issue in their classic work, "Ghosts in the Nursery." They observed that some of the mothers were "condemned" to repeat the tragedy of their own childhoods with their babies. The authors' task was to try to understand why this occurred in some families and not in others. They noticed that mothers who were not in touch with the associated affective (emotional) experience of events of their childhood identified in a pathological manner with the psychopathology of their own parents.

When a psychoanalytically informed expert listens to the developmental history of each parent from childhood through adolescence, adulthood, marriage, and to this point of evaluation, divorce, the expert is listening for examples of such repetitions and reenactments that may not be within the conscious awareness of the parent being evaluated. The forensic expert is attempting to assess how these repetitions and reenactments may have affected or could affect the parenting ability of the parent.

Furthermore, when evaluating parental capacity, the forensic expert assesses the constancy or reliability of the parent's emotional availability to the child (see chapters 4, 13, 14, 16, and 17). Robert and Erna Furman (1984) have made a remarkable contribution to our understanding of a particular kind of parental dysfunction that they have termed "intermittent decathexis." They note that parents vary widely in their ability to remain emotionally available to their children. On the two extremes of the continuum, parents can be over-involved ("anxiously preoccupied") or manifest total decathexis, in which parents are emotionally unable to enter into the developmental phase of parenthood, which leads to severe deprivation for the child.

Between these two endpoints on the continuum there is a group of parents who do enter the developmental phase of parenthood, investing themselves in their children, but who intermittently withdraw from the children, unconsciously and almost totally. The children of these parents report being physically lost or being unattended.

Such parental inattentiveness leaves them in emotional distress, physical danger, and even in situations where they are potentially molested by strangers or family members. These children report very low self-esteem and have difficulty mastering ordinary transitions and separations, as they constantly fear they will lose their parent completely. As Fraiberg, Adelson, and Shapiro (1987) have noted, when these children become parents themselves, they are capable of becoming "decathectors" with their own children, unconsciously reenacting the same parental deficiency.

There are several misconceptions about developmental terms within forensic and legal disciplines. These come from incomplete knowledge. One such term is narcissism. Narcissism is considered one of the many developmental lines referred to earlier in this chapter. In normal development, children move from primary to secondary narcissism. Narcissism fuels positive self-esteem when it progresses from the primary to secondary level. Often parents are referred to as "narcissistic," and with the label comes a negative connotation of being selfish and egocentric. As Katan (1981) noted in mothers who intermittently decathect their children, narcissistic refueling of the mother's self state is necessary for survival, and this can at times be done at the child's expense.

It is much easier to evaluate parenting capacity by looking to see how, when, and under what circumstances a parent's narcissistic withdrawal intrudes upon parenting capacity, rather than condemning the parent outright, seeing the parent as immature, and seeing this as all-encompassing psychopathology. Healthy narcissism depends heavily on the quality of internalized relationships. That is, the parent who feels he was loved, adored, and appreciated as a child will internalize this positive parent–child relationship and positive self-esteem, and call upon these internalized images even when narcissistic supplies are not readily available in the parent's present life, as is often the case at the time of divorce.

Levels of Awareness:
Unconscious, Preconscious, and Conscious

Freud believed that mental life could not be explained in terms of conscious motivation alone (Giovacchini, 1982). In his paper on repression, Freud (1915) posited the dynamic unconscious as an extraordinary and powerful element that determines both pathological and ordinary behavior. Because the unconscious remains repressed for most people, there are forces inside them of which they are unaware that control them and their destiny.[2]

For example, a husband and wife who are already divorced are involved in a custody battle over their child. The father is seeking to reverse custody and gain sole custody of the boy. In a very heated first meeting with the forensic expert, he said, "Danny's biggest problem is the difficult situation between myself and my mother."[3] Although the father caught his grammatical error and corrected it, he did not seem to have any awareness of the possible underlying meaning of his statement. To the analytically trained forensic expert, it is clear that part of this father's motivation to seek custody of his son is to rescue his son from his son's mother due to the father's transference of his difficulties with his own mother onto his former wife and their son. Too often these kinds of transferences from childhood propel parents into custody battles without their having a clue as to the origins of their motivations.

Freud (1900) believed that the dream was the "royal road to the unconscious." Similarly, the less available layers of meaning are available to the forensic expert in the home visits of mother and father with their children, and in the use of projective psychological testing (see chapter 16). The forensic expert is more likely to see the parent–child relationship in vivo, in the home environment, where they are more comfortable. One can say, the home visit and projective psychological testing are the "royal road to the less conscious."

The Usefulness of the Concept of Projection in Family Forensic Evaluations

Freud (1900) referred to projection as the psychological mechanism used by the individual to push *inner* feelings onto the *outside* world so as not to have to take responsibility for the internal origin of the

---

[2]The task of psychoanalysis is to unleash these unconscious forces by breaking through the barrier of repression. The belief is that as the patient becomes more aware of all the forces inside him, he will become more in control of his behavior, thoughts, and life. Although psychoanalytic theory distinguishes between the conscious, preconscious, and unconscious levels of mental functioning, for the purposes of this chapter the author will distinguish only between the conscious and unconscious.

[3]Throughout this chapter, pseudonyms are offered in case examples to protect the confidentiality of the patients or litigants.

feelings. Now, via the mechanism of projection, the individual experiences these feelings as coming from the outside world towards him, rather than onto the outer world from him. Although projection has been viewed primarily as a defense mechanism, it is used by everyone as a strategy in dealing with stimulation from the outside world, even where there is no internal conflict (Freud, 1938).

There is a group of psychological tests, referred to as projective tests, in which the individual (child or adult) projects his thoughts, feelings, conflicts, and fantasies onto the stimulus provided. These tests are based on open-ended questions to which there are no right or wrong answers. In many cases, once the individual feels comfortable, he responds without feeling he is directly revealing his inner self. Murray (1943) the psychologist who developed the Thematic Apperception Test, claimed that the person not only reveals aspects of himself that he ordinarily would not choose to admit, but that he could not admit because they are not in the domain of conscious thought. The projective tests include the Thematic Apperception Test, The Children's Apperception Test (Animals), The Children's Apperception Test (Humans), the Rorschach Inkblots, the House-Tree-Person Drawing Test, the Kinetic-Family Drawing Test (Draw a Family Doing Something), and the Sentence Completion Test.

Although these tests have been criticized because their scoring systems are not adequately refined, they are invaluable clinical tools if they are looked at as methods of obtaining less accessible levels of data (Anastasi and Urbina, 1997; Weiner, 1997). Projective testing is compatible with the psychoanalytic method. Both involve free association as a tool for arriving at the unconscious. Data derived from these tests can generate working hypotheses that can be considered in conjunction with data collected from multiple other sources in the family forensic evaluation.

In family forensic evaluations, parents wish to portray themselves as the good parent, and often portray the other parent as the bad parent. Family psychopathology is often projected onto the other parent, rather than the parent taking ownership or even rightfully attributing psychopathology to the children. The forensic expert's goal is to obtain data from the less accessible levels in order to evaluate each family member, the parent–child interactions and communications, and the functioning and dynamics of the family (see chapters 4 and 16).

Although conscious and unconscious material can conceivably be derived from the clinical interviews in the forensic expert's office, home visits, or in psychological testing, it is more likely that the material will unfold differently in the various settings. Conscious material will be offered in the clinical interviews with family members in the expert's office, or over the telephone with collaterals. Less conscious material is most available in the home visits, where parents may try to "clean up" for the forensic expert but really do not succeed. The home can be seen as a projection of the individuals living in it. Psychological testing is where the unconscious data are derived.[4]

Transference and Countertransference as Projections in Family Forensic Evaluations

When a forensic expert sees a new family for evaluation, she lives, eats, and breathes the case. She is preoccupied with it from the moment she starts until she hands her report in to the court, and sometimes even longer. Even though the evaluation is conducted from the perspective of the best interests of the child, or in Goldstein et al.'s (1996) terms, the least detrimental alternative, the forensic expert can have strong reactions to the children and parents, individually and collectively, that are likely to fluctuate during the course of the evaluation (see chapter 14). The family members are also capable of having strong reactions to the process of being evaluated, as well as to the forensic expert as a person, which can shift during the course of the evaluation. It takes time for the forensic expert to "right" herself; that is, to go through all the intense feelings in response to the family and their plight, their reactions to her and her responses. Although much of this is not verbalized, it may in fact be another level of data collected which is relevant to the family forensic evaluation.

Judith Wallerstein (1997) defines transference in divorce as the patient's "crisis-driven transference," in other words, transference that comes from the experience of divorce proper, not necessarily

---

[4]In family forensic evaluations, I typically give projective tests to both parents and all children three years old and older.

transferences from early life experiences.[5] She defines countertransference as all the clinician's responses to the patient. Although Wallerstein's paper does not address the reactions of the forensic expert per se, her conceptualization appears to be relevant to the forensic situation in divorce and custody.

Wallerstein (1997) notes that working with families of divorce can lead to "cumulative anxiety, irritability, and depression, intensified by physical fatigue and a sense of depletion that can provoke a strong impulse to take flight and avoid professional contact with this demanding population" (p. 118). Wallerstein also comments on the guilt and anxiety that can be experienced by a psychotherapist for having too much (an intact marriage and children) in comparison to the mother or father in a divorce. Alternatively, even with so much being lost in the divorcing situation, there is a lot that these families have that is positive, and which can be envied by the psychotherapist or the forensic expert.

What, then, is the way out of this mess of projections, feelings, fantasies and thoughts that the forensic expert experiences while trying to do an impartial, thorough family forensic evaluation? I "right" myself or self-correct my position vis-à-vis the family by allowing my feelings and fantasies to be explored privately. I realize that many of the countertransference feelings engendered in me during the course of the evaluation are actually feeling states which correspond to feeling states of the child.

I might discuss the case with colleagues to see if my thinking is clouded as a response to my countertransference (see chapter 4). Being trained as a psychoanalyst, I am fairly comfortable acknowledging these feelings and fantasies, and have been trained to use these feelings, thoughts, and fantasies as potential clues to aspects of the family's dynamics. Forensic experts who are uncomfortable with these feelings and fantasies may need to push them away and ignore this window into the unconscious of the family being evaluated. Or, their unexplored and unresolved countertransferences may strongly color their integration of data and their reported findings. Lifson (2000) reports the rejection of a forensic expert's findings in a motion for a change of custody as being due to several factors, one

---

[5]Traditionally, transference has been defined as the transferring of important fantasies and key elements of the relationship with a central parental figure in early life either to the psychoanalyst or to someone in the person's present life.

of which was a negative countertransference on the part of the forensic expert towards the respondent.

DANIELLE, SIMONE, AND GORDON: WHAT SHOULD THE COURT DO ABOUT VISITATION BETWEEN DANIELLE AND HER FATHER?

Danielle, age six, would visit her father for periods of time without reported difficulty. Then she would tell her mother she did not want to see her father. She would give as reasons that her father would yell at her, fall asleep and not play with her, or prevent her from phoning her mother. Her mother, Simone, found herself in a conflict. On the one hand, she believed Danielle's reports, having witnessed and experienced similar behavior in her husband Gordon when they were married. However she had a good relationship with her own father and wanted her daughter to have the same. She tried to talk with Gordon about Danielle's reluctance to see him, but Gordon was quick to externalize responsibility for the problem. He blamed Simone for telling Danielle bad things about him and reinforcing her reluctance—perhaps even creating it.

After not seeing or speaking to her father for a few months, Danielle would request time with her father again, but on different terms. She did not want overnights. She wanted shorter, afternoon visits, and she wanted them to take place in public places, such as libraries, museums, and restaurants. The question was, why? In order to evaluate this situation, the forensic expert interviewed mother, father, daughter; mother and daughter; father and daughter; home visit with the father without Danielle, because the evaluation took place during a several month period when Danielle refused to see her father; projective psychological testing (House-Tree-Person Drawings, father and daughter; Rorschach, father and daughter; Thematic Apperception Test, father; and Children's Apperception Test, daughter); and collateral interviews with father's brother, who spent considerable time with Danielle and Gordon, Danielle's camp counselor, Gordon's psychotherapist, and Gordon's psychopharmacologist.

Home Visit With Gordon

As part of the forensic evaluation, I made a home visit. Gordon's hobbies included art projects and photography. When I walked into the apartment, I smelled fumes from chemicals that Gordon was using for art projects. He seemed entirely comfortable with the fumes. After 45 minutes, my eyes were burning. I wondered how this affected Danielle when she visited.

In Gordon's bedroom there was a double bed, with a futon stored under it. Above the bed was one of Gordon's art projects, a spider in its large web, with a butterfly trapped in the web. I wondered if this display might frighten Danielle, since she slept in this room, right under the web.

In addition, Gordon showed me plastic replicas of hands he had created that showed every vein and line of the original hands. After he showed me the replica of Danielle's hand, he left it on the table between us during the entire interview. There was something strange about having his daughter's disembodied "hand" sitting between us. Another replica of Danielle's hand had been incorporated into a penholder. On the left side of the penholder was an alligator or crocodile swimming, its mouth open, toward Danielle's hand, which formed the base of the penholder. Gordon showed me as well a dollhouse room he had created for the purpose of simulating explosions for his photography.

In conclusion, Gordon's home is filled with aggressive, strange, and eerie images and objects. These not only reflect his inner life, as will be reported in the psychological testing section, but may also frighten Danielle. Danielle's discomfort at her father's house has not been expressed in terms of the environment; rather she has focused on the similarly aggressive aspects of her father's behavior.

Interview with Gordon

In my final session with Gordon I was late in arriving to my office. I met him in the lobby of my building. He berated me for being late. His upset turned into belligerence very quickly. His voice escalated until he was yelling at me, totally unaware of my reaction or the reaction of people nearby. I saw that this episode began as a panic attack, stimulated by his thought that I had forgotten my appointment with him (an abandonment). I knew that this was the behavior Danielle had described to me several times. Her father got very angry all of a sudden in a manner that could be frightening to an adult, and even more so to a child.

Psychological Projective Testing: Gordon

The psychological testing indicated that Gordon is suffering from a thought disorder, has had auditory hallucinations, understands first-hand the process of going mad, and is filled with persecutory thoughts. The testing was done when he was taking psychotropic medications to help him control his disorder.

When asked to draw a picture of a tree, Gordon drew an apple tree with apples falling, and offered the following story: "This is the only apple tree in the county. It's been the only tree for the past 60 years. Nobody picks up the apples or picks from the tree. There seems to be a very frightening story behind this—actually, there seem to be as many stories as people in the county."

When I asked him what the frightening story was, he added: "Somebody who had eaten an apple 60 years ago ate a worm or some kind of little insect creature and it grew—once they ate it, the creature grew inside the person and it took them over psychologically and they acted very strange in front of other people and the person was an outcast because of his strange behavior."

I then asked, what were the strange things that the man did? Gordon replied: "At first, he told offbeat scary stories. Then the pain became even stronger so he had to get away from the tree, but there was such pain in his head he couldn't move any distance. At that time there was no cure, and he thought he would be put away for madness. One of the townspeople moved him further away from the tree and the insect within him died which was causing his madness. But he was in a sense exiled from the town he loved. If he moved closer, the insect would reawaken (revitalize) itself."

In my opinion Gordon was describing how crazy he felt and acted when he was living with Simone and Danielle. He can only feel close to sane when he removes himself from them (the tree).

On the Rorschach inkblot test, five of the ten cards elicited menacing figures, ready to fight. The themes on the Thematic Apperception Test included how life was more hopeful when he was younger and he was more resilient; how the desire for vengeance and power can erode the natural goodness of a person; how intense his feelings are, and that things have been eating him up for years.

Psychological Projective Testing: Danielle

Danielle had bad dreams about crocodiles (the animal in her father's artwork in his house) and did not like anyone (for example, little boys) to touch her against her wishes.

On the Rorschach cards she saw a man screaming, alligators with their mouths open wide, and a huge butterfly that came into her face. Her associations were to dragonflies, whose two eyes really contain eight million eyes. Although she referred to her alligators and butterfly as "amazing," she was frightened. But nothing scared her more than the weird person screaming (Rorschach card II). This man must personify her father: "Person who's screaming (laughs). He has a beard—red beard and then he continues to be black and his eyes look like socks for some reason and up here looks like beaver teeth."

Interview with Danielle

It became clear in the interview that Danielle, and no one else, was making her own decision about when she did not want to see her father. This was usually after he had treated her in a way she did not like. She needed to back off from him in order to regain positive feelings about him. When she did not see him for a while, she started to miss him, and the danger here was that she began to idealize him. Although this process allowed her to see him again, she set herself up for great disappointment. She believed that he would have changed during the time she had not seen him. In reality, he could upset her again in the same ways. She wanted to believe that, as she got older and she could talk more directly with him, things between them would get better. What she does not yet understand is that she is quiet for good reason. She does not yet understand that if she upsets him, he may have a psychotic episode.

She preferred to visit her father outside of his house because when they were outside, he seemed to be in better control. Danielle said he stayed awake outside, but fell asleep at home. She described how her father had involved her in his artwork. When I asked her about the spider's web above her father's bed she told me that he had told her to have her mother braid her hair so that he could take a picture of a little girl afraid. Here, Danielle was being used by her father for his own purposes. He wanted her to model as a frightened child. These projects may have been attempts to master his own early fears and anxieties. Danielle drew a picture of a girl, her braids standing straight up out of fear, next to a spider in its web. By spontaneously positioning the frightened girl next to the spider in its web,

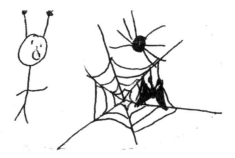

Danielle indicated her fears of the spider in her father's bedroom and of his involvement of her in his aggression tinged projects.

Concluding Remarks about Danielle and Gordon

The next task was to explain my recommendations to the court. These recommendations were based upon data from multiple sources, tapping different levels of awareness, and derived from a psychoanalytic understanding of the psyche. I explained to the court why Danielle could not tolerate visits with her father. The discovery of her father's psychosis would not have been made without the projective psychological testing. The opportunity to draw a tree and create a story, the projection onto the outside of what exists in Gordon's internal world, allowed for this discovery. The projective testing of Danielle, particularly the Rorschach, as well as the opportunity to draw a picture of a frightened girl standing near a spider in its web (after my observation of this in the father's bedroom during the home visit), brought all the pieces of the mystery about time with Gordon into focus.

It became clear from his drawing of and story about the tree, and from her specific requests for time with her father, that both Danielle and her father on some level understood that their relationship suffered when they were together for long periods and was enhanced when they were together for short periods, in public places where he functioned best. Furthermore, breaks, even of long duration, between visits facilitated the restoration of positive feelings. Forensic findings after the divorce did not support the father's self-perception that he would feel better in time.

Thus, specific recommendations for father–daughter visitation were for two afternoons (12 noon until 6 P.M.), Saturday and Sunday, every other weekend. It was recommended that during these afternoons they visit museums, libraries, and other public places that would serve to provide external structure to their time together. Mother agreed to be home in case Danielle felt the need to return there before 6 P.M. (owing to Father's psychic disorganization). Overnight visits were not recommended then or in the future, since Father's mental state was progressively deteriorating.

Summary

In a family forensic evaluation, there is an assessment of the developmental evolution of each family member, with an attempt to understand how each person functioned before the upheaval of the separation and divorce. It is important to try to ascertain this baseline for everyone, in order to be able to assess how much of the family picture at the moment of the evaluation is characteristic of the family's functioning, how much is responsive to the disturbance caused by divorce, and how much of what we see is reaction to the divorce as trauma or, in some cases, as relief. By studying interactions between children and their parents, we get a glimpse into the family tapestry up to this moment in time (see chapters 4 and 16). This kind of understanding of each family member and of the family takes time, and thus, the process of the forensic evaluation has its own developmental evolution. This corresponds to a developmental evolution within the forensic expert. That is, the formulations of the expert regarding each family member and the family as a unit can change as new data lead potentially to a reorganization of previously collected data.

Finally, the family has to separate from the forensic expert, and the forensic expert has to separate from the family (see Interlude I). The forensic expert process is intense for both the family and the forensic expert. Often the expert lives, eats, breathes, and sleeps thinking about the family and is often preoccupied with the family and the challenge of figuring out recommendations for the court. The family can experience this preoccupation as well, because the forensic evaluation is a major, if not *the* major, life event while it is conducted. To move from a state of preoccupation to letting go and separating without the experience of abandonment either by the family of the expert, or by the expert of the family, is a developmental process.

The forensic expert has a personal responsibility to the family when writing the final report for the court. Although in some courts parents are not permitted to have copies of the report (nor are lawyers), in others the parents receive their own copies. The report can often be interpreted as a report card for the parent. Remarks made by the forensic expert may be construed as critical of the parent and critical of the parent's parenting ability. The parent may read and reread the report. The report can either be helpful in facilitating the family's progression into the postdivorce stage or it can keep the parent fixed in time, that is, in the divorcing phase.

The court has asked for more developmental information from the forensic expert (see chapter 1). I believe the court is asking for psychoanalytic developmental information; that is, information not only on whether the child matches his peers in terms of developmental milestones, but also for information about the child's inner life. With more complete information from various levels of the child's inner life, the court can feel more confident in its decision regarding custody and visitation. It is the responsibility of the forensic expert to present her psychoanalytically derived and informed findings with clarity and precision, so that they can be understood by and useful to both the lawyers and the court.

Once the court digests the psychoanalytic developmental information it has been offered, it may be challenged by the fact that, often, we cannot achieve good external solutions for internal problems, whether this be for a child, a parent, a child–parent relationship, or for the entire family. Sometimes, a referral for psychotherapy (see chapters 24–27) and reevaluation at a later date may make more sense than a change in custody or a decision about visitation. Although this may require a longer Court involvement with the family, it may indeed be a wiser course of action, since a premature and potentially wrong decision would affect family life for many years to come. In essence, the court would also participate in a developmental evolution in its thinking about each family.

REFERENCES

Anastasi, A. & Urbina, S. (1997), *Psychological Testing*. Englewood Cliffs, NJ: Prentice-Hall.

Colarusso C. & Nemiroff, R. (1981), *Adult Development*. New York: Plenum Press.

Erikson, E. (1950), *Childhood and Society*. New York, NY: Norton.

Flavell, J. (1977), *Cognitive Development*. Englewood Cliffs, NJ: Prentice-Hall.

Fraiberg, S., Adelson, E. & Shapiro, V. (1987), Ghosts in the nursery: A psychoanalytic approach to the problems of impaired infant–mother relationships. In: *Selected Writings of Selma Fraiberg*, ed. L. Fraiberg. Columbus, OH: Ohio State University Press, pp. 100–131.

Freud, A. (1965), *Normality and Pathology in Childhood, Vol. 6: The Writings of Anna Freud*. New York: International Universities Press.

Freud, S. (1900), The interpretation of dreams. *Standard Edition*, 4 & 5. London: Hogarth Press, 1953.

—— (1905), Three essays on the theory of sexuality. *Standard Edition*, 7:31–122. London: Hogarth Press, 1953.

—— (1913), Totem and taboo. *Standard Edition*, 13:1–161. London: Hogarth Press, 1955.

—— (1915), Repression. *Standard Edition*, 14:141–159. London: Hogarth Press, 1957.

Furman, R. & Furman, E. (1984), Intermittent decathexis: A type of parental dysfunction. *Internat. J. Psychoanal.*, 65:423–434.

Giovacchini, P. (1982), *A Clinician's Guide to Reading Freud*. New York: Aronson.

Goldstein, J., Solnit, A., Goldstein, S. & Freud, A. (1996), *The Best Interests of the Child*. New York: Free Press.

Katan, A. (1981), Discussion of "Intermittent decathexis: A type of parental dysfunction" by R. Furman & E. Furman. Scientific Meeting of the Cleveland Psychoanalytic Society, November 20.

Lifson, (2000), *K.T. v C.S. NY Law J.*, July 6.

Mahler, M., Pine, F. & Bergman, A. (1975), *The Psychological Birth of the Human Infant*. New York: Basic Books.

Mayes, L. & Cohen, D. (1996), Anna Freud and developmental psychoanalytic psychology. *The Psychoanalytic Study of the Child*, 51:117–141. New Haven, CT: Yale University Press.

Murray, H. (1943), *Thematic Apperception Test Manual*. Cambridge, MA: Harvard University.

Piaget, J. (1958), Equilibration processes in the psychobiological development of the child. In: *The Essential Piaget*, ed. H. Gruber & J. Voneche. New York: Basic Books, 1977, pp. 832–841.

Stumbo, B. (1993), *Until the Twelfth of Never*. New York: Pocket Books.

Tessman, L. (1975), *Children of Parting Parents*. New York: Jason Aronson.

Tyson, P. & Tyson, R. (1990), *Psychoanalytic Theories of Development*. New Haven, CT: Yale University Press.

Wallerstein, J. (1997), Transference and countertransference in clinical inter-
ventions with divorcing families. In: *Countertransference in Couples Therapy,*
ed. M. Solomon & J. Siegel. New York: Norton, pp. 113–124.
—— & Blakeslee, S. (1989), *Second Chances.* New York: Ticknor & Fields.
—— & Corbin, S. (1999), The child and the vicissitudes of divorce. In: *The
Scientific Basis of Child Custody Decisions,* ed. R. Galatzer-Levy and L. Kraus.
New York: Wiley, pp. 73–95.
—— & Resnikoff, D. (1997), Parental divorce and developmental progression:
An inquiry into their relationship. *Internat. J. Psychoanal.,* 78:135–154.
Weiner, I. (1997), Current status of the Rorschach inkblot method. *J. Personal.
Assess.,* 68:5–19.

Chapter 16

Empirically Assisted Assessment of Family Systems

BARRY BRICKLIN
GAIL ELLIOT

A CUSTODY PLAN IN THE BEST INTERESTS OF THE CHILD

A child custody plan "in the best interests of the child" makes available to the child the most powerful array of skills and resources each parent is capable of offering, optimizing the child's ability to: (1) feel safe in the world; (2) develop effective and comfortable interpersonal skills, and (3) master gradually unfolding age-appropriate developmental tasks and other skills of competency. The plan may have to be implemented in the midst of significant levels of interparental conflict. Traditional approaches to creating such plans based on standard clinical methods and/or the findings of postdivorce research frequently omit the most important data needed: those that reveal the degree to which a specific parent's interpersonal responses lead to emotionally comfortable and effective behaviors for a particular child within various family systems. As the context or system within which a child and caretaker interact changes—for example, the child alone with each, with both together, within other actual (or psychologically internal) family groupings—the value of each parent to a child can shift, sometimes radically. For example, a parent who has little value for a child as a day-to-day manager of daily routines may have great value as the more ardent proponent of postdivorce family unity (Bricklin and Elliot, 2002a, b). An empirically assisted way to detect unique systemic values will be offered.

Since the plan will be used most frequently within our legal system, it must address the choice of a legal custodian, and the choice of a time-share plan (see chapter 15). From a legal perspective, whatever else the plan depends on as assessment targets, it must consider those based on the statutory guidelines and case law of the state of legal jurisdiction. The legal custodian refers to the parent who has the right and responsibility to make critical decisions for a child (for example, educational and nonemergency medical) often in spite of objections by the other parent. Legal custody may be awarded to both parents jointly, to one parent only, or to neither parent. The time-share plan, also called physical custody, refers to the manner in which the child's time is divided between the parental homes.

There are four main custody dispositions. (1) Sole custody means one parent retains both physical and legal custody of the child. (2) In a joint custody arrangement, the parents may share both legal and physical custody, or one parent may be the primary physical custodian while both parents share legal custody. When parents share physical custody they do not necessarily share a fifty-fifty time-share plan. An equal distribution of time is rare. (3) Under a divided or alternating custody plan, each parent retains physical and legal control when he or she has physical custody of the child. This is a plan normally employed when a child alternates between the parents but within longer blocks of time, for example, up to as much as a year with each parent. (4) Split custody means the splitting up of siblings. Each parent has sole custody of one or more of the children, while the other parent has sole custody of the remaining sibling(s). Each disposition allows for a time-share plan in regard to the noncustodial parent.

In our judgment, the time-share plan should take into account how well each parent's range of behavioral styles lead to comfortable and effective behaviors on the part of the child. At present, judges around the country (in our experience) are showing a trend toward recommending joint legal custody unless there are blatant reasons not to. The reasoning seems to be that this will keep both parents involved in a child's life without imposing any particular time-share plan on either the child or the parent. Shared legal custody is *not* warranted under three sets of conditions: (1) if a parent suffers serious impairments in judgment regarding the child; (2) if the parents can never agree; and (3) if logistical considerations rule out sufficient parental contact.

A Comprehensive Model Using Family Systems Data

The evaluation must be comprehensive and address not only what parents know and do, but the impact of this knowledge and behavior on each specific child. The comprehensive nature of the assessment is illustrated in ACCESS: *A Comprehensive Custody Evaluation Standard System* (Bricklin and Elliot, 1995). Since the parents should know ahead of time what is involved, a detailed contract should be read and signed by the major parties and their attorneys. Interview forms are provided for parents, children, stepparents, live-in companions, grandparents, pediatricians, psychotherapists, educators, and neighbors. Observation formats *that utilize statistically generated nonverbal behaviors as scoring categories* discern not just what parents do, but the *impact* of parental behaviors on the children. Our protocol and normative data are presented later.

Our system combines quantified (formal) procedures and an informal model. While not data-based, semiformal models have many advantages. They guarantee that somewhere in one's assessment similar data will be gathered from each main participant. Without this, meaningful comparisons are difficult if not impossible to make. Free-form interviews, for example, do *not* allow meaningful comparisons. This model guarantees that an evaluator will assess every area deemed pertinent in legal and psychological writings and not unwittingly (or subjectively) fail to consider relevant information. And because these pertinent areas are articulated, they can be challenged as well as continually fine-tuned. Information about parenting knowledge and skills is gathered. The Parent Awareness Skills Survey (PASS), a series of questions asking how a parent would handle critical childhood situations, reflects a parent's awareness of optimum child care strategies. The Parent Perception of Child Profile (PPCP) and the Assessment of Parenting Skills: Infant and Preschooler (APSIP) reveal the degree to which a parent is attuned to the developmental and unique needs of a particular child. These tools ask about the range, depth, and specificity of the information each parent has about the child's daily routine, interpersonal relations, health, developmental history, school issues, fears, personal hygiene, communication style, and disciplinary matters. *The Bricklin-Elliot Home Visit Booklet* guides home studies, including the investigation of complex topics like relocation.

A *Critical Targets* form organizes ACCESS information in about

40 custody-relevant areas formulated from a review of state statutory guidelines, case law, and the opinions of experts. An *Aggregation Booklet* presents a formal and informal model to assist the mental health professional to prioritize the gathered information. Should an evaluator suggest a primary custodial parent (called the placement parent in some states), it is essential to *distinguish between issues relevant to selecting a legal custodian and those germane to the time-share arrangement*. The BPS and PORT, described later, are most relevant to the time-share arrangement. Other parts of ACCESS address the former issue.

At the heart of ACCESS is the core concept later developed in the Uniform Marriage and Divorce Act, section 203 (1979), which directs that a decision-maker should evaluate parenting factors that directly and possibly indirectly have impact on the child. It is clear that (except at extreme ends of a continuum) "parental competence," as a concept, cannot be applied to any single individual, that is, "parental competence" does not "reside" in a parent. *Parental competence can only be understood as the property of a specific system.* For example, an abrupt, perfunctory style on the part of a father may greatly bother one child and hardly be noticed by another. The former child assigns meanings such as "I guess Dad doesn't have much time for me" to such utterances, while the latter child does not. In fact, if the latter child has information-processing strategies that work well only with short rather than lengthy communications, the child would actually prefer such communications. To this child, brevity constitutes either a useful cost/benefit ratio for utterances seen as a bit short on positive affect, or, at some deeper level, this child may even symbolize such behavior as a deep respect for the child's ability to fill in the "gaps" on his or her own.

The *Perception-of-Relationships Test* (PORT) and *Bricklin Perceptual Scales* (BPS) aim to provide data-based assistance in understanding the impacts different caretakers have on a child in selected family systems (Bricklin, 1984, 1989, 1992, 1997, 1998, 1999, 2002; Bricklin and Elliot, 2001, 2002a, b; Bricklin and Halbert, 2004a, b). Their theoretical bases derive from systems concepts. A system must have two or more elements and each element must have an effect on the *whole* system. The elements (and their effects) are not only interdependent but, however subgroups form, none can have an independent effect on the system as a whole. Within this definition of a system, one cannot affect a system of which one is part and then not oneself be impacted by this effect (Ackoff, 1999, pp. 15-17). Most people are more used to mechanistic than systems models. The former approaches understanding and/or prediction via a deconstruction process, in which the elements are analyzed one by one, after which their interactions with other elements are analyzed. With systems, synthesis precedes analysis. This is why mechanistic models are more concerned with structures and systems analyses with functions, the former with "knowledge," the latter with "explanation." Systems complexities affect both validational issues (some predictions will be true only in limited contexts), and the choice of one's measurement reference standard, as well as measurement units. The units must be adequate for a test's aims. A reference standard is the entity to which a measurement score is compared in order to derive relevance for a specific decision. The reference standard is a previously examined group (normative paradigm), a previously examined individual (the single-participant paradigm), or it may be criterion-referenced (arbitrary). It is not always clear what the reference standard should be, especially in the postdivorce world—a nightmare of shifting allegiances within a framework in which the child may have only two main choices. To the extent that mental health professionals think of systems at all, they think of models in which stable traits interact. This manner of thinking is evident in the way they write their evaluations, with sections called "Mr. Jones," "Ms. Jones," child "Mary Jones," child "Sam Jones," as though one can assess each element in a system as a separate entity and then somehow add up the parts. *In systems-based decisions, the elements of the system cannot be evaluated apart from the interactions of those elements within the system.* Further, as systems change, the relevant reference standard can shift. In a child custody context, the way Child 1 assigns value to his or her parents is not always meaningfully comparable to the way Child 2 or 3 would assign value either to his or her own parents or to the parents of Child 1. Except perhaps at extremes, knowing how a parent compares to other parents tells little about the unique and specific value a parent has to a particular child. To measure an individual's unique assignment of value, a single-participant reference would be used. However, in other circumstances, including "termination of parental rights" cases (see chapter 14), it might be useful to use a group reference standard (although there is currently no accepted "minimal-parenting" standard). Further, if a decision is to be made based on the extent of the discrepancy between how a given child assigns value to one parent as opposed to the other across a number of life areas and how children in general assign differential value to each parent, a group reference standard could be relevant. Ordinal data can address the issue of how a child assigns value to his or her caretakers in specific life areas, while interval measures are needed to address how a child assigns differential value to his or her parents across multiple life areas. The decision to use an ordinal scale (A>B; B>A; A=B) was deliberate. For one thing, it would be difficult to create a suitable measurement unit—except grossly—by means of which a child could express differential value between A and B in circumscribed areas, especially if the values for each are similar. *More important, the use of an ordinal scale was meant to reduce the influence on a decision-maker of parental value to a child in any single life area.* The ordinal measures are subsequently summed, so that the parent-of-choice suggested by a test is based on an interval scale that reflects a child's assignment of value across multiple life areas, seven with the PORT and 32 with the BPS.

Note also that systems complexities can have profound effects on the choice of validating criteria. The parent from whom a child seeks emotional closeness and/or active help can change dramatically depending on the family subsystems in which the child–parent interactions take place (Bricklin and Elliot, 2002a, b; Bricklin and Halbert, 2004b).

Our data-based tests assess the degree to which child–parent interactions lead to emotionally comfortable and behaviorally competent behavior on the part of the child in various family systems. The PORT generates data relevant to several systems, while the BPS is relevant to dyadic systems. They also seek ways to understand useful cost/benefit ratios. An anxious child may need that parent who can best calm him or her down, even though this parent may be less good at modeling competency, while such a pairing may be a poor one for a secure child. Each test elicits its main information nonverbally, which eliminates both the need for a child to say anything directly negative about a parent and bias resulting from the limited expressive vocabularies of young children.

Clinical data suggest that the impacts reflected in the tests are best explained by the degree of congruence in symbol systems and information processing strategies between communicators (Bricklin, 1995, pp. 54–73). Symbol systems refer to the manner in which people assign meaning to their worlds. Information processing strategies refer to the manner in which a parent communicates to a child in ways that are compatible with that child's way of taking in, storing, retrieving and using information. We believe such data can be helpful in custody-decision making, although by no means considered a full assessment of a child's "best interest." Existing and new data on 3888 cases will be given later, including future as well as concurrent validity numbers. We will describe our validity procedures in more detail than was done before, since it is only here that a decision-maker can discern whether the data are relevant to a specific decision. The tests have previously been used only with a single-participant reference paradigm: a person's scores are compared to other of his or her own scores. New research (Bricklin, 2002) has added the use of a group reference paradigm: a person's scores are compared to those established with experimental groups. A group reference allows us to see the degree to which a caretaker's parenting skills, as reflected in PORT data, compare to standards created by group norms. An evaluator can detect when one or both of the parents are creating signs in the child's PORT that are characteristic of groups known to manifest poor parenting skills. It is helpful to use both reference paradigms. Since the theoretical basis of this research stems from systems thinking, the information yielded would be compatible with any approach that recognizes the importance of context in understanding behavior. A main systems tenet is that, unless predictive tools can pinpoint the system or context in which predicted behaviors are likely to be manifested, they will most likely fail or be so vague as to be of little use in specific cases.

How Do Observations Contribute?

Early in our research, we had begun to formulate the systems concepts at the core of our approach. We could see how a given parent's range of behaviors might be positive for one child and negative for another. This led us to search for the observational cues that would help understand not what a given parent *intended* to achieve when interacting with a child, but rather what actually *was achieved*. Forty years of research has convinced us that spontaneous nonverbal behaviors, often quickly occurring, yield more accurate data about an individual's gut feelings than do more consciously controlled verbal data. How we operationalized this is described later. A very obvious challenge in using observational data involves determining whether what is being observed is really typical of the observed person. We concluded that observations in one setting were not necessarily generalizable to others. Another pitfall is that too many assessors choose only to observe each parent alone with each child. We believe, with Gardner (1998), that whatever momentary discomfort the child may suffer by being with both parents simultaneously is worth it, since it is essential that the evaluator observe what happens when the child, seeking either information, guidance, solace or support, can directly select which of the two parents is the more desirable choice. Further, a child's behavior with both parents simultaneously needs to be compared with what occurs when the child is alone with each. A child who is uncomfortable with parent A when B is present but is comfortable when alone with A may be the only non-test clue available that, among other things, the child fears allowing B to view his affections toward A, suggesting the possibility of alienation (see chapter 9), intimidation, or attempts to save an impaired parent. Since our observation protocol was critical to validation studies, it is described in more detail later, along with normative statistical information.

Assessing Parental Behavior Directly

Our comprehensive system (Bricklin and Elliot, 1995) includes parental skill categories such as the following: A parent's ability to model the skills of competency and generate feelings of warmth and safety, a parent's insistence about consistency and follow-through, a parent's ability to model admirable traits, such as honesty and altruism, and a parent's knowledge of a child's daily routine, interpersonal relations, health and developmental needs, educational strengths and weaknesses, fears, personal hygiene, and communication styles.

We can illustrate this by describing a father who is theoretically "ideal" in parental attunement. "He offers information to his daughter in amounts she can readily assimilate and use. He knows the importance of choosing the right words, not just from a developmental perspective, but also from a perspective that recognizes the deeper emotional meanings the child assigns to them. He is careful with his facial expressions and tones of voice. He knows the specific importance to this child of letting her have a say prior to offering her information. He takes into account her physical and mental state before interacting with her. He realizes how she feels in stressful and frustrating situations. He takes into account her unique past history before responding to her. He pays attention to her use of proffered information so that he can fine-tune his responses."

Interview Data in Custody Evaluations
Since it is obviously impossible to conduct a comprehensive evaluation without using interviews, one must find ways to reduce their pitfalls. We explain our use of interviews to parents in the following ways:

"We will listen carefully to your concerns. We will address each and every one of them in our report. But we want you to know that the heart of our report will be based upon a search for every strength each of you can make available to each child. We will primarily look for these strengths in our data-based tests, in our observations, and in our parenting skills inventories."

The hidden message is this: If you want to do well in this evaluation, we want you to spend far more time wondering how to be a better parent and far less time regaling us with a list of the other parent's shortcomings. We also advise each parent that while we can assess interview "facts" reported to us for relevance, there is often no way we can check them for credibility and accuracy. Therefore, most interview-based data will simply be listed in our report as "information reported by so and so." An important part of the data base is compiled by asking each parent the exact same sets of questions. From a scientific point of view, free-form interviews are much less useful. We also seek sense-based, not conclusionary, information ("What did you see and hear?" not "What do you believe to be true?").

The Role of Traditional Tests
Most psychologists use the MMPI-2, the MCMI II/III, the Rorschach, an intelligence test, and the Thematic Apperception Test (Ackerman and Ackerman, 1997) when evaluating adults. However, there are no clear relationships between the diagnostic categories typically yielded by these tests and the impacts of the parental behaviors associated with these categories *on specific children*. Further, there is no good way to recognize helpful versus nonhelpful cost/benefit ratios. A highly organized but mildly depressed parent may constitute a good match for a child who needs a highly organized parent, and a mismatch for a child who is already highly organized and more importantly would profit from exposure to positive and vital affective patterns.

While we always use traditional tests in custody evaluations, we do so mainly to red-flag serious psychopathology and/or to generate hypotheses about information derived from other sources. We rarely use them to make first-level inferences about parenting skills. Should one choose to use traditional test data in a more direct fashion, they need to be combined with other data so as to be able to address impact-on-the-child issues (see chapter 15).

CASE EXAMPLE: ACCESS IN USE

Father was 38 years of age, Mother 37, the two children, a girl and a boy, ten and eight years old, respectively. Each parent sought sole legal and physical custody of the children. While Father was a responsible, highly paid professional, Mother said that around the home he was inattentive, "laissez-faire with the children," and "only worries about whether everyone's having a good time." She complained that when the children needed discipline, he either ignored them or yelled at them. Father described Mother as socially isolated, "way too serious and uptight," and demeaning toward him. Mother was also a working professional.

The daughter, aged ten, did well in school and was obviously bright and quite social. The boy, aged eight, was described as being similar to "ADHD children," although no one thought the symptoms rose to a level that would warrant formal diagnosis. He was more restless and inattentive than his sister, although he performed satisfactorily in school. Collateral-source interview data yielded the usually encountered pattern: Mother's informants gave her rave reviews and Father poor reviews, while his informants did the opposite.

The Parent Awareness Skills Survey (PASS), which reflects how each parent deals with typical childcare situations, showed Mother to be superior to Father in every measured category (awareness of critical issues, adequacy of solutions, empathy, clarity of communications, attention to the child's unique qualities and to feed-back data needed to fine-tune an offered response). Additionally, Father demonstrated a rather clipped, overly authoritarian tone.

The Parent Perception of Child Profile (PPCP) demonstrated the sine qua non of the "attuned parent" for Mother and the reverse for Father: she recognized all the things that made the daughter and son very different from one another and he recognized hardly any. If we had been conducting a typical custody evaluation and stopped our evaluation at this point, Mother would be seen as superior to Father in just about all areas. While we still would have suggested shared legal custody, we would have recommended a time-share plan heavily or almost exclusively weighted in Mother's favor.

But the BPS and PORT (and observational data) yielded some interesting findings. While Mother was the overall parent-of-choice for both children, the daughter's responses showed a fairly close range of scores between Mother and Father items. The boy's scores did not show this pattern. His scores indicated that Mother's behaviors were having a much more positive impact on him in almost all areas than were Father's. In other words, the daughter could deal emotionally, socially, and scholastically with Father's autocratic, clipped, unattuned style, while the boy, who really required the attentions of an organized, diligent, hands-on, firm parent, fared poorly with him. Further, the PORT showed that *both* children valued and appreciated Father's greater range of social contacts and greater interest in extended family.

With this key information, we were able to recommend a much more flexible time-share plan for the children, particularly the daughter, than would have been indicated *without* the system-specific data— that is, a plan based only on how the father compared with normative data from other parents rather than with system-specific data. We were able to obtain yearly follow-up data on this case. In spite of repeated therapeutic attempts to upgrade the father–son relationship, it remains, almost by mutual agreement, distant. Mother, who is definitely no champion of Father, reports that the daughter still looks forward to her increased visits with Father and seems to enjoy and profit from them.

CRITICAL COMMENTARY

Several important issues have been raised about the methodologies described here (Krauss and Sales, 2000; Otto, Edens, and Barcus, 2000). New data, not available when these issues were raised, address some, but not all of them. A few of the negative criticisms are impossible to address briefly, since they deal with complex epistemologic issues involving: measurement *theory* (for example, when ordinal scales are scientifically adequate for a predictive purpose and when interval scales are needed), measurement *relevance* (expanded clarification of reference standard controversies), what a test actually measures (what it consistently predicts and a complete description of how this is determined), detailed descriptions of one's predictor and criterion concepts, especially the empirical equivalents of the concepts, the totally value-driven choices of what in the world of sensory experience exemplifies a concept, (Bricklin and Bricklin, 1999) and the value of measurement data to a decision-maker. This involves knowledge of how the decision-maker will use new information, what is already believed about the area of concern, the strength of these beliefs, what other information is currently available, the probability that certain choices will be made with and without the new information, the time-urgency of the needed decision, and the risk level of making less than an optimum choice (Bricklin and Halbert, 2004a, b). Psychometric data are needed but not sufficient for such an assessment. For example, tools with low (but known) accuracy rates may have considerable value in certain situations. When critics of a test have a dispute, they may all be right, since they could be making different assumptions about the listed areas. Collectively, what is required is a highly explicated chain of the reasoning that links evidence to conclusions. Hence, we will summarize our data with a more fully explicated chain. Before reporting statistical data, we will spell out the major validational procedures. PORT and BPS estimations for a parent-of-choice (POC) were compared to many independent validating criteria.

These criteria focused on the degree to which child-caretaker interactions lead to a child's emotionally comfortable and behaviorally competent behavior in a wide variety of settings. How these concepts were operationalized is spelled out in Bricklin and Elliot (2002 a, b) and Bricklin and Halbert (2004a, b). A brief description is given below. Having knowledge of validating procedures is the main way a decision-maker can determine whether a test's data reflect the area of concern. Please note the variety of sources of criterion data and the use of a quantified normative protocol with certain samples.

The original and much of the subsequent validity research with the PORT compared PORT estimations of the particular parent with whom a child more comfortably and efficiently shared information than with the other to estimations derived from extensive observations, often over several years. In all instances, these observations were made by mental health professionals on the bases of criteria independent of PORT scores. The original observation protocol is (briefly) summarized.

Emphasis was on (mainly nonverbal) ways a child demonstrated comfort and effectiveness during or immediately subsequent to interactions with each caretaker. These interactions took place in spontaneous, structured, and instructional contexts. The basic dimensions were a child's movements: toward (positive); against (aggressive); away from (fearful) (Bricklin and Halbert, 2004a, b). Research interest was on what impact parental behavior had on a child, not primarily on what parents knew or did. At the outset of our research we tracked positive *and* negative reactions. Our research goals were adequately achieved if we counted only positive reactions. This is a practical "plus," since fewer raters are needed. The following categories apply when the child is speaking (initiating or responding), listening, or listening and acting: smooth breathing patterns; body movements nonhurried; relaxed and/or smiling facial muscles (no grimaces, contortions, etc.); leans toward other person; maintains reasonable eye contact (evaluators were taught to distinguish fearful eye contact from relaxed eye contact—the former is motivated by the child's fear of saying or doing something the parent would object to); moves closer to or initiates physical contact; willing to be hugged; few signs of restlessness (even if a child is ADHD-like, one parent usually has a more calming influence than the other). Categories used when the child is speaking, initiating, or responding: willing to express annoyance, doubts, or confusion (*not* trying to be the perfect little child); pauses without fear of losing caretaker's attention; willing to ask questions; noting from whom the child most frequently and spontaneously seeks help. Categories used when the child is listening or listening and acting: accepts limits in comfortable manner; muscularly comfortable with failures (no agitated moves); focused attention; facial expression animated and interested; no evidence of leaping-to-action before waiting for the entire "sent message" to be received; open and ready to receive information; willing to explore and take chances; willing to try novel approaches. More statistical data on the observation protocol is given in Bricklin and Halbert (2004a, b). Briefly, in two samples ($n = 60$; $n = 37$), the ages, ethnicity, and SESs were directly similar to the norms given elsewhere in this paper. In each sample, a child was observed with both parents present, so he or she could make choices about interactions.

In a one-hour session, the distribution of positive scores ranged from 0 to 12. The mean number of positive reactions was 7.4; the Standard Deviation was 1.2. Six to nine positive reactions characterized 70 percent of the cases. A point difference greater than two represents a significant difference between two caretakers. These results are *not* comparable to protocols that count the number of positive and negative interactions *initiated by parents* (Lahey et al., 1984; Kerig and Lindahl, 2002). Interrater agreement (three raters) was high, 90 percent, partly because the range of categories used was narrow: $A > B$; $B > A$; $A \cong B$; neither A nor B. The actual number of positive interactions noted by each rater achieved an agreement rate of 82 percent.

Mental health professionals who offered validity designations used judgmental categories that reflect the narrow range of choices utilized by our legal system. Decisions are given in two main categories: legal custody (the right and responsibility to make key decisions for a child) and a time-share plan (or physical custody). In the former category, three choices are typically used: sole custody; shared custody; and, very rarely, neither parent should have custody. In our experience, judges currently favor shared legal custody, unless there are very strong reasons to exclude a parent from this role. As for time-share plans, few judges venture beyond two choices: sole custody or joint custody. If the former is chosen, the noncustodial parent is usually given a boilerplate arrangement in which he or she has the child every other weekend, plus an overnight in the middle of those weeks when he or she does not have the child for the weekend. *When complex time-share plans are awarded, they are almost always worked out by the parents and/or their attorneys, not by the data or the judge.* Further, complex plans are usually based on parental-convenience, not best-interest, factors. Judges rarely venture beyond simplistic dispositional categories. This choice range has advantages in a research setting, decreasing hair-spitting arguments about how much better one parent is than the other. In real life, mental health professionals can and do offer complex plans. New research is encouraging complex plans (Kelly and Lamb, 2000) but is currently considered controversial (Solomon and Biringen, 2001). Judges usually ignore these plans unless the two sides agree on their own to implement them.

PORT validity data collected between 1961 and 1997 consisted of 1381 cases. The sources of independent validity designations involved: (1) three observers watching each child and two parents interacting from behind a one-way screen; (2) two psychologists who had access to family therapy notes and consultations with the family therapists over a two- to five-year time span; (3) scores derived from the BPS; and (4) psychologists' findings based on all clinical and life history data available to them, usually gathered over a multimonth period. The average percent of agreement between PORT suggestions for parent-of-choice or POC and those of the independent experts was 88 percent. The agreement rate between courtroom judges and the POCs selected by the PORT was 92 percent, although this is reported as information only and not as validity data, since PORT data may have influenced the judges. PORT validity data collected between 1997 and 2002 involved 127 cases. The independent validity experts were mental health professionals who had had at least eight months of contact with each involved family. They were instructed to use all sources of information including the observational format already described. Future validity was measured by comparing the PORT POCs at Time Point 1 with expert opinion carried out at Time Point 2, eight months later. Future validity was 89 percent agreement. Concurrent validity was estimated by comparing the PORT POC at Time Point 2 with the validity designations made at Time Point 2. This figure was 91 percent. BPS validation from 1964 to 1997 was available for 2279 cases. The same validational sources were used as with the PORT, only here the family therapy data extended from two to seven years (the validity designations were never based on less than two years' worth of data). The agreement rate between the BPS and the criterion experts was 88 percent. The agreement rate for courtroom judges was 93 percent. BPS validity data collected from 1997 to 2002 on 93 cases showed a future validity score of 87 percent and a concurrent validity score of 91 percent.

Test-retest reliability will be given only from the most recent data, since the time span was longer than those previously used. Between 1997 and 2002, on 127 cases, the PORT showed a stability in POC, over an eight-month span, of 97 percent. That is, 97 percent of the POCs remained stable over this time span. However, the test-retest reliability drops sharply as the so-called Task Difference Score approaches 0 or 1 (a 21 percent chance that the POC will shift over an eight-month period). If the TDS is three or more there is a 3 percent chance of shift. With the BPS, if the item difference score is 0, 1, 2, or 3 there is a 19 percent chance the POC will shift over eight months. If the score is 4 or more, there is a 3 percent chance of shift. Three test patterns were identified that, when present, greatly suggest that there will be a shift in POC. It is a scientifically interesting issue as to whether they represent changes in the measured variables or errors of measurement.

PORT normative data gathered from 1961 to 1997 involved 797 women and 784 men. The mean age was 7.76, the SD 0.17. The SES was low to high middle. There were 98 percent Caucasian in this sample and 2 percent all others. On data gathered between 1997 and 2002, there were 61 women and 66 men. The other numbers are all similar, except there were 8 percent non-Caucasian. For the BPS, on 2389 cases between 1964 and 1997, there were 1202 women and 1187 men. The mean age of the BPS sample was 8.94, the SD 2.40. All other data were similar to the PORT. Interrater reliability of PORT scoring was obtained from two samples of seminar attendees ($n = 36$; $n = 41$), in which more than half of the scorers had no prior experience with the PORT. Four different percent-of-agreement scores were obtained: (1) the points scored on Task I (the most complex task); (2) the POC on Task I; (3) the overall TDS score for all seven tasks; (4) the overall POC based on seven tasks. The percent-of-agreement rates, respectively, were: 74; 90; 82; 92. No interrater data for the BPS were gathered, since scoring it is mechanical and requires only the ability to read arabic numbers and to recognize when one is larger than another. It is also assumed that an evaluator can add and subtract numbers between zero and 32.

The next research is the first in which PORT data were used with a group reference (Bricklin, 2002). A consistent relation between PORT signs and the adequacy of parenting was noted from PORTs collected over a 40-year span. Twenty-three hypotheses about them were developed. Following this, from the huge pool of data available, four experimental groups matched in age, income, absence of ADHD signs and age-correct grade placement were formed. Group I ($n = 16$) were children examined for minor reasons, mostly underachievement; none involved the quality of parenting. Group II ($n = 34$) were children whose parents were involved in mild custody disputes, centered on who could provide a better school, neighborhood, or extended family, or that the child had more friends at one place rather than the other. There were no concerns about parenting by either side or the evaluators. Group III ($n = 40$) consisted of children whose parents were involved in continual conflict, characterized by ongoing hostility, often within the courtroom, for two or more years. The involved children, "caught in the middle," were used as "message carriers" to deliver scathing messages from one parent to the other or to involved mental health professionals (Doolittle and Deutsch, 1999, pp. 425–440; Bricklin and Elliot, 2000, p. 501). Parental adequacy sinks to a serious low point when parents become so engaged, and the damage to children, whether from divorced or intact families, is alarmingly high (Hoppe, 1993, 1997; Hoppe and Kenney, 1994, 1995, 1997; Bricklin and Elliot, 1995, pp. 38–40; Bricklin and Elliot, 2000, pp. 501–505). Group IV ($n = 40$) consists of children whose caretakers represented on the PORTs had either been threatened by the court with a possible termination of parental rights or actually had had their parental rights terminated in the past and/ or were accused of substantiated abuse or neglect. In order to match the socioeconomic status of the parents in this group, and to match the intelligence of these children to those in other groups, the majority of these cases were derived from various private practices.

Seventeen of the 23 PORT signs yielded a probability of .05 or less so that the differential occurrences of the PORT signs among the groups could be random. Several caveats are listed to show that the manifestation of one or even several of these signs should be interpreted currently only as red-flags to launch expanded evaluations, since it is not completely clear that the signs are additive, nor is the interdependence among them known.

More information is available at www.DrBarryBricklin.com.

REFERENCES

Ackerman, M. J. & Ackerman, M. C. (1997), Custody evaluation practices: A survey of experienced professionals (revisited). *Profess. Psychol. Res. & Pract.*, 28:137–145.

Ackoff, R. L. (1999), *Ackoff's Best.* New York: Wiley.

Bricklin, B. (1984), *The Bricklin Perceptual Scales.* Furlong, PA: Village Publishing.

—— (1989), *The Perception-of-Relationships Test.* Furlong, PA: Village Publishing.

—— (1992), Data based tests in custody evaluations. *Amer. J. Family Ther.*, 20:254–265.

—— (1995), *The Custody Evaluation Handbook.* New York: Brunner/Mazel.

—— (1997), *Test Manuals Supplement Update.* Furlong, PA: Village Publishing.

—— (1998), Sequence of steps and critical assessment targets of a comprehensive custody evaluation. In: *Psychologists' Desk Reference*, ed. G. P. Koocher and J. C. Norcross & S. S. Hill III. New York: Oxford University Press, pp. 499–502.

—— (1999), The contribution of psychological tests to custody-relevant evaluations. In: *The Scientific Basis of Child Custody Decisions*, ed. R. M. Galatzer-Levy & L. Kraus. New York: Wiley, pp. 120–156.

—— (2002), *The Frequency of Appearance of Twenty-Three PORT Signs Among Four Groups Representing Different Degrees of Parental Competence*. Furlong, PA: Village Publishing.

—— & Bricklin, P. M. (1999), Custody data as decision-theory information: Evaluating a psychological contribution by its value to a decision-maker. *Clin. Psychol. Sci. & Pract.*, 6:339–343.

—— & Elliot, G. (1995), *ACCESS: A Comprehensive Custody Evaluation Standard System*. Furlong, PA: Village Publishing.

—— & —— (1997), *Test Manuals Supplement*. Furlong, PA: Village Publishing.

—— & —— (2000), Qualifications of and techniques to be used by judges, attorneys and mental health professionals who deal with children in high conflict divorce cases. *Univ. Arkansas Little Rock Law Rev.*, 122:501–528.

—— & —— (2001), *The BPS and PORT*. Furlong, PA: Village Publishing. *www.VillagePublishing*.Homepage.com.

—— & —— (2002a), What can empirical data on 4,500 child custody cases tell us? Presented at the American College of Forensic Psychology, San Francisco, CA, April.

—— & —— (2002b), *The Perception-of-Relationships Test (PORT) and Bricklin Perceptual Scales (BPS)*. Furlong, PA: Village Publishing.

—— & —— (in press), The BPS and PORT: Test-retest data on 127 cases. *Test Manuals Supplement*.

—— & Halbert, M. (2004a), Can child custody data be generated scientifically? *Amer. J. Family Therapy*, 32:119–138.

—— & —— (2004b), Perception-of-Relationships Test and Bricklin Perceptual Scales: Validity and Reliability. *Amer. J. Family Therapy*, 32:189–203.

Gardner, R. A. (1998), *The Parental Alienation Syndrome*. Cresskill, NJ: Creative Therapeutics.

Hoppe, C. F. (1993), Test characteristics of custody-visitation litigants: A data-based description of relationship disorders. In: Empirical approaches to child custody determination, S. Podrygula (Chair). Symposium conducted at the meeting of the American Psychological Association, Toronto, Ontario, Canada, August.

—— (1997), Perpetually battling parents. In: *The Handbook of Infant/Child and Adolescent Psychotherapy, Vol. 2*, ed. B. Mark & J. Incoravia. Northvale, NJ: Aronson, pp. 485–501.

—— & Kenney, L. (1994), Characteristics of custody litigants: Data from the southern California group. Presented at the meeting of the Psychological Association, Los Angeles, CA, August.

—— & —— (1995), MMPI-2 and Rorschach profiles of custody litigants: An intercorrelational study. Presented at the meeting of the American Psychological Association, New York, NY, August.

—— & —— (1997), Therapeutic intervention in high conflict divorce: Countertransference and the horrible decision. Presented at the meeting of the American Psychological Association, Chicago, IL, August.

Kelly, J. B. & Lamb, M. E. (2000), Using child development research to make appropriate custody and access decisions for young children. *Family & Conciliation Courts Rev.*, 38:297–311.

Kerig, P. K. & Lindahl, K. M., eds. (2001), *Family Observational Coding Systems*. Mahwah, NJ: Lawrence Erlbaum Associates.

Krauss, D. A. & Sales, B. D. (2000), Legal standards, expertise and experts in the resolution of contested child custody cases. *Psychol., Public Policy & Law*, 6:843–879.

Lahey, B. B., Conger, R. D., Atkeson, B. M. & Trieber, F. A. (1984), Parenting behavior and emotional status of physically abusive mothers. *J. Consult. & Clin. Psychol.*, 52:1062–1071.

Otto, R. K., Edens, J. F. & Barcus, E. (2002), Use of psychological testing in child custody evaluations. *Family & Conciliation Courts Rev.*, 38:312–340.

Solomon, J. & Biringen, Z. (2001), Another look at the developmental research: Commentary on Kelly and Lamb's "Using child development research to make appropriate custody and access decision for young children." *Family & Conciliation Courts Rev.*, 39:355–364.

Uniform Marriage and Divorce Act (1979), *Uniform Laws Annotated*.

Chapter 17

Parents' Sensitivity to the Child's Creative and Spiritual Core

An Overlooked Consideration in Child Custody Determinations

ELAINE SCHWAGER

*I*n attempts to apply the standard of the "best interests of the child" (see chapters 1, 4, 5, 10–12, 15, and 16), some states have developed guidelines for determining which parent in a custody suit has the greater capacity to meet the needs of the child. These guidelines focus on parental ability to meet the child's physical, emotional, and financial needs and to provide for safety, continuity, and stability in the home life. But "best interests of the child" often falls short of seeing the child, at his or her core, as a spiritual and creative being who, from the start, actively participates in creating meaning and goals for his or her life. Consequently, it does not consider parental capacity to nurture this aspect of the child.

DEFINING THE SPIRITUAL AND CREATIVE ASPECT OF THE CHILD

The spiritual nature of the child is composed of *desire*, related to talents and inner disposition, what the child is inclined to and develops passion for; *creativity*, the innate capacity to express and find ways to fulfill this desire or talent in ways unique to him or her; *faith*, the trust that he or she can uncover the truths and insights within that will further growth and development of innate potential; and *freedom*, the space and unimpeded emotional environment to continually transcend his or her own level of development and move on to more integrated and mature ones, as well as to constructively challenge the social and interpersonal levels of integration and values in the environment. These aspects of the child coexist with needs for physical survival and comfort, sexual needs, cognitive needs, and interpersonal needs and will guide and deepen the level of fulfillment of these other needs in accordance with the depth and direction of spiritual and creative development the child has achieved. Psychoanalysts, including Balint (1968), Winnicott (1971), Shengold (1989), Miller (1981, 1984), and Coles (1990) have expanded awareness of children's needs to include play, creativity, being alone, validation of their perceptions and individual sensibility, initiative, meaningfulness, explorations about God or the nature and value of life.

The spiritual in the child reaches for understanding of life beyond "the given" and established, and seeks to be a participant in life's creative evolution. This may or may not involve a belief in a supreme being or theistic force or come out of, or gravitate toward any organized religion. Many children make use of existing religion, myths, stories, and morality to grope toward their own spirituality, but others start from scratch and invent their own stories, enactments, and characters to represent how their mind and soul are struggling with the deepest questions and concerns within them. As Coles (1990) states, "Children try to understand not only what is happening to them, but why; and in doing that, they call upon the religious life they have experienced, the spiritual values they have received" (p. 100). However, if organized religion is too condemning of certain aspects of a child's experiences or behaviors or too demanding of conformity to existent dogma, it can be a threat to the development of the child's spiritual life.

Children's struggle for meaning and value, how they have made sense of life, and what they consider of utmost importance will show up in what they put their attention to, how they treat other people, the richness of their inner life, and their flexibility in dealing with difficulty. The development of this side of children may require periods of detachment from relationships, solitude, encountering difficult negative feelings, and at times sacrificing comfort in relationships and groups where they have learned to feel secure because of commonality in shared values and beliefs. If only the dimensions of relationship, affect, and intelligence are looked at, and not seen in relationship to children's ongoing struggle to make more meaningful sense of themselves and life and thus realize their potential, periods of withdrawal and negative emotion could mistakenly be pathologized rather than be viewed as necessary cycles in the children's spiritual development.

THE PARENTAL ROLE IN NURTURING THE SPIRITUALITY AND CREATIVITY OF THE CHILD

The capacity for creativity takes root if the mother–infant bond provides ongoing recognition and nurturance of it. The parents who target the child's spiritual life as central will view the child as an active participant in the evolution of her own life, see the child's motivation and needs as primarily good and directed towards aims necessary to her growth and fulfillment, and relate to the child with non-possessive empathy (Stern, 1985, 1990). As Bowlby (1989) has emphasized, it is the presence of the person who has been most responsive to the child's deepest needs that will be conjured up when the child is anxious, sad, or depressed. The child's deepest needs require of the parent that he value the child's inner world and inclinations over conformity and compliance to external demands, and see as a central aim of the child's life a capacity for solitude, creative participation in the evolution of her life, and a growing sense of authority over her own soul and self. The parent's faith in the child's ability to accomplish this and a positive responsiveness to this aspect of his or her development will help the child value that dimension of life and develop faith in living out his or her deepest desires and callings.

The child needs to feel free enough of the fear of hurting or disappointing his or her parents, or of his or her fear of the parents' retaliation, to move through each developmental phase in a lively, self-initiating manner. If the need to survive with a particular parent necessitates putting one's own urgent developmental needs second, the pain and conflict resulting from this will be manifested in various symptoms (see chapter 7). The child may become (1) overly withdrawn or schizoid to protect his or her inner life; (2) overly aggressive or demanding to protest having to sacrifice too much of his or her real self and be overly concerned with the other; (3) overly depressed, clinging, or fearful to express hopelessness at her invisibility or not being heard; (4) overly rigid, competitive, or ambitious in terms of achieving what parents expect, to express capitulation or resignation to external demands and loss of contact with the self; or (5) develop psychosomatic symptoms that reflect despair at not being heard or validated.

Being aware of and empathic with how children's pain and conflict manifests itself in how they negotiate their true needs with doing what they need to survive requires of a parent openness to what is unlike himself and may initially be experienced as injurious to the parent's narcissism (Donaldson-Pressman and Pressman, 1994). The parent who makes children feel supported and seen in their most urgent callings will elicit feelings of love. When the child feels thwarted or unrecognized, the parent is likely to experience the child's hate. In this author's view, anger and love are motivated by the "soul" of the child, generating love when they are allowed to fulfill themselves, and anger when they are not. Children are never "basically" bad or angry. When a child is angry, provocative, difficult, or "bad," the question is, what is not being seen, recognized, or given validity? And one keeps asking that question until the innocent motivation, a reason that may not be reasonable, but is totally understandable, given this particular child's predicament, is discovered. The way back to this innocence or undiscovered meaning, for a young child, is often through play. Imaginative play will reflect the child's experience and lead a child to where he or she needs to heal and grow. Playing with a child is thus often the best way to understand him or her (Singer and Singer, 1990). A parent who has experienced and enjoyed freedom in the creative process will be most likely to be able to provide the emotional space and nurturance to facilitate the creative process in the child. Such a parent is aware, as Gablik (1991) has stated, that "imagination is the deepest voice of the soul and can be heard clearly only through cultivation and careful attention."

In the most extreme examples, Shengold (1989) describes damage done to the child's soul that can dampen spontaneous aliveness and curiosity. Soul murder is "the deliberate attempt to eradicate or compromise the separate identity of another person [see chapter 7]. The victims of soul murder remain in large part possessed by another, their souls in bondage to someone else" (p. 2). In this situation the child is torn between maintaining his or her own perceptions and so being true to him or herself and retaining the love of the parents by meeting their expectations. When the child excessively sacrifices his or her perceptions to maintain the love of the parent, and restricts or denies his or her experience or perception to appease the rage or narcissism of the other, the self narrows rather than expands. Shengold goes on to say, "It is exactly the ability to feel that is so vulnerable to ruin and mutilation, especially the ability to feel love" (p. 84). When a child feels unvalidated by one parent he may turn to the other, but may find the second parent allied with the more feared parent. Where there is not receptivity to the child's own spontaneous perceptions and self, it can result in shutting down feelings, obsessive defenses, displacements of blame and fragmentation; that is, an ongoing, inner attack on the spontaneous, self-confident, creative capacity. When this abuse becomes normality, future relationships tend to reflect this pattern. Attachment can go hand in hand with abuse when this is all the child has known (when he or she does not experience a viable alternative in the other parent). Where there is divorce and parents differ greatly in their values and expectations of the child and are feuding with each other, the child often feels he or she has to develop two different personas. The resulting conflict and confusion can greatly impede her own integration and discovery of her true self (see chapter 8).

In extreme situations, the child who identifies with a psychotic or psychopathic parent may herself lose touch with reality. The parents' fragility, immaturity, and/or rigid narcissism may not allow them to tolerate difference or opposition in their child. Beneath the child's sense of unreality there may be dissociated patricidal and matricidal feelings toward the parent, who refuses to recognize the differing or opposing reality of the child. When there is soul murder or abuse the child's "no" is frequently pathologized, which can be crippling to the child's creative and imaginative functioning, her ability to retrieve the images that help her know who she is and why she hurts, and to her creatively constructing meaning and discovering new relationships.

In the creative realm, "no" is as necessary as "yes," black as white, hatred as love. The child's negativity is often a clue to something missing, hurting, frustrated, or deadened, and can be an opportunity, on the parent's part, for greater empathy. Lack of empathy or rejection when the child is negative may be overlaid by the parent's being affectionate or showering the child with gifts when he or she is "good" (as defined by the parent), confusing the child further as to whether he or she was in fact previously rejected. Where there is soul murder, the child often tries to please or accommodate to the parent he or she is most afraid of rather than the one to whom he or she is attached in a healthier way. This can "appear" to be attachment or preference, when in fact there is deep fear and rage at this same parent.

INTEGRATION OF EVALUATION OF THE CHILD'S
SPIRITUAL AND CREATIVE HEALTH
INTO CUSTODY DETERMINATIONS

In custody evaluations, discerning dynamics between parent and child that promote a healthy spiritual and creative life as opposed to those that do not is often difficult because overt interactions can exist in contradiction with more subtle unconscious dynamics (see chapters 15 and 16). In order to assess the true state of the child's spiritual and creative health, it is important to assess the child's capacity for play, self-expression, inner freedom to explore questions that are pertinent to him or her, and self-directed interests. It is also important to look at the parent's capacity to participate in, promote, and validate these aspects of the child. In order to validate the child's spiritual and creative life, the parent must value creativity in him- or herself. Richards et al. (1988) have developed a research tool designed to identify creativity in adults in their everyday life. Adult creativity is often an outgrowth of the ability and freedom to fantasize and be creative in childhood. Creativity can also be expressed in Rorschach responses and the Thematic Apperception Test stories told by the child or adult (Rapaport, Gill, and Schafer, 1968).

Custody evaluations should optimally include play sessions with the child alone, and with the child along with each parent in order for the examiner to get a sense of the child's freedom of expression alone and with each parent (see chapters 15 and 16). Play can include dollhouses, sand tray, drawing, or imaginative play like "house" or "school." With older children, dreams can give voice to the deepest cries of the soul and be a means to glean how longstanding patterns of behavior in the family have impacted on them and also how the present trauma of parental separation is affecting them (Piaget, 1962; Sutton-Smith, 1988; Singer and Singer, 1990).

In observing the child at play with the parent, the forensic evaluator looks for whether or not the parent allows the child to initiate play, follows the initiative with curiosity and openness to what the child is trying to express, and shows pleasure in the child's spontaneous, innovative, and creative productions. One is also alert to a parent being too controlling, imposing his own direction, and showing harsh judgment of certain topics or types of expression that offend his values. This desire for control may manifest itself in the parent trying to steer a child away from themes or topics in play or self-expression that might embarrass him, reveal him as being in some ways inadequate, or present the child in a way that the parent finds disagreeable. Essentially, the forensic evaluator is sensitive to ways in which the parent's narcissism, rigidity, or narrowness affects the child's ability to fully express him- or herself (see chapters 15 and 16).

It is also important to conduct an interview with the parent alone that will help determine whether he is open and receptive to the child's spirituality and creativity. One might include questions like, "tell me about an incident with your child in which you were not happy with her behavior or what she said, and how you resolved it with her." Another question might be, "what kinds of questions does your child ask you and how do you respond to them?" Questions can be asked that reveal what the parent and child enjoy doing together and what kinds of activities, lessons, books, music, and objects the parent offers the child. This questioning is likely to reveal a great deal about how the parent perceives the child and what aspects of the child he or she would like to develop and expand. With older children, where play is not a means of relating, one might ask questions that help determine whether the parent has specific information about what books, music, and activities the child prefers and what understanding the parent has of the value of these choices to the child.

Questions in the interview should help to reveal whether a parent can introduce doubt about a child's behavior or feelings so that a dialogue can open between them that allows the child to add to what the parent understands of him or her in a particular situation. This allows the child to have a sense of agency in affecting the parent's understanding, and in contributing to the meaning of her own behavior or feelings. One might also discern a parental capacity to sense in the child motivation coming from hurt or fear rather than reacting to the behavior as if it is bad, destructive, mean or stupid; that is, to reach for the sense in the behavior from the child's point of view. Anger or disgust towards the child may reflect how the parent was treated. One might ask, in this regard, how the parent feels when he catches himself acting like his own parent, or how he feels when he sees his child enjoying something that he was not allowed to enjoy.

The parent need not agree with how the child is dealing with his feelings, but if the child is not made to feel bad, he or she is more likely to be a participant in thinking about alternative ways to act. A parent educates a child spiritually by listening for the positive in the negative feelings or behavior and helping the child reflect on this. For example, there might be an element in a child's behavior labeled stubborn that is assertive or determined; or there might be in depression a non-verbal plea to be listened to or a protest that cannot easily be verbalized.

Is the parent able to see and accept that his child has goals and values different from his or her own and still love the child unconditionally? When the parent disagrees with what is important for the child, can he or she be reflective about available choices for the child and not impede the child's independent struggle? Are there times when a parent can see the child as a teacher, embodying missing aspects of him or herself, from which he or she can learn? If a parent has the capacity to be reflective in these ways he or she will model the empathy, kindness, and concern that are essential for children to grow in accord with their own dreams and goals. Then the child is able to internalize a parent that allows him or her the inner freedom and reflectiveness to develop a strong and flexible-enough self to genuinely and productively engage in creative work and intimate relations. A parent's spiritual task is to sacrifice how he embodies the existing world and be open to a new vision. Accomplishing this likely will contribute to the child's ability to imagine beyond the existent and create new ideas and possibilities for him- or herself and others.

CUSTODY EVALUATION OF JANICE AND HER PARENTS

I evaluated Janice, aged 12, in a custody dispute between her mother and her father. At that point Janice resided with her mother. Her father was asking for a modification of custody of his youngest daughter because of an eating disorder and what he saw as deteriorating behavior that he believed was related to conflicts and stress she experienced with her mother. Janice's sister was five years older and about to go away to college. She was not involved in the dispute or evaluation.

Janice's parents separated when she was one month old and her sister was five. Janice's mother was awarded sole custody of the girls, and her father saw them every other weekend. From interviews with all three, it appeared that the mother was warm and playful in their early years. The girls were well taken care of and sent to good schools with extracurricular lessons when they were older. The mother had ongoing bouts with depression, experienced difficulty being alone, and did not feel she fulfilled her own life goals to be a concert pianist or music teacher. Her father had been a music teacher and very much wanted her to follow in his footsteps.

From a young age, Janice experienced her mother's neediness as a demand to fulfill her mother's dreams, which involved Janice's feeling she needed to be perfect. Janice felt that she was her mother's "work of art" and her mother lived vicariously through her. While Janice's mother encouraged her creativity where it was congruent with her wishes for Janice, she was not attentive to Janice's thoughts when they moved in divergent directions. As a school-age child, Janice was overtly well treated, but she often got very depressed and could not say why. She could not reveal this to anyone because she was ashamed and felt that she should be able to snap out of it. She felt that her mother's depression was justified, because of her difficult life, the divorce, and her having to support two young children, whereas her depression was not.

When Janice was twelve her father remarried, her sister was looking ahead to college, and Janice's mother became more focused on her as a companion. Janice's growing antipathy to the performing arts (she said she felt that performing was not her "calling") seemed also to be a way of differentiating her self from her mother. She was gravitating towards visual arts, which she could do in her own space; if someone wanted to see her paintings she did not have to be there to feel embarrassed. She also found herself gravitating toward exploring esoteric religions as a way to find meaning and greater understanding of herself. Her mother belittled these interests and became frightened her daughter might be swept away by some cult, so she became more restrictive. Janice's inability to express anger and to set boundaries for her mother's intrusiveness contributed importantly to the development of an eating disorder. She was losing weight, but her mother could not recognize the problem because it was too narcissistically injurious for her to acknowledge that her perfect daughter had such a serious problem. Her father noticed her changed eating habits, long stays in the bathroom, increased sullenness, and occasional reluctance to return home to her mother after a weekend.

After a period of deliberation and discussion with his new wife, the father decided to try to get custody of Janice. Janice was interviewed alone and seen with her mother and her father. When asked directly what her preference was, her eyes teared and she shrugged her shoulders. She spoke overtly of loving both her parents. She admitted that she felt tension with her mother in regard to her mother not letting her have more freedom, not allowing her privacy, and expecting her always to be in the house when her mother came home from work. She said that, more and more, there was a strain between doing what she wanted and being there for her mother and that she often felt bad and did not understand why. The explanations she gave herself were either that she was born bad or that she was too selfish and was being punished by God. She felt being skinny was a way to get love and attention and to feel in control. Throughout the interview she never expressed anger and repeatedly tried to make the interviewer understand things from her mother's point of view. She often talked of herself in negative terms, telling the examiner how ungrateful and selfish she was. She said she did not feel as close to her father, but often felt more relaxed with him. He did not try to talk her out of what she wanted to do. He would ask questions about what she was doing and he gave her space in the garage to paint so that she could be alone.

When they were interviewed together, Janice's mother repeatedly spoke for her and tried to talk Janice out of what she had said. She seemed very nervous about impressing the examiner and got agitated when anything Janice said might reflect badly on her as a mother. Janice did not fight back. Because he did not feel it reflected on him as a bad parent, her father did not try to control the outcome of the session or the interviewer's opinion and had less of a need to deny Janice's depression and anorexia. This allowed him to be curious about why she felt bad, creating a more empathic environment for Janice to express her feelings. He expressed regret that he had not been more available and wished to make some of that up to her. She was carrying a sketch pad with some pastels in it, which her father asked to see. He asked thoughtful questions about her choice of colors and what she was trying to express, but respected her boundaries when she did not want to explain further. The nonintrusive questioning brought out an articulateness in Janice which allowed her to feel more confident. There was also playfulness between them in which Janice became like a giggly little girl.

In a second interview, alone, Janice told her dreams to the evaluator. In the first dream, she said, "I was given the opportunity to go back in time to meet my six-year-old self. When I introduced myself, I was overwhelmed at how trusting my younger self was. She accepted the stranger that was me. I was moved by how innocent the younger self was. I hugged her." In the second dream she was in a drugstore. "Two young guys are paying for something—it is obvious—with counterfeit bills. I observe their deceit. I make it clear to them that if they had forged something they would be in big trouble. I am bemused that they are pulling off such a badly done forgery."

In her free associations to the first dream she said it felt like she was embracing the child she was. Somewhere in her was an innocent child, labeled bad and selfish. She was trying to heal the little girl in her. She said how depressing it was to carry around a sad child everywhere, that thought of herself as bad. She said her mother made her feel that she never did enough, so she always felt bad. "I want to tell myself it's okay, to do what I want. It's huge to say what I need." The second dream brought up how she often felt counterfeit at home and had to shield herself from her mother's attempts to invade or influence her. Sometimes she was unable to tell the difference between her real thoughts and the shield. She said she was worried that, if she kept doing that, she would no longer be able to tell the difference between the real her and the counterfeit her. She said she hated to say it, but sometimes it was easier to be at her father's house because she could say anything without worrying about being bad or hurting someone. The dreams revealed feelings that were difficult for her to know she had and created images that expressed the deep concerns of her soul.

In doing this forensic evaluation I was aware of Janice's deep attachment to her mother, in spite of the conflicts, as well as how crippled Janice was in being able to follow her own feelings, thoughts, and creative interests, because she felt it would make her mother feel abandoned or angry. At this point in Janice's development, I felt her father could offer relief from the conflicts with her mother. I recommended joint custody, with Janice spending half the week with her father, half with her mother and summers with her father, except

for two weeks with her mother. Within a year Janice was happier
and the eating disorder had disappeared.

CONCLUSION

The forensic evaluation of Janice and her family illustrates symptoms
or behaviors in the child that can warn of damage to the child's creative or spiritual life. This evaluation highlights the importance of
including in a definition of "best interests of the child" not just the
child's overt physical, emotional, and social well-being, but the child's
spiritual and creative well-being as well. When a child's world ceases
to make sense and creative ways of searching for a meaningful connection to herself and her world feel blocked, symptoms appear in
all areas of her life. At times these symptoms can be life-threatening.
It is impossible to separate the spiritual and creative from other
aspects of the child. They are always intertwined.

REFERENCES

Balint, M. (1968), *The Basic Fault.* London: Tavistock.
Bowlby, J. (1989), *The Making and Breaking of Affectional Bonds.* London:
    Routledge.
Coles, R. (1990), *The Spiritual Life of Children.* Boston: Houghton Mifflin.
Donaldson-Pressman, S. & Pressman, R. (1994), *The Narcissistic Family.* San
    Francisco, CA: Jossey-Bass.
Gablik, S. (1991), *The Re-Enchantment of Art.* London: Thames & Hudson.
Miller, A. (1981), *The Drama of the Gifted Child.* New York: Basic Books.
—— (1984), *Thou Shalt Not Be Aware.* New York: New American Library.
Piaget, J. (1962), *Play, Dreams and Imitation in Childhood.* New York: Norton.
Rapaport, D., Gill, M. & Schafer, R. (1968), *Diagnostic Psychological Testing.*
    New York: International Universities Press.
Richards, R., Kinney, D., Benet, M. & Merzel, A. (1988), Assessing everyday
    creativity: Characteristics of the lifetime creativity scales and validation
    with three large samples. *J. Personal. & Soc. Psychol.,* 54:476–485.
Shengold, L. (1989), *Soul Murder.* New Haven, CT: Yale University Press.
Singer, D. & Singer, J. (1990), *The House of Make Believe.* Cambridge, MA:
    Harvard University Press.
Stern, D. (1985), *The Interpersonal World of the Infant.* New York: Basic Books.
—— (1990), *Diary of a Baby.* New York: Basic Books.
Sutton-Smith, B. (1988), Creativity and the vicissitudes of play. *Adoles. Psychiat.,*
    15:307–318.
Winnicott, D. W. (1971), *Playing and Reality,* London: Tavistock.

Chapter 18

Evaluation of Allegations of Child Sexual Abuse in Child Custody Disputes

B. J. CLING

*E*xpert opinion is particularly needed in child custody cases where possible criminal assault is suspected within a family, as for example when allegations are made of child sexual abuse (Brooks and Milchman, 1991). In these instances, the mental health professional is asked to give a professional opinion on whether such criminal acts are likely to have occurred and what the impact of these acts should be in terms of future custody and visitation arrangements. Because these types of evaluations are a growing area of forensic practice, this chapter has been devoted to the special aspects of such evaluations.

In the past 20 years, child abuse reporting has increased significantly. This increase has been attributed not to an increase in child abuse itself, but to an increase in the reporting of the abuse (Ceci and Bruck, 1995; Poole and Lamb, 1998). In recent years, state power has been exerted to find and punish those who abuse children. New laws have been enacted to protect children, and the definition of abuse has broadened. Law enforcement is taking the reporting of abuse seriously, and the public is being encouraged to report abuse. In fact, many professions now mandate that suspected child abuse be reported.

Along with the increased reporting of child sexual abuse in general has come an increase in alleged child sexual abuse in the context of a custody dispute. Such charges are generally leveled against the father. While some of the allegations are true, some percentage are also false. Clearly, the implications of custody and even visitation by a father who is in fact sexually abusing a child are profound, and must be taken into consideration by the court awarding custody. On the other hand, false accusations of abuse may be very damaging to the accused parent, the child, and their relationship, and can also negatively influence the court even if such charges cannot be proven. In fact, it is quite difficult to prove such charges, since they are criminal allegations, and when prosecuted require the highest standard of proof ("beyond a reasonable doubt").

Because of the possibility of improper use of allegations of child sexual abuse in custody disputes, some authors have been very concerned about the increase, perceived and real, in such reporting (Benedek and Schetky, 1985; Green, 1991; Gardner, 1994). In spite of the logic of this concern, there is an ongoing dispute as to how many allegations there actually are. Many authors in the child custody field maintain that it is difficult to know whether there has been an increase since there are no prior broad-based statistical studies, but that, even if there has been an increase, the total number is small, about two per cent (Faller,1990; Hlady and Gunter, 1990; Thoennes and Tjaden, 1990).[1] Others believe there is a current epidemic of sex abuse allegations (Benedek and Schetky, 1985; Green, 1991; Gardner, 1994).[2] The latter authors are also concerned that these allegations are being made frivolously or even malevolently by angry mothers. The fear of false accusations has even carried into the courtroom, so that in some courts the woman bringing the charge is met with a severe judicial backlash against her (Ellis, 2000).

SUSPECTED INCREASE IN CHILD SEXUAL ABUSE ALLEGATIONS IN CHILD CUSTODY PROCEEDINGS

It may be difficult to assess accurately either the number of allegations of sexual abuse that were made in the past or the number being made now. Studies gathering data from a broad base of cases

---

[1]Faller studied 136 cases and examined the question of purposely false allegations. She found two percent were knowingly false.

[2]The articles indicating recent increases in sexual abuse allegations and reporting currently high percentages are not based on broad-based statistical studies. Green has been justifiably criticized for his use of small unrepresentative sample sizes and his lack of corroborative evidence for "false allegations."

rely on official reports to determine whether or not such allegations have been made. Thus the allegation must be serious enough to be included in an official document in order to be counted (for example, a police report, court testimony, or a child welfare report). The majority of the research in this area indicates that, whether or not the number of child sexual abuse allegations in child custody disputes have increased, the overall numbers are very small (Finkelhor, 1986).

The most comprehensive study, conducted by Thoennes and Tjaden (1990), looked at 9000 cases across the United States from 1985 to 1986 and found that the number of sex abuse allegations in custody cases was approximately two percent. No such broad-based statistical studies exist for earlier time periods, but the authors noted that this figure was higher than that of allegations of child sexual abuse not made in the context of a custody dispute. Even if there has been a modest increase it is certainly in line with the observation that sex abuse in general is being reported more frequently. Thoennes and Tjaden found no difference in number of false allegations between general sexual abuse allegations and those brought as part of a child custody dispute. Even though officially the number of allegations in custody disputes may be relatively low, it is likely that, in the context of custody negotiations, the number of unofficial threats of abuse allegations by parents battling against each other has increased (though they have not been serious enough to become part of an official record).

A separate but related issue to the reporting of child sexual abuse in the context of child custody is the frequency of true versus false allegations. One of the problems in evaluating frequency is the fact that, as stated above, it is often difficult to determine whether or not abuse has taken place. If a case is not clear cut, the conclusion may be that the allegation is unsubstantiated. This conclusion may be owed to the fact that the child is too young to give clear testimony or simply to the lack of corroborating extrinsic evidence, since abuse usually occurs in private. Further, criminal charges may not have been brought, or may have been withdrawn. Of course, cases that are unsubstantiated are not necessarily cases of false allegation, but they have sometimes been counted as such in studies. Because of the many different measures of "not true" in the studies on allegations of sexual abuse in custody disputes, this author has found figures ranging from 2 percent (Faller, 1991) to overview figures of 20 to 80 percent, depending on the sample and on the measure used

(Wakefield and Underwager, 1991; Ellis, 2000). False and unsubstantiated allegations, although not provable or simply incorrect, may
have been brought in good faith. Although some previously cited
authors allege that malevolence often drives false and unsubstantiated allegations, there is no broad-based evidence that this is true in
a significant number of cases (Thoennes, 1988; Romero, 1990; Faller,
1991). In fact, misinterpretation rather than deliberate misrepresentation is thought to account for many false allegations, even in litigious circumstances such as custody disputes (Poole and Lamb, 1998).

A remaining issue based on the apparently conflicting reports
within this field is the problem that judges and those in the legal
community may read only those authors who have written of their
own clinical experience (Green, 1986; Gardner, 1987) and those
whose work is based on those authors (Farr and Yuille, 1988; Schaefer
and Guyer, 1988; Cramer, 1991), without being aware of the broader-
based studies detailed above. Lawyers and judges may read clinically
based material uncritically (Gordon, 1985), lacking the psychological
expertise to analyze the data on which they are based. Legal articles
based on these anecdotal accounts may wrongly persuade lawyers
and judges to dismiss any consideration of serious allegations even
in visitation considerations (see chapter 22), or to require burdens
of proof that are beyond the usual requirements of the non-criminal
situation. Luckily, a number of legal scholars writing on the issue
are aware of all the relevant research in this field, and some judges,
using cases in their courts as their sample, are aware of how small
the numbers of false allegations of sexual abuse actually are (Berliner,
1988; Snyder, 1988; Romero, 1990; Schudson, 1992; Toth,1992).

CONDUCTING FORENSIC EVALUATIONS
OF CHILD SEXUAL ABUSE IN CHILD CUSTODY CASES:
CONSIDERATIONS FOR THE EXPERT

I. Evaluation of the Parent

Some authors have tried to characterize parents' personality traits to
help clinicians recognize when a parent might be misrepresenting a
situation of suspected sexual abuse (Gardner, 1987; Wakefield and
Underwager, 1990; Ellis, 2000). However, it should be noted that the
fact that a disturbed or angry parent *may* accuse falsely does not

mean that every disturbed or angry parent *is* accusing the other falsely. Thus, evaluators should guard against forming an early impression of truth or falsehood based on the personality of a parent. Here again, corroborating evidence is needed to reach a more reliable conclusion. Furthermore, knowledge of unconscious psychological processes is necessary for a complete understanding of the parent's allegation and the child's support of such an allegation.

To illustrate, a mother who has suffered psychological abuse or even sexual betrayal in the form of extramarital affairs on the part of a husband she is now divorcing may see certain behaviors on the part of their child as indicating sexual abuse. Assuming that there is no actual abuse, psychoanalytic understanding of the situation allows an important distinction between conscious malevolent lying by the mother and a true belief that something sexual is amiss, based on her unconscious need to see the father in a particularly negative light. To complicate the scenario, if the child is very young (under three years old) and has difficulty communicating, he or she may not be able to dispel these suspicions or may exacerbate them by confusingly reporting touching that is really nonsexually motivated. The child may have the need to maintain strong ties with the caretaking parent, particularly if the parents are separating. Thus, there may be some motivation (albeit unconscious) to skew a report of touching, or simply not to object to the mother's interpretation.

On the other hand, assuming that the alleged sexual abuse has in fact taken place, psychoanalytic training and insight can also be helpful in teasing apart unconscious fantasy and the reality of the adult misbehavior. The fact that the mother may want to see the father in a very negative sexual light and the child may feel compelled to support her does not mean that the alleged sexual abuse did not occur. A detailed understanding of how the unconscious works indicates that fantasy and reality are always interwoven into a whole that is perceived by the individual as simply the reality of what is happening in the external world. Thus, after the forensic expert assesses the external information as to whether there is confirmation or disconfirmation of abuse, she must deal with the complex motivations of the parties in a sophisticated way in order to understand what the true situation is. It is critical for the expert to understand the conscious and unconscious motivations on the part of an accusing parent and child as well as the way those fantasies may be intermingled with the reality of the situation, which may indeed include abuse. In the context of the forensic evaluation, and particularly one involving sexual abuse within a custody dispute, unconscious thoughts and intense feelings which are triggered by either parent or the child may also affect the psyche of the expert (see chapter 15), without his or her knowledge (Jackson and Nuttal, 1997). That is why it is important for the evaluator to have a high level of self-awareness to help counteract this tendency. Many psychodynamic training programs focus on developing this kind of insight.

II. Evaluation of the Child

The age of the child is quite important in taking into consideration two controversial issues: (1) the ability of the child to distinguish what actually happened from a fantasy of what may have happened, and (2) the suggestibility of the child to views of prior professionals who have questioned her or adults to whom the child is close who may have pushed their ideas onto the child. Suggestibility is always a problem, and in the past has led to the undoing of cases regardless of the evidence.

In cases involving allegations of sexual abuse, mental health professionals have to be particularly careful to conduct interviews in a non-suggestive manner. Due to the early mistakes of professionals in child abuse cases, guidelines now exist on how to conduct interviews with children of various ages to establish what did or did not happen to them with an accused adult (Garb, Wood, and Nezworski, 2000a, b; Olafson, 2004).

Considerable research in the area of suggestibility (Doris, 1991; Ceci and Bruck, 1995) indicates the following. First, although there is some disagreement in the field (Ceci and Bruck, 1993; Yuille, 1996), it is generally acceptable to use anatomically correct dolls with children of all ages in such interviews. Children who have not been abused are not overly influenced by such dolls. However, children who have been abused may find them very useful in helping them articulate what happened (Morris, 1989; Everson and Boat, 1990). Second, although very suggestive questions, particularly if repeatedly asked, have clearly been shown to influence answers (Loftus, 1992), vague questioning leaves too much up to the child. Again, research has shown that specific questions bring forth more specific information from children who have been abused (Goodman and

Clark-Stewart, 1991; Saywitz, 1991, 1992). Vagueness in the examiner's inquiry is likely to lead to errors of omission in cases where children are uncomfortable about what happened (Powell and Thomson, 1994; Flin and Spencer, 1995; Warren and McGough, 1996). However, as noted above, interviewers still must exercise caution so as not to unduly influence a child's report of what happened (Ceci and Bruck, 1995).

The issue of whether a child, particularly a young child, can tell the difference between fantasy and reality, and thus accurately report sexual abuse, is still controversial. Research indicates that below age three it may be difficult to get reliable testimony (Goodman, Aman, and Hirschman, 1987; Ceci and Bruck, 1995). Although young children might be suggestible, they are unlikely to engage in outright lies or to confuse specific reality and specific details with contrived fantasies (Sivan, 1985; Saywitz, Goodwin, and Myers, 1990; Goodman and Clarke-Stewart, 1991). And, in the absence of suggestion, young children's memories can be clear and accurate (Fivush, 1993). The results of this research are particularly helpful, since the concept of discarding most testimony by children leaves them vulnerable to sexual attack.

The research on suggestibility generally informs us at what ages children are most susceptible to subtle pressure from authority figures (both parents and examiners) and what types of pressure even inadvertently applied may cause a child to report abuse that did not happen (Ceci and Friedman, 2000). For more precision in understanding a specific case, the psychoanalytic concept of "transference" is helpful. It is important to understand the relationship between the child and his or her parents in order to understand to what extent the child is influenced by authority figures. This is generally a function of age, but there is also a great deal of individual variation. The extent to which a child is subject to parental influence will also determine the extent to which he or she is likely to be suggestible to other authority figures via the mechanism of transference.

Thus, a child who can be easily influenced by subtle pressure from the mother is also likely to be influenced by a suggestive examiner. In a case like this, it is especially important that the evaluator be very neutral and pay close attention to the guidelines developed for neutral questioning techniques. Or a child who is afraid of her father may tend not to reveal problems that are actually occurring, and an evaluator may not be able to allay her anxiety. In this case, neutral but more directive questioning might be appropriate.

Much research has been devoted to the distinction between fantasy and reality, yet clinicians often feel that the research situations miss some of the complexity of what is revealed in the clinical setting.[3] According to the psychoanalytic view there is always some mixture of fantasy and reality, particularly in young children. However, the development of a firmer concept of reality is an ego function which matures as the child gets older.

This mixture of fantasy and reality can also be influenced by the psychosexual stage a child is in. For example, during the oedipal phase (ages three to five) a child develops a strong attachment to the opposite sex parent and has intense romantic longings and fantasies. These sorts of longings and fantasies are easy to observe even without the benefit of psychoanalytic theory. A child in this stage is very prone to childlike "sexual" feelings toward the opposite sex parent. Ambiguous behavior on the part of that parent may get wrapped up in a child fantasy that is more romantic than was intended by the parent. Understanding this possibility theoretically can be very useful in interviewing the child and observing her play with an eye toward teasing apart whatever fantasy elements may be present and the possibility that there has been real sexual behavior with a parent.

CONCLUSION

Allegations of child sexual abuse in large numbers are a relatively new phenomenon. Such allegations have become part of child custody disputes as well (Schuman, 1999). The early part of this chapter examined the scope and breadth of child abuse allegations in child custody disputes and found that while they may be on the rise, the total number is rather small, even though the perceived number might

---

[3]Some researchers, such as Loftus (1991, 1993), have created experimental situations in which children of varying ages are manipulated into reporting that neutral events that did not occur have occurred. Although these results are certainly powerful, clinical researchers working with child victims of actual abuse (Terr, 1988; Alpert, 1995) argue that children of various ages react differently to traumatic events than they do to experimentally created neutral events. While they may distort or omit them in their reports, they do not invent entire scenarios that did not take place.

be larger. Although there is no epidemic, as some have imagined, allegations of sexual abuse are still quite serious, and it is useful to consider the effect of such allegations on the dissolving family unit: the child and the two battling parents.

If the allegations are true and the child is being sexually abused, it is often uncomfortable for the child to communicate this. Actual psychological damage is being done, possibly on an ongoing basis. On the other hand, most cases are not clear cut, and once these allegations are brought, it may be very difficult to establish their veracity. Unfortunately, inconclusive results have a deleterious effect on all the parties. A parent's reputation may be destroyed and an element of caution and fear can enter the parent–child relationship. Naturally, the relationship between the mother and father becomes even more strained, making visitation in child custody cases more difficult. If the alleged abuse is not proven, judges may feel angry at the accusing parent and punish this parent in the area of custody (for example, sole custody may be changed to joint custody, or increased visitation may be awarded to the other parent), even when these decisions are not necessarily in the best interests of the child. In cases where the accused parent is innocent (even if the accusation was believed to be true by the accuser), the damage to the accused as well as the child, may be severe. Conversely, although exposure of criminal acts by a parent against a child is always painful, failure to expose and stop such abuse is far more harmful.

REFERENCES

Alpert, J. (1995), Professional practice, psychological science, and the delayed memory debate. In: *Sexual Abuse Recalled*, ed. J. Alpert. Northvale, NJ: Aronson, pp. 3–26.

Benedek, E. & Schetky, D. H. (1985), Allegations of sexual abuse in child custody and visitation disputes. In: *Emerging Issues in Child Psychiatry and the Law*, ed. D. H. Schetky & E. P. Benedek. New York: Brunner/Mazel, pp. 145–158.

Berliner, L. (1988), Deciding whether a child has been sexually abused. In: *Sexual Abuse Allegations in Custody and Visitations Disputes*, ed. E. B. Nicholson & J. Bulkley. Washington, DC: American Bar Association, pp. 48–69.

Brooks, C. M. & Milchman, M. (1991), Child sexual abuse allegations during custody litigation: Conflicts between mental health expert witnesses and the law. *Behavioral Sci. & the Law*, 9:21–32.

Ceci, S. J. & Bruck, M. (1993), The suggestibility of the child witness: A histori-
cal review and synthesis. *Psycholog. Bull.*, 113:403–439.
—— & —— (1995), *Jeopardy in the Courtroom.* Washington, DC: American
Psychological Association.
—— & Friedman, R. D. (2000), The suggestibility of children: Scientific re-
search and legal implications. *Cornell Law Rev.*, 86:33–106.
Cramer, J. (1991), Why children lie in court. *Time,* March 4.
Doris, J. (1991), *The Suggestibility of Children's Recollections.* Washington, DC:
American Psychological Association.
Ellis, E. M. (2000), Evaluations of sexual abuse allegations in child custody
cases. In: *Divorce Wars: Interventions with Families in Conflict.* Washing-
ton, DC: American Psychological Association, pp. 270–294.
Everson, M. D. & Boat, B. W. (1990), Sexualized doll play among young chil-
dren: Implications for the use of anatomical dolls in sexual abuse evaluations. *J. Amer. Acad. Child & Adoles. Psychiatr.*, 29:736–742.
Faller, K. C. (1990), *Understanding Child Sexual Maltreatment.* Newbury Park,
CA: Sage.
—— (1991), Possible explanations for child sexual abuse allegations in divorce.
Amer. J. Orthopsychiat., 6:86–91.
—— (1992), Can therapy induce false allegations of sexual abuse? *APSAC Ad-
visor,* 5:3–6.
—— & Corwin, D. (1995), Children's interview statements and behaviors: Role
in identifying sexually abused children. *Internat. J. Child Abuse & Neglect,*
19:71–82.
Farr, V. L. & Yuille, J. C. (1988), Assessing credibility. *Preventing Sexual Abuse,*
1:8–12.
Finkelhor, D. (1986), *A Sourcebook on Child Sexual Abuse.* Beverly Hills, CA:
Sage.
Fivush, R. (1993), Developmental perspectives on autobiographical recall. In:
Child Victims and Child Witnesses, ed. G. S. Goodman & B. Bottoms. New
York: Guilford Press, pp. 1–24.
Flin, R. & Spencer, J. R. (1995), Annotation: Children as witnesses—legal and
psychological perspectives. *J. Child Psychol. & Psychiat.*, 36:171–189.
Garb, H. N., Wood, J. M. & Nezworski, M. T. (2000a), Projective techniques
and the detection of child sexual abuse. *Child Abuse & Neglect*, 24:437–438.
—— —— & —— (2000b), Projective techniques and the detection of child
sexual abuse. *Child Maltreatment: J. Amer. Profess. Soc. Abuse Children,* 5:161–
168.
Gardner, R. A. (1987), *The Parental Alienation Syndrome and the Differentiation
Between Fabricated and Genuine Child Sexual Abuse.* Cresskill, NJ: Creative
Therapeutics.
Gardner, R. (1994), Differentiating between true & false sex abuse allegations
in child custody disputes. *J. Divorce & Remarriage*, 21:1–20.
Goodman, G., Aman, C. & Hirschman, J. (1987), Child sexual and physical
abuse: Children's testimony. In: *Children's Eyewitness Memory,* ed. S. J.
Ceci, M. P. Toglia & D. F. Ross. New York: Springer-Verlag, pp. 1–23.
—— & Clark-Stewart, A. (1991), Suggestibility in children's testimony: Impli-

cations for sexual abuse investigations. In: *The Suggestibility of Children's Recollections*, ed. J. Doris. Washington, DC: American Psychological Association, pp. 92–105.

Gordon, C. (1985), False allegations of abuse in child custody disputes. *New Law J.*, 135:687–689.

Green, A. (1986), True and false allegations of sexual abuse in child custody disputes. *J. Amer. Acad. Child Psychiat.*, 25:449–455.

Green, A. (1991), Factors contributing to false allegations of child sexual abuse in custody disputes. *Child & Youth Services*, 15:177–189.

Hlady, L. J. & Gunter, E. J. (1990), Alleged child abuse in custody access disputes. *Child Abuse & Neglect*, 14:591–593.

Jackson, H. & Nuttal, R. (1997), *Childhood Abuse*. Thousand Oaks, CA: Sage.

—— (1991), *Witness for the Defense*. New York: St. Martin's.

—— (1992), The malleability of memory. *APSAC Advisor*, 5:7–9.

—— (1993), The reality of repressed memories. *Amer. Psychol.*, 48:518–537.

Morris, S. J. (1989), Sexually abused children of divorce. *J. Amer. Acad. Matrimonial Lawyers*, 5:27–46.

Olafson, E. (2004), Child sexual abuse. In: *Sexualized Violence against Women and Children*, ed. B. J. Cling. New York: Guilford, pp. 151–187.

Poole, D. & Lamb, M. (1998), *Investigative Interviews of Children*. Washington, DC: American Psychological Association.

Powell, M. B. & Thomson, D. M. (1994), Children's eyewitness-memory research: Implications for practice. *Families Soc. J. Contemp. Human Services*, 75:204–216.

Romero, S. (1990), Child sexual abuse in custody and visitation disputes: Problems, progress, and prospects. *Golden Gate Univ. Law Rev.*, 20:647–680.

Saywitz, K. J. (1992), Enhancing children's memory with the cognitive interview. *APSAC Advisor*, 5:9–10.

—— Goodman, G. S. & Myers, J. E. B. (1990), Can children provide accurate eyewitness reports? *Violence UpDate*, 1:1–3.

—— —— Nichols, E. & Moan, S. F. (1991), Children's memories of a physical examination involving genital touch: Implications for reports of child sexual abuse. *J. Consult. & Clin. Psychol.*, 59:682–691.

Schaefer, M. & Guyer, M. (1988), Allegations of sexual abuse in custody and visitation disputes: A legal and clinical challenge. Presented at 96th Annual Conference of the American Psychological Association, Atlanta, GA, August.

Schudson, C. (1992), Antagonistic parents in family courts: False allegations or false assumptions about true allegations of child sexual abuse? *J. Child Sexual Abuse*, 1:111–114.

Schuman, T. (1999), Allegations of sexual abuse. In: *Complex Issues in Child Custody Evaluations*, ed. P. Stahl. Thousand Oaks, CA: Sage.

Sivan, A. B. (1985), Preschool child development: Implications for investigation of child abuse allegations. *Child Abuse & Neglect*, 15:485–493.

Terr, L. (1988), What happens to the early memories of trauma? A study of twenty children under age five at the time of documented traumatic events. *Amer. J. Child & Adoles. Psychiat.*, 27:96–104.

Thoennes, N. (1988), Child sexual abuse: Whom should a judge believe? What should a judge believe? *Judges J.*, 27:4–18, 48–49.

—— & Tjaden, P. G. (1990), The extent, nature, and validity of sexual abuse allegations in custody/visitation disputes. *Child Abuse & Neglect*, 14:151–163.

Toth, P. (1992), All child abuse allegations demand attention: A commentary. *J. Child Sexual Abuse*, 1:117–118.

Wakefield, H. & Underwager, R. (1990), Personality characteristics of parents making false accusations of sexual abuse in custody disputes. *Issues Child Abuse Accusations*, 2:121–136.

Warren, A. R. & McGough, L. S. (1996), Research on children's suggestibility: Implications for the investigative interview. *Criminal Justice & Behavior*, 23:269-303.

Yuille, J. (1996), Investigating allegations of child abuse: An interview protocol. Training Workshop, 12th Annual Midwest Conference on Child Sexual Abuse and Incest, Madison, WI.

Interlude V

The Dilemma of Visitation

The poignancy of the plight of a nonresidential parent was driven home to me during a custody evaluation in which I asked eight-year-old William to draw a picture of his family. The picture depicted William and his sister holding hands with their mother and her live-in boyfriend. Separated from this newly configured family by heavy black vertical and horizontal lines is William's father, who has struggled to remain actively involved with his children, to the point of moving to a house around the corner from their home. Although I observed the warm ongoing connection this father still maintains with his children, William's drawing betrayed his father's real position in relationship to the family: on the outside of it.

It was Goldstein, Freud, and Solnit (1973) who asserted that the child's interests are best protected if the custodial parent has unilateral decision-making in the life of the child, including the regulating of ongoing contact with the nonresidential parent. Tuckman (see chapter 22) takes issue with this position in his chapter on supervised visitation, forcefully arguing on behalf of the right of the noncustodial parent to visit the children. Nevertheless, he does allow that adhering to the guidelines recommended by Goldstein et al. would result in a vast reduction in litigation. Additionally, the limited impact that visitation with the nonresidential parent may have on the child is noted by J. Wallerstein (personal communication, 2000), who observes that, in the large majority of families, the nonresidential parent plays a relatively marginal role in the child's life. Such realities, however, have been moderated by a considerable increase in dual parenting arrangements, in which fathers have come to assume significant care taking responsibilities.

The contributors to this section are united in keeping their focus on the primacy of the needs of the child. Such a guiding focus however, leaves considerable room for a different emphasis. General agreement that the child's best interests must be preserved then gives way to the relative weight one places on protecting the security of the attachment of child and primary parent versus the struggle to maintain the active involvement of two parents in the child's life. Such competing concerns run like a fault line through decisions that the courts must face on a daily basis.

Professional groups can be as contentious as fathers' versus mothers' rights activists. To make a gross generalization, forensic experts often emphasize the developmental needs and capacities of the young child. Lawyers, in their role of representing their adult clients, may emphasize the rights of the parent to have access to his child. Judges note that it is frequently difficult to establish the primary attachment figure.

In light of such inevitable contentiousness, Dember and Fliman (see chapter 19) report on the inspiring work of an interdisciplinary group in Ohio that drafted a Standard Order of Visitation for their county. They acknowledge having had to compromise on issues such as the young child's overnight visitation (which they opposed), but admit to shifts in their own certainty about the child's resilience in adjusting to two separate households. Perhaps this resilience reflects some diminution of the exclusive primary parent/child bond, one indicator of the changing family constellation. Hauser focuses on the impact of visitation on the child's inner life and, in so doing, achieves a heartbreaking, child-centered view of the kinds of loyalty conflicts and dual existence into which children of divorce are inevitably drawn. She goes on to illustrate how the child becomes the repository for the often clandestine efforts of both parents to monitor and shape the child's relationship with the other parent.

Solomon (see chapter 20) presents a clear and elegant overview of attachment theory before describing her own research on infant and toddler visitation arrangements. In contrast to those in the field who have come to despair of ever believing that social science results can have policy implications, Solomon blends theory with empirical data to convincing effect. Her dispassionate tone aids in presenting a balanced and subtle picture, which allows her to steer clear of the polemics that have too often dominated the explosive issue of the young child's visitation versus attachment needs. Although she does not take a formal stand, Solomon certainly indicates the complications of overnight visitation with the nonresidential parent, particularly in high-conflict situations.

Hymowitz (see chapter 23) weighs in as well on the competing demands of estranged parents and children in the particularly high-stakes context of relocation. A geographical move, so common in today's society, sets in boldest relief the divergence between what is ideal for a child and what are the realistic needs of her parents. It should be acknowledged that no correlative restrictions have been, nor are likely to be, placed on the nonresidential parent's freedom to move. The improbable idea of so restricting the nonresidential parent is one reflection of society's wish to deny the reality of divorce and its impact on children.

REFERENCE

Goldstein, J., Freud, A. & Solnit, A. (1973), *Beyond the Best Interests of the Child.* New York: Free Press.

Paul Hymowitz

Chapter 19

Tailoring Parental Visitation Orders to the Developmental Needs of Children of Divorce

CYNTHIA DEMBER
VIVIAN FLIMAN

A major issue in divorces that involve children is the allocation of parental time. In many divorces, parents work out, with greater or lesser difficulty, time-sharing arrangements that satisfy both them and the Court. In many other situations, parents cannot agree on how to allot time, and the Court must decide on temporary or long-range plans. While sensible people have always recognized that no single time-sharing arrangement is optimal for all children, often the Court has to order temporary custody and time-sharing rapidly and without access to much information about the children or the family circumstances.

In Ohio, when the Court has to order temporary or permanent allocation of parenting time and there are no compelling reasons for special arrangements, the Court typically relies on a plan, outlined in more or less detail, commonly known as the Standard Order of Visitation. This plan varies from county to county and may be more or less specific about the timing of regular visitation, holiday arrangements, and vacation time. In practice, the Standard Order of Visitation serves as a guideline for attorneys advising parents as well as for the Court in traditional custody arrangements involving a residential and a nonresidential parent. This chapter describes efforts to revise the Standard Order for Ohio's Hamilton County and the outcome of those efforts. It is offered in the hope that the process and principles that we employed will prove applicable in other jurisdictions.

In 1993, when we began efforts at "reform," many counties in Ohio, including Hamilton County where we reside, paid little or no attention to the changing needs of children as they grow and develop. As clinicians, we often encountered well-intentioned parents who planned visitation schedules for very young children that involved extended separations between the child and the primary care-taking parent. The Standard Order of Visitation in use at that time called for a child, independent of age, to spend every other weekend (Friday evening to Sunday evening) and one weekly three-hour visit mid-week with the nonresidential parent. The nonresidential parent was also allotted four weeks of additional time each year, two of which could be consecutive. Holidays were also allocated. There was no acknowledgment in the standard order of any variation in children's needs from birth to age twelve.

It was clear that the standard order did not incorporate a developmental orientation. It was also evident that many parents and attorneys operated on what we considered unfounded assumptions, for example, if parenting time is infrequent, it should be longer to compensate for lost time. We were also concerned with the paucity of basic information about children's needs that was in the hands of at least some parents and their advisors. Because the standard order was so widely disseminated in the Court, among family law attorneys, and among divorcing parents, we hoped that a revised standard order could serve a significant educational function as well as provide a guideline that met the needs of many, although certainly not all, children.

A task force was formed to revise the standard order. It consisted of two attorneys (one of whom is a mediator); a magistrate from the Division of Domestic Relations of the Court of Common Pleas; two social workers, one a mediator and one the head of the counseling department of the Court's Division of Domestic Relations; and two clinical child psychologists.[1] The multidisciplinary composition of the group turned out to be critical to the successful

---

[1]Members of the task force of the Hamilton County (Ohio) Court of Domestic Relations were Cynthia Dember, Vivian Fliman, John McElwee, Paul Myers, Sherri Goren Slovin, Evelyn Wallace, and Jayne Zuberbuhler.

completion of its mission, which was to produce a standard order that acknowledged somewhat better than the then-current one the developmental needs of children and that was acceptable to the Court, to the legal community and, ultimately, to families.

In revising the Standard Order of Visitation, we were guided by psychological formulations that included attachment theory and our understanding of the factors that optimized attachment of the infant and child to both parents, children's changing sense of time and the gradual development of children's ability to maintain a mental representation of attachment figures even when separated from them. We also considered children's increasing need, as they grow, for sustained relationships with peers and uninterrupted relationships with community institutions like schools, teams, and clubs. Finally, we were concerned with the special needs of adolescents both for contact with parents and for separation and independence.

Children, of course, live in a real world in which there are practical considerations like parents' work schedules, needs of siblings of different ages, needs to have contact with extended families and a host of other realities. We tried to incorporate some of these concerns into our schedules, along with the wisdom of some of the task force members as to what the Court and the legal community were likely to tolerate, what Ohio law required, and how long a document attorneys and parents would read. The final product was the result of a remarkably congenial, conscientious, and productive multidisciplinary collaboration. At the risk of being overly detailed, we would like to present, verbatim, extensive portions of the revised standard order, entitled, "Allocation of Parental Rights and Responsibilities Parenting Schedule for Hamilton County Court of Domestic Relations."[2]

> During and after a divorce, there is often a crisis period (from several months to years) during which families are under great stress because of loss, conflict and change. Most studies show, and psychologists uniformly agree, that the children who 'do best' following divorce are from those families which maintain a low level of conflict. The absence of conflict is even more critical than the amount of time either parent spends with the child.

---

[2]Copies of the Hamilton County's visitation schedule (adopted in 1995) can be obtained on request from Vivian Fliman, 438 Ray Norrish Drive, Cincinnati, OH 45246.

However, children clearly profit [except under very special circumstances] by continued meaningful exposure to both parents. Children need the continuing and regular involvement of both parents to feel loved. No specific schedule will satisfy the change in needs of both children and parents over the years. Critical to the success of any schedule is that each parent be flexible based upon the changing needs of a child, as the child grows older.

This court order takes into account the changing developmental needs of children. It is recognized that each situation and each child is different, and it is preferred that parents tailor the parenting schedule to meet the specific needs of their children.

A good parenting plan developed for a family should be based on the following considerations:

1. The developmental needs and age of each child.
2. The psychological attachments of each child.
3. The way the child-rearing tasks were shared during the marriage.
4. The preservation or development of a close relationship with each parent.
5. A consistent and predictable schedule that minimizes the transition between the households.
6. Each child's temperament and ability to handle change.
7. Parents' career demands and work schedules.
8. The need for periodic review of the plan, [to note] trouble signs and [to revise it] as each child's needs and circumstances change.

If parents have not filed with the Court their own agreed plan, for good cause shown, the following schedule of parenting time . . . is hereby ordered:

* * *

PARENTS WITH CHILDREN IN MORE THAN ONE AGE GROUP:
The policy of the following time allocation is to provide a schedule which is best suited for the particular age of the child(ren). When a family has children in more than one age group, the parents should either adapt the schedule to fit the needs of each child or follow Schedule C [described below].

WEEKLY SCHEDULE
Basic Principles: Birth to Five Years
i. Particularly with very young children, the more frequently the nonresidential parent sees the child(ren), the more appropriate it is to have longer periods of time with the nonresidential parent.
ii. If the nonresidential parent has not had regular contact with the child, short periods of parenting time must precede extended periods.
iii. With children over the age of three months, and particularly with children in the preschool years, more overnight [with the nonresidential parent] time may be appropriate, subject to the temperament of the child and the circumstances of each family.

The nonresidential parent shall have parenting time as follows:
A. Birth to Three months: frequent short visits in the baby's home, unless otherwise specified. If the residential parent is not working outside the home, daily from 6:00 P.M. until 8:00 P.M. If the residential parent is working outside the home, every other day from 6:00 P.M. until 8:00 P.M. The nonresidential parent may take the child for walks or drives if sleeping and feeding are provided for.
B. Three months to Three years:
Frequent short visits per agreement or, Tuesday and Thursday evening from 5:30 P.M. until 8:30 P.M.
One day every weekend, alternating Saturday/Sunday from 10:00 A.M. until 6:00 P.M.
Beginning at 12 months, the Saturday parenting time shall begin on Friday at 6:00 P.M. until Saturday at 6:00 P.M.
C. Three to Five years:
Tuesday and Thursday evening from 5:30 P.M. until 8:30 P.M.
A rotating four week schedule as follows:
Week 1—Friday 6:00 P.M. until Saturday at 6:00 P.M.
Week 2—Saturday 6:00 P.M. until Sunday at 6:00 P.M.
Week 3—Friday 6:00 P.M. until Sunday at 6:00 P.M.
Week 4—Residential parent's weekend.

Basic Principles: Six to Eleven Years
i. Elementary school age children can adapt to longer periods of separation from their principal caretaker than younger children can.
ii. The needs of the 6–11-year-old child with regard to school schedules, homework, and extracurricular activities must be respected.

iii. Adjusting to and moving back and forth between two households increases the complexity of life for a child in a divorce situation. It may, therefore, be necessary to simplify other aspects of a child's life, for example, by reducing the number of outside activities.

The nonresidential parent shall have parenting time as follows:
D. <u>Six to Eleven years:</u>
Alternate weekends from Friday evening at 6:00 P.M. to Monday morning before school, or summer care.
Overnight on the Thursday evening following that weekend from 6:00 P.M. to before school or summer care on Friday morning, and from 6:00 P.M. to 8:00 P.M. on the following Tuesday evening.

Basic Principles: Twelve and Teenage Years
Parents should respect a teenager's need to spend time with peers and in organized activities, and less time with each parent, especially during weekends and summer holidays.
Quality of time is more important than a rigid schedule. Flexibility in scheduling is necessary. When possible, it is preferable to consider the teenager's wishes as long as the parents agree.

The nonresidential parent shall have parenting time as follows:
E. <u>Twelve to Eighteen years:</u>
Tuesday and Thursday evenings from 5:30 P.M. until 8:30 P.M.
A rotating four-week schedule as follows:
Week 1—Friday 6:00 P.M. until Saturday at 6:00 P.M.
Week 2—Saturday 6:00 P.M. until Sunday at 6:00 P.M.
Week 3—Friday 6:00 P.M. until Sunday at 6:00 P.M.
Week 4—Residential parent's weekend.

3. <u>HOLIDAY SCHEDULE/EXTENDED PERIODS</u>
B. When a child reaches the age of two, the nonresidential parent shall be entitled to four weeks of additional time each year. After the age of five, two weeks may be taken consecutively. . . . For children ages two to five, said four-week extended time may be taken in one-week increments. Under the age of two there will be no extended periods.
C. The residential parent shall be entitled to two weeks of consecutive time each year.

DISCUSSION

Our task force met approximately monthly for about a year. Although meetings were amicable and pleasant, there were areas of disagreement and compromise. There was probably a time when the authors would not have recommended overnights before the age of three. We have to admit that we have shifted our thinking in recent years. We were no longer as adamant as we had once been about the potential harmfulness for toddlers of relatively brief separations from principal caretakers if the youngsters were with someone they knew well. Similarly, the provision for as much as a continuous week with the nonresidential parent, starting at age two, reflected a compromise between those of us who were more concerned about issues of separation and those of us who were more attuned to the often desperate wish of nonresidential parents to spend time with their children.

The task force struggled with the issue of the complexity of the schedule, especially for the three- to five-year age range. We all favored simplicity and predictability as desirable goals for both parents and children. However, we recognized that weekend time is special and worked hard to find a way for both parents to have the experience of periodic uninterrupted weekends with their child(ren). The attorneys in the group were especially persuasive, pointing out that such weekends facilitated contact with extended family and short trips out of town. We decided that the benefits of periodic full weekends with each parent outweighed the disadvantages of complexity of schedule.

It was the experience of all of the members of the task force that specificity of scheduling was desirable in that it helps to undercut parental conflict. Also, it is easier for parents, attorneys, and the Court to modify specific arrangements than to create them de novo for each family; hence the recommendations for particular times for the onset and termination of parenting time for the nonresidential parent. We recognized that those times might require accommodation to family and work schedules. We had no easy solution to the problem of families with children of different ages. Our compromise solution—to work out a schedule to meet the needs of each child or to follow the schedule for three- to five-year olds—was based in part on the premise that time away from the residential parent is different for a child with siblings than it is for a single child. For example, a two-year-old can find support and continuity from being with the same beloved brother or sister in both parents' households.

Approximately four years after adoption of the revised standard order, we requested copies of time-sharing schedules from a sample (unsystematic) of Ohio counties to see whether there had been any change in what had been the near absence, in 1994, of developmentally-guided Standard Orders of Visitation. What we found was that the number of counties with age-adjusted visitation schedules had increased, but that most counties still recommend or order the same scheduling for children of all ages. We also interviewed by telephone a sample (again unsystematic) of Hamilton County domestic relations judges and magistrates. Their responses were predominantly positive. They emphasized that they urge parents to work out their own plans, but find the revised standard order useful in situations in which parents either like this plan or cannot agree on another one. One magistrate noted that this plan requires a lot of commitment on the part of the nonresidential parent. Nonresidential parents who cannot or do not want to spend the allotted time with their child may wind up feeling guilty or inadequate as parents, she thought, and she questioned whether that was a good thing.

Attorneys, who were generally pleased with the revised order, expressed the most dissatisfaction with the adolescents' schedule. Our sense is that adolescents, under ideal circumstances, would participate actively in developing a flexible time-sharing arrangement that would allow for time with each parent and would not interfere excessively with their activities and other relationships. They also would need parents to be sensitive to the importance for them of access to peer activities.

However, flexible plans in which young people have major control over time-sharing are vulnerable to abuse by both teenagers and their parents. Thus, children sometimes press parents for privileges or money as a condition for spending time with them. Similarly, parents sometimes use withholding of, or excessive generosity with, money and privileges to barter with their teenager around time-sharing. It is not in a young person's best interests to have the power to manipulate parental rules and limits by refusing, for example, to go to one or the other parent's house. Similarly, it is not in a young person's best interests to be enticed to spend time with a parent in order to obtain money or privileges. To reduce the likelihood of such abuses, and their potency if they do occur, it is helpful for parents and teens to have the structure of a fallback time-sharing schedule.

Finally, we were delighted that it was possible to have a mutually enriching multidisciplinary collaboration characterized by openness and compromise with an end product that was accepted into the system and mostly appreciated by the community. We are accustomed to working intensively with individual families, in therapy and in the courtroom, as they struggle with the knotty problems that derive from divorce situations. It has been refreshing and gratifying to influence the legal system by participating in the development of a revised Standard Order of Visitation that may be having an important effect on the lives of many children and families.

Chapter 20

An Attachment Theory Framework for Planning Infant and Toddler Visitation Arrangements in Never-Married, Separated, and Divorced Families

JUDITH SOLOMON

Decisions about time-sharing or visitation schedules are a common source of concern and conflict in never-married, separated, and divorced families with very young children. Frequently, conflicts revolve around the issue of overnight stays for the infant or toddler in the home of the father. Typically, it is the mother who is anxious and resistant to overnight plans, and the father who is insistent, fearful that his relationship with his child will suffer without overnights in the schedule. Such conflicts often are presented to court mediators and judges, who in turn struggle to balance their notions of what is "in the best interests" of the nonverbal child with judicial policies that favor increasing involvement of fathers in their children's lives. When parents and court personnel turn to the mental health profession for guidance in these cases, they are likely to receive conflicting advice (Goldstein, Freud, and Solnit, 1973; Hodges, 1986; Leiberman, 1993; Kelly and Lamb, 2000; Lamb and Kelly, 2001; Solomon and Biringen, 2001).

Experts disagree for several reasons. First, questions about time-sharing for infants evoke strongly held values and prejudices about what is best for children. Second, there is little uniformity in the training and background of mental health professionals, who make use of different theoretical models to understand the needs of the child. Few mental health professionals have received a thorough grounding in the empirical literature on the changing needs and nature of children over the course of maturation; fewer still have the experience necessary to interpret the behavior of the preverbal child. Finally, and most important, systematic research about the consequences of various schedules has, until recently, been entirely absent.

In order to assist parents and professionals, this chapter outlines the ways in which attachment theory, as first proposed by Bowlby (1973, 1982), and the research that has developed from this theory provide a framework for thinking about and planning for the needs of very young children and their separated parents.

THE NATURE OF ATTACHMENT

Bowlby developed attachment theory to explain why loss or separation from the primary caregiver, or the threat of these, sometimes lead to pathological behavior and personality development. Trained in psychoanalysis, Bowlby attempted to revise Freudian and other psychodynamic models of personality development by placing these theories on a more solid scientific basis. In order to do so, Bowlby forged an integration of ethology, psychoanalysis, and cognitive and developmental psychology that elucidated the nature and function of the child's tie to the caregiver in terms of evolution, adaptation, development, and underlying mechanisms.

Mary Ainsworth, an early colleague of Bowlby's, put the core of Bowlby's theory to an empirical test (Ainsworth et al., 1978). Due in large part to the rigor and success of Ainsworth's research and thinking, attachment theory now provides the dominant scientific model for the study of early relationships. Once rival perspectives, attachment theory has now been largely assimilated into modern day psychoanalytic theory; indeed, in some contexts it can be difficult to say where one theory ends and the other begins (Fonagy, 1999). For this reason it is helpful to summarize the core elements of Bowlby's approach.

The young child's attachment to his caregivers is now understood to reflect a biologically based behavioral system that develops over the course of the first year of life and remains active in one form or another throughout the life span. Freud and others, including the early behaviorists, believed that the attachment bond developed from the infant's experience of nurturance from the caregiver. That is, the caregiver acquired desirability by virtue of her ability to provide the infant with certain positive experiences, such as nursing (and to protect the infant from certain negative ones). It is now accepted that the attachment behavioral system is independent of, although integrated with, other behavioral (or motivational) systems, such as the feeding, exploratory, and sexual systems, and has its own adaptive function, developmental course, and internal organization (Hinde, 1982). The attachment system corresponds to and, presumably, was selected for in evolutionary history, by the infant's and child's particular need for protection from harm of many sorts, including illness, predators, and aggression from others (Bowlby, 1982; Polan and Hofer, 1999).

Attachment behaviors are any acts that function to bring the infant to the caregiver or the caregiver to the infant. They include smiling, signaling sounds and gestures (e.g., arms up), approaching and following the caregiver, and the like. Once the infant has developed an attachment to a specific person, any of a number of "natural cues to danger" will mobilize the infant to insist on proximity and contact with the attachment figure, that is, to display attachment behaviors clearly and persistently. These include internal discomfort (such as illness, fatigue), any unfamiliar or threatening persons or situations, and, separation from the caregiver. Once the infant is alarmed, only proximity to or contact with the attachment figure will be comforting. Under nonthreatening conditions, the attachment figure can be seen to provide a secure base for exploration, that is, the young child is most open to learning about new objects and persons in the reassuring presence of the attachment figure.

Understanding how the attachment system functions allows us to appreciate the emotional significance of attachment figures to the infant and the effects of attachment-related experiences on infant mental health. Separation, or the threat of it, including signs of the caregiver's psychological unavailability, leads to intense anxiety, distress, and anger in the child. In contrast, proximity to the caregiver and confidence in his or her psychological availability leads to a feeling of safety, security, and of being protected. Although attachment is only one of several motivational systems, it has behavioral and emotional priority over them: When threatened, the infant wants the attachment figure *now*. The urgency with which attachment needs are experienced by the young child makes sense when we consider that the attachment system serves the most immediate of survival functions. The vulnerable child needs protection at once. Other needs, such as exploration, usually permit some leeway for satisfaction, and, are therefore usually experienced with less urgency than is the need for the attachment figure.

Attachments to caregivers develop slowly over the first year of life. Social responsiveness becomes increasingly intentional and discriminating, culminating toward the end of the first year in the active and persistent display of attachment behavior toward particular individuals. Attachment behavior is also one of the most salient features of the infant's social behavior in the second and third years of life. By the end of this period, as a consequence of experience and cognitive development, fewer situations will be frightening to the young child, and his or her capacity to use internal mechanisms and other social partners to tolerate separations from the attachment figure improves. Attachment behavior therefore becomes a less salient aspect of the young child's day to day behavior by the end of this period. Nevertheless, whenever the child is frightened or otherwise vulnerable, he or she will experience intensely the need for reassurance from and proximity with attachment figures.

Given the organization of the attachment system, it is hardly surprising that, through the preschool years, separations from the attachment figure of a week or longer elicit intense protest and distress. Importantly, the nature and duration of the young child's reactions to separation depend strongly on the conditions of that separation. The longer the separation, the more unfamiliar and therefore threatening the alternate caregivers and placement are, and the less opportunity the child has to find a stable and sensitive alternate caregiver, the more intense will be the child's negative response (Bowlby, 1973, 1982; Robertson and Robertson, 1989).

Classic studies of children placed in foster care for one or more weeks have shown that, under adverse conditions, initial protest is followed by a period of withdrawal or depression, followed by an apparent adjustment to the new circumstances (Heinicke and Westheimer, 1965; Robertson and Robertson, 1971, 1989). This adjustment actually reflects a walling-off of attachment-related thoughts and feelings. Upon reunion, the child's behavior toward his or her attachment figures is characterized by a dissociated-like state called detachment. Some time after reunion, detachment gives way to disturbances in attachment behavior that may last days or even weeks. These include heightened attachment behavior, an inability to tolerate everyday separations including bedtime, and provocative, angry, and distressed behavior. The more tolerant and available to the child the caregiver is following reunion, the milder and briefer this transition period is likely to be. When the conditions of separation are more optimal, the child's initial distress is less intense, and withdrawal and detachment do not develop. Nevertheless, persistent attachment behavior, distress, and anger are almost inevitably directed toward the attachment figure for some time after reunion.

THE FORMATION OF ATTACHMENTS AND "MONOTROPY"

There are two aspects of attachment that are poorly understood but which seemingly have great relevance to the divorce context. First, it is not entirely clear what conditions are necessary in order for an attachment to develop. We know that infants who grow up in group-care conditions such as those found in some Romanian orphanages, in which there is no stability of caregivers, do not develop attachment relationships (Chisolm, 1998). Indeed, failure to establish an attachment of any kind past approximately two years of age sometimes results in a persistent inability to form one or severe distortions in secure base behavior, even when the child is then placed in a more stable situation (Bowlby, 1982; Talbot, 1998; O'Connor and Rutter et al., 2000). Whether there is some necessary or sufficient threshold of contact that is required for formation of attachment and how this threshold may be influenced by the stability, frequency, or duration of contact is unknown.

On the other hand, all home-reared infants develop an attachment to at least one individual. Even when the toddler is removed from the care of that individual and placed in foster care, the child's attachment to the parent can persist under conditions of limited contact (Jacobsen and Miller, 1999). The receipt of actual care from an individual is neither a necessary nor a sufficient condition for an attachment to develop. All that seems to be required is a(n) unknown, but, presumably, low and repeated level of interaction between the infant and the social partner. Among never-married or separating couples with custody disputes, it is often the case that one of the parents (usually the father) has never lived with the infant, or has lived with the infant for only a few months. In these cases, it is not clear how frequently the infant must see that parent, for how long, or in what context in order for an infant–father attachment bond to develop.

A second and more controversial aspect of attachment is that infants seem to have a predisposition to form a single "primary" attachment, however many additional attachments they also form. This characteristic is often referred to as monotropism (Bowlby, 1982). When the infant is under stress, this particular individual is not only preferred but may, from the infant's point of view, be required; that is, only this individual will be truly comforting when the infant is greatly alarmed, ill, or fatigued. Here again, we do not know what determines this preference. Based on anecdotal information, it is not strictly tied to caregiving experiences with the alternate figures or to differences in the amount of time the infant has spent with them (Freud and Burlingham, 1943; Lamb, 1976). When infants live continuously with both parents, this preference may wane by the time the infant is about twenty-four months, but the data on this question are incomplete (Lamb, 1976, 1977).

One consequence of monotropism is that, following separation, infants tend to be angrier and more insecure toward this primary figure even after they have, apparently, "forgiven" nonprimary attachment figures (Heinicke and Westheimer, 1965; Robertson and Robertson, 1971, 1989). In the context of divorce and visitation, an apparent consequence of caregiver preference is commonly reported by parents: the mother may find that the infant is needy and angry toward her at reunion and for some time thereafter; the father experiences nothing of the sort during his time with the child. Fathers sometimes believe that this difference in the child's behavior is a result of the mother's anxiety and over-protectiveness (since the child seems fine with them); mothers sometimes interpret this as reflecting the father's inadequate care. Although this differential behavior pattern can be exacerbated inadvertently by the actions of one or both of the parents, it may be considered as an expected reaction to separation from the primary caregiver, reflecting his or her psychological importance to the child. The fact that attachment figures are not interchangeable for the very young child greatly complicates the task of devising time-share schedules for parents of very young children. It suggests that we must be especially cautious about disrupting the infant's relationship with his or her primary attachment figure.[1]

ATTACHMENT SECURITY: ETIOLOGY AND CONSEQUENCES

Ainsworth found that important differences in the patterning or organization of infant attachment behavior following brief laboratory separations were systematically linked to stable differences in maternal behavior, especially the mother's sensitive and prompt response to the infant's attachment and other signals (Ainsworth et al., 1978).

Ainsworth identified three patterns of relationships based, not on the infant's response to separation, but on interaction with the mother upon reunion following brief laboratory separations. These three groups are by now well known. Infants classified into the normative or secure pattern (50 percent or more of infant-parent dyads in community samples) are unambiguous in their desire for contact or interaction with the mother following a separation and, if distressed, are comforted by that contact and able to return to comfortable exploration of the environment. The two insecure patterns identified by Ainsworth are characterized by some perturbation in the balance between attachment behavior and exploration, either emphasizing exploration and distance from the mother over the display of attachment (the avoidant group) or insisting on close contact with the mother at the expense of exploration (the resistant group).

---

[1]In the attachment literature, it is often assumed that the primary caregiver is the mother. For purposes of research this is a reasonable assumption, but in the clinical sphere it cannot be assumed. There is nothing in attachment theory proper that favors women over men for this role. As applied to clinical or real-world matters, attachment theory is conservative, in that it tends to "favor" whoever already *is* the primary figure over potential figures that might also serve in this capacity. In the context of custody evaluations, the question of whether one parent is indeed used by the child as a primary figure should be examined explicitly. Unfortunately, there are not well-established rules or measures of this phenomenon. Thus, whether a particular infant has a preference and who the primary source of security is must be determined by looking for differential behavior with the two parents under conditions of real stress, such as when the infant is ill or frightened. As we have already discussed, the amount of time spent with a parent figure or the kinds of activities parent and child engage in together does not necessarily predict this preference.

A fourth, more recently identified insecure group is characterized by incoherent and/or contradictory combinations of attachment and other behaviors (the disorganized group; Main and Solomon, 1990). This group seems to represent the most insecure of the attachment patterns and is most common in high-risk populations, such as maltreatment, maternal anxiety disorder, and alcoholism samples (Lyons-Ruth, 1996).

Thirty years of research with Ainsworth's classification system has shown that the infant or child's attachment security with mother predicts a wide range of social and emotional outcomes in early childhood and adulthood. These outcomes include the capacity for appropriate regulation of emotion, social competence and cooperativeness with peers, finding comfort and reassurance with others, avoiding personally and psychologically dangerous situations, and providing sensitive care to one's own children (for recent reviews of this extensive literature see, for example, Solomon and George, 1999a; Thompson, 1999; Weinfeld et al., 1999).

THE EFFECTS OF REPEATED BRIEF SEPARATIONS ON ATTACHMENT SECURITY

In considering time-sharing schedules for young children in divorced families, we have not only to consider their acute distress, but the long-term consequences for their psychological development. As with the temporary separations described above, Bowlby and others, notably Rutter, proposed that these long-term negative effects would be *context-sensitive*, that is, would depend on conditions before, during, and after the separation or loss (Rutter, 1972; Bowlby, 1982). A great concern was the possibility that major or repeated separations and losses might lead to long-term deleterious changes in the mother–child relationship, resulting in the perpetuation of the heightened insecurity, dysfunctional defenses, and symptomatic behavior of the immediate post-separation period. If Bowlby was correct, these enduring problems should be evidenced in the form of insecure attachment classifications in the context of laboratory separations and reunions.

Although in some of his writing Bowlby emphasized the context-sensitive view of the negative effects of repeated or extended separations, in others he advised that even practices such as day care should be avoided, that is, he placed an emphasis on the separations themselves rather than the context. This emphasis echoed the concerns of earlier investigators, who believed that separation, in and of itself, inevitably had negative effects on the child (Heinicke and Westheimer, 1965; Robertson and Robertson, 1971, 1989). This view was also influential in some of the early studies of the effects of brief separations on quality of attachment (Blehar, 1974; Thompson, Lamb, and Estes, 1981; Belsky, 1986; Bargalow and Vaughn, 1987).

The most recent, large-scale national investigation of day-care effects, however, reported no overall negative effects of amount of early day care (NICHD, 1997). Consistent with Bowlby's original context-sensitive view, the investigators found that long hours in poor quality day care and insensitive mothering interacted to produce higher than expected rates of insecure attachment. In the only large-scale study of the effects of sleeping away from the mother, Israeli investigators found that insecure-ambivalent attachments were more common in kibbutz infants who were cared for at night in a separate infants' house than among kibbutz infants who slept with the parents. The effect was attributed to poor quality of care by the alternate caregivers and the lack of compensatory supportiveness on the part of the parents (Sagi et al., 1994).

A LONGITUDINAL STUDY OF ATTACHMENT
IN SEPARATED AND DIVORCED FAMILIES

The limited data available on the effects of brief, repeated separations thus raise the possibility that such practices can have a negative effect on infant–mother attachment *in some circumstances.* Until recently, however, it was unclear whether the findings from classic and contemporary studies of separation might also apply to co-parenting arrangements in never-married, separated, and divorced families with infants.

A few years ago, my colleague Carol George and I undertook the first systematic longitudinal study of infants and toddlers in these "divided" families. Our goals were to determine whether or not overnight schedules away from the mother were associated with attachment insecurity and to delineate the circumstances in which these arrangements seemed to function well or poorly from the infant's point of view.[2] Key results of the study have been published elsewhere (Solomon and George, 1999b, c, d). Here I summarize the methods and findings very briefly, pointing out their links to attachment theory and research and their major implications.

The study involved 145 mothers and their first-born or oldest child. These families were divided about equally into three groups: separated families in which the child stayed overnight with father on a regular basis; separated families in which the child saw father regularly but did not have overnight stays, and dual-parent (maritally intact) families. Typically, in the overnight group, the infant stayed overnight with the father for one or two nights weekly or biweekly. Only 20 percent of infants stayed with the father for three or more nights in a row. There were no families in which the father was the primary physical caregiver. Mothers and fathers were mature (on average, about 30 years old) and the sample was ethnically and economically diverse. The children were 12 to 18 months at the start of the study (baseline). Many fathers could not be reached or declined to participate; only 83 fathers participated (42 from dual-parent families). It is noteworthy that the couples had separated, on average, by the time the infant was four months old, and a substantial minority had never lived together. Seventy percent of the divorce sample was referred to us by Court agencies. Therefore, the sample primarily comprised families in which there was a dispute about custody or scheduling.

At baseline, we observed infants separately with mother and father (as relevant) in Ainsworth's strange situation, a structured laboratory procedure that includes two separations from and reunions with the parent. Parents also were extensively interviewed about the history of their relationship (divorce groups only) and their relationship with the child and filled out questionnaires about themselves, the infant, and the relationship with the child's father. One year later, the majority (85%) of the families returned for a follow-up. The results at baseline, when the infants were about a year old, were generally in line with what would be predicted from attachment theory. About two-thirds of the infants who had overnights with father were classified as disorganized or unclassifiable in at-

---

[2]This research was funded by a grant to Judith Solomon from the Bureau of Maternal and Child Health Research Program (MCH-060616).

tachment to mother in comparison to one-third such classifications among infants from dual-parent families; this difference was statistically significant. The number of disorganized attachments among infants whose parents were separated but who did not have overnights was intermediate between these two extremes.

In accordance with attachment theory, the *context* of overnight visitation, not just the separations themselves, seemed to explain the unusual levels and types of insecure attachment in the overnight group. Neither the particular pattern of overnight visits nor the total amount of time away from mother predicted disorganized attachment. Insecure attachment in the overnight group was associated, however, with high parent conflict and low parent communication (and was unrelated to parents' current psychological adaptation). In addition, mothers who described themselves in interviews as failing to take the infant's needs into account in the context of overnight visitation with father, or who described themselves as unable to do so, were most likely to have infants whose attachment to them was classified as disorganized.

Paralleling what is known about infant–father attachment in maritally intact families, neither overnight visits nor the amount and patterning of the infant's time with father were related to security of attachment to father. Whether or not the infants had overnights with their fathers, infants in the separated and divorced groups were about twice as likely to be classified as disorganized in attachment to father in comparison to infants in the maritally intact group. Across all groups, including the maritally intact ones, low communication between the parents about the infant was associated with disorganized infant–father attachment which, at the most general level, suggests how important the father's relationship with the mother is for establishing an adequate infant–father relationship.

Results from the follow-up period, when the children were two-and-a-half, indicated that the children's difficulties with overnight visitation continued through the third year of life (Solomon and George, 1999d). They also shed light on the meaning of the high levels of attachment disorganization observed in the earlier period. At follow-up, children who currently were participating in overnights with father performed as well as other children during a challenging problem-solving task with the mother. Their mothers also were judged to be as sensitive in this context as other mothers were. In comparing children with and without overnights who performed well in the problem-solving task, however, we found that, following a second laboratory separation from the mother, overnight children were significantly more angry, resistant, and provocative with the mother. This breakdown in interaction suggests that overnight children were exceptionally sensitive to their mothers' departure and had difficulty "forgiving" her even in the obviously different context of a brief laboratory separation. Additional studies will be needed to determine how long these difficulties persist and what their ramifications may be for the children's subsequent social and emotional development.

CONCLUSIONS OF THE STUDY

The results of our longitudinal study demonstrated that some separated families with young children are able to create a generally supportive environment for overnight visitation regimes. In these families, parents create open lines of communication about the baby, which seem to facilitate sensitive caregiving on the part of both parents toward the child. In these families, the young child enjoys an adequate (organized) attachment to the mother; there is little or no reason to be concerned about the long-term developmental outcome for such children.

On the other hand, in two-thirds of the families who were participating in overnight plans, the parents apparently were unable to maintain a sufficiently supportive environment. These parents engaged in frequent verbal and even physical conflict and shared little or no information about the infant. In some of these families, based on mothers' reports, the mother's distress and anger at the father came to be directed at or displaced onto the infant. In the moment at least, her absorption in conflict with the father supplanted her responsiveness to her child.

In other cases, mothers described themselves as ineffectual at consoling or controlling their insecure infants. Such mothers usually described themselves as equally helpless and ineffective at negotiating a modification of the visitation plan with the father who adamantly guarded his time and independence with the infant. Our impression is that, depending upon the case, this helplessness might reflect a number of factors. These include the realities of the mother's circumstances (e.g., an intractable former spouse, unsympathetic court personnel, a hypersensitive baby), distortions in her perception of these circumstances (for instance, a belief that the father would emotionally abuse the infant as the mother feels he mistreated her in the marriage), or some combination of the two.

Regardless of the underlying cause, the infant was very likely to experience his helpless mother as unresponsive or even aversive at precisely those times when his attachment system was activated strongly, that is, during transitions between his parents' care. We believe that the prevalence of disorganized attachment relationships in the overnight group is a reaction to this state of affairs. By the age of two and a half, when many toddlers had been participating in overnight visitation for over a year, a substantial portion of those whose attachment to the mother originally had been judged disorganized were highly sensitive to a laboratory separation. They continued to be intensely angry and uncooperative with mother for some time after reunion.

CLINICAL IMPLICATIONS OF ATTACHMENT THEORY AND RESEARCH

Clinicians who work with separated couples, whether as a therapist, mediator, or evaluator, in one way or another must help parents decide on an appropriate visitation arrangement. They are also concerned with how best to support parents and child in such a way that these arrangements enhance rather than detract from the development of harmonious and secure relationships. Attachment theory and research can be applied straightforwardly to planning for visitation in separated and divorcing families. Following Robertson and Robertson (1979) these guidelines can be summarized as follows (see also Lieberman, 1993):

1. Familiarity of the Alternate Caregiver and the Environment in which the Child Stays

Following our earlier discussion of the organization and functioning of the attachment system, one of the most potent activators of the attachment system is *unfamiliarity*. When separated from his attachment figure and cared for by another person in an unfamiliar situation, the young child will be anxious and preoccupied with returning to his attachment figure, either intermittently or throughout the separation. Furthermore, the more anxious the child, the more difficulty he or she will have with separation and the more insecure and angry he or she is likely to be upon reunion with the primary caregiver. Although we know that even very young children adapt over time to new places, persons, and caretaking routines, the more familiar the alternative environment and caretaker, the more prompt and easy will be the child's adjustment.

In many never-married and separated families, the infant has had little or no experience with the alternate caregiver or with the house that will be a second home. In such cases, many briefer stays in the care of the alternate caregiver during a prolonged period of familiarization, lasting up to several weeks or even months, should precede the shift to an overnight schedule.

By the same token, familiar objects can help to provide a psychological bridge between people and places. Bringing familiar objects from home, including favorite blankets and toys as well as pictures (of the mother in the father's home or of the father in the mother's home), can provide a reassuring sense of continuity for the young child. Separation and reunion rituals, however simple, become comforting by virtue of their familiarity and help the preverbal child anticipate transitions and therefore be less concerned about them. For example, the routine of packing a bag with objects to take to mother's or father's in the child's presence, and even with his or her participation, can help to routinize or familiarize the transition in a way that can be very comforting.

2. Sensitivity of the Alternate Caregiver

Attachment security grows from the young child's experience of protection, contact, and reassurance that comes *in response to* his or her distress or fear. Thus, security grows out of repeated experiences in which the caregiver meshes his or her behavior with the young child's needs and signals, and the child repeatedly experiences the caregiver's psychological attentiveness. Fathers who seek overnight schedules with their young children often have had little or no opportunity to learn about this specific child and his or her needs. The period of familiarization described above can serve as an invaluable learning period in this regard. Signs of the infant's anxiety and ambivalence about separations can often be quite subtle. For example, the young child might mix biting or hitting with hugging and kissing. Superficially, this behavior may look like rough and tumble play—an indication of the child's happy rather than anxious mood. Developmental guidance and discussion about the child with a knowledgeable clinician can be helpful to fathers who are learning to read these signals.

Outside the context of divorce, alternate caregivers usually learn a great deal about the child—likes and dislikes, schedule, techniques that work well with him or her—from the child's primary caregiver. In well-functioning day-care contexts, for example, mothers and caregivers talk daily and at length about the infant, sharing insights and coordinating their activities in a way that smooths the transitions for the young child.

This communication can be seriously hampered and distorted when mothers and fathers have very little familiarity with one another, as is sometimes the case with never-married parents, or when there is residual conflict and disappointment. Often, fathers wish to avoid communication about the baby, especially during transitions, in order to prevent renewed conflict or intimacy with their child's mother. Many fathers interpret the mother's attempts to share information about the baby as an attempt to control them personally. When their young child has difficulties with transitions or calls for the mother while staying with him, some fathers suspect that the mother has made the child too dependent or insecure. These beliefs are understandable; in some cases, they may reflect, an accurate assessment of the situation. Nevertheless, they can interfere with the infant's experience of his father's responsiveness to him. The challenge to the alternate caregiver is to communicate fully with the primary caregiver and respond sensitively to the infant despite these obstacles.

3. Sensitivity of the Primary Caregiver after Reunification

Sometimes, even in the best circumstances, the young child will return to his or her mother's care with heightened attachment needs, will be easily distressed or angered, and may have difficulties returning to a sleeping routine. Mothers often are worried by such behavior, fearing that the child's experience with the father has been intolerable or that the schedule is harming the child or her relationship with the child. Clinicians can help the mother to understand and interpret the child's behavior, encouraging her to find ways to accommodate to the child's heightened needs without undue anger or anxiety.

The timing of the child's transition to the home of the primary caregiver can be an important factor. Although it is sometimes inconvenient, the primary caregiver should be psychologically prepared to focus only on the child for a good hour or so after reunion. Distraction from other family members or tasks should be avoided at this time. Similarly, transitions should be scheduled so that there is enough time before bedtime or other commitments for mother and child to work through the young child's distress and permit the mother to reassure the child of her psychological availability and responsiveness. Many parents report that limiting the number of transitions the child must deal with (even when this means slightly longer separations) helps to contain the young child's distress. In contrast, at least one psychologist has suggested increasing the number of transitions (Kelly and Lamb, 2000). There is no hard and fast rule—and no hard data—on this issue, however, so parents must be ready to flexibly adjust the schedule around their particular child. Both mothers and fathers may also find it helpful to work with a clinician to decide whether the current schedule needs to be modified, for example, to better suit the infant's natural daily routine, or to accommodate a child whose temperament makes transitions between homes particularly stressful.

CONCLUSIONS:
UNDERSTANDING THE PARENTS' PERSPECTIVE

When parents are able to focus on what works best for their infant and can accommodate one another in ways that support the development of the infant's relationships with both, helping parents to think through the application of the guidelines to their own situation is a relatively straightforward task. As our study shows, and as clinicians often experience, however, many couples are unable to achieve these goals on their own. If we wish to protect young children's relationships with their primary attachment figures while fostering the growth of their relationships with secondary attachment figures, then we must also begin to develop models for working with such divided families.

In the divided family, the primary caregiver must find new ways to provide psychological and physical protection to her infant despite repeated separations and given a necessarily diminished ability to monitor the infant when he or she is with the other parent. The primary caregiver's protective and anxious stance, which may be to some degree inevitable, necessarily places the alternate caregiver in a defensive position—one that may be intolerable. This role of the alternate caregiver is a complex and ambiguous one, as he or she attempts to contain the fear of being excluded from a relationship with the infant and humiliated by the seemingly more powerful primary caregiver. When these issues are intermingled with gender-related sensitivities regarding dominance and power, they can be especially difficult to resolve (Solomon, 2003). Being in the position of the primary caregiver in relation to the child inevitably brings with it a heightened attention to the infant's or toddler's needs. Yet, paradoxically, the father in the divided family often is asked to show his sensitivity to both infant and mother by taking a subordinate role. Fathers benefit when the mother can sympathize with how difficult it is to maintain involvement with the infant in a temporarily secondary role. As a rule, the child's relationship with the father takes on ever-increasing salience over the course of early childhood, frequently taking center stage during the critical adolescent period (Parke, 1995; Grossman, 1997; Horn, 2000). It is to the mother's as well as the child's future benefit to lay the foundation in the early years for the growing importance of the father's contribution.

These normative issues often will be intertwined with the parents' personal issues and sensitivities, requiring both clinical skill and time to unravel. Nevertheless, clinicians may find it helpful to reframe parents' disputes in these more normative terms. Thus, the naturalness of mothers' anxieties can be acknowledged, while the mother is helped to sort out realistic from unrealistic concerns about the father's care of the baby. Fathers who can be encouraged to communicate fully with the mother about the baby will, in turn, do much to allay mothers' anxieties. On the other hand, mothers often must be guided in how to seek this information from fathers without undue intrusiveness. Structuring occasions in the home or office when parents can interact together with the child can also be valuable in allaying mothers' fears and providing a basis for communication between the parents about the child.

In concluding, it is important to highlight the areas in which attachment theory and developmental research cannot help us. Parents, court personnel, and clinicians often would like to know quite specifically what kind of time-sharing plan works best for infants of various ages, and particularly at what age the infant can tolerate overnight visitation best. Beyond the very broad outlines summarized earlier, however, neither theory nor my own data speak to this question. Indeed, it is likely that there is no definitive answer; rather each situation may require a unique solution, reflecting the particular infant and the parents as individuals and as a couple. Theory and research also cannot tell us whether it is better to encourage parents toward more or less time-sharing with infants and toddlers. Is it better to stress the infant in the service of including two parents in his or her life at the earliest possible age? Or is it better to require one parent to wait in the wings, so to speak, until a later time? The answers to these questions await further research, of course, but ultimately will depend on the value parents and society choose to place on the psychological protection of the very young child.

REFERENCES

Ainsworth, M., Blehar, M., Waters, E. & Wall, S. (1978), *Patterns of Attachment.* Hillsdale, NJ: Lawrence Erlbaum Associates.

Bargalow, P. & Vaughn, B. (1987), Effects of maternal absence due to employment on the quality of infant–mother attachment in a low-risk sample. *Child Develop.*, 58:945–954.

Belsky, J. (1986), Infant day-care: A cause for concern? *Zero to Three*, 6:1–6.

—— Gilstrap, B. & Rovine, M. (1984), The Pennsylvania infant and family development project: Stability and change in mother–infant and father–infant interaction in a family setting at 1, 3, and 9 months. *Child Develop.*, 55:692–705.

Bowlby, J. (1973), *Attachment and Loss, Vol. 2.* New York: Basic Books.

—— (1982), *Attachment and Loss, Vol. 1.* New York: Basic Books.

Chisolm, K. (1998), A three-year follow-up of attachment and indiscriminate friendliness in children adopted from Romanian orphanages. *Child Develop.*, 69:1092–1106.

Fonagy, P. (1999), Psychoanalytic theory from the viewpoint of attachment theory and research. In: *Handbook of Attachment*, ed. C. Cassidy & P. Shaver. New York: Guilford Press, pp. 595–624.

Freud, A. & Burlingham, D. (1943), *War and Children*. New York: International Universities Press.

George, C. & Solomon, J. (1999), The development of caregiving: A comparison of attachment and psychoanalytic approaches to mothering. *Psychoanal. Inq.*, 19:618–646.

Goldstein, J., Freud, A. & Solnit, A. (1973), *Beyond the Best Interests of the Child*. New York: Free Press.

Grossmann, K. (1997), Infant-father attachment relationship: Sensitive challenges during play with toddler is the pivotal feature. Presented at the biennial meetings of the Society for Research in Child Development, Washington, DC, April.

Heinicke, C. M. & Westheimer, I. (1965), *Brief Separations*. New York: International Universities Press.

Hinde, R. A. (1982), Attachment: Some conceptual and biological issues. In: *The Place of Attachment in Human Behavior*, ed. C. Parkes & J. Stevenson-Hinde. New York: Basic Books.

Hodges, W. F. (1986), *Interventions for Children of Divorce*. New York: Wiley.

Horn, W. F. (2000), Fathering infants. In: *WAIMH Handbook of Infant Mental Health*, ed. J. D. Osofsky & H. E. Fitzgerald. New York: Wiley, pp. 271–297.

Jacobsen, T. & Miller, L. J. (1999), The caregiving contexts of young children who have been removed from the care of a mentally ill mother: Relations to mother–child attachment quality. In: *Attachment Disorganization*, ed. J. Solomon & C. George. New York: Guilford Press, pp. 347–378.

Kelly, J. & Lamb, M. E. (2000), Using child development research to make appropriate custody and access decisions. *Family & Conciliation Courts Rev.*, 38:297–311.

Lamb, M. E. (1976), Effects of stress and cohort on mother– and father–infant interaction. *Develop. Psychol.*, 12:435–443.

—— (1977), The development of mother-infant and father-infant attachments in the second year of life. *Develop. Psychol.*, 13:637–648.

—— & Kelly, J. B. (2001), Using the empirical literature to guide the development of parenting plans for young children: A rejoinder to Solomon and Biringen. *Family Court Rev.*, 39:365–371.

Lieberman, A. (1993), *The Emotional Life of the Toddler*. New York: Free Press.

Lyons-Ruth, K. (1996), Attachment relationships among children with aggressive behavior problems: The role of disorganized early attachment problems. *J. Consult. & Clin. Psychol.*, 64:64–73.

Main, M. & Solomon, J. (1990), Procedures for identifying infants as disorganized/disoriented during the Ainsworth Strange Situation. In: *Attachment in the Preschool Years*, ed. M. Greenberg, D. Cicchetti & M. Cummings. Chicago: University of Chicago Press, pp. 121–160.

NICHD Early Child Care Research Network (1997), The effects of infant child care on infant–mother attachment security: Results of the NICHD study of early child care. *Child Develop.*, 68:860–879.

O'Connor, T. G., Rutter, M. & the English and Romanian Adoptees Study Team

(2000), Attachment disorder behavior following early severe deprivation: Extensions and longitudinal follow-up. *J. Amer. Acad. Child & Adoles. Psychiat.*, 39:703–712.

Parke, R. D. (1995), Fathers and families. In: *Handbook of Parenting*, ed. M. Bornstein. Mahwah, NJ: Lawrence Erlbaum Associates, pp. 27–63.

Phillips, D., McCartney, K., Scarr, S. & Howes, C. (1987), Selective review of infant day-care research: A cause for concern. *Zero to Three*, 7:8–21.

Polan, H. J. & Hofer, M. A. (1999), Psychobiological origins of infant attachment and separation responses. In: *Handbook of Attachment*, ed. C. Cassidy & P. Shaver. New York: Guilford Press, pp. 162–180.

Robertson, J. & Robertson, J. (1971), Young children in brief separation: A fresh look. *The Psychoanalytic Study of the Child*, 8:288–309. New York: International Universities Press.

—— & —— (1989), *Separation and the Very Young Child*. London: Free Association Books.

Rutter, M. (1972), Maternal deprivation reassessed. *J. Psychosomat. Res.*, 16:241–250.

Sagi, A., van IJzendoorn, M. H., Aviezer, O., Donnell, F. & Mayseless, O. (1994), Sleeping out of home in a kibbutz communal arrangement: It makes a difference for infant-mother attachment. *Child Develop.*, 65:992–1004.

Solomon, J. (2003), The caregiving system in separated and divorcing parents. *Zero to Three*, 23:33–37.

—— & Biringen, Z. (2001), Another look at the developmental research: Commentary on Kelly and Lamb's "Using child development research to make appropriate custody and access decisions for young children." *Family Court Rev.*, 39:355–364.

—— & George, C. (1999a), The measurement of attachment security in infancy and early childhood. In: *Handbook of Attachment*, ed. C. Cassidy & P. Shaver. New York: Guilford Press, pp. 287–316.

—— & —— (1999b), The development of attachment in separated and divorced families: Effects of overnight visitation, parent, and couple variables. *Attachment & Human Develop.*, 1:2–33.

—— & —— (1999c), The caregiving system in mothers of infants: A comparison of divorcing and married mothers. *Attachment & Human Develop.*, 1:171–190.

—— & —— (1999d), The effects of overnight visitation in divorced and separated families: A longitudinal follow-up. In: *Attachment Disorganization*, ed. J. Solomon & C. George. New York: Guilford Press, pp. 243–264.

Talbot, M. (1998), Attachment theory: The ultimate experiment. *The New York Times Magazine*, May 24.

Thompson, R. A. (1999), Early attachment and later development. In: *Handbook of Attachment*, ed. C. Cassidy & P. Shaver. New York: Guilford Press, pp. 265–286.

—— Lamb, M. E. & Estes. D. (1981), Stability of infant–mother attachment and its relationship to changing life circumstances in an unselected middle-class sample. *Child Develop.*, 53:144–148.

Weinfeld, N. S., Sroufe, L. A., Egelund, B. & Carlson, E. A. (1999), The nature of individual differences in infant–caregiver attachment. In: *Handbook of Attachment*, ed. C. Cassidy & P. Shaver. New York: Guilford Press, pp. 68–88.

Chapter 21

Visitation in High-Conflict Families
The Impact on a Child's Inner Life

BARBARA B. HAUSER

*I*n the aftermath of parental separation, critical decisions must be made that have significant effects on the shape and structure of the postdivorce family. Parents and children alike are profoundly affected by these decisions, which guide the family from its former ways, through the disruptive period of dissolution, to the time when previously familiar relationships are shaped into new patterns. Indeed, much of the writing and research on the postdivorce life of children centers on the issue of custody. Considerably less has been written on the issue of visitation. Unlike custody, which has specific definitions covering sole legal custody, sole physical custody, shared legal custody, and shared physical custody, visitation in the law has no such preset formulas or guidelines.

Parents, therefore, have only to formulate a visitation plan that is *reasonable*. What is reasonable to the court, and may also have some air of reasonableness to parents, however, is frequently unreasonable in the eyes and experience of children. Visitation presents an array of challenges and dilemmas, often confusing, frequently distressing, and always complex to children, who struggle to maintain stability in the wake of their parents' separation.

CHILD ACCESS: CONSIDERATIONS

As distinct from custody, visitation is an evolving process. It presents to parents and their children a staggering array of choices.

There are, to begin with, the many specifics of scheduling time for children to be with the noncustodial parent. Often, the division of time between weekends and weekdays mirrors the desires and convenience of adults rather than the natural rhythms of a child. There are the ordinary and expectable demands on the child's time: school events, peer relationships, extracurricular activities, birthday parties, summer recreational programs, all of which derail visitation schedules and are often seen by the nonresidential parent as interferences on "*my* time."

Such are the external factors with which parents work to frame their visitation arrangements. It is critical, however, that these factors work in concert with issues intrinsic to the child, which, more than questions of day and time, shape the child's relationship with the noncustodial parent. The child's developmental stage is a central consideration in the formulation of visitation plans (Wallerstein and Corbin, 1996; Johnston and Roseby, 1997). The child's individual temperament and personality characteristics, which affect his ability to manage transitions and separations, are also factors to be considered.

For all children, each time of visiting can be an event that begins and ends with a sharply defined experience of the simultaneous combination of separation and reunion. There are countless ways children respond to these experiences, ranging from frenzied activity to marked withdrawal. But this challenge for children is best captured by a four-year-old boy who for months greeted his father each time with one word: "Hellogoodbye" and his mother, on returning, with a different one: "Goodbyehello." Visitation frames a relationship over time, beginning in the post-separation period and spanning the life of the parent–child relationship. It shapes what is and what is to become of the relationship with the noncustodial parent and, as such, also influences the child's relationship with the custodial parent. It is the arena in which loyalty conflicts can flourish, fueled by parental hostility.

For children, there is no equivalent of a visiting relationship in the predivorce life of their family. There are threads in the experience of time spent away from home with grandparents and other trusted relatives, but this is truly the most minimal rehearsal for visitation. Above all, visitation is a reminder that, despite the parents' profound wish to separate, which guides divorce proceedings, children's wishes, needs, and relationships to both their parents must guide visitation decisions, thereby continuing to link parents together

(Arditti and Kelly, 1994; Emery, 1999b; Madden-Derditch and Arditti, 1999).

POSTDIVORCE PARENTING STYLES

The literature contains innumerable studies documenting the range of parental styles following divorce. Of the 1000 divorcing parents in Maccoby and Mnookin's study (1992) 25 percent maintained a cooperative parenting style, while fully another quarter remained mired in hostility. The remaining 50 percent attained a pattern of disengagement, often called parallel parenting (Furstenberg and Cherlin, 1991), characterized by limited communication and lack of mutuality. These patterns appeared to be relatively stable over time despite expectations that with time and the prevalence of mandatory divorce education programs, disengaged parents would become more cooperative and hostility and conflict would decrease. Thus, it would seem that, for the majority of children of divorced parents, visitation occurs in a climate of enduring open hostility or disengagement, which can masquerade as a neutral or even harmonious state. Both conditions, however, can be burdensome for children.

Studies of samples both small and large, time-limited and longitudinal, based on questionnaire or interview data, frequently emphasize the adverse effects of hostility and conflict between former spouses on children's adjustment. Conflict between separated parents takes a variety of forms. It may be absent in the predivorce life of parents, only to emerge during the period of separation and continue long after the divorce is final. Emery (1999a), in a twelve-year follow-up of divorced couples, noted that parental conflict persisted unchanged over time. Hostilities evident in parents' expressed negative views of each other, competition for their children's loyalties, arguments over parenting practices, and use of children as messengers are the patterns most destructive to children's well-being.

An example of such difficulty is clearly evident in the psychological testing report of eleven-year-old Amy. Her parents separated when she was two, and the "divorce has been conflictual for all." Amy has "a strong need to make everything fit together. The need is so strong that at times it interferes with her reality testing. . . . She seems to be working very hard to pull everything together and keep things whole. . . . Issues of separation and attachment are most likely related to her need to make everything fit together." What to parents has become a chance to grow and change feels unfamiliar and confusing to children. They, unlike their parents, are the family members who are privy to the range of characteristics of *both* households: the spatial configurations, sizes and colors of rooms, the contents of the refrigerators, and, perhaps most important, the others who occupy the space. Their picture of the lives of their mothers and fathers is far more complete than those of their parents, each of whom has only a partial view. Children are exquisitely aware of the burdens of this familiarity with vast quantities of information known to them but unknown to one of their parents. Under benign conditions of transitions from one household to another, there is minimal discomfort in decisions to share such storehouses. When parents are in conflict, there is perceived danger in those revelations.

CLINICAL VIGNETTES

Jonathan and MaryLou

Jonathan, whose parents divorced when he was three years old, had a unique but understandable response. His mother, intensely protective of her son and enraged at her former spouse, whom she felt was an inadequate parent, wished to limit Jonathan's visitation schedule to two hours per week. When the court ordered whole day visits, and after a year, weekend overnights, her anxiety increased. Partings were difficult and, when he returned, she asked Jonathan countless questions about his activities at his father's house: What did he eat? Where did he go? What programs did he watch on television? Did his father allow him to ride his bike unattended? Were there others caring for him? Jonathan's father, equally angry at his former wife for restricting his contact, asked him similar questions about his mother's household. Often his mother or father would stuff angry notes in his suitcase. When Jonathan entered second grade, he precipitously ceased talking outside the home. With his parents, his former chatter was reduced to monosyllabic answers. Brought to therapy, he remained silent throughout the beginning three months of treatment; his first word in the therapy hour was "please," when he signaled his desire for a puppet. Although with continued treatment Jonathan grew into a talkative fourth grader, he remained markedly inhibited, and restricted in his communications with both parents as they continued their battles well into his adolescence.

Seven-year-old MaryLou's response to her parents' conflict was quite different from Jonathan's. Separated when MaryLou was two, her mother and father had not spoken directly to each other since that time; all communications were through their new partners or in court proceedings. On MaryLou's shoulders fell the burden of establishing some contact between the households, which she accomplished by furtive phone calls to her mother, often late at night. Her mother was painfully aware of her daughter's anxiety and distress as expressed in her entreaties to her mother to remain on the telephone. However, she also felt helpless to change the lengthy overnight visitation that had been ordered by the Court after extensive litigation.

Separating families and those professionals who guide them through the process of divorce confront a myriad of dilemmas in structuring access arrangements (Benedek and Brown, 1995). A central challenge that is clear from the beginning of the time parents separate is how to satisfy their children's need for both parents and how to minimize one of their children's primary fears, that of abandonment. The task of meeting the children's needs is daunting, indeed, particularly when it occurs in the climate of parental conflict. Instituting access arrangements insures that parents must continue to be in regular and reliable contact, which for many children means regular and reliable conflict. Significant reduction or elimination of contact with a noncustodial parent may protect the child from conflict, but raises the specter of abandonment and the reality of loss. It is necessary to balance the relative risks of continual exposure to parental conflict against the experience of loss of contact and the sadness and stress that accompany such a loss.

These dilemmas are mirrored in the responses of children whose parents' conflict has resulted in innumerable ruptures in contact with their noncustodial parents (Arditti and Kelly, 1994). These ruptures, fueled by the resistance of custodial parents to encourage or enable visitation to occur, may be short-term until repaired, often by legal remedies, or they may last for months, even years. Children experiencing these ruptures demonstrate a remarkable congruence in their responses, which contain feelings of sadness, fear, and curiosity, as well as fantasies concerning the parent who is absent, fantasies that they cannot share with the one who is present.

Michael and Jason

When Michael was three, his young parents divorced after a marital relationship marked by episodic separations, experimentation with alcohol and drugs, intermittent violent exchanges, and economic difficulties. He saw his father irregularly for the first year after the separation. His mother, distressed over his father's unreliability and irregular child support, allowed no further visits after Michael was five. Just prior to seeing his father again after a three-year absence, Michael said the following, "I've thought about seeing him again . . . I remember what he looks like . . . he has brown hair like my brown hair. But I don't remember much 'cause I was only a baby. I do have a daddy," he says, referring to his stepfather, "who's nice. He plays with me and gets me things . . . But I've always wondered about my dad, where he was, what he was doing, if he'd ever, ever see me again. I felt happy inside when I knew I would see him again. But I didn't tell mom because she might get mad. She yells every time I say his name."

Meeting his father, Michael smiles and welcomes his hug. "I missed you," he says spontaneously, to which his dad responds, "It was tearing my heart out." Says Michael soberly but emphatically, "I know just what you mean about that."

Seven-year-old Jason had a similar history. He lived with his mother, frequently visiting his father, after his parents' separation. His mother's severe discipline, erratic care-taking, and abusive boyfriend resulted in his father obtaining custody. Following this custodial change, Jason's father began to restrict visits with his mother, claiming that experiences with his mother had frightened Jason. He was resistant to allowing even supervised contact. Jason's mother appealed to the court to begin visits with Jason. In preparation for their reunion, Jason told the following story:

"Sometimes I have thoughts. What if dad is asleep and I am asleep and I feel this hand on my shoulder? I have just lost a tooth. Maybe it's the tooth fairy that has come. She says, 'Come with me,' and I go to the car and lie down—like I am in bed. Then I wake up and it's mom saying I am going with her."

With his mother, Jason is cautious, but soon they play games together while he easily tells her of school activities and the new baby in his family. When the visit ends, he is initially subdued, but the seeming sadness turns quickly into anxiety. To the interviewer he says, "I was supposed to tell her, 'I don't love you,' but I made a mistake. Dad asked me to say that. I was afraid she'd cry. . . . Inside I was happy but outside was the dark side. The dark side makes me try to hate her. I was supposed to say bad things about my mom that are very hard to say." He brightens briefly, "But it made me feel happy. Very happy—no, very, very happy." "What," he is asked, "made you happy?" Jason says simply, "My mom."

INTEGRATING TWO WORLDS

Embedded in these children's narratives are entrenched loyalty conflicts, limitations on spontaneous expression, and restrictions in their ability to weave tales of their life when in the care of the other parent. They tell their stories with heightened vigilance to the reactions of the parent they are with, searching the landscape for clues in a gesture, a look, or a phrase of each parent's sentiments about the other. Too often they are aware only of pervasive resentments and the abundance of negative images that often conflict with the reality of their own more positive relationships with each of their parents.

As these children grow, there is often little change in two distinct domains: the legal arrangements that define their visitation schedule and the hostile emotions that fuel and shape their parents' chronic conflicts. New partners, alterations in economic status, and geographical relocations may result in shifts in scheduling or a parent's temporary distraction from negative interactions. However, such diversions are often short-lived. Thus these children's developmental trajectories, flexible and fluid, proceed against a background of rigid legal agreements and static parental disagreements.

Unlike their parents, whose lives are now separate from each other, these children confront and contain a past, present, and future history of *all* of the relationships in their family. Lisa made such a history come alive in a single picture. Unable to give words to the experience of living with eight years of her parents' constant litigation over visitation, she elected to draw her family. All the figures in her world have smiling faces, and stand on green grass, in bright sunshine under a blue sky filled with puffy, white clouds. It is only on closer study that one sees that the woman designated as her mother is about to lose her footing and that her father is placed at a distance from his daughter. Standing closest to her brother, Lisa depicts herself with her stepmother's brown hair, her father's blue eyes, wearing an outfit identical to her mother's.

The stories that pictures like these and the children composing them tell are compelling representations of their often fragmented and confusing inner lives. These children's public faces are, like Lisa's figures, frequently smiling and even tranquil. Yet their private narratives reveal that far too often these children have become repositories of shared information, guardians of secrets, keepers of scores, and purveyors of messages. All of these are uncomfortable roles, but they are distinctive postures borne of the necessity to adapt to their parents' open or, at best, thinly-veiled warfare.

Throughout childhood and adolescence, the emergence of patterns of resilience allows for the necessary containment of these children's underlying distress and pain about their families' dissolution. Nonetheless, reflecting on their many years of experience dodging the persistent conflicts that filled the space between their parents' households, two adolescents, on the threshold of their own separation from their parents, remarked with considerable resignation: "You don't get over it; you get used to it."

REFERENCES

Arditti, J. A. & Kelly, M. (1994), Fathers' perspectives of their co-parental relationships post-divorce: Implications for family practice and legal reform. *Family Relations*, 43:61–67.

Benedek, E. P. & Brown, C. F. (1995), *How to Help Your Child Overcome Your Divorce*. Washington, DC: American Psychiatric Press.

Brant, J. (1991), *Law and Mental Health Professionals: Massachusetts*. Washington, DC: American Psychological Association.

Chambers, D. L. (1984), Re-thinking the substantive rules for child-custody disputes in divorce. *Michigan Law Rev.*, 83:477–569.

Czapanskiy, K. (1999), Interdependencies, families and children. *Santa Clara Law Rev.*, 39:101–178.

Emery, R. E. (1999a), Grieving divorce. Presented at meeting of Society for Research in Child Development, Albuquerque, NM.

—— (1999b), Post-divorce family life for children: An overview of research and some implications for policy. In: *The Post-Divorce Family*, ed. R. A. Thompson & P. R. Amato. Thousand Oaks, CA: Sage, pp. 3–27.

Furstenberg, F. F., Jr. & Cherlin, A. J. (1991), *Divided Families*. Cambridge, MA: Harvard University Press.

Goldstein, J., Freud, A. & Solnit, A. J. (1973), *Beyond the Best Interests of the Child*. New York: Free Press.

—— Solnit, A. J., Goldstein, S. & Freud, A. (1996), *In the Best Interests of the Child*. New York: Free Press.

Johnston, J. R. & Roseby, V. (1997), *In the Name of the Child*. New York: Free Press.

Kelly, J. B. (1997), The best interests of the child: A concept in search of meaning. *Family & Conciliation Courts Rev.*, 35:377–387.

Maccoby, E. & Mnookin, R. H. (1992), *Dividing the Child*. Cambridge, MA: Harvard University Press.

Madden-Derditch, D. A. & Arditti, J. A. (1999), The ties that bind: Attachment between former spouses. *Family Relations*, 48:243–249.

Massachusetts Gen. Law ch. 208 § 31 217 (1998).

Novinson, S. L. (1983), Post-divorce visitation: Untying the triangular knot. *Univ. Illinois Law Rev.*, 1:121–200.

Stewart, A. J., Copeland, A. P., Chester, N. L., Malley, J. E. & Barenbaum, N. B. (1997), *Separating Together*. New York: Guilford Press.

Wallerstein, J. & Corbin, S. B. (1996), The child and the vicissitudes of divorce. In: *Child and Adolescent Psychiatry*, ed. M. Lewis. Baltimore, MD: Williams & Wilkins, pp. 1118–1127.

Chapter 22

Supervised Visitation

*Preserving the Rights of Children
and Their Parents*

ALAN J. TUCKMAN

*E*nforcement of visitation with noncustodial parents and their
children presents decision makers with one of the most difficult problems encountered in the field of family law. When
access is a problem, it is one of the toughest to resolve.

When parents divorce, the mother, who is usually the custodial
parent, often blends the father role with the husband role and divorces both, viewing visitation as something she may terminate at
will. Similarly, many fathers withdraw from active visitation because
they view marriage and parenthood as a package deal. They often
include among other reasons for withdrawal from the family such
things as unwillingness to pay child support, a new father figure in
the home, competing demands of a new family, and unrewarding
relationships with the children of the divorce. If access is interfered
with, this also contributes to their withdrawal.

It is my opinion that visitation is nearly always appropriate and
necessary following divorce and cannot be foreclosed unless there is
clear and convincing evidence that it significantly endangers the
child's physical, mental, or emotional health (see chapters 1, 10–12,
21, and 23). Even in cases where one spouse has abused the other,
both may still be loving to the children. When children do not see a
previously violent parent, they may exaggerate the danger in their
minds or may repress memory of the violence and overidealize the
absent parent (see chapter 6). They may even blame themselves,

believing that if they had been better children, the absence would not have occurred.

This self-blame may result in a significant drop in self-esteem as well as future depression, or the children may even hold the custodial parent accountable for the break-up and lack of access to the absent parent, producing a rift in that relationship as well, and causing them to feel alienated from both parents. Even a noncustodial parent with few redeeming qualities may have something to offer a child and, at the least, the presence of that parent in the child's life may tend to avoid inappropriate fantasies and reactions.

JUDICIAL INTERVENTION

Parental divorce does not leave children without parents, although it often leaves them feeling abandoned by the noncustodial parent, especially when visitation is minimal. A New York court, in a holding in a custody and visitation case, stated "visitation is always to be premised upon a consideration of the best interests of the children . . . however, denying visitation to a natural parent is a drastic remedy and should only be done where there are compelling reasons . . . and there must be substantial evidence that such visitation is detrimental to the child's welfare" (*Parker v Ford*, 1982) (quoted in Tortorella, 1996).

Requiring supervised visitation is often a too-easy way out of a perplexing dilemma. Children are subject to many traumas in the midst of an acrimonious custody dispute, including the loss of the intact family, parental fighting, negative statements by the parents, repeated separations, and financial changes. Since custodial parents are frequently hurt and angry and may be vindictive, they may wittingly or unwittingly produce symptoms in the children which are then attributed to the visitation with the noncustodial parent.

THE BASIS FOR SUPERVISED VISITATION

Given that the courts have accepted the premise that there are advantages to the child's having ongoing contact with the noncustodial parent, there remain an array of circumstances under which supervised visits may be required. Prior to requiring supervised access between a noncustodial parent and children, my recommencation is that there must be clear evidence and sufficient findings of one or more of the following:

   a. Serious mental illness in the noncustodial parent that has resulted in markedly inappropriate behavior damaging to the children.
   b. Past history of physical abuse with lack of remorse and little appreciation of its impact on the children.
   c. Vindictive behavior toward the children or toward the custodial parent that is having an obvious damaging effect on the children's perception of the custodial parent.
   d. Arrests for antisocial behavior against people (see chapter 13) and disobedience of court orders during the pendency of the custody and visitation proceedings, indicating a marked impairment in judgment and an impairment in the ability to conform and to control one's behavior even while being observed.
   e. Abuse that has had a direct impact on the children. (While parental fighting or abuse within the marriage may become the basis for a recommendation of supervised visitation, frequently the abuse ends with the end of the marriage and the abuse may not have been directed at the children.)
   f. Substantiated sexual abuse of the child (see chapter 18). Allegations of sexual abuse arising in the midst of a custody and visitation action, when unproven, should not be utilized as the sole basis for depriving a parent of all visitation.
   g. Active alcohol and substance abuse, especially where there are allegations of the parent driving while under the influence or where the children have been under the supervision of an intoxicated parent.
   h. Persistent violations of or interference with custody or visitation orders.
   i. Threats or past acts of abduction. There is no basis to impose supervised visitation on a parent who was simply born (or who has family members living) in another country. This does not, in and of itself, indicate a parent's likelihood of absconding with the child.

j. Attempts by a noncustodial parent to impose religious views on a child against the custodial parent's wishes. Like it or not, the custodial parent sets the rules.

k. Ongoing (postdivorce) parental conflict produced by a noncustodial parent, that is having a detrimental effect on the child.

l. Little or no contact between noncustodial parents and their children over an extended period of time, (6–12 months or longer) followed by attempts to reestablish contact. Under these circumstances, a period of supervised visitation may allow time for the children to become comfortable with their formerly absent parent. Lack of contact may occur due to prior terminations of visitation, an abandonment, an inability to find the children, or extreme resistance by a custodial parent.

m. An alienated child who is strongly allied with the custodial parent, taking on that parent's identity as a victim and retaliator, and thus, consciously or unconsciously, appropriately or inappropriately, views the noncustodial parent as dangerous and damaging (see chapter 9). This has recently been termed parental alienation syndrome (Stahl, 1994).

CASE ILLUSTRATION

A middle-class suburban couple, married for 13 years and separated for 18 months, presented themselves to the family court upon petition by the mother for supervised visitation for the father, claiming that the father had physically abused her during the marriage and sexually abused the children. Their children were two girls, seven and nine years old, living with the mother since the separation. The allegations of sexual abuse immediately triggered an investigation by Child Protective Services, including a sexual abuse evaluation. No evidence of any sexual abuse was found, nor was there evidence that the children had viewed any alleged physical abuse of the mother by the father. Yet during the evaluation, the children made statements about the father that seemed inconsistent with their emotional presentation while making those statements and that were too sophisticated for their developmental level. The comments, referring to their father's lack of interest in them, abandoning them, and tormenting their mother, were presented in a manner that led the evaluator to consider whether the children had been coached to offer this material.

The father presented as a somewhat passive man, seemingly devoted to his children and without any significant psychopathology. The mother, on the other hand, presented as extremely possessive and enmeshed with her children, dressing them identically and wanting to educate them at home because she did not believe the school appreciated the children's problems (both children had a history of asthma). The school authorities described the children as functioning well, but also commented about the mother's intensely intrusive behavior.

Psychological testing of the father was essentially unremarkable. Psychological testing of the mother revealed significant underlying identity conflicts, conflicts with authority figures, a narcissistic character structure, and mistrust of others. The forensic psychiatric recommendation was for unsupervised visits for the father, psychotherapy for the mother, and an admonition to the mother that she refrain from intruding upon the visits between the father and children.

Six months later the family was back in court with the mother again petitioning for suspended or supervised visits between the father and children, claiming that he still was molesting them. Again, there was no evidence, but it became clear that the children's conduct and academic performance had been deteriorating. They both appeared more regressed. The father had continued to see the children despite the mother's attempts to obstruct the visitation. The school records were reviewed, including notations about the mother's attempt to obstruct the school's prerogatives and the children's learning processes.

Despite objections by the law guardian and the attorney for the mother, I made a recommendation for a change in custody. This recommendation was made due to the intense bond between the children and mother, who had attempted to isolate the children both from their father and from other social contacts, including the school. The court strongly admonished the mother for undermining the relationship between the father and the children and mandated psychotherapy for her. She was allowed unsupervised visitation with her children.

Several months later the case was brought back into court for review. The children appeared to have adjusted well to the change in custody, with significant improvement in their conduct and academic performance. The mother, on the other hand, continued to violate the orders of the court, intruding upon the father's custodial prerogatives and continuing her attempts to undermine the children's relationship with their father. At this time, supervised visitation was instituted between the mother and the children based upon the recommendation of the children's therapist, who saw the children as being harmed by the mother's inappropriate behavior. The saga continues.

TYPES OF SUPERVISED VISITATION

Supervised visitation may take two general forms. It may occur with a nonprofessional or with a mental health professional supervisor. The nonprofessional may be a family member, such as a grandparent; a college or graduate student (either untrained or trained); a supervisor who only considers safety during visits; or a supportive supervisor, who might offer parenting suggestions during the visit. The mental health professional supervisor is licensed and trained in parenting interventions and has special expertise in domestic violence, child sexual abuse, child abuse/neglect, and substance abuse (New York Society for the Prevention of Cruelty to Children, 2000).

When the supervisor is not a mental health professional, there are three basic types of supervision provided by most child access programs:

1. *One-to-one supervision* is the most intensive supervision. The parent and child are at all times involved with the supervisor, who can both observe and hear the details of the interaction. This occurs in situations where issues of safety or manipulation or coercion of the child are of most serious concern.
2. *Transition monitoring, or exchange supervision* involves supervision of the transfer of the children between parents at the start and end of the visits, but not of the actual visit between parent and child. It is especially useful where there is a history of explosive parental conflicts that take place in front of the children or in cases where a child becomes openly upset at the transfers, but where the relationship between the parent and child is not at issue.

3. *Loose monitoring* is used in cases in which there is no real concern regarding the safety of the child and minute-by-minute supervision is unnecessary. The supervisor is nearby and occasionally observes or listens to the interactions. A number of families may be monitored at once in a common space or an outdoor play area. This is used where the children haven't seen the parent in some time or where there is a history of abuse or substance use.

All three types of supervision can be adapted to off-site visitation at a shopping mall or playground or even, as the visitation progresses, to the noncustodial parent's home. Obviously, off-site visitation provides a much more natural and varied opportunity for interaction between parent and child. Most supervisors are expected to make notes of their observations that will be accessible to the court. They should have some form of training in supervising visitation. At times they may be required to testify about their observations of the visitation.

In supervised therapeutic visitation, a mental health professional acts as both the supervisor of the visitation and a therapist for both the child and the noncustodial parent. The supervisor meets with the child a number of times to prepare the child for the visitation. This occurs in situations in which the child is resistant to visitation, or where abuse of the child has occurred, or where the child is significantly alienated from the parent. The supervisor also meets with the parent for several sessions to orient the parent to appropriate parenting skills. In the visitation, the supervisor provides supervision for the parent–child interaction and also provides guidance to the parent and helps the child to be more accepting of the parent (Strauss, 1995).

TERMINATION OF VISITATION

There are rare situations in which the drastic step of termination of visitation[1] may be appropriate. This is to be distinguished from termination of the parent's rights (see chapter 14). These include:

---

[1]Distinctions between termination of a specific supervised visit and termination of supervised visitation services are offered in the *Professionals' Handbook on Providing Supervised Visitation* (New York Society for the Prevention of Cruelty to Children, 2000).

a. Where the child categorically and vehemently refuses to see the parent even after several attempts at supervised, therapeutic visitation.
b. Where a noncustodial parent manipulates a supervision, disobeys rules and guidelines, attempts to manipulate the child through letters or other communications, or surreptitiously attempts to gather information from the child about the custodial parent, even after having been admonished not to do so.
c. Where the noncustodial parent is seriously mentally disturbed and has no capacity to maintain control of his/her actions or to follow the rules of the supervision.
d. Where a child has been seriously abused by the parent and becomes intensely anxious and disturbed at the suggestion or actual initiation of supervised visitation.

The trauma to the child of attempting to effect visitation may be greater than the benefit of the visitation itself. However, it must be remembered that because a child becomes disrupted for a day or two after visitation (a not uncommon occurrence), this is not an appropriate indication to terminate visitation. Even under the best of circumstances, children may become anxious and act out temporarily after seeing a noncustodial parent after visitation.

CHOOSING A SUPERVISOR

Supervised visitation is a costly process, generally entailing significant fees. Thus, many people have attempted to utilize family members or friends of the noncustodial parent, or even of the custodial parent, as supervisors. They are generally not neutral, attempt to minimize the need for supervision, or in the case of family members or friends of the custodial parent, attempt to overemphasize the need for protection of the child. They always have an allegiance to the parent with whom they are aligned.

Supervisors must be independent parties who have had some degree of training in what is appropriate and what is inappropriate parental behavior and must have the support of an agency or a supervisor of their own in order to discuss the case and their personal responses to various situations. They must be able to enforce guidelines, understand the protection of the child and understand a child's interests and needs at each phase of development. In addition, they must not have a bias against the parent who is being supervised.

The supervisor should be someone who can mirror for the supervised parent appropriate parenting skills, such as how to develop a relationship with a resistant child, how to divert an unruly or crying child, and how to maintain boundaries. Discussion in advance between the parent and the supervisor about what will occur, what the setting for visitation will be, and what guidelines are to be followed are crucial to the success of the visitation process.

CONCLUSION

Supervised visitation should be used only in the most extreme situations and for a limited period of time. It does have the effect of undermining the child's trust in that parent, it is very expensive, and if the parent does not demonstrate changes to more appropriate behavior (including absence of psychiatric symptoms or aggressiveness, abstinence from substance abuse, avoidance of derogatory statements about the custodial parent and strict compliance with the visitation schedule), within a reasonable period of time, the likelihood of future change becomes very small. Supervised therapeutic visitation is an alternative that has been under-utilized and that may meet with greater success than that of supervised visitation with a non-mental health supervisor. Supervised visitation can be protective of or punitive to a child and his or her noncustodial parent depending on how it is handled. Every attempt must be made to maintain the relationship between the child and the estranged parent (see chapters 1, 10–12, 21, and 23).

REFERENCES

James, B. & Gibson, C. (1991), Supervising visits between parent and child. *Family & Conciliation Courts Rev.*, 29:73–84.

Johnston, J. & Straus, R. (1999), Traumatized children in supervised visitation: What do they need? *Family & Conciliation Courts Rev.*, 37:135–158.

New York Society for the Prevention of Cruelty to Children (2000), *Professionals' Handbook on Providing Supervised Visitation*. New York: New York Society for the Prevention of Cruelty to Children.

Parker v. Ford, 453, NYS 2nd 465-466 (App. Div. 1982).

Stahl, P. (1994), *Conducting Child Custody Evaluations.* Thousand Oaks, CA: Sage.

Strauss, R. B. (1995), Supervised visitation and family violence. *Family Law Quart.,* 29:229–252.

—— & Alda, E. (1994), Supervised child access: The evolution of a social service. *Family & Conciliation Courts Rev.,* 32:230–246.

—— Blaschak-Brown, N. & Reiniger, A. (1998), Standards and guidelines for supervised visitation network practice: Introductory discussion. *Family & Conciliation Courts Rev.,* 36:96–107.

Tortorella, M. (1996), When supervised visitation is in the best interest of the child. *Family Law Quart.,* 30:199–215.

The following literature on supervised visitation is available: New York Society for the Prevention of Cruelty to Children has published a handbook on providing supervised visitation (2000). Strauss and Alda (1994), Strauss (1995), Johnston and Strauss (1999), and James and Gibson (1991), discuss supervised visitation from a psychological perspective. Tortorella (1996) addresses supervised visitation from the legal perspective. Straus, Blaschak-Brown, and Reiniger (1998) present standards and guidelines for supervised visitation which evolved from the launching of SVN, the Supervised Visitation Network, in 1994.

Chapter 23

Relocation

Parents' Needs, Children's Interests

PAUL HYMOWITZ

To rephrase Tolstoy, In happy families, all relocations are alike; in unhappy families, each relocation is unhappy in its own way.

Relocation cases, which concern the right of a divorced parent to move away with the children, set in bold relief many of the more vexing child custody issues the courts have to face. In these cases, the competing claims of a custodial parent's right to pursue his or her own goals, the noncustodial parent's wish to remain involved and actively present in the children's everyday life, and the children's best interests must all be juxtaposed. Because relocation often entails a more permanent and one-sided resolution of the family dispute than a standard custody case, it can be a far more bitterly fought battle.

Further complicating the resolution of custody disputes is the fact that our society is an increasingly mobile one, and divorced parents are, understandably, even more likely to move than married ones. It is estimated that, within four years of divorce, seventy five percent of custodial mothers will move at least once (Trusch, 1997). Relocation law has thus become a crucial battleground in which the primacy of the mother–child bond is pitted against the increasingly active involvement of fathers in the life of the child.

This chapter explores how the courts have traditionally handled relocation disputes in New York and California. It addresses limitations in many of the current relocation statutes and argues the need for recognizing each family's unique dynamics.

HISTORY OF RELOCATION LAW

The right of the custodial parent to relocate has traditionally been subject to legal restrictions. The restrictions have been implemented by requiring the relocating parent to demonstrate "exceptional circumstances" to justify her proposed move, in part to serve as a deterrent. Consistent with Goldstein, Freud, and Solnit's (1973) position, however, a number of scholars argue that the primary parent's understandable desire to reconfigure his or her life is unduly hampered by the severe penalties that have been imposed on a parent's desire to relocate in a society that is increasingly mobile (Miller, 1995).

As of 1990, there was considerable disparity in how states approached relocation litigation. In many states, a presumption in favor of the custodial parent prevailed. Other states placed on the relocating parent the burden of proof that the move would not undermine the children's best interests.

The most widely quoted decision at that time was *D'Onofrio v D'Onofio* (1976), which attempted to balance the competing interests of all family members. In this case, the New Jersey court ruled that, after divorce, children and their custodial parent comprise a new family unit. It held that what is advantageous for this new unit as a whole is obviously in the best interests of the children. Nevertheless, the court left the custodial parent with the burden of demonstrating that some real advantage would accrue to the family from the move. Once this threshold was met, the court would evaluate the compelling and competing interests of all family members. It was precisely the "best interest" standard that was often used to justify restrictions on relocation.

Recent changes in relocation law in New York and California have reflected shifts in sentiments about the parent who wishes to move. Until 1996, New York had a traditional two-pronged test, in which the burden of proof was on the custodial parent to establish "exceptional circumstances," such as new employment or remarriage, to justify this action. Indeed, at that point, New York and California had two of the more restrictive statutes concerning relocation. Absent exceptional circumstances, the nonresidential parent's right of access to his child followed almost as law. However, as Miller (1995) points out, this seemed to put best interests of the child considerations to the side by burdening and potentially punishing the custodial parent which, in turn, could be detrimental to the child. She noted that no such restrictions were placed on moves by the nonresidential parent. She further objected to the presumption that continued convenient visitation with the nonresidential parent is to be preferred to permitting the relocation.

The linked decisions of *Tropea v Tropea* (1996) and *Browner v Kenward* (1996) in New York aimed to restore the child's best interests considerations to relocation determinations by relieving the custodial parent of the burden of scaling a preliminary legal hurdle in planning a move. Following this decision, the obligation of the custodial parent in New York is to notify the jurisdiction of his or her intentions to move, then the burden shifts to the nonresidential parent to contest it. However, the Tropea and Browner cases both involved moves that permitted the nonresidential parent relatively easy weekend access to his child, and thus were not fully representative of the range of relocation situations.

In New York, lawsuits over relocation and reversals of lower court decisions have increased as Handschu (1998) predicted. Further, some custodial parents, emboldened by *Tropea*, act hastily on moves, only to be shocked by litigation with approximately the same sloped playing field that they would have faced in the pre-*Tropea* days. For example, as Handschu states, moves justified by the desire of the custodial parent simply to make a "fresh start" typically have not been upheld.

In the *Burgess v Burgess* ruling in California (1996), the courts went a giant step further than the decision in New York by asserting that, in today's mobile society, the custodial parent should have the automatic right to relocate with the children. Judith Wallerstein's amicus brief (1995) for the State of California probably comes closest to codifying Goldstein, Freud, and Solnit's (1973) position in the area of parental moves, by focusing on protecting the autonomy of the primary parenting figure and hence the primary parent/child bond.

Wallerstein and Tanke (1996), in an expanded version of the Wallerstein brief, allow for a restriction on moves that appear to be spiteful or frivolous in nature, but they then go on to emphasize that divorce itself is predicated on society's interest in letting people reconstitute their lives. They argue that equal attention ought to be given to the repercussions of a move being allowed or not allowed. Perhaps most controversial is their contention that the well-being of the child is not correlated in any way with proximity to or frequency of contact with the nonresidential parent. Instead, they assert that intense, high-quality time with that parent can readily substitute for more frequent but often superficial contact.

CRITIQUE OF THE NEW STATUTES

Fathers' rights advocates, among others, have been quick to raise questions about the assumptions made in the New York and California rulings. For example, they have challenged Wallerstein and Tanke's (1996) association of a child's well-being so exclusively with the security and happiness of the custodial parent and the new family unit. In a recent comprehensive review of the national relocation scene (Terry et al., 1998), Phalen, a developmental psychologist, takes issue with the presumption that the court should automatically strive to protect that primary family unit. She argues that each case should be approached openly in terms of what is in the best interests of a particular child.

Further, Bryan (1997) suggests that identifying the primary parent is often more a legal designation than a concrete reality. He contends that the "broader impact" of the liberalized relocation acts is to force parents, trial counsel, and trial courts to attach great significance to the custodial labeling process in the early stages of separation, since only the designation of "joint legal" or "joint physical" custodian gives the nonresidential parent equal footing to contest the moving parent's plans.

Wallerstein and Tanke (1996) highlight a number of key issues to support their position on relocation. They cite the research findings of Johnston (1995) that suggest, in high-conflict situations, the child fares better if regular contact with the noncustodial parent is minimized, thereby limiting the child's further exposure to interparental hostility. They do not acknowledge in this context, however, that the majority of divorces and of relocation cases as well are not high-conflict in nature (Amato and Booth, 1997).

Wallerstein and Tanke (1996) state that, in cases where a parent's wish to move has been denied, the child will feel guilty that her parent's wishes have been thwarted. They fail to acknowledge, however, that a child can have many emotional reactions. The younger child's egocentricity might, for example, preclude a guilty reaction.

It is also possible that a parent whose plans are thwarted could work to contain his or her disappointment, thereby protecting the child from possible emotional repercussions. If the parent's focus were on the child's needs and he or she accepted the possibility that they might deny that request, negative reactions might again be moderated.

Wallerstein and Tanke promote the need to listen to the child's voice in all custody determinations and imply that the child will naturally speak in concert with the voice of the custodial parent. However, in my clinical experience, the child often is very reluctant to voice any opinion that might be hurtful to either parent. The child who does speak in concert with the primary parent may have been pressured into doing so. Wallerstein and Tanke state that "children who are seven or older should be carefully listened to in relocation cases" because they alone have an experience of each parent's residence and hence of what a move could entail. Again, based on my own work, young children are highly sensitive to the competing tugs of loyalty from both parents and they are unlikely to have a realistic appreciation of how relocation could affect them.

A related issue touched on by Wallerstein and Tanke is that joint custody has not been a success in California and, in the overwhelming majority of cases, the mother ends up being the primary residential caregiver. They acknowledge that, where a viable joint caretaking arrangement does exist, an assumption in favor of the relocating parent cannot be made. Although they appear skeptical about the frequency of genuinely shared custodial situations, Bryan (1997) reports a considerable number of such parenting arrangements.

THE ROLE OF THE FATHER

An essential assumption of the Burgess ruling is that the role of the father in his child's life must be subordinated to the security of the mother's bond with the child. In the ruling, the relationship with the nonresidential parent becomes a secondary consideration. Wallerstein and Tanke conclude that the relationship with the nonresidential parent is not a significant factor in the child's adjustment post-divorce. They bolster their position with research suggesting that the quantity and regularity of contact with the father is not essential to the maintenance of a bond with him. However, the often unintended effect of rulings such as *Tropea* and *Burgess* is that they drive, as well as respond to, social change. The increased latitude given to relocation requests may in fact be adding the woes of the "disenfranchised" father to society's larger problem of the "disappearing" father (Young, 2000).

Warshak (2000) has interpreted the research data differently than Wallerstein and Tanke. His view is that the literature supports the desirability of both parents remaining in close proximity to their children. Among his arguments is that children develop close attachments to both parents and that they do best when this is promoted. Kelly (1994) has questioned the presumption that a "primary" parent can easily be identified, especially in today's dual-wage earning families. This is related to a second point of Warshak's, that many of the studies Wallerstein and Tanke cite rely on data gathered before the explosion in the day-to-day involvement of fathers in, and their greater impact on, their children's lives. He further cites Guidubaldi and Perry (1985), who felt that the mother's attitude toward the father's involvement is a crucial mediating factor in assessing the qualitative influence of father-child contact. They found that, given a favorable maternal stance, the father's contact has a more positive impact on the child's adjustment.

Warshak (2000) refers to a large number of studies to bolster his argument, some of which seem more equivocal than he acknowledges. For example, he includes Maccoby (1993) in a group of studies that Wallerstein excluded and which, he claims, demonstrate a link between children's contact with divorced fathers and their subsequent behavior. Yet Maccoby's discussion states that, "we did not find evidence that sustaining a relationship with outside fathers made a difference in adolescent adjustment." Warshak himself describes the research of Furstenberg and Cherlin (1991) and Hetherington, Cox, and Cox (1982) as containing contradictory findings. Both Warshak and Wallerstein and Tanke thus cite research with more ambiguous results than either side acknowledges.

A PSYCHOANALYTIC/DEVELOPMENTAL PERSPECTIVE ON THE CHILD'S NEEDS

Freud's essay on the "family romance" (1909) concerns latency age (six to ten years) children's urge, at a time of some disillusionment with the parents, to replace their actual families with idealized ones in their fantasies, usually assigning themselves more elevated, aristocratic origins. In a divorce situation, children's longing for a reunited, harmonious family may supercede more fanciful and fantastic family romance wishes. Extrapolating to relocation arguments, it is as if each warring faction harbors its own fantasy of the reunited family. Fathers' rights supporters seem to believe that vestiges of the original family will somehow be preserved if the two parents are forced to remain in close geographical proximity to one another against the wishes of the custodial parent. Conversely, those siding with the rights of the relocating parent focus on the need to preserve the "stability and integrity of the post-divorce family unit." These supporters deny the likelihood of damage to the child's relationship with, and sense of loss about, the left-behind parent.

A psychoanalytic/developmental perspective reminds us always to consider the specific needs of the child in terms of gender and age-related factors in addition to the specific psychological makeup of the individual child (Roll, 1997). A developmental assessment includes the cognitive capacity of children of different ages and how well they can sustain an internal image of an absent parent (object constancy). It is difficult, for example, for a two-year-old child to maintain emotional ties to a parent whom he sees less than several times per week. Mahler, Pine, and Bergman (1975) observe that children do not reliably consolidate a stable internal image of the parent until age three. Consideration should also be given to the unique role of the interaction between the sexes of the parent and child at different developmental stages. For example, Cath (1989) states "both boys and girls living with the same-sex parent after a divorce do better in terms of social competency, superego development, and general maturation" (p. 462).

Such general developmental considerations must be viewed in the context of the particular child's cognitive and emotional capacities, stage of separation and individuation, and quality of relatedness and attachment. With such information, one can more accurately determine how much contact a child requires to sustain an emotional attachment to a parent. The psychological strengths and weaknesses of each child should also be considered. For the younger and more vulnerable child, the risk of psychological damage may require a delay in relocation, or at least more frequent visits and professional help in coping with the loss of a parent. In many cases, mental health professionals must help the courts to delineate a parenting plan that helps the child deal with the impact of the relocation or with the reactions of the custodial parent to its denial.

CLINICAL VIGNETTE 1: EVA

Developmental issues and the complexities of identifying the "psychological parent" are exemplified in this case. A mother attempted to move from New York to Tennessee, with her one-year-old daughter, Eva, without having first established herself as the sole custodian. The parents, Mr. A and Ms. B, had been living together when Ms. B unexpectedly became pregnant. The relationship became more acrimonious during her difficult pregnancy, and ultimately she decided to return to her family home in Tennessee for the delivery.

Four months after Eva's birth, Ms. B returned to New York to live with Mr. A, albeit with misgivings. Soon her relationship with him was as troubled as it had been before her pregnancy. Following a violent encounter, the couple separated. According to Mr. A, several months went by in which Ms. B "disappeared" with Eva and, indeed, he laments missing his daughter's first birthday. He says that he subsequently learned that she had moved to Harlem, making frequent trips to Tennessee, where she was attempting to establish her permanent residence. Legal wrangling between the two states eventuated in Ms. B's being forced to remain in New York, where Mr. A initiated a custody suit in which a forensic evaluation was ordered.

The evaluation revealed numerous instances of Ms. B's limited sensitivity to the needs or reactions of other people, including her daughter. This emerged, for example, in her dismissive remark, when asked to describe her daughter, that "all babies do is eat, sleep and poop all day." This attitude was also dramatically illustrated when she brought Eva, fast asleep, to my office for a visit with her father. When I attempted to question her about Eva's schedule, Ms. B acknowledged that Eva was unaware that she was being taken to my office, but assured me that Eva rarely slept so late into the afternoon and was easily awakened. In fact, Eva was deeply asleep and could not be aroused during the scheduled hour.

In contrast, I found Mr. A to be a soothing and nurturing caregiver, particularly compared to the more cerebral and emotionally cool Ms. B. His attunement to his daughter's need for consistency was illustrated by his attempt to link together his sometime visits by singing the same little tune to her each time they were together. This instinctive "bridge" was fortuitous given the repeated threats to the continuity of his relationship with her.

It was not surprising that Ms. B and her lawyer made ample use of the new relocation rulings to bolster her request to be able, as the de facto custodial parent, to move with her daughter. One might readily discern that the legal situation had actually become knottier in this case with the advent of *Tropea*. Ms. B justifiably contended that she need not demonstrate exceptional circumstances but only her good faith desire to return to her ancestral home and raise her daughter there with the support of her extended family. The glitch in her argument was that she had not yet established herself as the custodial parent, and her de facto status with Eva had been gained only because she had deprived Mr. A of consistent access to his daughter.

In addition to the difficulty of addressing a request to move in the absence of a designated custodial parent, this case raises several other concerns germane to the broader relocation question. First, there are the developmental needs of a twenty-month-old, in the midst of the throes of separation-individuation. At this age, object constancy is still being established (Mahler, Pine, and Bergman, 1975), and it is likely that a move halfway across the country would effectively sever any mental representation of a parent in the toddler-child's mind. For a child this age, the assumption that it is quality not quantity of time with the nonresidential parent seems hard to sustain. Second, the personal strengths of these two very different adults highlight how frequent it is that a child benefits from the complementary qualities of each parent.

Third, there remains an ambiguity as to which party bears the burden of establishing that a proposed move either is or is not in the child's best interests. Ms. B's self-centered motives for her move raise further questions for determining when such an action is being undertaken in good faith.

CLINICAL VIGNETTE 2: SAM

A second case underscores the pitfalls of the not unusual circumstance in which caretaking responsibilities and physical custody have been evenly shared. It involved a mother with legal custody wishing to relocate (from New York to Florida) with her ten-year-old son, Sam. While there was no joint custody agreement, Sam's parents, Ms. C and Mr. D, were essentially sharing equally in parenting responsibilities. Ms. C's new marriage was somewhat precipitous and resonated with her history of making rapid and self-centered life decisions which, in the past, had included a proposed move to California and marriage to a man with HIV who became actively involved with Sam before he died of AIDS.

The forensic evaluator found Ms. C to be limited in her recognition of or commitment to Mr. D's ongoing relationship with his son, which clearly would be attenuated by the distance of the move. Despite the court's efforts to follow Wallerstein and Tanke's (1995) admonition to "listen to the child," Sam was extremely reluctant to express any preferences, except to indicate his wish to continue to have his time split between his parents.

Sam had established meaningful relationships with peers, two half siblings, and his school and larger community. He had already faced divorce, death of a stepfather, and separation from his stepbrother. The New York State courts (*Friederwitzer v Friederwitzer*, 1989) had previously cited considerations of a child's personal stability in such decisions. Ms. C had made a unilateral decision to move without Sam (and had done so), giving the court an opportunity to see how he had adjusted to being away from his mother.

This case, occurring shortly after the *Tropea* decision, illustrates the difficulties in rigidly applying any of the statutes in existence. Ms. C, in planning to remarry, might well have had difficulty passing the pre-*Tropea* requirement of "exceptional circumstances." While she could demonstrate that her husband's business required him to remain in Florida, her personal life was marked by persistent instability, with the impulsive nature of her recent betrothal being no exception. Under the *Burgess* ruling, she, as legal custodian, would automatically be given priority since malicious motives were not involved in her move. With the new *Tropea* guidelines in place in New York, the court was in a dilemma, and the decision-making process was prolonged and torturous.

With the judge's intervention, Sam's parents were able to reach a provisional settlement whereby he would spend the remainder of the current school year and the following one with his mother, spending summers with his father, and then the third school year in

New York. This settlement was at considerable variance from the expressed opinions of the forensic evaluator and the law guardian as well as from the judge's own leanings. Each of these had concerns about Ms. C's history of instability and its impact on Sam. However, Mr. D's shaky financial status, which included being in arrears on child support and difficulty paying his legal expenses, may well have compromised his bargaining position.

The judge was concerned enough about the impact of the settlement on Sam that she conducted an additional interview with him in an effort to try to elicit his genuine feelings about the relocation. The interview was arranged in late October after he had already spent six weeks with his mother in her new home in Florida and in his new school. The meeting proved to be no more informative than had previous contacts with Sam. He was clearly uncomfortable about speaking of his parents with the judge or anyone connected with the evaluation, although one could surmise that he was torn between the disruption of his life and his close bond with his mother.

The transcript of the judge's interview with Sam (in the presence of the law guardian) vividly illustrates the reticence of a child who is fearful of alienating either of his parents. Sam repeatedly asserted that he had no opinion about where he preferred to live, but that, "if I mixed both of them, I could have a perfect world." He added that, even though he knew it was impossible, he would choose to go to his former school in New York and his current school in Florida, each for half the year. Clearly trying to get around Sam's even-handedness, the judge then asked, "If you got the chance to go to Disneyworld and only had two tickets, which parent would you choose to go with"? Sam answered, "I don't know." The judge then asked, "Okay, would you ask somebody else to choose for you?" Sam replied, "No, I wouldn't choose either of them, I just wouldn't go." The transcript then reflects a sigh of exasperated resignation on the part of the law guardian.

This case illustrates the difficulties in adhering to the new *Tropea* ruling (1996). Unlike *Tropea* and *Browner*, this case involved considerable geographical distance. Further, the two parents had essentially been equal caretakers. Also, Ms. C's justifiable desire to relocate had to be weighed against a ten-year-old child's rootedness in a particular community and school. Sam's need for continuity in his daily existence, given the frequent disruptions of his recent past, added extra urgency to this issue. Finally, his reticence to speak to the judge or any of the professionals regarding his feelings about the move, particularly one that was by now a fait accompli, may be more typical than is realized.

DISCUSSION

Best interests standards are notoriously murky and can invite more litigation. Yet guidelines have been offered in a recent New York Supreme Court decision. In *Samaroo v Samaroo* (2000), it was determined that, where the move would interfere with regular contact with the other parent, the relocating party bears the burden of establishing, by a preponderance of the evidence, that the move is in the child's best interests. This determination seems tantamount to establishing two prongs, with the first prong entailing evaluation of the circumstances of the move and of its potential interference with the other parent's visitation.

In *Samaroo*, it was acknowledged that the mother had been the primary caretaker and psychological parent for her child throughout his life. However, her economic argument for relocation appeared to be "completely speculative." These considerations would constitute a first prong and, in this case, since the mother's reasons for her relocation were deemed insufficient, the necessity of a "best interests" determination, and a far lengthier evaluation, would have been obviated.

Basic issues that should be taken into account in determining the best interests of the child include: the overall stability of the child's life, the relative fitness of the respective parents, the effect that the move would have on the relationship with the other parent in terms of the relocating parent's commitment to that relationship, and evidence of ways in which the move would enhance the child's life (*Samaroo*, 2000).

CONCLUSIONS: IMPACT OF RELOCATION ON THE FAMILY

Because relocation cases often entail a potentially permanent and one-sided resolution, they dramatically highlight the conflict between parents' rights and the child's best interests. Legislative and judicial efforts to deal comprehensively with the myriad family situations that can arise seem doomed to create as many new problems as they solve, and one parent may be left feeling—and in reality may actually be—disempowered.

For the left-behind parent, diminished contact with the children can lead to resignation and increased withdrawal from them. Conversely, the custodial parent who is denied the freedom to move may be faced with an intolerable choice between her children and new life opportunities. Understandably, he or she will be resentful of a ruling in which her plans are thwarted while the noncustodial parent faces no such restrictions.

Of course it is children who face the greatest loss, inevitably having to confront an irreconcilable rift between their needs and those of at least one of their parents. There is not much room for "family romance" fantasies in such a scenario.

REFERENCES

Amato, P. & Booth, A. (1997), *A Generation at Risk*. Cambridge: Harvard University Press.

Browner v Kenward (1996), 87 NY2d 727, 642 NYS 2d 575.

Bryan, R. (1997), Beyond Burgess. *Family Advocate*, 20:14–17.

Burgess v Burgess (1996), 51 Cal. Reporter 2d 444.

Cath, S. (1989), Afterword: Disrupted families. In: *Fathers and Their Families*, ed. S. Cath, A. Gurwitt & L. Gunsberg. Hillsdale, NJ: The Analytic Press.

D'Onofrio v D'Onofrio (1976), 144 NJ Superior Court, 200, 365 A.2d 27, 29–30.

Freud, S. (1909), Family romances. *Standard Edition*, 9:235–241. London: Hogarth Press, 1959.

Friederwitzer v Friederwitzer (1989), 55 NY2d 89, 93–94.

Furstenberg F. & Cherlin, A. (1991), *Divided Families*. Cambridge: Harvard University Press.

Goldstein, J., Freud, A. & Solnit, A. (1973), *Beyond the Best Interests of the Child*. New York: Free Press.

Guidubaldi, J. & Perry, J. (1985), Divorce, socioeconomic status and children's cognitive-social competence at school entry. *Amer. J. Orthopsychiat.*, 54:459–473.

Handschu, B. E. (1998), Relocation case law: *Tropea* and its offsprings. Unpublished manuscript.

Hetherington, E. M., Cox, M. & Cox, R. (1982), In: *Nontraditional Families*, ed M. Lamb. New York: Wiley.

Johnston, J. (1995), Children's adjustment in sole compared to joint custody families and principles for custody decision making. *Family & Conciliation Courts Rev.*, 33:415–419.

Kelly, J. (1994), The determination of child custody. *Future Children*, 4:130–131.

Maccoby, E. (1993), Postdivorce roles of mothers and fathers in the lives of their children. *J. Family Psychol.*, 1:24–31.

Mahler, M., Pine, F. & Bergman, A. (1975), *The Psychological Birth of the Human Infant*. New York: Basic Books.

Miller, S. (1995), Whatever happened to the "best interest" analysis in New York relocation cases? *Pace Law Rev.*, 15:339–389.

Roll, S. (1997), How a child views the move. *Family Advocate*, 20:26–31.

Salichs v James (2000), *New York Law J.*, June 30, 33–36.

Samaroo v Samaroo (2000), *New York Law J.*, March 8, 29–34.

Terry, E., Proctor, K., Phalen, C. & Womack, J. (1998), Moving forward, moving backward. *J. Amer. Acad. Matrimonial Lawyers*, 15:167–228.

Tropea v Tropea (1996), 87 NY2d 727, 739.

Trusch, N. L. (1997), A panoramic view of relocation. *Family Advocate*, 20:8–23.

Wallerstein, J. (1995), Amica Curiae Brief of Judith S. Wallerstein, Ph.D., filed in Cause No. So 46116, *In re Marriage of Burgess*, Supreme Court of the State of California, Dec. 7, 1995.

——— & Tanke, T. (1996), To move or not to move: Psychological and legal considerations in the relocation of children following divorce. *Family Law Quart.*, 30:305–332.

Warshak, R. (2000), The role of social science in relocation. *Family Law Quart.*, 34:83–113.

Young, C. (2000), The sadness of the American father. *Amer. Spectator*, 14:40–45.

Interlude VI

Aftermath and Healing

D ivorce can be traumatic for both children and parents. It can have even more serious repercussions when it is the most recent of a string of traumatic events (for example, abandonments) in the life of a child or parent.[1] Divorce is not only a disruption in family equilibrium affecting all family members; it can also propel development along a course that might never have otherwise occurred and it can lead to changes in the personalities of all family members (see chapters 4, 15, 25, and 27). As a result, there is no way to predict the "shape" of the divorce from the family's predivorce history, and there is no way to predict postdivorce parent–child relationships or the mental health of each family member from the information gathered about the marriage prior to the divorce.

Family life just before divorce has not received proper attention. This gives us the inaccurate impression that the family disequilibrium suddenly occurs in the divorce proper. However, some children who enter treatment during the divorce seem emotionally drained from the disruption in the predivorce family.

Wallerstein and Resnikoff (see chapter 27) emphasize the dramatic change in parents as a result of divorce. They suggest that the parents have conscious and unconscious desires to rid themselves of their children. The children remind them of the failed marriage and impede their freedom. At the same time, the children may be held onto tightly, much of the time for the wrong reasons. The children may be required to parent the parent, act as a sibling or as an ally against the spouse, or even be a substitute lover.

---

[1]Cumulative trauma has been addressed in the psychoanalytic literature by Khan (1963). Divorce often centers on issues of abandonment and can be traumatic when it comes on the heels of previous episodes of abandonment early in life.

Wallerstein and Resnikoff highlight the interplay between internal or intrapsychic factors and external factors in divorce, and between conscious and unconscious factors within each member of the family, and in every interaction between family members (see chapters 15 and 16). We get a glimpse of this interplay both in child psychotherapy (see chapters 24–27) and in psychoanalytically informed clinical longitudinal studies (Wallerstein, Lewis, and Blakeslee, 2000).

A variety of treatment approaches are outlined in this section: individual child psychotherapy (Siskind); parent consultation (Siskind); brief, focused clinical work with high-conflict divorce families (Johnston); and brief intervention (Tessman). Siskind and Johnston emphasize the importance of an assessment phase, whether it is prior to the beginning of treatment, or in a good forensic family evaluation for the court. For Siskind, it is in the exploratory phase of treatment that important information about the child is obtained and the working alliance between parents and psychotherapist is established. She reminds us of the importance of protecting the child's treatment from the litigation process. For Johnston, the history-taking is important in developing a working hypothesis about the "divorce impasse." In contrast to Siskind's private practice model, Johnston's work with high-conflict divorce families requires the availability of the court.

The therapist becomes the holding environment (Winnicott, 1962) for the child and parents during a phase of their lives filled with chaos and disorganization. However, the divorce, or premature termination of a marriage, can be mirrored in a premature termination of the child's psychotherapy. The handling of the parents is the hardest, perhaps most frustrating, part of the child's treatment.

Even though it is best that both parents participate in the selection of the psychotherapist for the child, this is complicated in divorce. One parent may feel that if the psychotherapist was recommended by the spouse, that the spouse will have an "edge" with that therapist, and vice versa. The child may be in crisis and a decision about beginning treatment may not be able to wait for these issues to be worked out. The parent who feels left out of the decision may sabotage the treatment by telling the child he or she does not like the therapist or that the other parent made a unilateral decision, leaving the child unsupported in the psychotherapeutic endeavor. The child then may lose interest in the treatment because participation is equivalent to the betrayal of one parent.

The treatment of a child in the throes of a divorce has phases. In the beginning phase there is a greater likelihood that feelings about the divorce and the impact of the family disruption will be discussed. This phase may be affected by whether or not the family is in the process of divorce litigation. If the family is in litigation, the child often does not want to talk about the divorce for fear he or she may say something that will affect the litigation outcome. This is so even when the child has been reminded by the psychotherapist that what he says in the treatment remains confidential. Thus, it may be only after litigation is completed that the child begins to talk freely, especially about the parent who has custody of the child.

In the next phase, the child turns to the world of his friends and school. Even though issues related to the family are expressed in the arena of school and friends, there can be resistance to thinking about this linkage by the child, who is trying to rid him- or herself of family troubles, wanting "fun" and a clean slate. This is reminiscent of the case example of Noah in Wallerstein and Resnikoff's contribution (see chapter 27).

Finally, although psychotherapy can promote positive growth for children of divorce, the therapy and the therapist are not able to help a child get used to *anything*, or work through the impact and ramifications of *anything*, such as custody and divorce arrangements ordered by the court. Thus, the court must make its decisions based upon what this child can legitimately handle in the present, without relying on therapy. Even if the child is in psychotherapy, the therapy may come to a premature ending, leaving the child on his or her own to handle the fallout of the litigation and the court's directives. One critical aspect of both separation and divorce is the loss of the noncustodial parent, often the father. Tessman (see chapter 24) poignantly illustrates the vicissitudes of trying to hold onto the absent father internally. If we really listen to the child's sense of loss, we can empathize with his pain not only in the divorce process, but in the continued loss that is experienced for years to come.

REFERENCES

Khan, M. (1963), The concept of cumulative trauma. *The Psychoanalytic Study of the Child*, 18:286–306. New York: International Universities Press.
Wallerstein, J., Lewis, J. & Blakeslee, S. (2000), *The Unexpected Legacy of Divorce*. New York: Hyperion.
Winnicott, D. (1962), *The Maturational Processes and the Facilitating Environment*. New York: International Universities Press, 1965.

Linda Gunsberg

Chapter 24

Experiencing the Absent Father
In Sight and Inside

LORA HEIMS TESSMAN

THE FATHER IN SIGHT AND INSIDE:
THEORETICAL CONSIDERATIONS

O ne morning an analysand, a married mother, arrived in my office tired and mentioned that the family had been annoyed to be awakened before 6:00 A.M. by the noise of the garbage being collected. The only family member not annoyed was her toddler daughter, almost three, who emerged from bed in a sunny mood, exclaiming: "Daddy, this morning you were outside singing!" This little girl, secure with both parents, has an inner representation of a singing Daddy that turns garbage trucks into music. This is not the case for most children of divorce. This chapter discusses the impact of divorce on children's external and inner encounters with the father who is no longer at home. I focus on the relation to the absent father because in the majority of cases the mother is the home parent. However, although disruptions in maternal and paternal functions have different developmental impacts, many similar issues are at stake when mother is absent. I will consider how the child's experience of the father is also affected by the particular ways the child's mother, the rest of the family, and the broader social network view

An earlier version of this chapter was presented at the symposium "Divorce from the Child's and Adolescent's Perspective" sponsored by the Center for Study of Child and Adolescent Development, Cambridge, MA, November, 1991.

the father (see chapters 8 and 9). Internal images of father, conscious and unconscious, are transformed in his absence in ways that can foster or impede the child's attempts to cope with the loss and the changes that accompany it.

The consequences of divorce for a particular child are as diverse as are cultures, families and marriages. A circle of influence includes the parent's individual and cultural values, as well as those aspects of parental character that determine what range of emotions can be borne by them. For example, the child's experience is affected by whether a parent can allow for the vulnerability of grieving, or emphasizes and values only active modes of coping. When divorce forces a family into poverty, with a change of neighborhood and a depleting workload for the mother, the child may experience a different degree of demoralization than when a supportive social network can be preserved. My discussion will be biased in the sense that it is based on clinical experience with children in families with enough cohesion so that at least one family member brought the child for psychological evaluation or psychotherapy because of evident emotional difficulties. The children I will refer to were seen either in the psychiatry clinic at the Massachusetts Institute for Technology, which offered short-term, limited service, or in private practice, which offers more leeway for suiting the treatment to the needs of the child and family. When an opportunity for extended psychotherapy could be sustained, the yield was often considerable.

In previous writings (Tessman, 1978, 1984) I compared the psychotherapy and well-being of 50 children who parted from a parent because of divorce with 19 children and adults whose parent had died during their childhood. Although the well-being and parenting capacity of the home parent was most predictive of overall coping capacity, the child's view of the relationship to the absent parent remained crucial. Its meanings to the child emerged in long-range effects such as later choice of love objects, the formulation of aspirations or life goals, or a lingering propensity to depression (see chapter 2).

When a parent has died, idealization of the dead is often encouraged by the social network. In contrast, when parents divorce, denigration of the absent partner is often the stronger force. For example, when a previously loved parent is now referred to as "that bastard," the child experiences an assault to his own self esteem as well. In that bind, the child might attempt to keep the absent parent psychically alive by secretly idealizing him, while devaluing himself or herself.

Divorce involves a rupture in continuity of loving. Such a rupture has different implications for each child according to the child's developmental level, individual character, gender, and particular family dynamics. For example, a four-year-old boy, who may be in need of a prolonged affirming male sense of "WE," will experience the deprivation of a valued relationship to father differently than a four-year-old girl whose excited love for father ends in shame or in a sense of futility about having anything of value to offer, which, if unresolved, may make her feel disqualified in adulthood for the love of a good man. Elaborations of differences according to developmental level are beyond the scope of this chapter, but the point I want to make is that boys as well as girls thrive on *both* an identification with and a love relation to each parent.

The child must evolve a reliable internal father for fantasied interactions as well as eventual identification with qualities he or she values in him. With selective highlighting, aspects of the internal image of father become part of the self, of inner structure. Until that happens a lot of dialogue (in words and deeds) goes on between parent and child, and between the child and the inner presence of the father. However, when the father is no longer in sight, internalization or identification happens abruptly as a defense against loss. In this process the image of father may be frozen in time, rather than being a gradual construction that lends itself to ever-changing elaboration in fantasy—a melding of fathering functions the child needs at that very moment in development sifted through his or her actual continued experience with the father. Identification with father as a defense against loss is apt to be based on those memories that are most laden with exquisite affective pleasure or pain, magnified by their intensity and cut off from growing along with the rest of the child. And the integrity of the image may be more vulnerable to contagion from other views. In order for the internalized father not to be frozen in time (a time of intense distress in divorcing families), the child needs the opportunity for an active engagement with a father figure that will let the father "inside" develop as the child does.

In addition to internalization culled from the particular ways of loving and hating in the father–child relationship, the child is affected by what he or she sees in the interchange of feelings between mother and father. Some hope about a man's and woman's adult relationship to each other also becomes integral to the child's capacity to venture from investing only in dyadic (consisting of two) relationships, with the inevitable accompaniment of vulnerability to separation anxiety (or the counter-dependent defenses against it), to the complexities of negotiating triads (consisting of three), such as oedipal involvements and the broadened horizons which are sequelae.

Even when the external father is disappointing, the child's need is to create an inner fathering presence he can love, from whom he can accept fathering functions, and whose identity is sustaining to him. The father "inside"—that is, the internalized father—does not necessarily match the external father, the father "in sight." The unmatch (not necessarily a mismatch) can be in either of two directions: father can be steadily present in an intact family, but in a context of emotional obstacles to constructive internalization; or, conversely, what the external world views as a tarnished father may shine in the child's experience in a deeply sustaining way.

Divorce impels a discrepancy between the father "inside" and the father "in sight" more naturally than almost any other situation. Mother and father have had reasons to part, to disentangle their union in the external world as well as their inner representation of each other as best beloved. Differences between parents are necessarily highlighted while each spouse mobilizes whatever mixture of anger, grief, and acute awareness of disappointment seems required to protect self esteem while accomplishing the separation.

ERIK AND PETER

Here is an articulate child's version of what is involved. Erik, age eleven, is struggling to diminish his sense of irreconcilable differences in his divorcing parents' natures. As he puts it, it is not packing the clothes and playthings that he minds in going back and forth between houses each week, but that he has to switch imaginary companions (imaginary companions are no longer usual at age eleven) each time because neither could exist at the other parent's house. He had accepted quietly the news of his parents' intention to divorce, telling me he had known for a long time it would happen, that he noticed they never called each other darling and sweetheart. Father did call her that sometimes, but only when he was very angry and didn't sound as if he meant it. Also they didn't sit together, while his friends' parents snuggled on the couch.

But Erik is an optimist. He wants to be an anthropologist, specializing in the Pygmies and the Watusis, who, he informs me, live together in a small space near Uganda. He enlightens me about the obstacles:

> Erik: The tribes are complete opposites! The Pygmies are three or four feet tall and the Watusis seven; the Watusis are serious but the Pygmies roll on the floor the minute they hear a joke; the Pygmies get emotional while the Watusis keep strong feelings inside.
>
> LT: So how do you figure they manage to share their small space and live in peace?
>
> Erik: But it's more than just living in peace! [He fairly shouts at me, fighting me because I sounded ready to settle for so little, and fighting himself because he knows that with his own "opposite" parents it did not work like this.] It's because neither tries to rule the other and they respect each other—that they can want different things and still have deep friendships between them. But just think of what they had to go through. . . . When the one tribe worships the elephant as sacred, and the other eats it for food!

When therapists feel weighed down by the pain of children of divorce, it may be because we and our patients are regularly saddled with just such elephants. As Erik's shifting imaginary companions suggest, when one listens to each of two divorcing parents, one realizes that the child has to live with two quite different realities—different truths about what is important in life and why things went awry (see chapters 8, 25, and 27). Still, Erik is lucky for he has, with effort, evolved a vision of how things could be between adults and pictures himself as an anthropologist, exchanging helplessness for the mastery of becoming a legitimate observer of the scene. His belief in effort has a basis, for his parents, who also believe in effort, came for consultations before their divorce rather than in its aftermath. They both supported him emotionally during three years of psychotherapy. Erik is already a boy who is committed to integrity about his deeply felt values and will not short-circuit the conflicts that surge in their wake.

But compare Erik with eight-year-old Peter, a pessimist about his parents, whose emotional depletion during divorce caused them to experience the care of their son as a burden. Peter keeps himself constantly in motion and hits children in school. At the school's insistence, the parents agreed to an evaluation, but did not follow the recommendation for therapy. Asked how he felt about his parents splitting up he said, "I feel tipsy-topsy, like I never know who will pick me up at school." He tells me:

> Peter: The big people are trying to hurt the little people who get in their way. The big people like to tell lies. The little people are sad.
>
> LT: Can the little people do something about that?
>
> Peter: Not that much, they can just do the same thing the big people do to them. The big people even destroy the buildings, that's why there aren't many little people left.
>
> LT: How awful, how scared they must be! Who comforts the little people and who comforts you at your house?
>
> Peter: Nobody, my Daddy always has to leave when I'm scared.

For Peter, the father as reassuring internal presence simply was not home. In school Peter passed on his hurt to other little people—the children he hit.

SOME PSYCHIC COSTS OF COPING

In the context of incompatible realities, each invested with the self-esteem of a parent, the child may have difficulty preserving the integrity of his own perceptions of the absent father, feeling strongly pulled to take on the mother's or the broader social view. I do *not* mean this is the mother's fault. He is drawn because he needs a close alliance with mother even more than before, while she is disengaging from father, either regretfully or with the force of venom. However, *some* mothers do not give emotional permission for the child to value the absent father (see chapter 9). In that case the child is forced into a variety of negative options: (1) to mistrust his own perceptions; (2) to carry on a secret quest for reminders of the father, preserving the lost love relation (in this case the image of the loved father becomes unconscious, but expresses itself in a variety of symptoms and behaviors); (3) to unconsciously identify with the degraded or negative aspects of the father. The child may then be true to father by acting out the negative identity in self-defeating ways rather than being able to mourn his real limitations.

Shifting erotic feelings in the divorcing family are volatile, powerfully felt, and very hard to describe. In some families, desires previously directed toward the mate find their niche in the child; in others, they are withdrawn from the child as involvements with new lovers or whole families take their place, while in still others the bond to the child had been the past glue between the parents. Each puts the child in a profoundly different position. A common dynamic as father leaves is that the mother now begins to see his traits in the child. As the previous balance of intimacy breaks down, the child is exposed to the erotic vulnerability of the parent. Often the child desires to be the means of restitution.

The child may develop a kind of vigilant empathy, used to maintain an excellent rapport with each of the two parents. He learns habitually to isolate and hide the sense of emotional contact with one from the other. Such vigilant empathy may be highly adaptive in future emotional intimacies as well as certain fields of work. Yet when its defensive functions remain central as well (that is, the assumption that one cannot maintain connectedness without vigilant empathy), then anxiety and depression may appear wherever it is disrupted. Behaviorally, along with the vigilant empathy, many children develop a heightened adaptability, seeming to cope extremely well with going from home to home in joint custody arrangements.

Each divorced parent may turn to the child in ways that lessen the generation gap in both emotional and practical areas. The emotional complications (for example, for the boy who feels he should act as the man of the family now) are many. Yet the child may also gain in feeling him- or herself to be a needed, participating family member successful in mastering responsibilities, holding things together, and having his or her opinions count. It is sometimes not until young adulthood that the other side of this adaptation emerges in the haunting sense of having lost one's childhood at high psychic cost.

JASON

Jason was three years and three months when I met him. A guardian ad litem had insisted on the final separation of the parents six months earlier because Jason's fearfulness and weight loss were increasing while the parents' attempt at reunion foundered. When exposed to pained and angry yelling on his father's part, Jason would run to his mother's bed, hiding his head under the pillow until his father had left the house. Jason was in weekly psychotherapy.

During his first few sessions, Jason busied himself with extension cords, connecting one side of the room to the other, plugging them into each other in the middle. "I'm a telephone repair man, I have to fix the turnpike," he announced. Mommy's house was on one side, daddy's on the other, but the turnpike was broken. It was full of holes. I wondered out loud if it was awful for the turnpike, being broken between mommy and daddy. For several sessions the theme shifted to fixing everything in mommy's house. He was the plumber and the carpenter; all her pipes needed fixing and she needed new doors. Jason would fix my pipes and doors too. He was very vigorous in this play; we sawed, nailed and hammered to repair with energy. Alternately he was a tiny mouse, hiding under my table while his voice could only squeak. But when the mouse's "eyes and ears grew big" he could jump out at me in gleeful laughter (as he had not done from under the pillows). At home he was now reportedly less fearful, more raucous and hard for mother to control. He was enchanted with actual repair men who were working next door to his house and offered to help.

The theme of repairing the parent and attempts to manage the fear of further loss are common for children of divorce. Attunement to parental emotional states becomes more complicated as the child elaborates, pushed by his own desires and growing capacities, what his role in the parental relationship might be. As an illustration, Jason, by age four, incites his father to deal openly with his role in the divorce.

Jason's mother, in distress, was indeed trying to force shut the doors of her body and house, as well as her inner plumbing, to father's invasion. Meanwhile Jason, was the center of her delight. In addition, at age three, he was ripe for the kind of castration concerns that might make holes in the turnpike quite urgent for filling. Whether he should be male, with a penis, like father, was an unsettling question for him.

About six months later, Jason is a doctor, operating on the baby doll, "so that his ears and heart will be okay." Suddenly Jason brings the saw to cut off the baby doll's penis. I find myself blurting out about the penis: "He may want to use that again!" and stop his saw. He tells me that "the doctor has to be very strong and eat a big breakfast." He picks out a full-sized ear of plastic corn—the doctor's breakfast—stuffs it into his own pants, laughing, and asks me, "where did it go?" Then, gleefully, he pulls it out to show me. Jason's ability to suddenly "use" the big corn in his pants (probably symbolic of his penis) with pride, rather than needing to destroy it, becomes emblematic of revisions in his images of what he, as little boy and as man-to-be, might safely risk. At home, later that week, Jason urinates standing up for the first time. In the same mode he brings romantic feelings to the next session, singing to me, "I'm in the mood for love—simply because you are near me!"

About thee months later, the Gulf War dominates the news and is on television. Peter Pan and the bad Pirates are Jason's current characters for playing out fantasies about biting, losing a limb, getting children without mother, and so on. In his play, pirates drink rum, babies drink milk. When the Gulf War begins, he adds the "newborn baby prisoner" to his play, tying him up with rope and crochet yarn and subjecting him to all kinds of torture (with blindfolds, hammer, and saw), at times putting his head under a pillow and taping his eyes and ears shut. The baby prisoner is in Kuwait, the bad pirate is Saddam Hussein.

The next session he begins as the bad pirate. Mixing clay and confetti, he announces:

Jason: This is a real bad bomb the bad guy is making.

LT: Like in Kuwait, that you were playing last week?

Jason: No, it isn't as bad as Kuwait. . . . it's more like a preview. . . . it's like a bad preview of Kuwait. Now I'm the pirate throwing the bomb and this is the bad pirate's drill and his sword. [Jason comes to me for help in tying the woodworking drill and sword on himself.] Now I'm taking a big grown bomb which can hurt people. [He throws the bomb and the sword across the room.] I made a big mess and now I'm brooming all the bomb back in a big lump. [He sweeps the clay and confetti together. This led to exploring lumps and bombs.] Jason: When Daddy shouted I got scared but I had to poop. Daddy was shouting bombs and my poops were almost bombs too. But I tried to hold it in. Jason explains that he had been scared because he thought Daddy had been mad at him, had been mad at everybody in

Mommy's bed. But Mommy can get rid of Daddy and did. Jason now wants to build a private pirate bathroom for pooping, where no one can come in. With cardboard bricks we construct his bathroom: he directs me to make a skull and crossbones "keep out" flag.

I am amazed at Jason's capacity to invent a "preview of Kuwait," invoking observing ego in lieu of actual devastation. A preview allows him some choice in mastery. It fits his valor in trying to modulate and contain explosiveness without father's help. He has endured the explosive, expulsive sensations of father's angry shouting, his own bowels, and mother expelling father, which are all associatively linked for him. He enacts the angry father, but in a more controlled fashion, and eventually makes mental boundaries (the private bathroom) between pooping, anger, and being thrown out.

The week after the cease-fire in the Gulf, Jason plays that Mommy and Daddy pirates aren't fighting right now. He unties the "newborn baby pirate" and, attempting to unite warring factions, insists: "Now we'll make rum and milk formula soup for the baby and everybody, and then they'll play together." He asks me to hold the baby doll in my arms while Jason feeds him rum and formula from the bottle. And so he tries to make peace, wanting to combine male and female nurturing, that is, he and I caring for baby together, not separately.

Jason is now four years, two months. Mother has broken up with a boyfriend to whom Jason was very attached, having dubbed him his "pirate-pal." Jason is once more the only contender for mother's love. He declares that he hates visits with Father and hates visits with me (which he tells each of us) because he wants to be with Mother all the time. For some time he gives up being a pirate, and becomes a plumber and repairman again. He tells me that Mother has lots of leaky faucets now and it keeps him busy to fix them all. He knows Mother has been weeping. However, when visiting Father, he now asks a lot of questions, saying he hates him and accusing Father of being mean to him and Mother. Father admits that when Mommy and he were living together they got nasty to each other. "Oh no," Jason tells father, "it was a one-way nasty." Father swallows his hurt feelings and the two keep talking and playing. In sessions he tells me about past boyfriends who have hurt Mother. "We think they get nasty and it was a good thing to say good-bye." I question the "*we* think," saying "let's figure out what *you* think and what Mommy thinks." Father reports that during a visit with him Jason told him: "Daddy, I had a dream that I grew a big beard just like you—but Mommy shaved it off" and "Don't you know I could only love you both if you weren't divorced. And I live with Mommy all the time so I can't love you!"

In voicing his worst fears, Jason evokes the response that he needs. He has experienced that the relationship to his father endures through the little boy's hatred, though being male with Mother alone has other dangers. Fortunately at this time Mother finds love with a man who treats her well and declares his wish to become her husband and the stepfather of Jason, whom he enjoys. Slowly, slowly Jason readied himself for a positive new male influence in his life, while also needing to maintain a tie to his father. When his mother did remarry and was happy again, Jason's stepfather became a loved and enriching figure in his life, and he flourished.

A NOTE ON SUSTAINING FANTASIES

When the father "in sight" cannot help but be disappointing in relation to the child's wish and need, the quest for a father who can be idealized inside psychic life may continue unrequited. Is this always bad? No. Derivatives of various illusions may have widely differing positive or negative effects on an individual's aspirations or experiences during the life course. For example, adolescent and young adult ego-ideal formation may be eventually consolidated from derivatives of an earlier period of emotional engagement with an idealized, emulated parent, and yet become a stabilizing aspect of the individual's identity and aspirations. Whether illusionary aspects of the child's motivation are useful or necessary to confront may depend on their interference with, or enhancement of life goals.

To illustrate the complex function of the child's inner construction, I draw on the life of Eleanor Roosevelt. Eleanor Roosevelt's parents were separated when she was eight, and a year later her mother died of diphtheria. Eleanor then lived with her grandmother. She wrote:

> My father explained to me that my mother was gone and she
> had been all the world to him and now he had only my brothers

and myself, that my brothers were very young, and he and I must keep close together. Someday, I would make a home for him again, we would travel together, and do many things which he painted as interesting and pleasant, to be looked forward to, in the future together. Somehow, it was always he and I. I did not understand whether my brothers were to be our children or whether he felt that they would be at school and college and later independent. There started that day a feeling which never left me—that he and I were very close together, and someday would have a life of our own together. He told me to write, often, to be a good girl, not to give any trouble, to grow up into a woman he could be proud of, and he would come to see me whenever it was possible. When he left, I was all alone to keep our secret of mutual understanding and to adjust myself to my new existence. Though he was so little with us, my father dominated all this period of my life. Subconsciously, I must have been waiting always for his visits [Erikson, 1964, p. 785].

Eleanor Roosevelt's love for her father sustained her against all odds, in spite of the fact that he was viewed as flawed by others because of his alcoholism and less than responsible behavior. The father "inside," rooted in her actual loving experience with him early in her life, compensated for the father who was so often not "in sight."

REFERENCES

Erikson, J. (1964), Nothing to fear: Notes on the life of Eleanor Roosevelt. *Daedalus*, 93:781–801.
Tessman, L. (1978), *Children of Parting Parents*. Northvale, NJ: Aronson.
—— (1984), The quest for the wanted absent parent in children of the divorced or deceased. In: *Marriage and Divorce*, ed. C. Nadelson & D. Polansky. New York: Guilford Press.
—— (1996), *Helping Children Cope with Parting Parents* (rev. ed.). Northvale, NJ: Aronson.

Chapter *25*

Psychotherapy with Children and Parents During Divorce

DIANA SISKIND

A divorced father called his former wife on the telephone and invited her to meet him for coffee. He told her that he was eager to "chat" with her because in recent months he had realized that she was the only person in the world who cared as much about their children as he did.

This telephone call took place after a period of sixteen years during which there had been no communication between these two once-married people. During the divorce process, and for many years following its legal completion, this father had been so chronically angry, threatening, and intrusive, and had cast such a shadow of fear and tension over the lives of his children and their mother, that she had stopped all contact with him as soon as the children were grown and she was no longer required by law to consult with him regarding decisions affecting their children. Then, after a sixteen-year hiatus, they accidentally met at the window of the newborn nursery of the hospital where their first grandchild lay sleeping.

It was on the day following this chance meeting that this man called his former wife and made his request. When she politely but firmly refused, he became as angry and threatening as he had been during the divorce process and its aftermath. His former wife, my patient, reported that she in turn found herself as shocked and para-lyzed by his attack as she had been in the past.

This chapter represents a distillation of my personal experience of several decades of psychotherapeutic work with children and their families. I emphasize aspects of the work that deal with parents in high conflict with one another.

I use this vignette to begin a chapter on the treatment of children of divorcing parents because it captures something of the scope, depth, and immutability of the painful feelings that so often come unleashed during this process. It makes the point that divorce does *not* always afford the divorcing parents much in the way of room to lead separate lives free of the shadow of the "other," at least not until their children have reached adulthood and emancipation. And by emphasizing that the father was *pathologically* angry, the vignette challenges three myths about divorce.

Myth I is that both parties are responsible for the collapse of a marriage. Myth II is that the terms of a divorce can be worked out smoothly and fairly if the parties involved *try* hard enough. Myth III is that children of divorce whose noncustodial parent continues to be significantly involved in their lives are *always* much better off than children whose noncustodial parent is less present (Goldstein et al., 1996). In addition to these myths, the vignette captures the essence of two of the most devastating consequences of divorce:

1. The interplay of hatred and dependency between the parents juxtaposed with their pain and loneliness at not being able to share with each other (or perhaps with anyone) their love for their children.
2. The erosion of parental authority and autonomy; the disintegration of the parents' role as adults in full charge of the care of their children. This second point may be the least understood effect of divorce on parents. And unfortunately, this tragic consequence of divorce is unavoidable when legally imposed terms and conditions replace the naturalness of parental prerogative. Sometimes the effect is so far reaching that the parents are never again completely at ease with their children.

In my example the volatility of a father was the major obstacle to finding a modus operandi. In other cases it could be the pathology of the mother or something in the interplay of the couple that prevents a gradual recovery from the divorce crisis—a settling into separate lives for the adults and the provision of a comfortable environment for the children. The degree of *parental pathology appears to be the principal determinant of the extent of divorce upheaval and of its immutability.*

ASSESSMENT OF THE DIVORCING FAMILY

Although there are divorce situations that are not as bitter and extreme as the picture painted so far, the strain is never absent. And for divorcing parents the fact of their parenthood is what makes it so particularly difficult to be free of each other. Now let us have a child therapist enter this complex family situation. How do we approach this most challenging aspect of our work and protect the essence and continuity of the treatment? How do we avoid being swept into the storms of divorce? When we take the time to carefully assess the child and his parents and the impact of the divorce on each of them and on the family unit, we are on the way to achieving an essential grounding that will prove invaluable to the treatment process.

As in all therapeutic situations, we learn a lot from our countertransference, and of course when the patient is a child, our countertransference extends to include his parents (Wallerstein, 1997). It is essential that we take our time and allow the treatment picture to emerge in its fullness and complexity and move slowly until we understand the terrain we are on. It is our most important safeguard to ensuring the continuity and effectiveness of treatment.

Our assessment should, as with all our patients, include observations about ego functioning, defense, adaptive functioning, object relations, identity formation, psychosexual stages with their corresponding anxiety states, and stability of mood states. Recognizing that divorce is a crisis for both parents and child, we need to consider that the person we are assessing might be in a regressed state due to this upheaval. Equally, we need to keep in mind the possibility of the reverse, a person in crisis is sometimes able to mobilize resources that are not usually available and that may fade when the crisis subsides. And we also need to remember that these regressive and progressive shifts are in constant flux, thereby requiring the therapist to view assessment as an ongoing process.

In short, our most effective approach to working with a child of divorcing parents is to understand both child and parents beyond, as well as within, the microcosm created by the crisis of divorce. Child therapists are often reluctant to think diagnostically about the *parents* (Siskind, 1997) of their child patient, but what better way to be equipped to do our work then to be clear about the personality structure of any person in our consulting room. The parent of a child in treatment might not be deemed to be the primary patient, but that does not alter the need for thorough assessment.

In the case of the angry father described earlier, it made an enormous difference that his son's therapist understood that this father's ability to reason failed him whenever he felt out of control. Because his son's therapist understood the nature and extent of this father's fragility, he avoided explosive subjects and this enabled constructive exchanges between them. The therapist also understood how *desperately* this man needed to feel in control of any decisions affecting his children. Although he expressed this need in an arrogant and overbearing manner, the therapist recognized this as a struggle for autonomy in a man who felt quite helpless, dependent, and inadequate. With this insight, the therapist's empathy generated tactful and sensitive responses.

While the child's therapist was consistently attuned to both parents, there was one condition from which he would not waver. He refused to take a position or comment on any divorce-related issues. He knew that even a simple comment on his part could have led to the dissolution of treatment because the father would not have tolerated anything less than total backing of his point of view. That, of course, would have been impossible.

FOUR THERAPEUTIC SCENARIOS

I would like to discuss four types of situations that are commonly encountered by child therapists when divorce is, or becomes, a factor in the lives of their patients. I will briefly describe each of these and then discuss some therapeutic dilemmas they present.

In situation 1 we are consulted by the parents because a divorce is imminent and they want their child to be in treatment in order to be better equipped to cope with the inevitable strain of the divorce. Again, the most rigorous evaluation is called for, because the therapist has no idea of what is really being requested. The purpose of the evaluation, which might include psychological testing, is to assess whether treatment would be useful at this time. Sometimes it is better to stay in touch with the parents, discuss the child's mood and behavior, but delay the child's treatment for a while. Some children find it difficult to see a therapist when divorce negotiations are very heated and the atmosphere at home is tense and charged. In some cases a child who is already worried about losing her parents cannot bear to be sent to a therapist because she experiences this as being abandoned and relegated to the care of a stranger. Two or three months later, with the atmosphere more settled, that same child might be ready for treatment. Another child might accept and welcome treatment even during the most explosive divorce proceedings. Carefully timing and particularizing each situation is always of paramount importance.

Should you decide that treatment for the child is a good plan, it is prudent to tell the parents that treatment will involve working with their child and working with them, but will *not* include taking a position on divorce disputes, meeting with their attorneys, or the provision of affidavits. If they are unhappy with this condition, you can explain the reason for it and tell them that another way to proceed is to have a therapist for their child and a separate therapist-consultant for them. That way the child's therapist is not involved in disputes between the parents, thus safeguarding the treatment process.

That leads us to situation 2. These parents consult a child therapist with divorce as the presenting problem, but the request for help is for themselves, not for their child. They are about to divorce and their one point of agreement is their desire not to upset their child more than necessary. They want the therapist to take the role of representing the best interests of their child by using his knowledge of child development to help make good decisions regarding various issues as they arise. They want help with how to tell the child about the divorce, how to answer his questions, and how much information he should be given regarding the break-up of the marriage and the changes in living arrangements that lie ahead. They want a place to come to when they feel uncertain about how to handle things with their child, or when they disagree. They envision that the therapist will stay in the picture and help to settle questions as they arise over time. These parents recognize that, as their child grows older, new issues will come up and new questions will arise and new disagreements will need to be settled.

Our role as therapist–consultant can be very effective as long as we understand that it is not our place to make decisions for parents but rather to help them think through the problems and understand the obstacles that are hampering their decision-making capabilities. Although this role appears somewhat different from that of treating an individual, the training and skills we offer are the same. We are not mediators or arbitrators, we are therapists acting as consultants. We promote reflection, self-observation, and self-knowledge. We do not give advice. We provide a milieu in which it is possible to think. Our presence lends an air of safety to the dialogue and we work hard to preserve and maintain it; providing a safe climate is part of what we are trained to do.

In situation 3, divorce proceedings have been under way for some months and the parents both note that the child is exhibiting signs of stress. The parents attribute the symptoms to the divorce crisis. This type of request comes in many forms. Sometimes the parents have already seen a dozen therapists and are as unable to agree on a therapist as on anything else in their lives. And sometimes the parents' concern for the distress they have observed in their child is a common ground that is not swept into the divorce disagreements.

In situation 4 a child comes to treatment because of excessive fears, phobias, difficulties with peers, or other such typical child-hood problems. Then, at some point after treatment has gotten under way, tensions in the marriage—not necessarily discernable or dis-cussed during the beginning phase—become pressing, and divorce proceedings are instituted.

In the first three examples the therapist and parents meet for the first time with divorce as the point of focus, while in the fourth case the therapist has had an ongoing relationship with the child and his parents prior to the divorce. There are many other versions of requests for help, but the underlying principles of our approach are the same. Of paramount importance is the fact that, while par-ents are in a state of crisis, the therapist is not. Thus the therapist is in the best position to take charge of the situation, and not let him-self be pressured by the parents' sense of urgency for immediate action and for solutions. As in all treatment situations, we have to listen to the presented request and then look beyond to what is un-stated and unknown at the beginning, but will emerge over time. We need to wait to know what we are dealing with and what needs to be done before we do anything (Siskind, 1997; Novick and Novick, 1998). Some parents will not be able to accept our exploratory phase and will move on to the next therapist. Others will feel reassured by our calm demeanor and comprehensive approach and feel relieved that help is on the way.

Do any of these situations present the therapist with a more favorable prognosis for effective therapeutic work? Plain logic might point to the likelihood of a more solid situation when the therapist had been in place for a period of time prior to the divorce. Using such logic we could argue that treatment prior to the divorce would have allowed the child and the parents time to form a working alliance with the therapist. Hence the parents would have the comfort of having a relationship with a therapist whom they have come to know and trust and who is there to help them. In such situations, the presence of the therapist provides effective anchoring for all family members. And this indeed was so in the case of the angry father presented earlier. But just as often, the positive picture quickly changes as new forces, fueled by the divorce upheaval, invade the therapeutic climate.

THERAPY WITH THE DIVORCING FAMILY

As in all therapeutic endeavors, the working alliance is a safeguard against the inevitable frustrations, disappointments, and periods of negative transference that are a part of treatment. In the treatment of children this situation is always complicated by the need to have that alliance extend to the parents. The fact is that, in many cases, the alliance with the parents is shaky and uneven. One parent might have confidence in the therapist while the other is skeptical or even antagonistic to the therapist and to treatment. While in some cases the presence of an unsympathetic parent proves to be an insurmountable problem, in others this condition may be managed and not become a major obstacle to the treatment. What appears to be essential to containing these difficult dynamics is the therapist's acceptance of the right of the skeptical parent to his point of view. That would include accepting the parent's choice to participate in or to stay away from the treatment situation. If a parent does not believe in treatment yet allows the child to come to sessions, we need to recognize that this willingness to allow the treatment to proceed is an important, though oblique, communication to us, a tacit acceptance that counterbalances the negative attitude (Siskind, 1992, 1997).

Now let us add to this precarious therapeutic arrangement the jolt of divorce. Suddenly everything is stirred by heightened affect; there is potential for regression and for transferential fluctuations. What was a quiet flaw turns into something akin to a fault line when an earthquake strikes. Affective shifts may unleash suspicion and distrust, even hatred. Add to this the often inflammatory effect of

lawyers and court appointed forensic experts, and the possibility of
the therapist becoming embroiled in the couple's territorial fights
over money, possessions, and custody grows into an unmanageable
situation. The therapist may then find himself transformed by the
parents, or one parent, into the representation of a "bad" object, an
enemy to be removed, thus placing treatment in great jeopardy. When
this results in the dissolution of treatment, we have yet another on
the growing list of losses suffered by the family.

It cannot be overemphasized that, in some of these bitter proceedings, a therapist can become discredited and fired by either or
both parents for capricious reasons. When that happens, the consequences for the child can be devastating. In the opinion of this author,
the therapist's best chance of safeguarding the continuity of treatment is to maintain the most rigorous professional stance, which
includes the firm resolve to abstain from involvement in any divorce-
related decisions.

I remember treating a boy of five whose parents began divorce
proceedings a year after treatment began. When the divorce process
was under way and disputes around visitation occurred, the mother
asked me to write a letter stating what I thought was a good schedule
for visitations considering the age of her child and the particular
fears that had brought him into treatment. I wrote a very simple
letter which basically stated that a flexible visiting schedule would
be most appropriate until it was possible to observe what arrangement was most comfortable for the little boy.

I had made a blunder quite typical of child therapists who find
themselves in what they experience as being on the spot. I had responded to a request without realizing how far it took me beyond
my role as therapist. Wanting to be "helpful," I had succumbed to
my countertransference; I reacted without reflecting. I did not realize
the extent of my error until it became apparent that the parents were
retaliating by sabotaging the child's treatment. Although it happened
gradually, in effect they fired the therapist. I had failed to realize
how desperately each parent wanted to retain the appearance of
power and autonomy, however illusory. My *simple* letter had represented me as having greater authority than theirs. Had I declined to
write the letter, I might still have failed to prevent termination, but I
would have been more at peace with my own behavior as a therapist
who had not stepped out of her professional role.

THE CHILD IN THERAPY

By now you might feel puzzled that a paper on the psychotherapy of the child and parents during divorce has gone on for all these pages with the focus solely on the parents, with hardly a word about the treatment of the child. The explanation is this: *The treatment of the child is not altered by the fact of divorce.* The child's life is altered, his anxieties are stirred, and he may regress or begin exhibiting such symptoms as bed wetting, nightmares, or phobias, as well as changes in mood and general behavior. But the essence of treatment remains the same. When the child is very young and play therapy is the primary mode of communication, or with latency-age children who may use games as a backdrop for verbal communication, or later yet in years when verbal communication is the exclusive tool, the child brings to the therapist the range of concerns, worries, anxieties, and conflicts that form the themes of his treatment. The therapist receives her young patient's pace and tone, forward movement, regressions, periods of resistance and, of course, the themes he brings to his hour. If a child misses his father, if he is frightened when his parents speak so grimly to each other, if he is ashamed of telling his friends that his mother has left the home, if he feels homeless living half time in mommy's house and half time in daddy's house, these are the divorce-related strains he brings to treatment. The way he interprets them and how they may exacerbate developmental lags, cause anxiety and regression to fixation points, or feed fantasies that create conflict are the issues that treatment is designed to address.

SUMMARY

The focus of so much of this chapter on the parents is in recognition of the decisive role they play in the treatment of their child. This is so even when divorce is not a factor. Divorce intensifies the complexity of the parents' role.

When parents request treatment for their child, we need to give them a general idea of what child treatment entails and explore their expectations. If they are ready to proceed, we move on to the assessment process. When treatment for the child follows this careful beginning, we have set as good a foundation as is possible. Once the child becomes our patient, our work with him or her will contain the normal challenges and complexities of child treatment exacerbated by the strain of the divorce. An important aspect of our work is to find ways of dealing with these strains therapeutically without becoming embroiled in parental disputes.

CONCLUSION

In conclusion, a divorce, particularly when children are involved, is a major crisis with the potential of causing pain and damage to all family members. The extent of the divorce upheaval and its immutability are determined by the degree of parental psychopathology. In many cases the strain and discord caused by the divorce invade all aspects of family life and, if the child is in treatment, these strains may disrupt treatment and cause premature termination. A child therapist entering this volatile situation has a difficult task and needs to adhere to some basic guidelines in order to protect the integrity and continuity of the treatment.

1. Before beginning treatment it is imperative to carefully assess parents and child to determine whether treatment is indicated at this time and, if it is, what the treatment objectives are, and who can benefit from treatment—the child, the parents, or all three.
2. The therapist must find a way to take charge of the treatment plan while at the same time being sensitive to the fact that parental autonomy has been undermined by the legal arrangements concerning the children.
3. Since the divorce situation is frequently a trigger for countertransferential responses, the therapist must vigilantly track his or her own reactions to the divorce upheaval and analyze any tendency to enact fantasies of rescuing the child and becoming the better parent.
4. The therapist can seriously endanger the child's treatment if she participates in legal decisions, has interviews with lawyers, or engages in any activity other than that of treating the child and being available to the parents in nondivorce matters. If the parents need the help of a therapist on divorce-

related issues concerning their child, they can consult a separate therapist to act as consultant on these matters.

5. When the therapist protects her special place in the life of the family, when she maintains her professional role and positions herself equidistant to parents and child (Siskind, 1997), she has the best chance of averting disruptions in the treatment or premature termination. When treatment is allowed to continue for as long as it is needed, the therapist will have had the opportunity to play a significant part in helping child and parents move beyond the divorce crisis and settle into a new way of life.

REFERENCES

Goldstein, J., Solnit, A. J., Goldstein, S. & Freud, A. (1996), *The Best Interest of the Child.* New York: Free Press.

Novick, J. & Novick, K. (1998), Parent work in analysis: Children, adolescents, and adults. Unpublished paper.

Siskind, D.(1992), *The Child Patient and the Therapeutic Process.* Northvale, NJ: Aronson.

—— (1997), *Working with Parents.* Northvale, NJ: Aronson.

Wallerstein, J. (1997), Transference and countertransference in clinical intervention with divorcing families. In: *Countertranference in Couples Therapy,* ed. J. Wallerstein, M. Solomon & J. Siegel. New York: Norton, pp. 158–165.

Chapter 26

Clinical Work with Parents in Entrenched Custody Disputes

JANET R. JOHNSTON

*H*igh-conflict parents in custody disputes are susceptible, to varying degrees, to the stresses of loss and rejection that are inherent in the divorce crisis and its aftermath. A few separating spouses are especially vulnerable by virtue of having experienced previous traumatic losses—such as the untimely death of a child, a parent, or a sibling—and they reexperience this earlier helplessness and grief along with the pain of the divorce (McClenney, Johnston, and Wallerstein, 1994; Bar, 1997; Johnston, 1998). More commonly, these vulnerable persons have never fully psychologically separated or individuated from their own primary caretakers because of early, pervasive emotional deprivation and childhood trauma. For them, the marital separation can trigger panic and intense anxiety about abandonment. When this happens, these parents cling to the child as a substitute for the ex-spouse or other lost object (Wallerstein, 1985; Garrity and Baris, 1994).

Parts of this paper are adapted from chapters 9 and 10 of Johnston and Roseby (1997). The therapeutic work described in Johnston and Roseby derived from a series of four empirical studies with a total of 200 high-conflict families in entrenched custody disputes, supported by grants from the Gerbode Foundation, Marin Community Foundation, Van Loben Sels Foundation, and the Zellerbach Family Foundation. All subjects in the study gave informed consent to their participation and the collection of data according to protocols for the protection of the human subject approved by the Judith Wallerstein Center for the Family in Transition. All personal identifying information in the clinical examples has been changed to protect the confidentiality of participants.

Many of them are narcissistically fragile and have chronic difficulty in maintaining a positive and stable sense of self (Ehrenberg,
Hunter, and Elterman, 1996; Baum and Shnit, in press). When the
separation occurs, old feelings of shame, failure, and "badness" are
evoked and become part of the emotional response to the rejection
inherent in the divorce and the threatened loss or perceived "betrayal" of the child. These feelings produce intolerable anxiety, which
tends to be defensively managed by the process of splitting and projective identification: the unbearable "bad" feelings and unwanted
aspects of self are projected onto the former partner (and others) so
that the self can be experienced as invulnerable and "good." Consequently these persons tend to view the other parent as irrelevant
and irresponsible, even dangerous, whereas the self is seen as the
essential, responsible, and safe caretaker (Hoppe and Kenney, 1994;
Walters, Lee, and Olesen, 1995). In cases of more severe narcissistic
vulnerability, one partner experiences the other's rejection, custody
demands, or accusations as a devastating attack, and in defense develops paranoid ideas of betrayal, conspiracy, and exploitation by
the ex-mate (Johnston and Campbell, 1988; Garrity and Baris, 1994).
The children, in order to receive any semblance of nurturance and
avoid their own abandonment, or even psychic destruction, are required to mirror what the rejected parent feels and perceives
(Johnston and Roseby, 1997).

The adversarial legal system that these disputing families enter
in order to resolve their custody disputes is particularly fertile ground
for this polarization and projection of blame. Moreover, as the parents
act out their projective identifications, new partners, families, and
friends—sometimes even the professionals involved—reify their negatively biased views of each other. In a culture where child abuse and
spousal violence are gaining increased recognition, the idea that
everyone is either a victim or a victimizer in failed family relationships
is receiving greater social validation, and this societal view also ex-
acerbates the parents' projection of blame (Johnston and Campbell,
1988; Garrity and Baris, 1994; Saposnek, 1998).

The problems presented by chronically disputing parents stem
partly from the acting-out of projective identifications that, in turn,
tend to be validated as reality by the social world of the divorced
family. In some cases and to some extent, these negative views will
have a basis in fact, that is, the real experience of the other spouse's
violent, neglectful, or substance-abusing behavior. The goal for the

clinician, then, is to help parents distinguish their unrealistic fears and phobias from their realistic concerns about one another's capacity to care for the child. In pursuing this therapeutic goal, the quintessential dilemma is how can the clinician manage these often intense and overwhelming transferences on the part of the parents and countertransference reactions on the part of the clinician and maintain an empathic stance toward both disputing parties in order to maximize parental functioning and protect the child's development.

The purpose of this paper is to describe parental counseling and conflict resolution with families in entrenched custody and postdivorce disputes from the viewpoint of the fairly dramatic changes in transference and countertransference dynamics that commonly occur throughout the phases of a successful family intervention. These phases are generally as follows: (1) initial referral and contract formation; (2) assessment of the impasse and its effects on the child; (3) reformulation of the problem; (4) challenge and crisis; (5) working through and resolution; and (6) termination and follow-up.[1]

The therapeutic approach used here draws broadly from neoanalytic object-relations, self-psychology, and similar interpersonal theories (Kernberg, 1976; Kohut, 1977; Spence, 1982; Masterson, 1985; Masterson and Klein, 1989; Singer and Salovey, 1993; Hedges, 1994). Specifically, the concepts of projective identification, countertransference, and empathy are congruent with Tansey and Burke's (1989) seminal interpersonal theory of the clinical process. Projective identification is a psychological defense wherein the projector stirs up in another person an experiential state that matches or complements the projector's immediate experience, either consciously or unconsciously. Countertransference refers to the totality of thoughts

---

[1] It is not within the scope of this paper to discuss the special nature of individual and group work with children involved in highly conflicted custody disputes, a large topic that has been addressed elsewhere (Johnston and Roseby, 1997; Roseby and Johnston, 1997). Some kind of access to the children as part of the family work is, however, essential in order for the clinician to remain focused on the needs and experience of the children rather than becoming caught up in the parents' projections and conflicting perceptions of their offspring. If the child is being seen in separate treatment, a close working alliance with the child's therapist is an alternative to direct access. Otherwise the child is seen from time to time as part of the family intervention, thus providing an opportunity for good observation of the child's defensive and adaptive responses to the parental conflict. This diagnostic information in turn provides credibility to the clinician's advocacy to parents on each child's behalf.

and feelings that are generated in the clinician by the client, including realistic responses as well as those distorted by the clinician's own idiosyncratic personal conflicts and psychological state. From this stance, countertransference reactions are viewed, not as impediments, but as essential clinical data that signal the state and quality of the clinician's relationship with the client. However, these reactions need to be sorted through and carefully processed by the clinician in order to achieve an empathic response to the client, at which point they can also be judiciously used in intervention.

THE LEGAL CONTRACT THAT GOVERNS THE THERAPEUTIC INTERVENTION

To begin working with these kinds of families in a haphazard manner, without a clear purpose and structure, is a prescription for disaster. The first task is to restrain the tendency of the parents to involve the courts, attorneys and other professionals, as well as families and friends, in acting out their conflicts (that is, in their projective identifications). For this reason, effective intervention in high-conflict custody disputes takes place within a legally defined framework (a legal contract or court order) that coordinates the actions of all professionals in the case and supports the focused role of the clinician in fashioning and maintaining a protective holding environment for the child in the fractured family. This legal framework also provides an overarching rule-governed process for managing the ongoing conflict and the involvement of the wider network should the conflict erupt beyond the capacity of the clinician to contain it. (See Baris et al., 2000; Johnston, 2000; Johnston, Walters and Friedlander, 2001; Sullivan and Kelly, 2001; Schephard, 2004) for a more detailed discussion of this collaborative, case management approach.)

At the outset, a legal contract or court order for the intervention needs to specify each of the following: (a) the goals of the service; (b) who will be seen in sessions; (c) the limits of confidentiality with the court; (d) the permissible lines of communication among parties and collaterals; (e) a timely procedure for resolving issues when parents are stuck; (f) payment for services; and (g) an agreed-upon process for terminating the intervention or transferring to another counselor. Specifically, the following kinds of provisions in the legal agreement have been found effective in containing conflict and promoting case control. First of all, the clinician needs to have access to all family members involved in the dispute on an as-needed basis. Second, in order to ensure that each parent is assuming responsibility for the resolution of the family conflict, each should pay for his or her own individual sessions, for half of each joint session, and for half of the children's sessions. (If a sliding scale fee can be provided to each parent, this can take care of real inequities in resources.)

Parents are usually asked to give their consent for all information to be held confidential from the court, with the exception of any child abuse or threats of violence, for which reporting is mandated. This means the parties must stipulate that the clinician will not be asked or subpoenaed to testify in court. The signed confidentiality agreement should be a three-way one, indicating that the consent of both parents and the clinician is required to waive it.

On the other hand, granting broad discretionary powers at the outset for the clinician to share information with other professionals and extended family members maximizes the potential for collaboration and limits the possibility of manipulation by the contending parties. It is particularly critical, if not imperative, for parents to sign releases for the clinician to share accumulating information with other mental health professionals involved with the family, especially the parents' and children's individual therapists. Releases to speak with teachers, childcare persons, and pediatricians can be added as needed. Permission for the clinician to speak with new stepparents and extended kin involved in day-to-day care of the children is also important.

To maximize coordination between parents who usually cannot communicate with one another directly, it must be specified that the clinician can use his or her discretion to exchange information freely between parents in separate interviews. However, to protect children who are often in a dangerously vulnerable position between parents, it should be made clear that the children's confidences will be privileged. The only kind of feedback parents receive about their child will be general clinical impressions, unless the child consents to the release of more specific information.

THE THERAPEUTIC MODEL OF INTERVENTION

The clinician's overall aim is to build a functioning organizational structure out of the family chaos that initially presents as a situation in which each parent is acting unilaterally, without reference to the child's needs or the other parent's wishes, and each is actively sabotaging and undermining the other's capacity to parent and protect the child. From the beginning, most elements of the new structure lie within the clinician who acts, in the best sense, as the charismatic center for the parents and child, and who calls upon the legal contract for constraints and limit setting when necessary. Typically what erupts in the family over the course of the intervention are a spate of issues, problems, and crises that must be resolved, one by one. Out of each successful resolution emerges clearer expectations as to how parents need to conduct themselves for the sake of the child. Gradually, a working group becomes organized, as the role of each family member is delineated and stabilized. Later, a family "constitution" is drawn up wherein these roles are codified into a set of principles and rules about how members are to treat each other, independent of intervention by the clinician or the court.

Initial Referral and Contract Formation

It is best if parents are jointly referred for this service, by attorney stipulation or judicial order. If there is no parenting agreement and referral follows a failed mediation or a custody evaluation, a temporary custody and access order needs to be in place. If only one of the parties or an attorney tries unilaterally to engineer referral of the family, the effort is often met with suspicion, resistance, and stalemate. In any case, initial contact with each party usually begins with a strategic "dance," as each parent vies for position and advantage. Telephone calls from all parties will consume considerable time, sometimes with demands that the clinician provide references, resumes, or disclosures about his or her attitudes toward controversial topics such as joint custody, fathers' involvement with infants, and domestic violence. It is especially important for the clinician to keep a balanced perspective and maintain the appearance of neutrality during this exploratory period. Both parents must agree to proceed before any information gathering or counseling sessions take place. During this phase, the terms of the contract need to be carefully explained.

Parents come to the intervention with a range of expectations and strong feelings, mostly negative ones. Most commonly, parents are ambivalent, skeptical, distrustful, even paranoid. Some feel quite hopeless and despairing, convinced that no one can help. They may appear exhausted by what feels to them like a life-and-death struggle. Others are highly focused and energized by the dispute. Almost all parents express fears that the clinician will be duped by the other side.

Some of these parents have a utilitarian, exploitative attitude: "What can you do for me? Can I use you to get what I want?" Simply put, they are in search of an ally in the power struggle. Their unspoken agenda may include: "Can I use counseling to delay or avoid an outcome I don't want (e.g., an unfavorable court decision, or a confrontation about my violence)?" They may see counseling as a way to prolong the marriage and deny the fact that the divorce is occurring. It is important for the clinician to tease out these various motivations and decide whether the case is a suitable one for confidential counseling and mediation, or whether a custody evaluation, court hearing, or arbitration is needed instead.

There are a number of unconscious or pre-conscious emotional responses of his or her own that the clinician needs to keep in check and avoid acting out. For example, the clinician might find himself or herself being vague and nonspecific about the terms of the contract (for example, whether reports will be made to the court); or the clinician may be tempted to abandon some of the necessary structure as a concession in order to capture an ambivalent or unwilling parent (for example, agreeing not to see the child). There may be a temptation to relinquish neutrality, favoring the less emotionally disturbed parent and backing away from the more disturbed one. Or, in response to intimidation and fear, the clinician may make unwarranted concessions in an attempt to placate a disturbed, controlling, or violent parent.

Assessment of the Impasse and Its Effect on the Child

Once the contract is entered into, the clinician undertakes a dispute-specific assessment of the divorced couple (giving special attention to any history of domestic violence in the spousal relationship) from courtship to separation. A synopsis of the early history of each parent is obtained together with a concise assessment of their current personal and occupational functioning. An overview of the developmental history of the child is also obtained with special attention to any allegations of abuse, what the child has witnessed of the parental conflict/violence, what separations and losses the child has experienced, the child's reaction to the parental separation/divorce, and his or her attachment to each parent. The child's symptoms of distress during transitions between parents as well as other emotional or behavioral problems (including somatic ones), school achievements, and peer relationships need to be reviewed and, if disputed, validated by information from collateral sources. This initial assessment usually takes from six to eight hours.

The point of gathering this information is to formulate a working hypothesis about the "divorce impasse," the intrapsychic and interactional factors in and between parents and others that maintain the family disputes (Johnston and Campbell, 1988). The actual or potential impact of the parental conflicts on the child's development is also hypothesized. This involves a specific assessment of the effects of the impasse on parenting and parent–child relationships and how all of these relate to the symptoms of distress, the defenses, and the coping style of the child. It is also useful to consider how the child's symptoms and defensive adaptation, in turn, contribute to the parental disputes.

> Mr. and Mrs. P were locked in a bitter dispute over the father's access to their eight-year-old daughter, Julie. Mrs. P, a young woman who had been abandoned by her own father, and who was unable to emancipate from her intrusive mother, was convinced that she needed to protect Julie from an "uncaring, brutal" man. There was some real, though exaggerated truth to Mrs. P's views. Mr. P, a product of rigid, punitive, and shaming parenting, was highly affronted by his daughter's refusal to visit him; he was also convinced that he needed to rescue Julie from a "sick dependency" upon her mother. Armed with a court order for visitation, he invaded the home, shoved the mother and grandmother aside, and dragged the extremely frightened child, kicking and screaming, to his car. An intrapsychic split within this child mirrored the ongoing struggle between her parents, which was fueled by tribal warfare between the extended families. Anxious and phobic, Julie struggled with an unintegrated sense of herself: she was unable to separate and differentiate from her "good" mother, and was fearful of becoming like her "bad" father. This was concretely manifested by her attempts to shave off one of her eyebrows that "looked like Dad's." Not surprisingly, the child's disturbed behavior reinforced the parents' negative views and blaming of one another.

The clinician's task, in such a situation, may involve coming up with a series of alternative hypotheses that will be carefully considered in designing the intervention. The idea is to formulate a strategic plan of attack: determining what elements of the impasse can be shifted, what must be bypassed or diffused, and how this will be done.

> In the P family, the questions were: who and what are amenable to change? Can we show this mother how to more effectively protect her daughter by helping Julie cope with visits to her father; or is she wedded to an intractably negative view of the husband who has humiliated and deserted her? Can she tolerate some interpretation of the origins of her fears? Can we teach this father to be more empathic and responsive to his daughter's fears, or is he too indignant, too obsessed with his "rights" as a father?

Typically, an "idealizing transference" will develop during the assessment phase wherein the clinician is revered as being perfectly understanding and capable of being completely gratifying. The clinician's empathic listening during the often intensely emotional individual interviews is experienced as a validation of each parent's perceptions, feelings, and reality. This is especially likely when the clinician is willing to accept any information the parent wants to supply, including talking with supportive others or reviewing video or audio tapes and prior evaluations. This kind of idealizing transference by the parents is valuable in that it can reinforce the hope that the clinician will be able to effect change, but it can also lead to unrealistic positive expectations. The challenge is to meet the parents' needs to be acknowledged in these ways without relinquishing neutrality and inadvertently confirming their distorted views.

Some clinicians can be seduced into wanting to gratify these fantasies during this "honeymoon" phase of treatment and will, with good but misguided intentions, hint at or promise what they cannot deliver. Specifically, a clinician may be seduced into trying to rescue one or both parents or the child in order to prove that he or she is a more effective therapist than the string of mental health professionals that have failed. Others, who are more skeptical—because they have been down this road before—will maintain a cool, dispassionate distance and an inscrutable demeanor that may be experienced as non-supportive and anxiety-provoking, and which may even induce paranoia in the client. The optimal response is to relate empathically to the feelings expressed by both parents, explaining that one is withholding judgment about the accuracy of their perceptions, while emphasizing to both that there are two sides to every story and that problems such as theirs are often very complex. This stance is likely to be experienced by parents as more understandable, even if not altogether reassuring.

Reformulation of the Problem

As in other brief, focused therapies, the intervention proper usually begins with the clinician's redefining or reframing the problems and issues under dispute, hopefully in a manner that each parent can accept. This reframing may involve direct interpretation of the impasse and an explanation of what the dispute is doing to the child. Here, the leverage for change is generally the parent's concern for the child.

> To Mrs. P, the clinician might say, "Your daughter sees you as the angel and her father as the devil! She is struggling with being either "all good" like you, or "all bad" like him. This means she can't allow herself to make any mistakes, for fear she will be less than perfect—"bad" like him. How can we let her know that it's okay and only human to make mistakes? Can you allow her to see that you, too, have strengths and weaknesses? Can you let her know that her father has good as well as problematic traits?"

Alternatively, the intervention may involve some careful modification of the parents' views, using their primary defenses as leverage for change. For example, one may make an appeal to the self-interest of the parent, using the fact that the parent has a vested interest in saving face and appearing to be the nobler parent.

> To Mr. P, the clinician might comment, "I've been impressed with how committed you are to having the opportunity to be a good father to your child, and helping your child separate from her mother. Your child wants and needs a good, understanding father too! Sometimes being a good parent, one who feels safe to a child, means rethinking the way we ourselves were parented." This can lead to a discussion of the father's own childhood experience of a rigid, punitive upbringing and parenting style.

The cognitive reframing of the problem in terms of the impasse generally relieves the parents' anxiety. It makes rational what may have been experienced as deeply shaming or as sheer craziness.

> When Ms. S was a young teenage mother, her six-month-old son was severely injured in a car crash as a result of her driving at excessive speed. Her relationship with the child's father fell apart irretrievably during the long stressful months of the baby's rehabilitation. At the time, feeling conflicted and guilty, the young woman "acted out" by darting in front of a bus and sustaining almost identical injuries to those her son had suffered. Then she allowed herself to be beaten by the father and relinquished the care of their baby to him. The father, rewriting history, concluded that the exciting young woman (whom he had once loved) was an "abusive, endangering" mother from whom his son needed to be protected at all costs. By both word and deed, the father conveyed his enormous fears for the child's safety at the hands of the mother, and soon the child was phobic, unable to be soothed or managed by his mother. When the now seven-year-old boy rejected his mother, reciting the family legend of the car accident as his reason, the young mother's unresolved guilt erupted into a narcissistic wound for which she fought a sustained, bitter battle for custody as a salve. The significant turning point in the clinical intervention with this young woman was an interpretation in which she was portrayed as a very caring, loving mother who could not forgive herself for her son's accident, and who effectively continued to punish herself by fighting for custody and forcing access in a manner that frightened and alienated her child.

This kind of intervention often works well at an intellectual or cognitive level; however, it is often difficult to know just how much the family members can truly absorb and understand psychologically, using this method. Most certainly, at this point, the bulk of the hard work in producing emotional and behavioral change still lies ahead.

If the clinician succeeds in being both accurate in interpretation and at the same time protective of the parents' vulnerabilities, the parents may be impressed and intrigued by the redefinition that is offered to them, and by the depth of the clinician's insight. When this happens, the idealizing transference is magnified. In some instances, the clinician will be experienced by one or more of the family members as the all-knowing, all-giving, omnipotent parent figure, who is somehow going to "fix" everything. If this feeling takes hold, it might be important to actively discourage or modify the transference by interpreting it and predicting the potential for trouble that lies ahead. This will prolong the clinician's power to effect change. Alternatively, if the cognitive reframing is clumsy, inopportune, or experienced as an attack, the clinician may be dismissed as naive, in which case he or she will be swept into the most troubled waters of the next phase of intervention—the rocky shoals of "challenge and crisis."

Challenge and Crisis

Sooner or later, the disputing parties will test and challenge the clinician by precipitating a crisis or series of crises. For example, one or both parents may act out by snatching or withholding the child, disputing or physically fighting at the transition between homes, or simply behaving as they always have, regardless of their new knowledge and the insights they have supposedly gained from the cognitive reframing. This acting-out behavior must be responded to in a timely and firm manner. Specifically, it must be confronted and interpreted according to the clinician's developing understanding of the impasse and its effects on the child. This is problematic because the crisis is, in part, generated by the needy parents' jealousy over the child, who is always the central concern of the clinician. It is crucial, however, that the clinician be available to deal with this crisis period and be willing to work through it by firmly confronting any behavior that either hurts or fails to protect the child.

> For example, Mr. P and Ms. S each lost patience with their own child's irrational fear of themselves as parents and attempted to force demonstrations of affection, which further alienated the child in both of these cases. At other times, they each demanded prematurely independent behaviors that further frightened these children.

At the same time the clinician is firmly confronting parents, he or she defines principles and rules for ways that situations like this have to be handled in the future. These principles or rules form the bases of the mediation agreements that will be drawn up later.

In these two cases, Mrs. P and Mr. S each reacted with outrage and increased demands for child protection, when they heard and entirely believed somewhat distorted accounts relayed by the child of the other parent's cruel/endangering behaviors. When the clinician carefully explored the critical incidents with both parents, far more benign interpretations arose. This affirmed the need for each parent to calmly check out stories the child brings home in the future and work to improve their child's reality testing.

During these crises, there is generally a precipitous de-idealization of the clinician. The parents may feel bitterly disappointed, even hostile; they may accuse the clinician of naiveté, bias, unethical conduct, or ineffectiveness and failure—just as all the others before this have failed them. They may become disillusioned and depressed about the chances of anyone being able to help them. In the worst-case scenario, the clinician can become a phobic object or the focus of the parents' paranoid projections.

Resolution of crises is critical to the successful treatment of a case. In order to be seen as a real, separate person and not a "part-object" of the parent's idealized or de-idealized self, the clinician needs to carefully, patiently, and persistently reiterate his or her point of view about the child's plight. Specifically, this means repeatedly focusing on the child's needs and experience. At the same time, the clinician empathically reflects the parents' own needs and feelings, appealing to and validating the positive attributes of each parent, all the while differentiating each parent's needs from those of the child. Throughout the family intervention, the clinician continues to confront aspects of the parents' behaviors that are destructive to their children or to themselves.

A common scenario is the fight over the child's possessions, which usually erupts at the time of transfer from one home to the other. One parent becomes infuriated when good clothes and toys that they have provided for the child "disappear into a black hole" when taken to the other parent's home. Consequently, the parents react in a number of ways that are highly distressful for the child. They may scream and yell at each other (frightening the child), demand that the child retrieve the items or steal back ones of equivalent value (burdening or undermining the child's conscience), insist that treasured belongings be left behind when the child goes to the other home (disenfranchising the child), completely strip the child at the point of transfer (objectifying the child), or send the child back in scruffy, ill-fitting clothes (embarrassing and demeaning the child). With each of these actions, the child's sense of self-continuity and control is undermined. While the clinician acknowledges to each parent the symbolic and monetary value of these items (connecting it to their convictions about being exploited, cheated, or ignored by the ex-spouse), he or she draws primary attention to the destructive results of the parents' attempts to solve the problem at the expense of the child's self esteem.

The clinician's role is neither a passive nor a neutral one; rather it involves taking a strongly supportive, active, but confrontational stance with both parents, while advocating for the child's needs. The idea is to align with the "good parent" attributes of each parent and to gently but firmly confront them about their negative attributes. This involves supporting their valid perceptions of the other parent and withholding support for those accusations that are invalid or cannot be confirmed. For example, the clinician may need to sort through a litany of objections that a mother makes about her three-year-old visiting his father, and help both parents to organize their issues in terms of those that are valid concerns, those that are less important, and those that may be invalid. The clinician points out to both parents that the father's failure to provide a child car seat for transportation is a critical issue and supercedes his reluctance to insist the child has a nap or his tendency to feed the child "fast food." And he/she suggests that, on the other hand, his including his new girlfriend on visits may actually be a benefit to the child.

Disputing parents are often puzzled and even suspicious of the clinician's active support for both sides. They may complain that he or she "speaks with a forked tongue," saying whatever each parent wants to hear. In actuality, the clinician is not being inconsistent or contradictory. He or she is painting a picture that each parent can tolerate, but also one that is part of a larger, more realistic, and less negatively biased view. Though the clinician starts with polarized partial positions gleaned from each parent, he or she tries to understand the whole situation from the viewpoint of the child's needs, teasing out the shared reality so that there will be less and less chance of saying to one parent something that would not be true to say to the other. It is this shared reality which the clinician will impart to the child and which the child can use for mastery. The stories or narratives that the clinician may later construct for and with the children, and send home with both parents to read as bedtime stories, become a metaphor for that shared reality (see Johnston et al., 1997).

> Mrs. Y was an attractive teenager when she married Mr. Y, a staid working-class man who was more than twice her age. This union had been precipitated by the accidental death of her high school sweetheart; the sorrowing girl found comfort in the older man's attentions. Shortly after the wedding, Mrs. Y came to realize the dreadful mistake she had made, but not before finding herself pregnant with twin girls. The marriage fell part when the babies were toddlers, and Mrs. Y resumed her lost teenage years by dating widely and taking up photographic modeling as a career. Mr. Y, feeling humiliated and betrayed by her desertion, began a concerted attack upon her mothering abilities. He denounced her as "a liar, manipulative, unscrupulous, materialistic, a user of people, inordinately concerned with the superficialities of appearances, a drug taker, and unfit to be the primary custodian." He, in turn, devoted himself to teaching the girls "good values," which included the rough and tumble of sports and expected academic achievement. Mrs. Y counter-accused him for his neglect of the girls' grooming, his carelessness with their diet, his working-class roughness, and his excessive drinking.
>
> The litigation between the parents, supported by their extended families, raged so fiercely that both nine-year-old girls became completely conflicted in their loyalties. They lied to both parents, and demeaned themselves and both parents on every one of the issues. The difficult task for the clinician in this case was to slowly redefine the problem as being their entrenched animosity towards each other rather than either parent's actual parenting skills, and to succeed in getting all family members to acknowledge that both parents were loving caretakers who made valuable, unique, and separate contributions to their daughters' upbringing. Finally, the girls were given an especially designed story about a fancy, prancing circus pony (the mother) that married a plodding draft horse (the father). The story included a thinly veiled rendition of the parental disputes along with a prescription on how the baby foals could solve the problem.

Countertransference feelings during the phase of challenge and crisis can be intense, even intolerable. The clinician may feel anxious, defensive, and angry. Clinicians, at this point, will be tempted to

abandon the case, or defensively withdraw into a passive, compromised stance. Others act out in retaliation, becoming hostile and
accusing the clients of provoking crises. Alternatively, the clinician
may participate in the splitting and projection of blame by
scapegoating the other professionals involved. The clinician, however, must accept the experience of absorbing the emotional responses that distressed parents are afraid of owning (the projective
identification), and this can be overwhelming. He or she may feel
stupid, confused, incompetent, unethical, sly, greedy, bad—or all of
these, at once. One clinician commented, "My brain felt like it was
being sucked out with a straw!" Another said, "I felt slimy and dirty,
and I wanted to take a shower." Yet another had disturbing dreams
of being condemned for some unknown horrible crime. It may be
necessary for the clinician to seek out consultations with an experienced and trusted colleague in order to tolerate and understand these
powerful feelings.

The clinician must be able to use his or her emotional reactions
both selectively and therapeutically in this process. We have not found
it helpful to be a passive-neutral recipient of the parents' rage and
contempt. They will not learn anything if they are allowed to act out
and project in this manner. Rather, they may become even more
frightened and chaotic, and the clinician can indeed become ineffective and even supportive of their pathological defenses. However,
in accord with Tansey and Burke (1989), we believe the clinician
needs to identify and process the origins of the countertransference
reactions before acting upon them.

What guidelines should govern countertransference disclosure?
First, the clinician may consciously and selectively use his or her
expectable emotional reactions (those that are normative to most
persons) as a confrontational mirror to the parents' outrageous or
inappropriate behavior. Second, the clinician may advocate for the
needs of the child and convey what most of these infants, children,
and even teenagers cannot possibly express to their parents. To this
end, the clinician may openly verbalize shock, distress, outrage, and
even anger in responding to these parents' actions that are destructive of their children, but always with therapeutic wisdom and in
moderation. Third, when reframing the issues and correcting the
parents' distorted perceptions, the clinician may express surprise,
curiosity, puzzlement, or incredulity at the stance they are taking.

At all times, the clinician must examine the motivation for his or her own observable stance, and continually ponder the question, "Am I helping this person by my emotional response, or am I merely protecting myself from further narcissistic wounds?"

Indeed, a high level of drama is likely to occur in entrenched custody disputes, and the clinician needs to know how to take over the role of stage director to the play. We have speculated that the high level of drama and emotional intensity that these parents both generate and demand may relieve their feelings of existential emptiness, incipient depression, and fears of emotional death.

> Dr. B would periodically become highly agitated when his ex-wife passive-aggressively refused to respond to his proposals for coparenting his son. Feeling cut off and abandoned, just as he had when his mother periodically abandoned him as a child, Dr. B would escalate his demands into a manic frenzy, transmitting multiple abusive faxes and telephone messages to all and sundry. At the point when he seemed to be losing all semblance of perspective and control, the clinician would intervene, empathically interpreting the origins of his desperate panic, but being highly offended by his abuse and disappointed in his self-destructiveness; insisting that he restrain his bullying behavior, and helping him organize his legitimate issues and proceed in a more rational manner.

The consistent availability of the clinician over the long haul is unquestionably an important component of successful treatment. While the clients have the right to withdraw at any time from the process, the clinician needs to make it clear that he or she will remain available to them and expects that the parents will try to be fair, honest, and civil. Unrealistic hopes and fantasies, however, (for example, that the other parent will disappear or be expelled from the child's life) need to be confronted as such: the clinician makes clear, over and over again, if necessary, what realistically can and cannot be done. The overarching message to these parents is that they will not be abandoned in their struggle. This is an unusual, if not unique experience for many of these people, who have indeed been abandoned and negated repeatedly, not only by their own early caretakers but also, within recent memory, by therapists, attorneys, and other professionals.

Working Through and Resolution

Progress is consolidated in an uneven manner, two steps forward and one step back. This means that the working-through phase often continues to be disrupted by intermittent crises, especially with more characterologically disturbed parents, or when the child's symptomatic behavior continues to reactivate the conflict between the parents. The techniques for handling these crises are similar to those described above although, if intransigence solidifies, the family may need to be referred to an arbitrator or returned to court to obtain a more structured agreement or a reality check on their unrealistic expectations about the kind of relief that the court can provide.

Psychoeducational child guidance work (see below), parent counseling, coaching parental communication about the children and, of course, monitoring parents' behaviors and agreements are the usual order of business at this stage. When elements of the core impasse recur, ongoing interpretation is offered and strategies are developed to help the parents cope without compounding the impasse.

The important products of this phase of the intervention are written drafts of a series of co-parenting agreements that not only specify time-sharing arrangements, but also define the principles by which parents are to govern their dealings with each other and by which they can make good decisions about their child in a timely manner. These agreements may need to be formalized as court orders by stipulation, in which case they need to be passed on to the parents' attorneys and the child's attorney for processing. The clinician will know that the co-parenting agreements have been internalized when parents telephone or meet together over a complaint or a dilemma and are fairly quickly able to reach a principled resolution. In the best of situations, the clinician fades into the background, leaving in place the knowledge and guidelines that will structure the family's ongoing interactions through the years until the child is able to psychologically and physically emancipate. These outcomes are what one hopes to achieve.

It is the mark of a successful intervention when parents view the clinician more realistically as a concerned helper and a benevolent (but human and fallible) person, who is profoundly interested in their child and in them as parents. He or she takes much pleasure in the child's growth and development and in their accomplishments as good parents. The family members now know that, despite their limitations, the clinician understands their history and their vulnerabilities, and values and cares about them. Moreover, the clinician continues to provide a model for the child as to how to relate positively to both parents. Problems may arise for the clinician, however, in managing his or her own boredom and frustration at the slow pace of change, manifested in the need to deal with the same old issues again and again.

Termination and Follow-Up

Optimally, the clinician does not terminate with these families; instead he or she remains available for the child and the parents to consult in the event of renewed conflict, developmental changes in the child, or changes in life circumstances throughout the child's growing-up years. Effective clinicians doing this kind of work become members of the divorced family's network, like the old-time family physician, akin to the stabilizing influence of elders in the lives of families that are buttressed by close-knit extended family, tribal, or community ties.

How can these families continue to be helped if the initial clinician cannot be consistently available to them over the long term? Unfortunately, many parents will not follow through on a new referral, in which case the most the clinician can do is to leave them with a good parenting plan and appropriate principles and parenting guidelines to follow. Or, if it seems reasonable to do so, and with the permission of the family members, the clinician may introduce a new clinician and transfer the family through a series of conjoint sessions. Alternatively, in family and professional conferences, the emerging structure and process can be passed on to grandparents, teachers, or child-care workers. These termination and transfer meetings should include a clear definition of what behaviors to flag for further help.

In summary, successful outcomes[2] in working with families engaged in high-conflict divorce are determined, in large part, by the

---

[2]This model of intervention has been evaluated in several outcome studies that are available from the author. The main findings are summarized in Kline-Pruett and Johnston (2004; Johnston, 1993).

extent to which the therapist can maintain a working alliance with all disputing parties, as well as maintain balance and equidistance in the face of the extraordinary polarization and demands for exclusive allegiance. That is, the idealization of the therapist by the clients usually gives way to de-idealization and rejection as both parents are bitterly disappointed and angry that their perceptions and actions are not fully validated by the therapist. Consequently, challenge and crisis, resistance and regression are expected features of this work and provide therapeutic opportunities for growth and change.

REFERENCES

Bar, M. (1997), The relationship of childhood trauma to adult adjustment to divorce. Unpublished doctoral dissertation, Western Graduate School of Psychology, Palo Alto, CA.

Baris, M. A., Coates, C. A., Duvall, B. B., Garrity, C. B., Johnson, E. T. & LaCrosse, E. R. (2000), *Working with High-Conflict Families of Divorce.* Northvale, NJ: Aronson.

Baum, N. & Shnit, D. (2003), Self-differentiation and narcissism in divorced parents co-parental relationships and functioning. *J. Divorce & Remarriage.*

Ehrenberg, M. F., Hunter, M. A. & Elterman, M. F. (1996), Shared parenting agreements after marital separation: The role of empathy and narcissism. *J. Consult. Clin. Psychol.*, 64:808–818.

Garrity, C. B. & Baris, M. A. (1994), *Caught in the Middle.* New York: Lexington Books.

Hedges, L. E. (1994), *Remembering, Repeating and Working through Childhood Traumas.* Northvale, NJ: Aronson.

Hoppe, C. F. & Kenney, L. M. (1994), A Rorschach study of the psychological characteristics of parents engaged in child custody/visitation disputes. Presented at the 102nd annual convention of the American Psychological Association, Los Angeles, August.

Johnston, J. R. (1993), *Developing Preventive Interventions for Children of Severe Family Conflict and Volence.* Technical Report of the Judith Walerstein Center for the Family in Transition, Corte Madera, CA.

—— (1998), *Prevention of Parent or Family Aabduction of Children through Early Identification of Risk Factors. Stage II, Part B.* Final Report to the Office of Juvenile Justice and Delinquency Prevention, Department of Justice, Washington, DC.

—— (2000), Building multidisciplinary professional partnerships with the court on behalf of high-conflict divorcing families and their children: Who needs what kind of help? *Univ. Arkansas Little Rock Law Rev.*, 22:453–479.

—— Breunig, K., Garrity, C. & Baris, M. A. (1997), *Through the Eyes of Children.* New York: Free Press.

—— & Campbell, L. E. G. (1988), *Impasses of Divorce*. New York: Free Press.

—— & Roseby, V. (1997), *In the Name of the Child*. New York: Free Press.

—— Walters, M. G. & Friedlander, S. (2001), Therapeutic work with alienated children and their families. *Family Court Rev.*, 39:316–333.

Kernberg, O. (1976), *Object Relations Theory and Clinical Psychoanalysis*. New York: Aronson.

Kline-Pruett, M. & Johnston, J. R. (2004), Therapeutic mediation with high-conflict parents: Effective models and strategies. In: *Divorce and Family Mediation*, ed. J. Folberg, A. Milne & P. Salem. New York: Guilford Press, pp. 92–111.

Kohut, H. (1977), *The Restoration of the Self*. Madison, CT: International Universities Press.

Masterson, J. (1985), *The Real Self*. New York: Brunner/Mazel.

—— & Klein, R., eds. (1989), *Psychotherapy of the Disorders of the Self*. New York: Brunner/Mazel.

McClenney, L., Johnston, J. R. & Wallerstein, J. S. (1994), *Adjustment to Divorce as a Function of Prior Trauma and Perceptions of the Marital Relationship*. Technical Report of the Judith Wallerstein Center for the Family in Transition.

Roseby, V. & Johnston, J. R. (1997), *High-Conflict, Violent and Separating Families*. New York: Free Press.

Saposnek, D. T, (1998), *Mediating Child Custody Disputes*. San Francisco, CA: Jossey-Bass.

Schepard, A. (2004), *Children, Courts, and Custody*. London: Cambridge University Press.

Singer, J. A. & Salovey, P. (1993), *The Remembered Self*. New York: Free Press.

Spence, D. P. (1982), *Narrative Truth and Historic Truth*. New York: Norton.

Sullivan, M. J. & Kelly, J. B. (2001), Legal and psychological management of cases with an alienated child. *Family Court Rev.*, 39:299–315.

Tansey, M. J. & Burke, W. F. (1989), *Understanding Countertransference*. Hillsdale, NJ: The Analytic Press.

Wallerstein, J. S. (1985), Parent-child relationships after divorce. In: *Parental Influences: In Health and Disease*, ed. E. J. Anthony & G. H. Pollock. Boston: Little Brown, pp. 317–347.

Walters, M. G., Lee, M. S. & Olesen, N. (1995), Rorschach findings about parenting capacities of parents in protracted custody disputes. Presented at the Society for Personality Assessment, Atlanta, GA, March.

Chapter 27

Parental Divorce and Developmental Progression
An Inquiry into Their Relationship

JUDITH WALLERSTEIN
DEBORAH RESNIKOFF

P sychoanalytic formulations about psychological development in childhood evolved within the paradigm of a stable intact family. The continued presence of both parents during the child's early years was given, except for the involuntary disruptions of death or severe illness. The impact of neurotic or psychotic illness of a parent on the child was a widely acknowledged concern; but marital breakdown was rare, and its developmental and clinical implications for the child were of little moment within the community or the mental health professions.

Divorce is by no means the time-limited, circumscribed crisis that it was expected to be, but often destabilizes adults for many years. It is not only the family structure that changes. What is striking is that the entire patterning of conscious and unconscious psychological needs, wishes, and expectations that parents and children bring to each other is profoundly altered under the impact of divorce and its multiple ripple effects. Psychoanalytic theory has shown us that the quality of the parents' marriage and the quality of the parent–child relationship are closely intertwined. A good marital bond has a powerful capacity to support and enrich each parent–child relationship, to shape and sustain it, in accord with the parents' identification with each other and with the child as the fruit of their union.

An extended version of this paper was published in the *International Journal of Psycho-Analysis* (1997), 78:135–154.

When this bond is broken, a wide range of passions, including rage, sexual jealousy, and depression, can and do spill over into all domains of the family. These passions, which can lead to uncontrolled behavior, including violence, in persons whose behavior had been previously well regulated or even reserved, have the power to modify, skew, or totally derail the parent–child relationships that were in place during the intact family. One immediate consequence is the eruption of anxiety in the child, setting into motion a hypervigilant tracking of each parent that can last for many years. The child's anxiety-driven responses contribute significantly to the potential for volatile changes in parent–child relationships (Wallerstein, 1985).

As a result, it is not possible to predict postdivorce parent–child relationships from those that existed during the intact marriage. Nor is it possible to predict parent-child relationships within the remarriage from the relationships within the first marriage or during the intervening divorce period. In effect, divorce introduces change— not only at the time of the marital break-up, but throughout the rest of life (Wallerstein and Blakeslee, 1989). In an earlier report about the more common alterations in parent-child relationships that emerge at the time of divorce, Wallerstein (1985) called attention to two contrapuntal trends in parental attitudes. The first reflects the parent's conscious or unconscious wish to abandon the child. The adult's magical wish at this time is not only to dissolve the marriage but also to eradicate it from history. Every adult wants to take back the wasted years. Tragically, the hapless child often represents an all-too-real reminder of the failed marriage and the heavy responsibilities that lie ahead. The diminished capacity to parent that is evident in the rising anger of parent and child, the lax discipline and greater household disorder, and the erratic physical and emotional care in all domains of the child's life, all reflect the parents' intense ambivalence as well as the real burdens and difficult decisions that they confront. "If I had my way, I would take my youngest and walk out of here and keep on walking," commented a divorcing mother of three (Wallerstein and Blakeslee, 1989).

Running counter to the wish to leave the child, and often coexisting with the parent's resentment, is a passionate attachment to and dependence on the child. This dependence on the child often translates into the adult's inability to distinguish his or her own needs and wishes from those that are attributed to the child. Following the divorce, parents often find they need the child with a new intensity, to fill their emptiness, to ward off depression, to give purpose to their lives, to give them the courage to go on. Consciously or unconsciously, parents may turn to the child for help, as surrogate spouse, confidante, advisor, sibling, parent, caretaker, lover, concubine, ally within the marital wars, or as extended conscience and ego control. The child at divorce has an extraordinary capacity to restore the parent's shaken self-image. Even very young children are pressed into this role: "He understands everything I say," declared the businessman of his three-year-old son; "sometimes I talk to him for hours" (Wallerstein and Blakeslee, 1989).

Given these unprecedented changes in the trajectory of parent–child relationships in divorce and remarriage, what do we know about the child's inner world in its strange new reality? How do these family changes affect the psychic reality of the child: fantasy life, self-concept, conscience formation, view of relationships between men and women, template of family life? How do they impact on the child at each developmental stage, and throughout the developmental sequence taken as a whole? Is the developmental course of the child whose parents divorced during his preschool years different from that of the child in the intact family, and if so, how can that difference be understood?

We present here the case of a preschool child and his parents, one of thirty families with preschool children seen at the time of the family breakup and during the two years that followed. Our contact with the family began within a year of the marital separation and spanned the legal divorce and two subsequent years, with a brief follow-up twelve years later. Our interest was in capturing the extraordinary changes that the child confronted in his external world during this period and the interplay of the external reality with the child's internal world as evident in his play, fantasy, and overall adjustment, including his relationship with the clinician. We were also interested in the parents' changing attitudes, fantasies, and perceptions of the child, and the combined impact of these and other changes on the child's psychic development. Finally, we were interested in the course of the post-divorce family and developmental status when the child graduated from high school.

This case is drawn from a clinical research project which began in 1980 to study 180 divorcing families with an average of 2.2 children per family, and which was broadly designed to record the psychological effects of divorce on children and their parents and to provide preventive treatment that would alleviate the children's suffering and help the parents make plans for the post-divorce family.[1] Clinical impressions of the child and his parents are based on five play sessions with the child and five interviews with each of the parents shortly after referral and from clinical interviews with all three, one year and two years later. Interviews conducted with both parents and the child a decade later are also reported. The interviews were supplemented with findings from a battery of psychological tests, including projectives devised for the project that were administered to the child and the parents at the outset and during each follow-up except at the final contact. Neither the child nor his parents were in psychoanalysis.

NOAH AND HIS PARENTS

Noah, an engaging, lively four-year-old, was referred to our program by his preschool teacher during the year following the marital breakup and prior to the legal divorce. Early in their marriage, his parents had enjoyed what seemed to be a reasonably amicable relationship. The child was loved and well cared for during his first three years. The parents separated without warning when the father left on a business trip and the mother impulsively moved in with a former boyfriend, placing Noah with her married sister. The father returned, angrily filed for divorce, and took the child to live with him, his new girlfriend, and her three daughters. Several months later the mother reclaimed the child, taking him as her constant companion into a surreal day-and-night world of drugs, sex, and alcohol. Our contact began at this time.

Mother

Noah's mother presented as an attractive, well-educated 32-year-old woman, the youngest child of a socially prominent family. When she was functioning well, she was capable of warmth and sensitivity to the child. At other times, her impaired judgment and immaturity

---

[1]This research was conducted at the Center for the Family in Transition, Corte Madera, California, which was founded in 1980 by Judith Wallerstein. The project was funded by the San Francisco Foundation.

were astonishing. She suffered with serious addiction to alcohol and drugs. There was evidence of severe underlying depression, preoccupation with suicidal thoughts, and more ominous indications of feelings of unreality and disconnectedness. She said, with seeming ease, "I've always been a very dependent person emotionally. I've hardly made a single independent decision in my life."

Following the marital separation, her care of Noah was like that of a young teenager. She was unable to tolerate the thought that he might be frightened and distressed by the many changes in his family and his environment. She was resentful of her responsibility for his care, describing the boy as her adversary in a battle of wills, as someone who humiliated and victimized her. (This was the exact accusation she leveled at her former husband.) She felt helpless as a parent, although ashamed and guilty about her failure. At other times, she was enchanted by Noah's playfulness and sociability. When asked to draw herself, as part of her psychological assessment, she drew her own mother holding a very large child. The grave lapses in her care of her son were, according to both her sister and the child's father, in sharp contrast to her careful mothering while the marriage was in place.

Some of the mother's unconscious sexual and hostile fantasies about the child, when he was four years old, emerged in the drawing that she did in response to our request for their jointly executed drawing of the family. She drew Noah with a well-developed muscular, manly upper body and a little bottom dressed in baby-like shorts, squatting on a potty. Noah was hurt and humiliated by her drawing and, using puppets he found in the playroom, he pretended to bite her repeatedly. The mother paid no attention to his crying or his attack and altogether throughout our joint assessment interview showed almost no responsiveness to the child's feelings. Surveying the playroom at the end of this session, the mother said wistfully, "I'd like to come here to play."

Mother was more stable a year later. She was in once-a-week psychotherapy and had enrolled in Alcoholics Anonymous. Except for a few lapses, she was sober and drug free and was working full-time. She had, however, changed boyfriends and residences several times and she was still anxious and discouraged. There were a few positive changes in her relationship with the child. Her anger at him had lessened; she was more aware of him as a charming child and was proud of his social progress. However, in her expectations of Noah, she continued to have trouble recognizing that he was a little boy, and treated him as if they were both growing up, side-by-side. At times she was controlling and intrusive, which the child feared and resented.

Mother made significant progress during the second year of our contact and was still drug and alcohol free at the next follow-up. By this time Noah was six years old. The frenzied pace of mother's life had finally come under control. As a result, for the first time since the breakup Noah had a predictable schedule. Mother had consciously undertaken her own growing up as a difficult but necessary mission. She lamented, "It's hard. I have a lot on my shoulders. Why do I always have to think about filling my car with gas or worry about money? There is not a lot of time for myself." One result of her emerging adulthood was that, for the first time, three years after the breakup, she could openly acknowledge that the child had also suffered. Unfortunately, her delayed recapturing of her maternal role went hand-in-hand with continual nagging, which the child continued to fear and resent.

Responding to a series of projective tests administered three years after the marital separation, the mother, responding to a stimulus picture of a child of uncertain age and gender looking into a mirror, recounted the confused thoughts and sexual feelings of a pubertal boy. The theme of a boy's sexuality combined with aggression emerged again in the Draw-Your-Family test that she and Noah were asked to do together. Despite his vigorous protest, she drew him holding a gun in one hand and a pencil in the other. Her unconscious image of the child as a sexual and aggressive boy-man seemed to persist unchanged despite her committed relationship to her new boyfriend, whom she characterized happily as "really grown up." Thus, although her external adjustment was more stable, her inner confusion about herself and the many cross-currents in her perceptions of her son were the central themes of the projective tests.

Father

Father was a 34-year-old stockbroker at the time of the breakup. He was a personable man, interested in his work and sports and concerned about his career. He and Noah's mother had met in college.

He was fond of her and had been content with the marriage. Her abrupt abandonment left him, in his words, "shattered and suicidal."

Father had a strong attachment to Noah and sought his help in the recovery process. He acknowledged, "I turned to Noah for comfort for two to three months after she left. My old friends were worried that I would kill myself." His need to deny the child's distress was very strong. Speaking of the child's needs, he volunteered, "I think he needs to learn to have good manners, just the way I was taught." He saw himself and the then-four-year-old boy primarily as pals who engaged in sports together. Unfortunately, Noah lacked the coordination that would appeal to this very athletic father, and both were uneasily aware that they were not meeting each other's expectations.

Noah was not in the forefront of his father's attention for long. The father's life very quickly centered on his newly acquired girlfriend and her daughters. He extolled her for providing him with a home and restoring his self-esteem. He was unable to understand that Noah might be uncomfortable in the new family unit. The father, like the mother, saw the child as an equal and talked about him with kindness, but as if Noah were another adult in the family.

A year later, the father turned on the child and blamed him angrily for the father's erratic visiting. Although the father had taken several extended trips that upset their visiting schedule, he demanded that five-year-old Noah take the initiative and call him. With no recognition that he was talking about a very little boy, he said, "I want Noah to take more responsibility for the visits. He has got to learn." A short time later, father became distressed and lonely because his new girlfriend had left him. His chief activities were work and sports, but he seemed to be spiraling downward into a serious depression. Like his former wife, he desperately wanted Noah to fulfill the role of companion and parent who would love him, comfort him, and restore his shaken self-esteem.

Three years after the separation the father was clinically depressed and untreated. Visiting with Noah had resumed, but the rest of his life was "wretched." He admitted, "After being on top of it all, I've really fallen." His work was going poorly and he had lost a lot of money. He was very frightened about his capacity to hold himself together: "I'm getting lost in my mind." He lamented the loss of his wife. He still felt committed to the boy but said that he had "little to offer him." He told the child that "growing up is a hassle." Father felt worthless, unloved, and weak. He was pleased with the growth that he was seeing in Noah, but he needed to feel pride in himself in order to truly enjoy the child's progress. The visiting was beginning to deepen father's depression. As a result, father's connection to Noah was gravely weakened.

Noah

Noah was on the verge of panic when we first saw him, a few months after his parents separated. His play was a frenzied portrayal of the turmoil of his internal and external worlds. He turned the doll house, the dolls, and the furniture topsy-turvy. With frantic movements he brought objects and people together and tore them apart again, in driven, random, continually shifting combinations, as if trying in vain to figure out who and what fit where, who would sleep where, what would be on top, who should be on bottom. Destruction threatened from all sides. Babies and adults crashed from the roof, were stung by bees, locked into refrigerators, attacked by fierce monsters.

Gradually, more organized themes emerged. One persistent figure in Noah's play was the needy baby who was engaged in a forlorn search for his mother. The baby needed food; he needed a diaper change. Always, when he reached the mother, she said, "I'm too busy. I'll do it later." Sometimes she said, "I can't stand to hear about it now."

Another theme was his valiant, sometimes successful effort to parent himself. In one sequence he lined up the babies, put them in cradles and covered them tenderly with blankets, saying, "Let's pretend that the whole floor is covered with food." In another sequence, as the toy cars swirled around in dangerous chaos, he called for the police to slow them down. Turning to the mother doll, he shouted defiantly, "She's too busy. I don't want her help." He then became the policeman, who slowed the cars to an orderly pace.

These themes threaded in and out of his early play, as Noah continued to seek order amidst chaos and protection in the presence of danger. There were no rescuers in his world. The main figures were himself as director of chaos, as needy baby, as tender parent, as traffic policeman—and the preoccupied, unresponsive mother.

A year later, Noah, now five, appeared initially much improved. He was taller by four inches, which he showed the therapist with pride. He described having had a good start in kindergarten. His living arrangement was better, although still unstable. He and his mother had recently moved to live in her new boyfriend's apartment. His manner was more relaxed and his expression was no longer openly sad or worried. But there was a marked discrepancy between his social presentation, in which he appeared outgoing, reasonably well organized, and more mature and his very troublesome underlying concerns, especially about his erratic contact with his father, which were causing him great pain.

He introduced the father–son relationship at the outset of his sand tray play, via a little airplane that was portrayed with mounting intensity and passion. (The father had taken several trips by plane during the year.) Noah's opening gambit was the little airplane whose flights were very hazardous but which managed "this year" to land safely. The play gained momentum when the plane began to spin and was unable to stop. After much technical checking, Noah diagnosed the problem as trouble in the cockpit and righted the troubled plane.

When he was invited to draw, Noah drew a picture of a "grown-up" whom he designated as "ten years old." He described the grown-up as "nice, happy, and someone who likes to play with toys." Asked to draw a child, he chose to draw a girl, assigning her the same age as his own. In his beginning doll house play, he indicated that all of the dolls were girls, including those that were clearly male. Thus he described a world without men or boys, in which adults and children were almost indistinguishable. This relatively calm overture ended abruptly, and the doll house play soon became as frenzied as his play of the year before. The needy baby reappeared as a central character, as father, mother, and babies got thrown back and forth, landed on hot stoves, and searched in vain for a safe or cool place. As the wild play continued, father and baby were caught up in a chaotic swirl. The figure of the flying and falling father was accompanied by the baby, who was looking for a place to hide but found none. In this frantic search the baby ended up, first, in the fire and then as a bullet on the father's head. Noah screamed, "He's on Dad's head! It's a bullet! The baby is the bullet!" The father doll then fell, broken and bleeding.

The frenzy subsided then, almost as quickly as it had begun, as the child played out a remarkably moving and eloquent sequence. It was played in slow motion, almost like a dirge. The father was walking backwards. As he backed away from the babies, the child said sadly, "He does not know that he is walking backwards." The babies and the father ended up in separate boxes distant from each other.

Then the child's bitterness reached its fullest expression. He drew a fat ghost drinking from a coffee cup. The ghost, he said, was a 16-year-old girl or boy. It had no children. It liked to fly, to scare people. "The ghost makes you as little as a telephone call. You slide out of the telephone." The child's anguish at what he experienced as his father's cruelty in reducing their contact to a telephone conversation that slides out of the telephone could not have been more poignantly expressed.

At the two-year follow-up when Noah was six (three years after the marital breakup), for the first time mother and child had a home of their own that was sunny and cheerful. The mother's life was well organized and she had a steady boyfriend. His father had reestablished regular visiting and the visits included overnight stays. Noah was doing well at school and in his relations with friends. He looked robust and was friendly, polite, and happy to see the clinician. In brief, the child's external world had at long last stabilized. Unfortunately, his father was clinically depressed and his personal life and work were in a shambles. A source of new concern was that Noah checked the response that he "had thought of suicide although would not do it," on the pencil and paper Kovacs test, which was administered at the time of the clinical interviews.

Noah began his play like a latency-age child. He chose a board game and built a model. His play was quick, competitive, and empathic. He won the game, happily abiding by the rules. His three wishes had to do with fast vehicles to drive. He spoke with pleasure of his physical growth, adding with excitement that his mother's new boyfriend "is big and tall." However, he soon returned to the theme of unprotected and uncared-for babies and inept parents. But this time the themes of his play had significantly shifted. The babies were running away from the mother, who slept a lot or wanted the babies to spend time with her in grown-up activities such as watching TV. The babies were in flight from the father as well. On the run from the grown-ups, the babies moved frantically from place to place looking for hiding places where they could fit, but to no avail. They fit nowhere. The father searched for them but when he did find them, they cried, and so he shut them back in the cabinet. He could not stand their crying. As if to emphasize the portrait of inept adults, when the rescue of a falling baby occurred, it was the work of a five-year-old boy.

The message repeated endlessly throughout the play was, "Stay away from the parents. They mess up or co-opt you for their own needs. They never help." It was especially interesting that in the TAT cards (which we had modified to suit divorce situations) where three family members are represented, Noah ignored the presence of a third person. He could deal with one person and with the dyad, and with grown-ups and children in groups, but the triad appeared to make him too anxious. Several sub-themes made their appearance. One story was of a child who lacked clothes and went out in a storm to beg, and returned to try on what he had been given. Another was about the toy plane: He explained that the plane needed a pilot. But the pilot was unable to reach the cockpit and the plane could not take off.

DISCUSSION

As we examine this child's play in relation to his experience, it is striking that the world he creates so vividly in his early play and reintroduces at the first follow-up realistically portrays the world in which he is living. The turmoil that he plays out in the doll house—the random, wild moving about of adult dolls and babies—captures his experience. The distortions are few. There are no windmills that are transformed into giants. There are no supernatural comic book heroes or fearsome, villainous monsters. The play is remarkable in its lack of disguises or symbols of his imagination or of the culture. With great clarity of vision, Noah at age four portrays a chaotic world in which parents and their children are driven randomly by forces that they do not comprehend and over which they have little control. It is a world that contains only victims, among whom the child is the most vulnerable.

Noah's view of his mother the year after the breakup is well within human dimensions. Despite the child's anger, the mother is not portrayed as malevolent or even cruel. Her sin is her failure to parent, not her failure to love. She is incompetent, child-like, and distracted, but not evil. He does not hurt her or punish her in his play. In his role as baby, he searches for her continually, and he records his repeated disappointments and his anger at her unresponsiveness.

But he maintains his positive and remarkably realistic image of her in his inner world. This good image rides in part on the good relationship that Noah had enjoyed during his first three years. He is searching for the good mother that he once knew well. This kind of compassionate image also reflects the generosity and concern of many children in divorce, often very young children, who have not suffered with longstanding neurotic illness in which their own fearful fantasies have obscured their perceptions. There is a very moving dimension to this child's understanding and implied willingness to forgive his mother. At the tender age of four, despite his own suffering, he recognizes her frailty.

Noah's warm welcoming of the clinician and the positive transference that develops at their initial meeting reflects the same reservoir of good feeling. In the car on his way to the third play session, Noah happily told his mother that he thought he just heard the therapist calling his name. Many children, like Noah, when they are seen at the height of the divorce crisis reach out eagerly for help, expecting that the new adult will rescue them. Many, like Noah, have a history of good parenting prior to the family breakup which shapes the transference to the clinician.

Based on the interviews at the first year post-separation, it is fair to conclude that despite his suffering Noah has maintained a balanced inner view of his predicament. His perceptions accord with his reality and his conclusions about his parents reflect remarkably mature judgment and compassion in a child this young. It is reasonable to speculate that the good parenting of his first three years has continued to sustain him, keeping his hope alive, muting his anger, and maintaining his inner equilibrium. Had the parents been able to reconstitute their personal lives, individually or together, after the first postdivorce year and rally to his support, the troubling threat to Noah's development that emerges later might have been avoided.

A year later, the child is better organized psychically partly because of his developmental progress. But he is angrier and less hopeful. His play is richer in symbols, more complex and less directly linked to the external reality. His central protagonists are his father and himself, represented by the unhappy baby. The father is treated roughly in Noah's play. He is hurled from the roof and acquires a broken leg and a bleeding mouth. But despite Noah's anger, the father, too, is no arch villain. He is depicted as retreating from the relationship with the child; but with compassion Noah says, "He does not know that he is walking backwards." The father is accused of being heartless for not understanding how much his inconstancy causes pain. He is threatened with the loss of his son (the adult is described as childless). And he is perceived, like the mother, as a child-adult, a disappointing failure, incompetent but not monstrous. The one breakthrough of the child's explosive anger occurs during the play sequence when he identifies himself as the bullet that presumably could destroy the father and is perched on the father's head with that threat in mind. But despite the child's rising excitement, the destruction he contemplates does not occur. Instead, the child searches in vain for ways that might empower the father to be a better parent. He concludes in anguish that the father he needs is vanishing.

Noah's play at age six takes a different turn, reflecting a radically revised view of himself and his parents which has important implications for his developing character. He no longer forgives their deficiencies as parents. Nor does he hope for the return of the protective parenting that he once knew. The new stability of his family seems to have little impact on his jaundiced view. The child's earlier quest for food from the mother and constancy from the father has ended. At age six, he is a fugitive on the run from both parents, because he sees them both as the central cause of his distress. He has changed from seeking solace from them to regarding them almost phobically as the problem. They are no longer fellow victims helplessly driven by forces beyond their control. They have become the danger.

Leaving the parents behind and seeking the company of peers is, of course, associated with latency. But Noah comes to this solution by a different route than the more familiar sequence following resolution of oedipal issues via internalization and identification. He enters latency as a runaway. He comes to latency by default, with the profoundly held grievance that his parents have failed him as they failed each other. He has given them every chance but the cumulative effect of their unresponsiveness is greater than he could withstand. There is little evidence of respect or a wish to emulate either parent. On the contrary, he is in full flight from both. As a consequence, he is profoundly worried that he fits nowhere. He makes very clear that all the hiding places are unsatisfactory. Nevertheless, keeping his distance, whether phobically or realistically, and turning to teachers and friends seems to him, at age six, the best course to pursue.

The timing of the change in the child's inner life deserves comment. There is an interesting theoretical and clinically important time lag between the several years of chaos in the boy's family and the child's anger and rejection of his parents, which occurs three years later when his external world has finally stabilized. During the acute disorganization, he clings in his fantasies to benign images of both parents. There are several possible explanations for the time lag between the external crisis and the child's conclusion that his parents are to blame and that proximity to either is hazardous. It may be that it is safe, or safer, to be angry and reject them when life is more ordered. It is also possible that he cannot reject them until he has reached the developmental milestone of latency. Until then, his total dependence on his parents for physical care and protection precludes the flight that he enacts so vividly in his play at age six. And it may also be that three years later he has recognized the permanence of the divorce and is no longer expecting that his parents will reconcile. (Many children cling to reconciliation fantasies well into adolescence.) The time lag, however, may be significant in and of itself. It may tell us about the natural course of the child's response to crisis and the capacity of the child to maintain his inner balance over several years by holding on to inner images of the parents that are still largely those of the pre-crisis family experience.

Noah's self-image in his play during the most disorganized part of his early years is the distressed baby who is in need of physical care and comforting. His troubled parents, like many other parents in crisis, could not bear to acknowledge his distress and could not comfort him. In fact, they expected him to comfort them. As a result, the distressed, needy baby is kept carefully hidden, initially out of love and loyalty to his parents, and later out of his realistic, angry recognition of their limitations.

The regressive pull represented by the figure of the needy baby is a common response to divorce among young children. Often it takes on special meaning, as it does here, because the family was intact when the child was a baby. By implication, being a baby magically restores the bountiful past. This hidden self-image that goes along with his lowered expectations of receiving love and comfort provides the basis for what may well become a depressive undertone to this child's developing character. His response to the psychological test indicating that he has contemplated killing himself is ominous in this regard. He may well feel bitter and unrewarded for his earlier patience and kindness. On the other hand, Noah's despair may be modified by his capacity to turn to others for help. This capacity was very visible in the transference, in his reaching out to the clinician.

Noah's ability to maintain a balanced, clear-eyed view of his family may keep him from over-generalizing his disappointment to other close relationships. His countervailing judgment, that other people are not like his parents, may reflect his own early good experience with them, his warm relationship with his aunt and uncle, and his proud claim that he can rely on his own resources. He may be able to maintain his emotional equilibrium, seek rewards outside the family circle, and avoid neurotic illness. All of these developmental tendencies are in dynamic play when we see him at age six. It was certainly, at that time, too early and too close to call.

It may be of critical importance in understanding the course of the child's psychological development that Noah enters latency at this time. The sad, angry, needy baby of his psychic reality is in marked contrast to the charming, competent, outgoing child that we begin to see at age five and more clearly at age six. The pleasures and challenges of the world of the latency child coincide remarkably with his own defensive needs and fantasies. The social norms of latency in our society impel him to move on and out to relationships with peers and teachers outside the family. And, fortunately, he is well able to enter this world successfully. At age six, he is learning well; he gets along in the group, he understands and accepts rules, and he is very much into boys' activities. Doubtless, Noah's alternative self-image as a child who can take care of himself, who can diagnose and fix the plane and get it off the ground, is a welcome child to his teachers, his classmates, and his parents. And of course, as a competent latency child, he relieves his parents of the anxiety and guilt of feeling responsible for his distress. He helps them by not requiring the parenting that they cannot provide. He, in turn, is protected by the society of his peers from becoming too closely involved in his mother's sexualized and aggressive fantasies and from the pull to take care of his depressed father. Thus the child's defensive flight from his parents serves his own interests as well as those of his parents and is rewarded at school and on the playground. His progress into the next developmental stage safeguards the integrity of his inner life.

What is lacking in the child's play is evidence of oedipal conflict. There is no part of Noah's play that addresses both of his parents

together. In responding to the stimulus cards, Noah blocks any perception of three figures together. Of course, we lacked the kind of
clinical material that psychoanalysis would provide. Nevertheless, it
is obvious that the unity of mother and father is helpful in resolving
the challenges of the oedipal period. But two parents together are
clearly not available for Noah, nor for millions of children of divorce
here and abroad. In fact, the thought of them together may be especially painful for him because it evokes memories of the intact family
of his early years and the sorrow of his loss.

There are traces of oedipal issues in the material. The brief play
at age five that shows only girls and women in the doll house and his
self-portrait as a girl are surely relevant to the child's concerns about
sexual identity. His yearning for his father is intense and his anger
at what he sees as his father's betrayal is powerful. He may well feel
that his father's rejection and absence emasculate him or that his
father would have stayed had Noah been a girl, especially in view of
the fact that father's new girlfriend had daughters. But there are no
triangles in his play and few themes of rivalry or competition. His
concern is his dyadic interaction with mother and father, each taken
separately; or he plans his escape from both.

We are left with many questions. Does the well-functioning
latency child we observe at age six conceal a troubled child whose
development is fixated at pre-oedipal levels? Or is it possible to move
forward developmentally without having fully dealt with oedipal
issues? Could these issues be put off, to be addressed more fully at a
later time, perhaps at young adolescence? Is the developmental sequence modifiable? What are the consequences of a foreshortened
developmental stage? We do not know how flexible the developmental timetable is, whether it can be stretched so that developmental
issues which have been marginally resolved or almost bypassed can
be addressed anew, with good resolution, at a later time. Our experience has primarily been with symptomatic patients for whom the
failure to traverse a particular developmental stage has been linked
to inner conflicts. But Noah is not symptomatic. He appears to his
teachers, peers, and parents to be developmentally on course, and
there would be no reason to seek treatment for him at this time.

Noah's final play may be prophetic although, as with many
prophesies, the message is cryptic. The child tells us that the little
plane cannot take off because the pilot cannot reach the cockpit. It
may be that the pilot will grow big enough to climb into the cockpit

and fly off. Or, it may be that identifications with adults, whether his parents or others, which the child appears to have rejected in his anger and disappointment, are necessary in order for him to fly safely. In any case, the child seems to have concluded from the vantage point of his six very full years that he will need to depend on the strengths and limitations of his own judgment and resources. Fortunately, he comes well-endowed with both.

EPILOGUE:
A BRIEF REPORT OF A FOLLOW-UP 12 YEARS LATER

Noah and both parents were interviewed separately by the clinician who had seen them at the divorce. The mother was now 47, the father was now 49. Both had remarried. Each had suffered with loneliness and sustained many unhappy changes in partners over the intervening years. At the twelve-year mark, mother was seriously depressed. Father, by contrast, had finally recovered and was happy in his fourth marriage and in his work. Noah, now eighteen, was living with friends and attending college.

Noah at eighteen was a physically attractive, appealing teenager who was very much at the threshold of young manhood. He came willingly to the interview, approaching it seriously with the expectation that the interchange would provide him with the opportunity for learning more about himself and reflecting on his plans for the future. His openness and candor throughout were striking. Although Noah did not remember the clinician, or much about the divorce and its aftermath, he assumed correctly that his early life was familiar to the interviewer, and occasionally he asked her questions to fill in the troubling gaps in his memory. The immediacy of this trusting, affectionate transference, which he sealed unexpectedly with a shy kiss at the end of the interview, was remarkably reminiscent of his earlier transference when, as a very young child, he reached out to the clinician and seemed to welcome the opportunity to portray the drama of his inner world in her playroom.

Noah spoke about his parents with sadness and disappointment, but without rancor. He began with his worries about his mother. He said, "Her behavior is confusing to me. Why can't she wake up and see what is happening to her? She is so submissive. It occurred to me when I was seventeen that her marriage is wrong and it is wrong of her to put up with it. I think she stays in the marriage because she needs the money. I'm still mad about it. It's hard for me to separate whether I am angry at my mom or my stepfather." With surprising moderation he observed, "My stepfather wants to reshape people to his wishes. He likes to be in charge. It was tough. It's better for my self-esteem to be out of there." Shaking his head, he concluded, "My mom will do what she will do. I'm glad I'm out of there." However, he confessed that "moving out, though, has not had as much effect as I had hoped. I'm not getting as much relief as I had hoped I would."

Noah also spoke movingly about his disappointment with his father, and his longstanding yearning for a more intimate bond between them. He asked the clinician, "When you met my Dad many years ago, was he open or closed? I wish that my Dad were more open. He's good at organizing and being practical, but I would like to be closer to him than I am. I really appreciate him now, though, in certain ways, because he is a good problem solver and he has good common sense." The boy evidently did not share the father's sense of having had a restored father–son relationship during his adolescent years. Instead he emphasized the limitations that he had experienced while acknowledging the father's recent efforts.

Noah went on to say, "What I lost from my father I gained from my mother. I grew up without the balance I would have had if they had stayed together. I know my Dad a lot less than if we had grown up in the same house. It's not a normal father–son relationship. It's awkward and superficial. I'd like to know him more. Since I turned sixteen, he's been more interested in me—more probing, more giving advice, more like a mentor."

Asked about his significant relationships during his growing-up years, Noah said, "My mom is my most important relationship. Then my aunt and uncle. Then my dad. But I rely a lot on my friends. I have two good friends in similar situations to mine, a boy and a girl. We talk a lot to each other." He talked about his values, directly and indirectly, within the context of describing his longstanding friendships. He emphasized the value of being independent, of holding on to friendships despite expectable tensions, and of maintaining a balanced outlook on life. "Independence is very important to me," he said. "I have one friend who is a real leader, who I have admired since I was thirteen. In high school, he had his own check book and handled his own expenses. I wanted to be like him and handle my own stuff. I've always wanted to do more on my own. As I've gotten more independent, it has created some tension between us. We both want to be leaders and it's been a threat to him. But we've worked it out and we are still good friends." He mentioned an unhappy friend. "She only sees the negative. She doesn't have a balanced view of life. Her perspective is way off. She doesn't have the capacity to see what there is to be happy about in addition to what there is to be upset over."

Noah expounded happily on his future plans, noting with sparkle that he is in favor of marriage. "It can be good. My father's current marriage is good. I've always assumed, and I still assume, that I will get married. I like the idea of having a partner, of doing things together, of doing it in a good way." He had dated a girl for six months but "she was too smothering and she wanted commitment." He decided to end the relationship, but he tried to do it so she would not be hurt. He said, "The relationship was good because I got to see what I like and don't like in a girl." He grinned. "Of course, I'm on the alert for relationships. I meet girls who are very attractive, and then I say to myself, "Be alert. What's good on the surface isn't necessarily what's good inside. You have to be careful."

Noah's current plans are to finish college, attend flight school, and become a commercial pilot. He had previously been accepted into flight school but decided, on the advice of the school counselor, to defer flight training until after college. His father and uncle have both offered financial help with tuition, and he plans to continue working part-time to support himself. He has already been promoted in his current clerical job and he thinks that his earnings will suffice.

Summarizing his personal outlook, Noah said, "If things get rough, eventually good stuff will happen. If you do good things, good things will happen." As he rose at the end of the meeting, he kissed the clinician gently on the cheek, thanking her for the interview.

CONCLUSION

Noah appears in this latest interview to be developmentally on course. He is an appealing young man with a lively curiosity about his own emotional life, a strong sense of direction about his future, and a spontaneity and ease that people undoubtedly find very attractive.

He is a vigilant youngster who is, as he tells us, a young man "on the alert," a careful, conscious observer who relies on himself and his friends to pick up what he did not learn within his family.

Unlike many children of divorce, who fear that their relationships will fail, Noah fully expects to marry and has begun a systematic exploration to determine what he needs and wants in a long-term relationship. Unfortunately, we lack information that would clarify this key question, except to note the striking difference in his self-image and expectations in man–woman relationships from those of his peers with a similar background. Also, unlike many young men from divorced families, Noah is hopeful about his future. He expects that the world will treat him well and that he will reach his goals through his own diligence combined with the help of others. This capacity to look ahead, to make full use of opportunities that become available (as he did with the follow-up interview), and to plan for various eventualities obviously stands him in good stead. It was already evident in the very young Noah, when he was able to foresee the possibility of his father's abandonment and, despite his pain and anger, to anticipate the blow before it fell. It was also evident in his ability to turn energetically to the anticipated gratifications of school and friends when the disappointments mounted in his family, both when he was six and again when he was seventeen.

Obviously, there is no way to be sure from this material that the boy is not more troubled than he looks. It would, in fact, be surprising not to find with further probing some general and specific anxieties, some of which he hinted at in the last interview, but which he preferred not to disclose. Nevertheless, this young man looks well despite the psychopathology and long-term disorganization of his family, which have extended far beyond a single traumatic event, or even a series of traumatic events, and which include his mother's lasting depression and chaotic life style, his father's three failed marriages and abandonment during most of his childhood, and his harsh rejection by his stepfather during his adolescence. He is realistically aware of the disappointments in his relationships with both parents. But he has maintained his compassion for his mother and his openness to his father since early childhood.

Furthermore, Noah has avoided identification with the disturbed aspects of both parents. Unlike many of his peers from divorced homes, who feel at young adulthood that they have borne the brunt of their parents' divorce, Noah's anger at his parents is muted but not denied. His efforts to achieve the balanced perspective that he values, reflecting neither his mother's ideology nor her behavior, appear to have been reasonably successful.

Unlike many children who come to the divorce emotionally depleted or symptomatic because of the turbulence in the predivorce family (Cherlin, Furstenberg, and Chase-Lansdale, 1991), Noah was an emotionally sturdy child who had been well cared for by both parents during the first three years of his life. Moreover, we were told that there was no overt conflict between his parents during the marriage or during the years that followed the divorce. The nature of a child's attachment to both parents and the capacity of these early relationships to maintain their power over many years, in intact families, is well established. The course of these early attachments in divorced families is less well known. But clinical observations and early research findings show that children's sense of trust, their access to their own feelings, and their reality testing can all be seriously eroded by ongoing high conflict between divorcing parents (Johnston and Campbell, 1988; Johnston, 1994). So Noah was fortunate not only in his early relationships but also in the fact that, whatever the shortcomings of his parents, they did not struggle over him.

From the follow-up, we learn that during his adolescence Noah was once again able, at a time of crisis, to move successfully into the developmental stage that lay ahead. At age seventeen, when his step-father ejected him from the family, he was able to distance himself emotionally from the intolerable circumstances in his home, to re-ject his father's offer to share his home and, again, to propel himself forward, away from both households, into independence. Fortunately for Noah, his father reappeared after an absence of seven years to facilitate the boy's developmental advance. The father's identification with his son, who had grown to attractive young manhood, contrasts sadly with the father's abandonment when the boy was small and needy. But the father's timely agenda following his return was to encourage Noah to separate from his close relationship with his mother and also to provide his son with a strong endorsement of love and marriage.

Thus we learn from this long-term follow-up that, at each critical developmental stage, when the child was caught in conflicts that threatened his psychic equilibrium, he managed, as a result of his innate capacities together with the social supports and opportunities available to him at the time, to propel himself forward along his developmental route and outward, away from the troubled family situation, in the direction of the greater independence and freedom that lay outside his family orbit.

There has been a striking consistency between Noah's inner life, as reflected in his play as a young child, and his real-life plans as he stands on the threshold of manhood. The yearning of the six-year-old for independence, competence, and escape, which was captured so vividly in the story of the toy airplane that could not fly because the pilot could not reach the cockpit, reappears as the real airplane of his adult ambition. In accord with his childhood hopes, he has grown tall enough to reach the cockpit and competent to handle the controls.

REFERENCES

Cherlin, A. J., Furstenberg, Jr., F. F. & Chase-Lansdale, P. I. (1991), Longitudinal studies of the effects of divorce on children in Great Britain and the United States. *Science*, 252:1386–1389.

Johnston, J. R. (1994), High conflict divorce. *The Future of Children, Vol. 4, No. 1*. Los Altos, California: The David and Lucille Packard Foundation.

—— & Campbell, L. E. G. (1988), *Impasses of Divorce*. New York: Free Press.

Wallerstein, J. S. (1985), Changes in parent-child relationships during and after divorce. In: *Parental Influences: In Health and Disease*, ed. E. Anthony & G. Pollock. Boston: Little Brown, pp. 327–348.

—— & Blakeslee, S. (1989), *Second Chances*. New York: Ticknor & Fields.

Epilogue

No matter what children are told about their parents' decision to divorce, they do not experience it as a mutual decision. One parent is seen as responsible for the breakup of the family. Also, there is a discrepancy between parents' and children's preparation for divorce. Parents may have been dealing with the possibility of divorce for a long time before the actual marriage breakup while the children may be shocked when the plan to divorce is announced. The children experience themselves as "divorced" and the victims of divorce and they may see one parent as the victim as well. For example, the parent who leaves may be seen as being forced out by the parent who stays. This may or may not dovetail with the reality of the marital separation.

Children of divorce are always missing someone. When they are with their mothers, they miss their fathers. When they are with their fathers, they miss their mothers. They are not alone in their reunion fantasies. Often the parents who have chosen to divorce have fantasies of getting back together, and these fantasies can re-emerge at any time. When children of divorce make a wish and blow out their birthday candles, often they are wishing for their parents to get back together again as father and mother, husband and wife. Later, when this wish is not realized, it is replaced by the wish that their mother and father would be friends. This is necessary to retain continuity and cohesiveness of the self. The cornerstone of identity is the family triangle—mother, father, and child.

Staal (2000) and Berman (1991) interviewed adults who were children of divorce. They both note that parental patterns, including divorce, are repeated. One important question to research would be how divorce in childhood impacts on these children when they become parents themselves. Parents regret the hardship they cause when they break up a family, as this hardly fits their own dreams of family when they originally fell in love. But, as Staal points out, one way the children of divorce move on is to forgive their parents.

Although this volume focuses on the problems and conflicts faced by families of divorce, there are some positive outcomes. Children can see a parent appropriately extricate himself from a bad situation. This can serve as a model for the child in facing future life challenges. Furthermore, in high-conflict divorcing families, the parental separation can be experienced by all family members as relief, with less conflict in the home. Most important, both parents have the potential, in time, to become better parents when they are out of the marital conflict (Furman, 1991; Hetherington, 1993). Many parents report that they spend more time with their children after a marital separation and divorce.

With divorce, each parent has the opportunity for a new beginning, which can bring with it both gratifications and complications. There is the possibility that the second time around the parent will be successful in marriage. This may afford the child the possibility of experiencing the positive husband–wife union that was missed in earlier childhood. In addition, if the biological parent who is not living in the home does not see the child often or at all, a stepparent may offer the child a second chance for a positive parent–child relationship (see chapter 12).

We have a lot to learn from our collaborative efforts. Each discipline has its own perspective, its own language (see chapters 1–4). Not only can this collaboration be exciting, but, most important, it can lead to good results for the families that come to our attention. Joseph Goldstein (1984) stated about Anna Freud's contributions to the interdisciplinary collaboration between law, psychology, and psychiatry:

> Our [Goldstein's, Solnit's, and Freud's] more than a dozen almost week-long meetings between 1969 and 1973 working on the first book began each day with a 2- to 3-hour session in the morning, a 2-hour session in the afternoon, followed by tea and an evening session of 1 or 2 hours. By the time we reviewed our final draft before sending it to the publisher we had discussed every line and nearly every word of the entire manuscript. We had found a common tongue [p. 7].

REFERENCES

Berman, C. (1991), *Adult Children of Divorce Speak Out*. New York: Simon & Schuster.

Furman, E. (1991), Children of divorce. *Child Anal.*, 2:43–60.

Goldstein, J. (1984), Anna Freud in law. *The Psychoanalytic Study of the Child*, 39:3-13. New Haven, CT: Yale University Press.

Hetherington, E. (1993), An overview of the Virginia longitudinal study of divorce and remarriage with a focus on early adolescence. *J. Family Psychol.*, 7:39–56.

Staal, S. (2000), *The Love They Lost*. New York: Delacorte Press.

Linda Gunsberg

Subject Index

Custody evaluations (*continued*)
ethics complaints, 46, 54–55
families referred, 31–32
forensic mental health expert-legal
system contrast, 40–43
informed consent, 49–50
interviews, 209, 227–228
judgments based on "established
scientific and professional
knowledge," 46–47
legal considerations, 52–53
legal *vs.* mental health perspective, 40–
43
non-threatening questions, 37
opinions about individuals not
evaluated, 51
parental competencies, 35
parent–child fit, 47
payment, 54
play, 226–227
professional guidelines for conducting,
33
psychological testing, 50–51, 54
purpose, 46
recommendations to court, 53
repeated, 83–84
research literature, 33
resources, 33
risk management strategies, 54–55
self-report, 36–39
sexual abuse, 236–240
skills, 34
specialized competence, 33–35, 46, 47–
48, 55
spirituality, 226–228
statutory criteria, 52
stepparents, 149–150
therapeutic *vs.* forensic roles
irreconcilable, 48–49
traditional tests, 209–210
training, 34
waiver of confidentiality, 49–50
Custody plans
alternating custody plans, 202
choice of legal custodian, 202
demarcated joint custody, 178
dispositions, 202
divided custody plan, 202
dual parenting arrangements, 245
interests of child, 201–210
joint custody, 52, 77, 202
sole custody, 69, 74, 202

split custody, 202
time-share plan, 202
traditional approaches, 201

D
Day care, 267
DeBoer case, *see* Jessica DeBoer case
Defensiveness, 50–51
Demarcated joint custody, 178
Denunciation, 111–112
Deprecation, 111–112
Depression, 371
Despair, 378–379
Detachment, 262–263
Devaluation, 111–112
gender identity problems, 112
Developmental assessment, 4
Developmental process, 181–183
creativity, 223–224
Developmental progression, divorce
case illustration, 368–386
relationship, 365–368
Disclosure, 19
Disloyalty, 117
Disorders of created reality, 110–111, 115
Dispositional hearing, 165, 169–170
Divided custody plan, 202
Divorce
absence of conflict, 251
aftermath, 315–316
consequences, 320
dead *vs.* divorced parent, 320–321
developmental progression, 368–386
developmental progression
relationship, 365–368
diminished capacity to parent, 184, 366,
369–370
dramatic change in parents, 315
effects on child, 140–141
family life just before, 315
healing, 315–316
immutability of painful feelings, 331–
332
impact on child, xxiv
least detrimental alternatives, 140–142
myths, 332
new beginning, 388
parent–child preparation discrepancy,
387
shifting erotic feelings, 325
Documentation, custody evaluations, 51–
52

Author Index